Care Services for Later Life

TRANSFORMATIONS AND CRITIQUES

EDITED BY
ANTHONY M. WARNES,
LORNA WARREN
AND MICHAEL NOLAN

Publishers for the British Society of Gerontology

Care Services for Later Life

of related interest

Geronticide
Killing the Elderly
Mike Brogden
ISBN 1 85302 709 X

Hearing the Voice of People with Dementia
Opportunities and Obstacles
Malcolm Goldsmith
ISBN 1 85302 406 6

Including the Person with Dementia in Designing and Delivering Care
'I Need to Be Me!'
Elizabeth Barnett
ISBN 1 85302 740 5

Training and Development for Dementia Care Workers
Anthea Innes
ISBN 1 85302 761 8
Bradford Dementia Group Good Practice Guides

Working with Elder Abuse
A Training Manual for Home Care, Residential and Day Care Staff
Jacki Pritchard
ISBN 1 85302 418 X

The Psychology of Ageing
An Introduction, 3rd Edition
Ian Stuart-Hamilton
ISBN 1 85302 771 5

Understanding Dementia
The Man with the Worried Eyes
Richard Cheston and Michael Bender
ISBN 1 85302 479 1

The Abuse of Older People
A Training Manual for Detection and Prevention, 2nd Edition
Jacki Pritchard
1 85302 305 1

Drug Treatments and Dementia
Stephen Hopker
ISBN 1 85302 760 X
Bradford Dementia Group Good Practice Guides

Social Work and Dementia
Good Practice and Care Management
Margaret Anne Tibbs
ISBN 1 85302 904 1

Care Services for Later Life

Transformations and Critiques

*Edited by Anthony M. Warnes,
Lorna Warren and Michael Nolan*

Jessica Kingsley Publishers
London and Philadelphia

Publishers for the British Society of Gerontology

The right of the contributors to be identified as authors of this work has been asserted by them in accordance with the Copyright, Designs and Patents Act 1988.

HV
1481
.G72
C37
2000

First published in the United Kingdom in 2000 by
Jessica Kingsley Publishers Ltd
116 Pentonville Road
London N1 9JB, England
and
325 Chestnut Street
Philadelphia, PA 19106, USA

www.jkp.com

Copyright © 2000 Jessica Kingsley Publishers Ltd

Library of Congress Cataloging in Publication Data
A CIP catalogue record for this book is available from the Library of Congress

British Library Cataloguing in Publication Data
A CIP catalogue record for this book is available from the British Library

ISBN 1 85302 852 5

Printed and Bound in Great Britain by
Athenaeum Press, Gateshead, Tyne and Wear

Contents

List of Figures and Tables   7

Acknowledgements   8

Preface
Anthony M. Warnes, Lorna Warren and Michael Nolan   9

1   Health, welfare and old age:
Transformations and critiques   15
Anthony M. Warnes, Lorna Warren and Michael Nolan

2   Beyond the body: An emerging medical paradigm   39
Charles F. Longino Jr, Wake Forest University, North Carolina

3   Towards person-centred care for older people   54
Michael Nolan

4   Rationing care   75
Alan Maynard, University of York

5   Designing and implementing a National
Service Framework   89
Ian Philp, Anne Ashe and Kate Lothian, University of Sheffield

6   Defining difference: Health and social care
for older people   103
Gillian Dalley, Centre for Policy on Ageing, London

7   The medical–social boundary and the location
of personal care   119
Julia Twigg, University of Kent, Canterbury

8   Older people, citizenship and collective action   135
Marian Barnes and Sandra Shaw, University of Birmingham

9   The entry to a nursing home:
Residents' and relatives' experiences   152
*Sue Davies, University of Sheffield, Jonas Sandberg
and Ulla Lundh, Linköping University, Sweden*

10   Discharge from hospital to care home:
     Professional boundaries and interfaces   171
     Jan Reed and David Stanley, University of Northumbria,
     Newcastle-upon-Tyne

11   The quality of home-care services in Sweden:
     Consumer expectations and changing satisfaction   184
     Gillis Samuelsson, University of Lund, Sweden

12   Death and dying: Changing the culture of care   204
     Amanda Clarke and Elizabeth Hanson, University of Sheffield

13   Design for later life: Beyond a problem orientation   219
     Roger Coleman, Royal College of Art, London

14   Older people, telematics and care   243
     Josephine Tetley, Elizabeth Hanson and Amanda Clarke,
     University of Sheffield

15   Chinese older people in Britain:
     Double attachment to double detachment   259
     Ruby C.M. Chau, University of Sheffield and Sam W.K. Yu,
     City University, Hong Kong

16   Bangladeshi families in Bethnal Green, London:
     Older people, ethnicity and social exclusion   273
     Chris Phillipson, University of Keele, Emadad Alhaq,
     Tower Hamlets Social Services, Saheed Ullah, Tower
     Hamlets Social Services, and Jim Ogg, Caisse Nationale
     d'Assurance Vieillesse, Paris

17   Averil Osborn and participatory research:
     Involving older people in change   291
     Lorna Warren and Tony Maltby,
     University of Birmingham

18   Care services for older people: The forward agenda   311
     Anthony M. Warnes, Lorna Warren and Michael Nolan

     The Contributors   333

     Subject Index   338

     Name Index   346

Lists of Figures and Tables

Figures

9.1	Coping strategies employed by relatives to develop and maintain relationships with nursing home staff	161
11.1	The tree hierarchy of quality attributes in home care	190
13.1	Programming the video recorder	222
13.2	Flip-top toothpaste tube	230
13.3	Good Grips™ grater	231
13.4	Good Grips™ gardening tools	232
13.5	RSA student design award winner: Gavin Pryke – a jar we can open	233
13.6	RSA student design award winner: Sally Muddell – finger-friendly door security	234
13.7	The Comfacto bed	236
13.8	B+W easychair	236
13.9	B+W range of 'domestic' style furniture	237
13.10	B+W chairs from the 'domestic' range	237
13.11	The 'Stedy', by RCA Industrial Design Engineering (IDE) student Etienne Iliffe-Moon, now in production by Arjo Ltd of Gloucester	240

Tables

1.1	A selective chronology of innovations in UK policy and services for older people	18
1.2	Principal influences and pressures upon the formal services	23
1.3	Sources of exceptionalism in older people's treatment, care and support	30
1.4	Principal stakeholders in the development of health and social services for older people in the UK	33
3.1	The potential goals of home care for older people	57
3.2	Rehabilitation: Contrasting models	63
3.3	Dimensions of interpersonal competence	67
5.1	Organising values and principles of the National Service Framework	94
5.2	Service models reviewed for the External Reference Group	94
5.3	Categories of reviewed evidence	96
5.4	Key features of the External Reference Group's report	99
7.1	The medical–social care boundary	122
7.2	Medical–social distinctions in health care	132
9.1	Ideal types of admission to a care home	158
11.1	Level one attributes of 'quality' in home care: Determining questions and ratings of importance by informants	191
11.2	Satisfaction with home help received in Malmö, 1992 and 1997	194

Acknowledgements

The editors and contributors wish to thank Anne Jamieson, Chair of the Publications Committee of the British Society of Gerontology, for her very helpful advice during the planning of this book. Kate Smith at the Sheffield Institute for Studies on Ageing worked for many hours on revisions of the chapters and we have been very fortunate indeed to have had her careful, skilful and uncomplaining help.

Preface

Origins and context of the collection

The seeds of this collection were sown at the 1998 annual conference of the British Society of Gerontology (BSG) in Sheffield. The meeting brought into contact the distinctive insights of its members with the special interests of the organising group, which was drawn from Sheffield's universities and health, social care and voluntary welfare organisations. The BSG aims to promote both the understanding of human ageing and later life through research and communication, and the application of this knowledge to the improvement of the quality of life of older people.[1] The membership, being drawn from many academic disciplines and welfare professions, is more eclectic than in many learned societies, and its viewpoints more diverse than those of the professional associations concerned with specific services, specialities, diseases or disabilities.

With a strong representation from, for example, social theory and developmental psychology, BSG members are as interested in healthy older people as they are in unwell older people. Sharing also a strong liberal and egalitarian ethos, they give prominence to issues of equity, cultural sensitivity, the respect of individuals' diversity and choices, and the promotion of user orientation and consultation. Most of all, the society and its members share a trained or learnt empathetic understanding of the situation of older people, and challenge through evidence and reasoned argument all manifestations of age discrimination and the marginalisation and social exclusion of older people and their carers.

The large organising group in Sheffield represented well the noviciate academic disciplines associated with the more recently established welfare services for older people and reflected their coalition with the city's voluntary and statutory services. It was a multi-disciplinary gerontological team, with specialists in architecture, clinical psychology, comparative social policy, domiciliary social services, geriatric medicine, gerontological nursing, information studies, palliative care, population epidemiology, rehabilitation therapy, residential and nursing home care, and services for homeless older people. All are associated through the cross-faculty Sheffield Institute for Studies on Ageing (SISA) at the University of Sheffield.[2] The organising group also reflected a major development in British universities during the 1990s, the upgrading to university level of the training of nursing and several other professions 'allied to medicine' and 'ancillary to social work'. University departments of academic nursing, therapeutic studies, health services and social work are primarily charged to expand and improve the education of practitioners. All display however a keen ambition to strengthen their 'evidence base' through high quality research and, on this foundation, to contribute to the formulation of health and social care priorities and policies.

During the 1998 conference there were many stimulating exchanges between researchers of and from the welfare professions and theoretical gerontologists. These were enhanced by the inputs of our visitors from Wake Forest University, North Carolina, and from Swedish gerontology and geriatric societies. It is pleasing that those contrasts are represented by three chapters in this book. When we, the editors, reviewed the conference proceedings, we found that many participants argued that care services for older people could be immensely improved, both in the respect they show for the dignity and individuality for their clients, and in prosaic efficiency and performance terms. The two are not independent, as was illustrated by the many constructive suggestions about how to bring about improvements in care and more thoughtfulness and respect for often anxious and vulnerable clients, patients and carers. Three deserve early emphasis: the adoption of more sensitive and holistic approaches to assessment; the faster and more reliable transmission of information through onward referrals, discharge and residential placements; and the more widespread sharing of information with clients and patients.

In short, the papers at the conference demonstrated both the weaknesses of elderly care services and that there are abundant opportunities for positive change. The delegates' thoughtful and informed work provided inspiration for the book and has strongly influenced its aim, to elucidate the broad issues raised by under-funded and over-stretched care services for older people. The authors have produced a rich set of essays informed by critical analyses, the reflective experience of practitioners, appraisals of evidence about the achievements and limitations of services and service innovations and, not least, the expressed opinions of clients and patients. Collectively they provide a strong foundation for reasoned debate.

The conventional apology for adding another title to a crowded publishing field is not here offered, even though during the last decade the well-established catalogue of textbooks and critical essays on relevant branches of health and social care has been supplemented with a spate of books on the reforms of the National Health Service, health service policy and economics, and comparative (and particularly European) health services and social policy.

This book attempts something more. All but a few current titles reflect the compartmentalisation of the welfare services, as between health and the social services and within them into myriad specialities (including the near segregation of the mental health from the primary care and social services), not to mention the further chasm which separates the 'social housing providers' of accommodation to special needs groups. While one book cannot examine all the resulting care hiatuses and the numerous fragile interconnections, much less propose comprehensive remedies, a consistent and perhaps distinctive characteristic here is the application of the perspectives of older people and their carers to the services they receive.

The chapters contain ample evidence of high ambitions: how to specify and implement the requirements of care services which do more than provide immediate treatment and minimal care; how they can be sensitive to the special anxieties of patients and clients who are (or perceive themselves to be) nearing the end of their lives; and how the staff at all levels of responsibility of the 'care complex' can comprehend and overcome both its complexity and the economic and political constraints which resist its reform. As well as working vigorously to establish their teaching and research credentials, the emerging welfare and academic fields inevitably and legitimately are ambitious for more influence on practice and policy. To achieve this requires demonstrations of competence and the granting of a voice. Among the pre-conditions are a solid foundation of knowledge and understanding, a track record of practical and worthwhile recommendations, and the standing that brings customary inclusion in influential debates and forums.

Changing their inherited subordinate status will not be easy. No profession is more hierarchical than medicine, and in none is the hierarchy more legitimated by graduations of responsibility. The most senior and responsible are ascribed high status and granted power and influence at all levels of the system, in clinical and multidisciplinary teams, upon boards of directors and trustees, and in national policy councils and committees. There is a comparable dominance in the personal social services of professional social workers over others. How then can the system be changed except within bounds acceptable to the currently dominant players? The answer is only with concerted effort, some charisma, and an overwhelming case that eventually persuades the only arbitrators with leverage, the electorate and governments or other paymasters.

Processes of change are fickle and can be generalised in only broad terms. As many of Britain's twentieth-century governments have found, to achieve significant change in the capacity, efficiency and performance of the health and social care services requires not only substantial amounts of money, but also the considerable feat of simultaneously redesigning the service and equipping it with the latest technologies and more highly trained staff, while continuing to provide at least the pre-existing level of care. This has to be done with staff that are characteristically frequently distrustful of and demoralised by change, and sometimes intransigent too, and with management whose level of flair and enterprise, if not their dedication and leadership, often matches their relatively low remuneration and the highly constrained conditions in which they work.

The desire to gain a better understanding of the health and social care complex is endemic. The general public and patients want to know what is available in their own cities or regions, and politicians about the system over which they have influence. Welfare analysts strive for a larger comparative view but find it very difficult to compile. The available evidence is often both partial and biased towards the longer established and more readily recorded services, as provided by hospitals. Most comparative studies have emphasised institutional and legislative histories or resort to sometimes revealing historical dialectic. There are also population-based evaluations which show, for example, that in most countries the more specialised and advanced branches of medicine are concentrated in the largest cities, especially national capitals and leading commercial centres, whereas provincial regions generally have much lower quotients of hospitals, clinics and physicians.

The comparative perspective also shows large national differences in the emphases, scope, organisation and financing of health and social care. They reveal sometimes marked differences in the 'performance' of the system, as indicated by mortality rates from specific causes, or satisfaction ratings with a country's domiciliary services. Broad international contrasts, say between southern Europe and North America, or between either of these and Japan, raise even greater challenges in understanding the influences upon health and social care development and current directions of change.

The perspectives, analyses and recommendations that feature in the chapters of this book might represent well the broad 'schools of opinion' about what is wrong with today's services for older people, and what might be done about them, yet the aggregate contribution is but a fraction of the research and advocacy that is required to bring about significant improvement. The reader will find diverse evidence and opinions in the chapters: there is variously strong support for some current policy and practice changes (such as the increased attention being paid to the 'voice' of older people and carers), strong endorsements of some recent proposals which the government has been slow to adopt (as by the Royal Commission on Long-Term Care), much consensus about the damaging consequences of the marginalised status of many specialist 'elderly care services', and some optimism that changes now in train, such as the moves towards a primary care-led

National Health Service and towards pooled budgets for domiciliary care, will bring worthwhile gains.

Structure of the book

The book begins with both the 'macro' or structural conditions of service delivery and manifestations of generic pressures, contradictions and change, and progresses towards more specific services and types of need. The first chapter attempts an overview of the most insistent pressures upon the health and care systems of affluent countries at the turn of the twentieth century. The conclusion reflects further on current policy initiatives and pressures for change, and identifies some priorities for research and service evaluation. As throughout the book, the focus is on current UK services, but the analysis strives to identify the structural features and pressures for change which are shared with formal care systems in other countries.

Notes

1.   Further information about the British Society of Gerontology is available online from: www.soc.surrey.ac.uk/bsg/

2.   The aims and activities of the Sheffield Institute for Studies on Ageing are set out online at: www.shef.ac.uk/~sisa/

Anthony M. Warnes, Lorna Warren and Michael Nolan,
University of Sheffield

CHAPTER I

Health, Welfare and Old Age
Transformations and Critiques

Anthony M. Warnes, Lorna Warren and Michael Nolan

This chapter identifies and illustrates the principal pressures and influences upon health and social services for older people in Britain at the beginning of the twenty-first century. The aim is to provide a framework in which to set the later chapters on the functions, organisation and performance of specific services and on current opportunities and change. The focus is on pervasive forces and long-term tendencies rather than specific legislative and administrative acts. While primarily concerned with the UK, a comparative view is deployed because many economic, social and political pressures, while common to all affluent countries, are difficult to observe and usually neglected in a field of study which is characteristically nation bound. The framework has been developed from a population-based and holistic conception of the needs of older people for treatment, care and personal support. Its scope is limited to formal health and social services provided by statutory, for-profit and voluntary organisations and largely excludes both the important welfare dimensions of income support, housing and education and the substantial contributions of family carers.

The chapter has three sections which, succinctly, are about legacies, the reasons for the low standing of services for older people, and current forces for change. The legacies of most interest are those that account to some degree for several characteristics of current services: the divisions of roles, their strengths, weaknesses and idiosyncrasies, their marginalisation, and the locations of established, waxing and waning power. The insights into the human elements of today's forces for change will be assessed alongside the also powerful bio-technological, macroeconomic, commercial and electoral influences.

Many who work in British human welfare services sarcastically or desperately complain about the constancy of reorganisations. Neverthe-less, there is a strong possibility that the early twenty-first century will mark greater changes than for fifty years. A new Labour administration is strongly committed to 'third way', 'one nation' or 'communitarian' policies which, however elusive of detailed definition, may institute radical transformations. The government has begun to increase signifi-cantly the proportion of the gross national product that is spent on health care and may engineer a radical pooling or reconfiguration of social and health care budgets and service delivery, may take from the medical profession the responsibility to regulate doctors, may achieve a patient-centred, primary care-led National Health Service (NHS), may improve public services through local authority-led inter-agency part-nerships with older people, may develop a co-ordinated strategy on older people, and may raise the comparative prestige of social care pro-fessionals, nurses and therapists. Yet for all the fascination and the exciting opportunities of today's welfare politics, in too many ways older people are likely to continue to be poorly served, particularly if they are without close relatives and friends to advocate for them and are financially dependent on the state. The book has therefore strived not only to identify today's forces for change, but also to evaluate whether the current reforms are likely to achieve real improvements in services for older people.

Simply to pose such questions directs attention to the interests that mould and frequently ossify policy and the institutions which tend to relegate older people's services to low priority. Health and social service debates are littered with venerable questions. Why are England's most prestigious teaching hospitals concentrated in London? Why are inner city areas under-served by modern health care centres with multidisciplinary staff? Why are the community health services, which have so much potential to raise the independence and quality of life of the most vulnerable older people, not only the perennial Cinderella services, but also totally uncertain about their continuing role and organisational structure? Why were the Labour government's initial public health targets silent about older people's health and specified exclusively for people aged less than 65 years? Hundreds of such questions can be asked and countless explanations result. There are common threads; for example, that the services become marginalised which are not critical for life, do not require rarefied knowledge, and predominantly serve a relatively powerless and taken for granted client and patient group. As Olive Stevenson (1989, p.110) said of the post-Seebohm 'unified' social work departments, 'elderly people [are] not assessed in the same way as children and families, with the same attention to their social and emotional situation..."generic" social workers with individual case loads cannot, almost by definition, maintain a balanced effort across all client groups'.

The development of the health and social services

Whatever some textbooks imply, any inquiry or the slightest direct experience of the modern welfare system reveals that it is not entirely a product of acts of parliament and government funding programmes. One reason is that many of its components, from befrienders and day centres to nursing homes and hospitals, are provided by volunteers and by voluntary and for-profit organisations. Another is that many specific services, not least for older people, arose not from a legislative stroke but incrementally from other (usually general) services through the local reallocation of staff, buildings and funds. Very often this has happened through agency or professional experiment and innovation, and not all have been well recorded. When was the first voluntary community car-ride service to hospital appointments for older people organised? When did a nurse in a general practice first give advice or administer influenza vaccinations to an older person?

Celebrated histories of the Poor Law and its workhouses (Webb and Webb 1929) and of the NHS have been published (Rivett 1998; Webster 1988, 1996, 1998), as have critical reviews of the development of modern medicine (Le Fanu 1999), hospitals (Abel-Smith

1964), nursing (Dingwall 1988), and British welfare services for older people (Means and Smith 1985, 1998; Tinker 1997a). There are several accounts of the development of residential and nursing homes (Means and Smith 1983; Parker 1988; Thomson 1983; Townsend 1962; Woodroffe and Townsend 1961), of mental health services and institutions (Jones 1972; Parry Jones 1972; Tinker 1997b), of geriatric medicine (Brocklehurst 1985, pp.982–985), and of psychogeriatric services (Wattis 1994). These and other sources have been drawn upon to compile a chronology of significant dates and innovations in the development of those services which are either dedicated to or significant for older people (Table 1.1).

Table 1.1 A selective chronology of innovations in UK policy and services for older people

Date	Service or facility	Source
C10?	Almshouse for older people.	
C19?	For-profit nursing home for older people.	
1894	Charles Booth *The Aged Poor* (Macmillan, London).	
1895	Royal Commission on The Aged Poor.	RAP
1908	State old age pension.	HG
1919	Ministry of Health.	HG
1927	Nursing Homes (Registration and Inspection) Act.	W&T
c1930	Publicly financed home nursing.	W&T
1930s	Geriatric hospital unit.	JGE
c1938	Local authority 'rest homes' for older people, as in Birmingham.	M&S
1941	Nuffield Foundation established.	KS
	National Committee for Old People's Welfare established, precursor of Age Concern co-ordinating bodies in England, N. Ireland, Scotland and Wales.	PGC
1944	Kidney dialysis.	JLF
1947	National Corporation for the Care of Old People founded (precursor of the Centre for Policy on Ageing).	PGC
1948	National Health Service.	GR
	National Assistance Act – local authorities to provide residential accommodation for persons who by reasons of age...are in need of care and attention. Abolished Poor Law, and created powers to provide domiciliary, day centre, adaption and aids, laundry and assisted holiday services.	M&S

	Consultant geriatrician. Intraocular lens transplant for cataracts.	JGE
1948	Specialised local authority housing units for older people.	BOG
1955	Open heart surgery.	JLF
1962	Prototype local authority sheltered housing scheme.	AT
1961	Charnley's hip replacement.	JC
1962	Help the Aged established.	PGC
1963	Kidney transplantation.	JLF
1964	Prevention of strokes. Professor of geriatric medicine.	JLF/JCB
1967	First heart transplant.	JLF
1968	Health Service and Public Health Act. Mandatory duty on all local authorities to provide home help service.	AT
1970	Local Authority Social Services Act (unified social services departments).	AT
1971	British Society for the Study of Social and Behavioural Gerontology founded (precursor of the British Society of Gerontology).	PGC
1976	Sheltered housing for sale.	W&L
1978	*A Happier Old Age* – first policy document exclusively on older people's welfare.	AT
1979	Coronary angioplasty.	JLF
1981	*Growing Older* – first white paper on older people's welfare.	AT
1982	National Council for Carers and their Elderly Dependants (now Carers' National Association).	BL
1984	Registered Homes Act and Home Life: A Code of Practice.	CPA
1986	Cumberledge Report on community nursing. Community psychiatric teams.	GR/P&B
1987	Thrombolysis (clot busting) for heart attacks.	JLF
1988	*Community Care: An Agenda for Action* (Griffiths report).	L&G
1989	NHS recognition of old age psychiatry as a speciality.	P&B
1990	NHS and Community Care Act – new GP contract and GP fund holding.	GR
1993	Community care provisions of 1990 NHS Act implemented.	L&G
1995	Carers' Act. Professor of gerontological nursing.	
1997	Hostel for older homeless people.	MC

Sources: BL British Library catalogue; BOG Butler, Olman and Greve (1983); CPA Centre for Policy on Ageing (1984); JCB Brocklehurst, Tallis and Fillit (1992); JC Charnley (1979); PGC Coleman (1975); MC Crane (1999); JGE Evans (1997); JLF Le Fanu (1999); HG Glennerster (1995); L&G Lewis and Glennerster 1996; M&S Means and Smith (1983); RAP Parker (1988); P&B Philpot and Banerjee (1997); GR Rivett (1998); KS Slack (1960); AT Tinker (1992); W&L Warnes and Law (1985); W&T Woodroffe and Townsend (1961)

As the chronology shows, many of today's services for older people have a short history. It has been said that 'in 1900 social care and welfare services [for any age group] hardly existed. The Poor Law provided support only for the destitute and then under deterrent conditions' (Parker 1972, pp.372–373). Progress during the first half of the twentieth century was slow and mainly associated with the enterprise of local authorities in hospital management and residential care (at that time mainly for orphans and mentally ill and handicapped people). Although the Ministry of Health was created after World War I and began with ambitious aims to create a unified health service, 'sectional interests prevented anything but incremental and opportunistic growth between the wars' (Glennerster 1995, p.46). It was of course the foundation of the National Health Service in 1947–8 that greatly increased the access of older people to primary and acute health care and established an organisational and funding framework in which geriatric medicine could grow; and the contemporaneous National Assistance Act laid the foundations for the expansion, initially slow, of local authority personal social services for older people.

These had hardly existed before 1940, for socially isolated and very dependent people had previously been cared for through informal family, neighbourly and community support, in long stay hospitals, or not at all. During the war, however, the National Council of Social Service promoted local Old People's Welfare Committees which stimulated voluntary organisation and local authority provision (Slack 1960; Titmuss 1950). But for more than a decade after the foundation of the NHS, 'local [community] health and welfare services were a low priority [and] a favoured target for cuts in each expenditure round… Even implementation of small policy advances, such as a chiropody service, or permitting local authorities to provide a meals-on-wheels service, were held back for years' (Webster 1998, p.54). As late as 1958 in the County of London, when the pensionable population was half a million, just 27,000 'chronic sick, aged and infirm' people received home helps, and 33,400 aged 65 years or more received visits from home nurses (Slack 1960). Through that period there was a lack of imagination about alternative forms of support and the developing social services formed a muddled mosaic (Means and Smith 1994). The complementary roles of informal, voluntary organisation and statutory service care have been in flux ever since.

It was the Seebohm report (Home Office Committee 1968) that created the 'unified' local authority social services departments with an enhanced role in providing domiciliary and day centre services for older people:

> To the existing responsibilities of the [local authority] children's departments, the committee added the various social workers in the health and welfare departments, their home helps and the residential care of elderly and disabled people... What Seebohm and the new NHS had done, however, was to separate into two statutory camps the social workers and the medical and related professions, like nursing... For those dependent on both, like the [frail] elderly, the mentally ill and the handicapped, the results were not to be good. (Glennerster 1995, pp.128–131)

Many subsequent developments, such as key reforms in the NHS (the internal market, the divesting of long-term care from acute hospitals, the promotion of primary care, and the 'modernisation' agenda of the current government), and in the social services (the promotion of private sector residential and nursing home care, the 1993 'community care' arrangements), are well covered in the chapters which follow. If the dominant tone is critical, Table 1.1 reminds us that attention to the needs of older people in policy, training and specialised services continues to elaborate and has never been greater. The rate of change and the prospects for real gains also appear unprecedented, which surely means that the need for rigorous analysis of needs and effectiveness, for fresh thinking, and for prioritisation, also surpass the requirements of the past.

General and exceptional pressures on health and social care for older people

A taken for granted duality pervades health and social care for older people. For the majority of services, as for accidents and emergencies, most acute treatments, general practice and the probation services, the age of the client is an irrelevance and 'elderly care' merges imperceptibly with 'care' (Jennett 1995). There are alongside many services designated for the age group but they tend to be fragmented, poorly co-ordinated and of low prestige. The co-existence reflects a taxonomic illogicality in both health and social care: the 'elderly' or 'geriatric' label is used only for the services that treat, care and support people with relatively severe and chronic disorders and who generally are in their late seventies or older. The nomenclature is both a source of confusion and a foundation for stereotyping 'old people' as having the more intractable diseases, disorders and disabilities.

The duality means however that elderly people's services experience both the pressures common to the generic health and social care services (Table 1.2) and those special to themselves. Paradoxes form, as in geriatric medicine, which shares the quasi-sacerdotal quality of all health care (doctors are gods, nurses are angels, and medicines magical) but has repeatedly been marginalised. The 'Cinderella standing' is common to the medical and social care of older people but has different multiple roots. This book elucidates many details of the perversities, inefficiencies and poor manners of services for older people. Many assertions are made that elderly care is different and, in various ways and degrees, marginalised, denigrated and deprived. The situation is however much more complicated. A majority of hospital episodes and physician consultations are with older patients (aged 60 years or more), so it must be that the massive expansion and undisputed improvements of the services – as in cardiovascular care, orthopaedics and general practice – have brought great benefits to older patients. To gainsay that there have been great advances during the last few decades would be absurd.

Table 1.2
Principal influences and pressures upon the formal services

Sources of long-term change	Timeless management, economic and political constraints pressures
Supply-led change	*Public or state sector*
Increases in capability: advances in clinical science and medical technology.	To maximise equity in the allocation of treatment and care, on moral, ideological and electoral advantage grounds.
Clinical innovators and entrepreneurs, including providers of complementary therapies.	To contain public expenditure and tax (fiscal burden) given policy (or volume of supply) decisions.
Voluntary organisation enterprise, as with hospices, day centres, services for people with dementia and older homeless people.	To maximise the private sector's contributions to capital investment, and patients' and clients' contributions to current revenue.
Corporate and institutional innovation and development, as most notably by pharmaceutical companies.	*All sectors*
	To contain costs and keep within budgets.
Demand-led change	To maximise performance (outputs, billing or welfare gains) and therefore efficiency of the services.
Rising expectations for treatment and care.	
Rising individual expectations: Secularism, ending belief in predestination.	To minimise fraud, excess remuneration among practitioners, and excess profits among suppliers.
Decreasing deference to professional opinion. Perfect body, full life norms of the life course.	To minimise media and public complaints, for profit or fiscal reasons (costs of litigation and compensation), and electoral reasons (mainly but not exclusively in the public
Rising societal expectations: Expanding and increasingly declamatory media coverage of biomedical science, health service and social dysfunction and deviation issues, from gene therapies to paedophilia.	*Only private (for-profit) sector* To maximise returns on capital (profit).
Rising prominence of health in political manifestos as the prominence of defence, housing and unemployment have waned. Growth of 'special interest' user groups, alliances and movements.	To increase the number of subscribers and customers, to enable the company to grow and protect itself against competitors.
	To maximise government and charitable subsidies and underwriting of fees, training costs and capital investment.

Many widely demanded goods and services have special features which lead to departures from open, free or perfect competitive markets, diverse examples being national security, law and order and education (the last because the benefits are societal as well as personal). Arguably, however, the most vital and economically unusual commodities of all are health, functioning and survival. It is frequently heard that one cannot put (too high) a value on a human life, although welfare economists disagree. Equally elusive is the value of being without disability or chronic pain. Unlike apples or pears, there are no substitutes for one's life or good health, nor can the consumption of a critical medical intervention be delayed. A young person may see these issues as theoretical, but they are supremely real for those who become seriously ill and for older people who perceive the onset of a condition as heralding the end of their lives.

This exceptionalism not only imbues much health and social care with special tensions and emotions, it immensely confounds both clinical and management decisions about which groups should and should not receive which kinds of care. Battlefield triage has its particular stresses, but generally deals with a relatively homogeneous patient group: young men. The ethical, utilitarian and managerial issues which are raised by the allocation of scarce health and social care resources among young, mature, old and very old people are immensely more complex, extend beyond the competence of 'clinical judgement', and have only recently been seriously addressed (Williams 1998). Later chapters present contrasting examples and views about these issues.

Competence, Outcome Indicators and Regulation

Egoistical reactions to finitude and the pre-eminence human beings give to their good health and functioning are not the limit of health and social care's exceptionalism, for others lie in the special roles that we require of the health and social services. Treatment, care and support comprise several kinds of interventions. At one extreme is the proven, scientifically demonstrated or evidence-based 'fix' – for example, a specific drug, prosthesis or surgical operation; at another are forms of care and support that respect the individuality, 'personhood' and dignity of the person even when and if they are permanently impaired, terminally ill, have severe cognitive deficits, or are from a powerless, socially outcast or 'deviant' group. Most health and social care interventions, not least for older people, lie between these two extremes and require the exercise of both 'technical' and 'humane' care. Questions then arise as to which groups of people and which organisations should provide the different types of intervention – including competing professional groups, (family) carers, religious organisations and practitioners of alternative and complementary therapies – and whether the 'contracted' organisations achieve an optimum pattern of care or privilege some kinds of intervention over others.

For many medical interventions the 'consumer' cannot realistically choose from the top or bottom of the range: there is no such thing as an acceptable second-class heart by-pass operation or anaesthetic dispensation. In any case, most patients and clients have little knowledge (and rarely claim an opinion) about the comparative merits of different courses of treatment, rehabilitation or care. Most are relatively uninformed about the likely benefits, attendant risks, side effects or comparative costs of the available treatments or of alternative approaches to the delivery of care. This is partly because of the intrinsic complexity and volume of the required information, but has been partly contrived by the exclusivism of the welfare professions and, until recently in Britain, the scarcity of both accessible information and comprehensible outcome indicators for either treatments or individual staff – although journalists now frequently call for the publication of the mortality rates of the patients of individual surgeons. Most people continue to put their health and social care-related quality of life prospects literally in the specialists' hands and minds. Attitudes may however change rapidly with the diffusion of the Internet and the NHS Direct telephone advice line, both of which are radically improving access to medical knowledge (Sandvick 1999). The potential value of using modern information technology to give older people and their carers more information about the residential and nursing homes to which a person might move is discussed in Chapter 9. This would help counteract a pervasive source of sub-optimality in residential 'placements', that many are made at a time of crisis and therefore are conditioned by the haphazard availability of vacancies at the time.

Medical and care interventions are potentially damaging in both apparent and rarely recognised ways. Surgical and pharmaceutical interventions can obviously be fatal or permanently disabling, but inappropriate or careless occupational therapies, bereavement counselling and institutional care can also cause serious and permanent harm. The criticality of health and social care interventions has resulted in special arrangements for staff training, accreditation and regulation. Training has to be both academically advanced and comprehensively practical: it is therefore protracted and expensive. Consider the exceptional requirements of the 'complete physician'. She or he needs a university grounding in physiology, anatomy, biochemistry, neurology and pharmacology, plus proven competence in diagnosis, prognosis, treatment decisions, treatment organisation, and communication with patients and relatives. For other staff, the duration of training varies with the responsibility, but those customarily seen as needing little instruction such as residential care assistants should be practised in appropriate interpersonal manners as well as the instrumental personal maintenance and care skills. Many reflective practitioners in nursing, mental health and social care take for granted these 'special factors', but are dismayed at their imperfect application in formal care for older people.

Because assured competence is vital and training is extended and expensive, the entry of many grades of health and welfare professionals into practice is regulated and in the short term all but fixed (some worrying exceptions are described below). The training lead times and investments are unusually large. Another consequence is the creation and legitimation of professional hierarchies. Within them, responsibility is associated with salaries, status, influence and power. Medical colleges and professional associations are licensed to serve the public interest through the promotion of training and qualification standards, and by reviews of performance and the operation of disciplinary procedures. Inevitably, however, professional associations become vehicles for the promotion and protection of their members' interests, which includes exerting their partial interests on policy. 'The [medical] professions lay claim to bodies of knowledge that it is difficult for managers or politicians to challenge [but] social work's knowledge base and its public esteem is far weaker' (Lewis and Glennerster 1996, p.21).

The effect is nonetheless universal: in this nurses, therapists and researchers are no different from hospital consultants. If the professionalisation of care commonly produces unconstructive tendencies, its absence is more inimical to high standards of care. The diagnosis and treatment of affective mental health disorders is largely in the hands of general practitioners, but few have adequate training for the role. Two recent reports have shown a more general weakness, that less than one-half of older people with a mental health need received treatment from a 'competent' professional (Audit Commission 2000; Health Advisory Service 2000).

One of the many subsidiary implications is the problem which arises if the trained workforce changes its career paths; for example, by voluntary exits from the profession. 'Workforce' planning and management issues also arise if the government (or a health service management company) wishes to tackle a specific cause of morbidity, by increasing the number of specialist clinics and professionals, as with the current drive to reduce cancer and cardiac mortality (DoH 2000). To correct a seepage of trained and accredited professionals, or to expand their numbers in a short time, requires substantial training investments or salary increases.

A related set of issues in the 'mixed economy' of residential care was illustrated by the unusual (and poorly handled) national and local 'capacity' management requirements raised by the expansion of the private sector during the early 1980s. When the profitability of nursing homes was boosted by Department of Social Security fee payments, new entrant proprietors were rapidly attracted – experienced welfare professionals, diverse petty entrepreneurs and well-meaning amateurs. This created a new vested interest or stakeholder group and hampered inspection and regulation, for 'restraint of trade' considerations bore on planning approvals for institutional homes, and legal standards of proof were required in courts to establish negligence in care.

The Exceptional Scale and Fiscal Significance of the Care System

A further 'special factor' differs in being a relative rather than qualitative differentiator: it is the huge scale and cost of health and social care. While not the largest sector of national economies in comparison to, say, telecommunications or retailing, welfare services involve substantial government funding and unlike, say, defence in any year serve face to face a high proportion of the electorate. The millions of consultations and contacts each week are riven with opportunities for both imperfect communication and failure to deliver the desired goods – especially cure, restored functioning or survival. Imagine paying a large sum for a car that does nothing to improve your mobility and quality of life. In this metaphor we see why treatment, nursing care and personal support have exceptional political sensitivity.

Governments are also much exercised by the substantial costs to the public exchequer of not only maintaining but also expanding year on year the services. This is so even in the USA, where training, capital expenditure, research and armed service veterans and elderly care are large charges on the federal budget. The macroeconomic importance of health and social care is witnessed by the Organisation for Economic Co-operation and Development's many concerted analyses (for example, OECD 1985, 1994, 1995, 1999). UK health spending in 1996 was 6.9 per cent of GDP, compared to 7.7 in OECD countries (OECD 1999, Table 2.3). In 1997 in Great Britain, the NHS directly employed 918,000 people, there were 52,000 general medical and dental practitioners, and 283,000 local authority personal social services staff (GSS 1999a, Table 8.10). The total amounted to nearly 6 per cent of those in employment; while a comprehensive count of those engaged in human health and social work (and veterinary) services raises the 1998 total to 2.49 million or 11 per cent of the work force (GSS 1999b, Table 7.5). In 1997, around 245,000 prescriptions costing £2,140 million were dispensed to people aged at least 60 years, 49 per cent of the total (*ibid.*, p.141). It is estimated that during 1996 and 1997, £9.2 billion was spent in England on older people's care in hospitals and by the community health services, and £4.6 billion was spent by local authorities (*ibid.*, p.145).

The Marginalised Standing of 'Elderly' Care

We come to the factors which underlie the perennially low standing of older people's services (Table 1.3). Today's concerns should be kept in perspective. No service today would justify the opprobrium that

Charles Dickens heaped on malpractice in poor law workhouse care: '[In] the majority of shameful cases of disease and death from destitution [in the workhouses]…the illegality is quite equal to the inhumanity' (Dickens 1865). Perhaps the most influential of modern 'attacks' was Peter Townsend's (1962) indictment in *The Last Refuge* of inhumane practice within residential care and nursing homes. Nearly four decades on and despite the hopes raised by the Registered Homes Act 1984, a new government promises an improved registration and inspection system to raise the quality of care in the sector and to sweep away neglect and abuse. It is reasonable to conclude that there is little chance of bringing about enduring and general improvement unless the reasons for the perennially humble state of older people's services are understood.

The deepest root is probably the timeless aversion of the not-old from sick and dependent older people for presenting images of their own possible destiny (see Cole and Winkler 1994; de Beauvoir 1970). As the oral historian Ronald Blythe described individual and societal attitudes:

> Much in our treatment of the old and our attitudes towards them is scandalously similar to that which governed nineteenth-century attempts to solve the 'intractable' problem of the poor. They are not us, is what we are saying (politely and humanely, of course), and there are so many of them! … The inescapability of old age is now secretly for many the new predicament. And even those who pray, and save, for a long life have the feeling that by eating and behaving in the way which they believe will encourage longevity, they are tempting fate. (Blythe 1979, p.20)

As negative attitudes towards old age are widespread in society, it is little surprise that they manifest in staff attitudes and the low priority for funds in the dedicated services. Attitudes are reinforced by the characteristics of older people's care needs and the forms of provision they require. Advanced age leads to a high incidence of acute health conditions and prevalent chronic and multiple disorders. The latter bring a considerable need for the sustained management of disease and disorders, for rehabilitation and for personal care and support to overcome dysfunction and disability. Few such services are of interest to

Table 1.3
Sources of exceptionalism in older people's treatment, care and support

Effect	Characteristics of the influence or bias

Reactions to older people

Carers' aversion from older people	Formal carers' fears of old age, chronic disability and death, unleavened by few non-kin social contacts with older people and no tutoring in older people's experiences, concerns and expectations.
Inter-generational distance and disrespect	Age or generation differences in values and attitudes associated with differences in both education and cohort (or 'period') experience lead to group legitimation and reinforcement of individual carer's disdain.
Societal devaluation of older people	The social construction of older people as 'unproductive' and a 'burden' mixes with rational and instinctive assessments that the health and lives of children and young people are 'more worth saving'.

Prestige of older people's services

Care not cure	High needs for chronic management, rehabilitation and care, but not cure.
Empathetic and holistic care	High requirement for holistic approaches which are sensitive to individuals' anxieties about irrevocable decline or impending death and the implications for
Complex funding and co-payment arrangements	The 'package' of care requires inputs from health and social care and non-professional domestic services, producing complexities in the allocation of costs to budgets, among the providing organisations and between them and the patient or service user.
Weak evidence base for reform	Low prestige reflected in late and modest development of related academic fields, producing a weak theoretical critique and evidence base about: (i) older people's needs and preferences; (ii) the attitudes of clinicians, professionals, managers and politicians; (iii) the effectiveness of different models of treatment and care organisation.

Isolation of some older people

Social vulnerability	Some patients and service users are socially isolated and have no relatives or friends to advocate on their behalf.

fundamental biological science or stimulate 'brilliantly heroic' clinical interventions, and they do not therefore attract scientific and professional prestige (or high remuneration). Instead the requirement is for a combination of frequent monitoring, fine therapeutic adjustments, protracted rehabilitation and palliative care, along with a humane, holistic and person-centred or empathetic approach to care. As exemplified in Chapters 7 and 12, there are now attempts to raise the awareness and prestige of humane and holistic care of older people, partly through a critique of disease or organ-based specialist 'disembodied' treatment.

Some older people therefore require a service panoply: specialist medicine from surgery to the management of, say, blood pressure or sugar and multiple medications; empathetic mental health interventions; highly skilled nursing care; and high amounts of personal and domestic support. The provision of such care normally requires several organisations, is intrinsically difficult to do efficiently and 'seamlessly', and generates multiple opportunities for cost shifting, neglect, service withdrawals and inequity. Provision is also confounded by ideological, ethical and policy questions, such as what are the 'minimum acceptable standards' for the care and quality of life of the weakest individuals, or about funding and payment arrangements; and by political and ethical judgements about redistribution among destitute, poor and not-so-poor older recipients of care.

A third source of marginalisation is the exceptional vulnerability, powerlessness and apathy of a minority of seriously ill and incapacitated older people. A small proportion of those who reach advanced old age are quite alone, with no spouse, children or other relatives in touch or concerned for them. Clinical depression and suicidal tendencies have a high prevalence in the group, and many are undemanding and supine. These traits combine with 'institutional ageism' to allow low standards of care, disrespectful and unprofessional treatment and, in the worst cases, financial, mental and physical abuse.

Interest groups, stakeholders and influence

Another way to gain understanding of the current state and the trends in older people's services is to identify and analyse who possesses influence and power. Five principal sets of interest groups (or stakeholders) can be identified: users, carers, practitioners, providing organisations and government (Table 1.4). Subsidiary interest groups or stakeholders can be identified, such as commercial suppliers (notably pharmaceutical and biotechnology companies), insurers and the legal profession, and the main five can be subdivided. 'Users' self-evidently include current patients and service users, but extend to their relatives and all potential patients and users; in other words, the general public and those not yet born. Their 'influence' is exerted through market mechanisms (more often in the USA or France than in the UK), through complaints to professional bodies, elected representatives and the courts, formal consultation processes, and sometimes through journalists and campaigners.

New forms of the collection and transmission of users' views are being tried. First, the inaugural National Survey of NHS Patients was undertaken in 1998 and concentrated on patients' experience of general practice services; 61,426 completed questionnaires were returned from a sample of 100,000 people in 100 English health authorities. It was found, for example, that 'doctors tended to spend longer with older patients, so that younger patients – particularly younger women – were more likely to be unhappy about the length of consultation', and that 'the older the [out-of-hours] caller, the more likely (s)he was to receive a [home] visit' (DoH 1999a). Second, as later chapters describe more fully, an alliance is now forming between academics and users in the development of 'involvement research', which is exploring innovative ways of enabling older people's informed and reflective views to be articulated and communicated to service providers.

Table 1.4
Principal stakeholders in the development of health and social services for older people in the UK

Major groups	Specific interest groups	Influence
Users	General public (including those not yet born). Current patients and service users. Advocacy and user-representative organisations.	Rising
Carers and relatives	Relatives and others directly involved in providing informal care and support. Other concerned relatives.	Recently rising
Practitioners	Physicians and their representative bodies. Other clinical and professional groups. Ancillary staff.	Falling
Managers, entrepreneurs and provider organisations	Statutory and publicly financed agencies. For-profit companies. Non-profit organisations.	Variable
Politicians, experts and technocrats	Financing organisations and their shareholders. Government treasuries. Government policy ministries. 'Think tanks', commissions and international advisory agencies.	Rising

The managerial and party politics associated with the periodic reforms and near continuous development of the welfare services are labyrinthine and immensely variable. For a first guide to the main issues and interest groups in recent reforms, Charles Webster's comments on the formulation of the internal market in the NHS during the late 1980s are instructive:

> [The internal market] was naturally attractive to the government's advisers, who were being pressed hard to come up with management and structural reforms capable of yielding big efficiency gains. They had stumbled upon an idea capable of

attracting support in medical circles among groups frustrated with limitations imposed by NHS bureaucracy. Many general practitioners aspired to break free of the Family Practitioner Committees and control their own budgets; consultants, especially in teaching hospitals, resented the intrusion of district and regional authorities... [It could] generate economies in public expenditure, without detracting from the financial rewards of the successful entrepreneurs. (Webster 1998, pp.188–189)

The main players were the government, Treasury and Department of Health civil servants, the medical and nursing professions (or specifically their associations and colleges), specialist advisers, and the NHS management. Through the twentieth century and particularly its last quarter, their relative influence has changed, most clearly with that of central government rising at the expense of the medical profession and the vanquished roles of local government, hospital boards and ancillary staff trades unions.

An interesting omission from the identified players are patients, service users and the public (which in the public services are readily conflated). Their influence has in a way been omnipresent: all principal stakeholders at times claim to represent their interests and preferences, in both misappropriations to further their own interests and in altruistic expressions. The great change of the last 30 years has been the heightened sensitivity of governments to the actual, supposed and selectively amplified representations of public opinion by the mass media. Webster noted two indicators of the change during the lead in to the 1990 reforms: the NHS review was announced by the prime minister on the television programme *Panorama*, and the reformers argued that in an internal market 'money would follow the patient', a catchphrase which knowingly implied that the producer interest had been too strong and was an early expression of the now consensual view that welfare services should be user orientated. Yet despite the declaration that 'empowerment' was to be the driving force of British health and social services (DoH 1991), the model which was implemented treated users primarily as 'customers' or 'consumers'.

One decade later, a distinguishing feature of the new Labour administration's 'modernisation plans' for the health and social services is the emphasis on meeting and managing the public's expectations and demands. As the White Paper on *Modernising Social Services* (DoH 1998, para.1.7) puts it, 'our third way for social care moves the focus away from who provides the care, and places it firmly on the quality of services experienced by individuals and their carers and families', and as a new Secretary of State for Health said in November 1999, 'I am setting out a new approach to the management of health care services in the NHS…around the needs and preferences of patients rather than the needs and preferences of services… Modernisation is about new ways of working that put patients first' (DoH 1999b). The likely effect and potential of the current reforms will be examined further in the final chapter.

Conclusion

This short introduction to formal health and social care services for older people suggests that there is a greater volume and wider range of provision in Britain today than ever before and that most is delivered by more highly trained staff and to a higher standard than in the past. There are more specialised services than informal care has ever provided and formal care continues to support and supplement the larger volume of spousal and filial care that remains the foundation of frail older people's care and support. But all is not well. Expectations continue to grow more rapidly than the volume and quality of provision, and of more concern to today's older people with serious health problems and functional restrictions, study after study reports that many perennial weaknesses persist. Services for older people are under-resourced, under-staffed and lowly regarded, and many are blighted by great variability in accessibility and standards of care. Every government announcement about its plans to modernise the relevant services documents a continuing weakness or endemic failure, as with the social services which, they say, 'are often failing to provide the services that we expect… Equally worrying are cases where…elderly people are neglected or mistreated, or live in conditions which nobody would want to call their home. Any decent society owes…to every elderly or disabled man or woman the right to live in dignity, free from fear of abuse. These duties must be given greater effect in future' (DoH 1998, Chap. 1).

Independent analyses and commissions lay down the same charges. Notwithstanding the huge achievements and advances during the first 50 years of the NHS, Charles Webster's summary assessment of developments outside the hospitals is telling and dismaying:

> Advanced ideas [i.e. proposals] concerning community health services or primary-care arrangements…have been realised in only limited instances and usually only approximately. For many groups, best practice remains as remote a prospect today as in 1939. The unemployed, the poor, the elderly, the physically disabled, or other vulnerable groups remain in a situation of disadvantage too reminiscent of before the existence of the NHS, while inequalities in resource distribution remain as glaring today as when they were first revealed. (Webster 1998, p.216)

In the following chapters of this book, the contributors report little to challenge these pervasive criticisms and indeed add discomfiting evidence of unacceptable attitudes towards older people and older people's services. They are not however altogether negative and identify several examples and opportunities for improvement and spreading good practice. Several chapters set out fresh and instructive analyses of the problems and agendas for positive change. They will be of great interest to all those concerned to raise the treatment of, regard for and well-being of older people.

References

Abel-Smith, B. (1964) *The Hospitals 1800–1948.* London: Heinemann.

Audit Commission (2000) *Forget Me Not: Mental Health Services for Older People.* London: Audit Commission.

Blythe, R. (1979) *The View in Winter: Reflections on Old Age.* Harmondsworth: Penguin.

Brocklehurst, J.C. (1985) 'The Geriatric Service and the Day Hospital.' In J.C. Brocklehurst (ed) *Textbook of Geriatric Medicine and Gerontology,* 3rd edn. Edinburgh: Churchill Livingstone.

Brocklehurst, J.C., Tallis, R. and Fillit, H.M. (eds) (1992) *Textbook of Geriatric Medicine and Gerontology,* 4th edn. Edinburgh: Churchill Livingstone.

Butler, A., Olman, C. and Greve, J. (1983) *Sheltered Housing for the Elderly.* London: George Allen & Unwin.

Centre for Policy on Ageing (1984) *Home Life: A Code of Practice.* London: Centre for Policy on Ageing.

Charnley, J. (1979) *Low Friction Arthroplasty of the Hip: Theory and Practice.* Berlin: Springer-Verlag.

Cole, T.R. and Winkler, M.G. (1994) *The Oxford Book of Aging.* Oxford: Oxford University Press.

Coleman, P.G. (1975) 'Social Gerontology in England, Scotland and Wales: A Review.' *The Gerontologist 15,* 219–229.

Crane, M. (1999) *Understanding Older Homeless People.* Buckingham: Open University Press.

de Beauvoir, S. (1970) *La Vieillesse.* Paris: Gallimard. (Trans. Patrick O'Brian (1977) *Old Age.* Harmondsworth: Penguin.)

Department of Health (DoH) (1991) *Managers and Practitioners: Guide to Care Management and Assessment.* London: HMSO.

Department of Health (DoH) (1998) *Modernising Social Services.* Cm. 4169. London: DoH.

Department of Health (DoH) (1999a) 'The National Survey of NHS Patients.' Press release 1999/0623. London: DoH.

Department of Health (DoH) (1999b) 'Patient Experience of the NHS to be Transformed.' Speech by Alan Milburn on 22 November. Press release 1999/0687. London: DoH.

Department of Health (DoH) (2000) *Modernising Health and Social Services: National Priorities Guidance 2000/01–2001/03.* London: DoH.

Dickens, C. (1865) 'Postscript' to *Our Mutual Friend.*

Dingwall, R. (1988) *An Introduction to the Social History of Nursing.* London: Routledge.

Evans, J.G. (1997) 'The Clinical Achievements of British Geriatrics.' In J. Phillips (ed) *British Gerontology and Geriatrics: Experience and Innovation.* Sheffield: British Society of Gerontology.

Glennerster, H. (1995) *British Social Policy since 1945.* Oxford: Blackwell.

Government Statistical Service (GSS) (1999a) *Social Trends 29 1999.* London: The Stationery Office.

Government Statistical Service (GSS) (1999b) *Annual Abstract of Statistics 1999.* London: The Stationery Office.

Health Advisory Service (2000) *Not Because They Are Old: An Independent Inquiry into the Care of Older People on Acute Wards in General Hospitals.* London: Health Advisory Service.

Home Office Committee on Local Authority and Allied Personal Social Services (1968) *Report of the Committee on Local Authority and Allied Personal Social Services.* (Chairman, Frederic Seebohm.) London: HMSO.

Jennett, B. (1995) 'High Technology Therapies and Older People.' *Ageing and Society 15,* 2, 185–198.

Jones, K. (1972) *A History of the Mental Health Services.* London: Routledge and Kegan Paul.

Le Fanu, J. (1999) *The Rise and Fall of Modern Medicine.* London: Little, Brown.

Lewis, J. and Glennerster, H. (1996) *Implementing the New Community Care.* Buckingham: Open University Press.

Means, R. and Smith, R. (1983) 'From Public Assistance Institutions to "Sunshine Hotels": Changing State Perceptions about Residential Care for Elderly People.' *Ageing and Society 3,* 2, 157–182.

Means, R. and Smith, R. (1985) *The Development of Welfare Services for the Elderly.* London: Croom Helm.

Means, R. and Smith, R. (1994) *Community Care: Policy and Practice.* Basingstoke: Macmillan.

Means, R. and Smith, R. (1998) *From Poor Law to Community Care: The Development of Welfare Services for Elderly People 1939–1971.* Bristol: Policy Press.

Organisation for Economic Co-operation and Development (OECD) (1985) *Measuring Health Care 1960–1983.* Social Policy Study 2. Paris: OECD.

Organisation for Economic Co-operation and Development (OECD) (1994) *New Orientations for Social Policy.* Social Policy Study 12. Paris: OECD.

Organisation for Economic Co-operation and Development (OECD) (1995) *New Directions in Health Care Policy.* Health Policy Study 7. Paris: OECD.

Organisation for Economic Co-operation and Development (OECD) (1999) *A Caring World: The New Social Policy Agenda.* Paris: OECD.

Parker, J. (1972). 'Welfare.' In A.H. Halsey (ed) *Trends in British Society since 1900.* London: Macmillan.

Parker, R.A. (1988) 'An Historical Background.' In I. Sinclair (ed) *Residential Care: The Research Reviewed.* London: HMSO.

Parry Jones, W.L. (1972) *The Trade in Lunacy.* London: Routledge and Kegan Paul.

Philpot, M. and Banerjee, S. (1997) 'Mental Health Services for Older People in London.' In S. Johnson and ten others (eds) *London's Mental Health.* London: King's Fund.

Rivett, G. (1998) *From Cradle to Grave: Fifty Years of the NHS.* London: King's Fund.

Sandvick, H. (1999) 'Health Information and Interaction on the Internet: A Survey of Female Urinary Incontinence.' *British Medical Journal 319,* 129–132.

Slack, K. (1960) 'Councils, Committees and Concern for the Old.' Occasional Paper in Social Administration 2. Welwyn: Codicote.

Stevenson, O. (1989) *Age and Vulnerability: A Guide to Better Care.* London: Edward Arnold.

Thomson, D. (1983) 'Workhouse to Nursing Home: Residential Care of Elderly People in England since 1840.' *Ageing and Society 3,* 2, 47–69.

Tinker, A. (1992) *Elderly People in Modern Society,* 3rd edn. London: Longman.

Tinker, A. (1997a) *Older People in Modern Society,* 4th edn. London: Longman.

Tinker, A. (1997b) 'The Development of Service Provision.' In I.J. Norman and S.J. Redfern (eds) *Mental Health Care for Elderly People.* Edinburgh: Churchill Livingstone.

Titmuss, R.M. (1950) *History of the Second World War: Problems of Social Policy.* London: HMSO.

Townsend, P. (1962) *The Last Refuge: A Survey of Residential Homes for the Aged in England and Wales.* London: Routledge and Kegan Paul.

Warnes, A.M. and Law, C.M. (1985) 'Elderly Population Distributions and Housing Prospects in Britain.' *Town Planning Review 56,* 3, 292–314.

Wattis, J.P. (1994) 'The Pattern of Psychogeriatric Services.' In J.R.M. Copeland, M.T. Abou-Saleh and D.G. Blazer (eds) *The Principles and Practice of Geriatric Psychiatry.* Chichester: Wiley.

Webb, S. and Webb, B. (1929) *English Poor Law History.* London: Longman.

Webster, C. (1988) *The Health Services since the War.* Vol. 1, *Problems of Health Care.* London: HMSO.

Webster, C. (1996) *The Health Services since the War.* Vol. 2, *Government and Health Care.* London: The Stationery Office.

Webster, C. (1998) *The National Health Service: A Political History.* Oxford: Oxford University Press.

Williams, A. (1998) 'Medicine, Economics, Ethics and the NHS: A Clash of Cultures?' *Health Economics 7,* 7, 565–568.

Woodroffe, D. and Townsend, P. (1961) *Nursing Homes in England and Wales: A Study of Public Responsibility.* London: National Corporation for the Care of Old People.

CHAPTER 2

Beyond the Body
An Emerging Medical Paradigm

Charles F. Longino Jr

As with so many other aspects of US society, the baby boom may be the catalytic factor that ultimately changes the way we treat our health. The culture of medicine is changing because the population is changing. Our bodies are ageing, but this is only the most obvious physical change. We are increasingly well-educated consumers, and our health-related attitudes and behaviour are changing. As a result, the American medical community is heading toward a new paradigm that combines scientific knowledge with a humanistic approach (Longino and Murphy 1995). This chapter examines several alternative or complementary models of and approaches to medicine that are challenging the biomedical model. It also examines the nature of the health care needs that are associated with advanced old age and which are expected to increase, and it will argue that, to meet those needs and in the face of mounting cost pressures, health care systems will have to revise their inherited emphasis upon curative approaches.

The existing paradigm of modern scientific medicine may be called the 'western biomedical model' (Freund and McGuire 1999). It relies on an essentially mechanical understanding of causation, one derived from science. Repairing a body, in this view, is analogous to fixing a machine. Furthermore, this view leads to the remarkably optimistic expectation that each disease has a specific cause, awaiting discovery by medical research. Finally, because the body is the appropriate subject of medical science and practice, it is also the appropriate subject of regimen and control. Although we may not consciously think of medicine in these terms, these are nonetheless the doctrines of the biomedical model. They form the subconscious cultural context out of which our thinking, medical education and professional conduct arise.

Because it has been so successful in dealing with deadly infectious diseases, medicine has worked itself out of much of its original job. It now faces a growing population of patients and potential patients who expect the same successes and advances in dealing with the chronic diseases and conditions that are more prevalent in old age. Unfortunately, scientific medicine cannot cure these ills. Medicine has to change its essential self-understanding to succeed in the future.

Out-of-date doctrines

Just as societies evolve ideas of truth, justice and beauty, they also develop philosophical conceptions of the human body, ideas that differ somewhat from culture to culture and change over time. The 'western biomedical model' is predicated on five related doctrines. The first to arise was the doctrine of mind–body dualism, instigated in the seventeenth century by the French mathematician and philosopher, René Descartes. The idea that the physical body is completely separate from the mind, soul and other less tangible factors may have been useful as a starting point for biomedical science, but it is increasingly difficult to affirm in the modern practice of medicine. It is a barrier to understanding the psychosocial component of medicine, including the placebo effect, the connection between stress and illness, the importance of support groups, and the more general relationship between social support and health. Although the doctrine is no longer strictly adhered to, psychosomatic phenomena are still often considered peripheral to scientific medicine.

The second doctrine is the mechanical analogy, which treats the body as a system of functionally interdependent parts and the physician as a mechanic. When disease is present, the structure of an organ is the first place to look for a cause. Thinking that a physician can repair one part of the body separately from the others is, however, a simplistic view and one unfortunately reinforced by much of academic medicine. Students often graduate without integrating their biomedical knowledge into an understanding of the human body as a whole, much less that of a total human being. Medical curriculum committees have struggled with the issue of integration, which usually flies in the face of departmental structure, funding allocations and the scope of their power. They are not unaware of the concept; they just find it logistically difficult to execute.

The third doctrine is physical reductionism. This focus excludes all non-material dimensions (social, psychological and behavioural) in the search for causes and interventions. It is the tendency to look for answers at progressively more basic levels. In biomedicine, this takes its ultimate form in attempting to locate causes largely in the genes. Again, the relatively greater power of the basic sciences in academic medicine promotes this outcome. Exposing students to behavioural and social medicine in the basic sciences curriculum would alleviate the problem.

The fourth doctrine is that the body is the appropriate focus of regimen and control. This principle is a logical corollary of physical reductionism. If disease exists in the body, then treat the body. Because of the emphasis that is placed on physiology, a patient is responsible for following the doctor's orders to get well, forming a power hierarchy with the doctor in control. The fifth, and final, doctrine of specific etiology relates to the idea that each disease has only one cause. This pushes medical research to discover 'magic bullet' cures and promotes a form of over-promising that has less and less credibility with the public today. Representatives of gay communities have already changed the paradigm under which its members operate with respect to the medical establishment and the treatment of AIDS.

The growth of medical consumerism

Medical consumerism, simply put, is the idea that the patient has rights and is an equal partner in the doctor–patient relationship. Criticism of science became increasingly prevalent in the late 1960s and 1970s, when authority of all kinds was being challenged by a baby boom generation come of age. Medical authority did not escape this onslaught. American physicians came to be regarded less like gods, and their sovereign profession came under fire for epitomising greed. The escalating cost of medicine and dwindling access to services under-scored a public sense of betrayal by both science and professional medicine. Many began to believe that scientific medicine was a monopoly designed to keep prices high and avoid competition (Starr 1982).

Nonetheless, with their narrow focus on the body and over-dependence on medical technology, doctors had become more and more removed from a human relationship with the patients. Zanner (1988) traces this growing distance directly to the biomedical model. Accordingly, the quality of the interaction came to be more impersonal and strained. Because scientific detachment was not offset by unques-tioning trust in the scientist-physician, malpractice suits increased. Patients, simply put, more often felt misunderstood, isolated and manipulated.

This issue is critically important in the context of chronic illness. Doctors may have lowered the priority they give to managing chronic conditions because this mode of treatment requires that they spend a lot of time talking with patients and in work that is ostensibly non-scientific. There is a lot to talk about: preventing or postponing disease, making early diagnoses, assisting in behavioural modifications, educating patients about treatment regimens, discussing options that could reduce disability, and modifications to home and workplace. These activities take too much time in the view of most physicians, not least because more patients can be seen when consultation time is reduced. As a consequence, nearly all the tasks are delegated to a nurse (Fox 1993).

Furthermore, during the 1980s there was a tendency to recognise medicine as an industry rather than primarily a profession and, of course, to encourage market mechanisms to control costs. Physicians were called 'providers' and hospitals 'provider organisations'. Consistent with this outlook, patients were called 'health care consumers'. Corporate medicine created the circumstances – and the consumer protection movement the values – that inundated American health care. Together they provided a setting in which the doctor–patient relationship came to be seen as commercial, impersonal and contractual. But clearly the values and attitudes that subtend commercial relationships are pragmatic and self-interested, and not idealistic. This shift eroded further the authority of the physician and subverted his legitimacy. This manoeuvering conveyed to the public the idea that health care was not something personal, but merely a commodity. Health care came to be seen less as integrated into daily life, and more as something that is periodically consumed. Rather than maintained, health is purchased from employers and the doctors they retain.

Consumerism empowers patients at the expense of at least some of the doctors' professional autonomy. The effect of this view has spread from the realm of practice to the halls of academia. In patient-centred interviewing courses, student doctors are encouraged to 'negotiate' a treatment plan with the patient. This is good medical practice because by buying into the plan patients are more likely to comply with it and less likely to blame the doctor for negative outcomes (Longino 1997).

The outlines of an emerging medical model

The new model has been established, one which focuses more broadly on health rather than only on medical interventions. It understands health to be both holistic and environmental, and it fully appreciates the connection between mind and body. It merges the cult of Asclepius and Hygeia (Dubos 1959). The orthodox biomedical model, by contrast, draws its lines tightly around the body and defines itself as scientific medicine.

In the USA other approaches to health and illness have grown up outside the fortress walls. They are acknowledged and sometimes appreciated by orthodox medicine but, because they go beyond the body, they are viewed as peripheral to its core mission. Although generally devalued and underfunded, they are gaining widespread acceptance among the public. Furthermore, their adherents publish in journals, often have postgraduate medical degrees, and conduct research funded by US federal agencies. These country cousins, to give them names, are holistic, environmental and behavioural medicines (Foss and Rothenberg 1987).

Of the three, holistic medicine is the least accepted by practitioners of orthodox biomedicine. Proponents of holism view patients as spiritual, psychological and cultural as well as physical beings, who relate dynamically to their social and physical environments. Holistic medicine emphasises 'wellness'. Within this framework patients are encouraged to become actively involved in their healing process, rather than being passive recipients of the healer's ministrations, placing an emphasis upon health maintenance rather than crisis intervention. Several treatment modalities are accepted that would not be considered reliable by the standards of biomedicine. Holism is broad and ecumenical, rather than narrow and exclusionary.

Environmental medicine stands closer to biomedicine than holistic medicine. Its understanding is that the causes of disease emanate largely from the physical and social environment and they afflict or burden the body. Environmental medicine does not deny the diseased body, but is not reductionistic; and searches for the causes of disease elsewhere. It emphasises the environmental, behavioural and nutritional ways of avoiding disease in the first place. The theoretical basis of this approach is rooted in an historical understanding of human evolution and environmental adjustments. That is, individual human biology is less important than the biology of populations. The understanding and practice of public health are rooted in environmental medicine.

Of the three, behavioural medicine stands the closest to biomedicine. Neuroendocrinology and psycho-neuroimmunology, for example, have emerged from this approach to medicine. Its most basic focus is on the connection between the immune system, the central nervous system and the endocrine system. The goal is to identify neurochemical mechanisms that operate in conjunction with subjective emotional states to trigger physiological reactions. Behavioural medicine, therefore, criticises mind–body dualism. The mind–body connection is recognised, along with the efficacy of coping mechanisms (not medicines) to reduce stress. Thus, it has one foot in biomedicine and the other in holistic medicine, although it talks the language of biomedicine. As with holistic and environmental medicine, humans are understood to affect and to be influenced by their social and physical environments.

The emerging paradigm sees connections between mind and body, in addition to between the person and the surrounding physical and social environments. In this model, the body and mind are embedded in, not separated from, the rest of the world. This paradigm is more attractive to specialists in family, geriatric and community medicine than to other medical specialities which tend to view the patients without reference to their contexts. British physicians from these specialities may wonder why the USA is so far behind the paradigm shift. In considering dementia, Kitwood (1998) expressed the new paradigm well. The answer is that there are far fewer physicians in America that specialise in the whole body, much less the person. Roughly half of British physicians are hospital consultants, whereas the US proportion is far higher.

A convergence of catalytic forces

Medicine's embrace of science has had profound and wonderful effects on human health. No one would want to give up the genuine benefits it has brought. Nonetheless, by the end of the twentieth century, the biomedical model is increasingly incomplete and deficient. In the fifteen decades between 1900 and 2050, the percentage of the US population aged 65 years and older will have increased from 4 to 20, and of those aged 75 to 84 years from 1 to 7. By 2050, those aged 85 years and older will represent nearly 5 per cent of the population, up from 0.2 per cent in 1900. This impressive growth has happened largely because public health initiatives have vastly increased the odds that people will reach old age, and that they will live longer once they get there.

The growth of the older population is relevant to biomedicine, because chronic illnesses tend to accumulate with advancing old age. Mittelmark (1993) made this point clearly when he asserted:

> Accident and injury are prominent concerns in childhood, adolescence and early adulthood, developing chronic diseases are a central feature of middle adulthood, morbidity and mortality from chronic

diseases characterise the period around retirement, and deterioration in functioning, disability and dependency are concerns mainly
of old and very old age. (Mittelmark 1993, p.135)

Functional ability tends to decline among very old people as
impairment leads to disability and disability leads to handicap, thereby
requiring increasingly comprehensive and expensive levels of care. Age
magnifies need not only for the older person, but also for their carers
and for society as a whole. Most important, however, is that an ageing
population increases the demands for certain types of care, namely
chronic as opposed to acute care (Friedland 1999). Unfortunately, this is
not the sort of condition that biomedicine is designed to meet. For
example, preventive strategies are called for to delay and diminish
health crises, while rehabilitation and disease management strategies are
needed afterwards. Environmental and holistic approaches stand ready
to step into the breach, but these are exactly the areas of medicine that
challenge the limitations of the biomedical model.

Most of the diseases that will eventually afflict an older person
cannot be cured, but their impacts can be postponed, reduced, and
sometimes partially reversed. At this time, however, preventive care is
viewed as the responsibility of those outside the medical profession
proper: nurses, social workers and others who work in community
health. The emerging paradigm presses for a merger of public health
and medicine into an integrated health delivery system.

Such changes cannot happen now because they presuppose the
existence of a broad consensus on health and healing. Nor can they
occur without major changes in academic medicine. Medical educators
are not ignorant of the problems posed by an inevitable increase in
chronic illness in an ageing population. The issue has created uneasiness
among physicians who are aware of the advantages offered by holistic,
environmental and behavioural medicine, but who feel trapped by the
biomedical model.

New paradigms grow out of the old, although the process takes
many decades. The decline in professional autonomy among physicians
and the rise of corporate medicine may speed up the process in this
particular case. If therapies from outside the western biomedical model
become popular and are less costly, the increasingly powerful man-

aged-care industry may simply mandate them. Already some companies are offering coverage for a limited number of chiropractic visits. 'Alternative' medicine is accordingly being redefined as 'complementary' medicine. Naturopathic and even homeopathic remedies, once hidden away in health food stores, are appearing on the shelves of major drug store chains. The high growth sector of the broad health care economy is no longer limited to orthodox western medicine. A visit to the 'PlanetRx.com' website and its links is instructive in this regard.

Major technological developments can also strain paradigms and increase the pace of change, just as in a previous era rapid urbanisation and economic growth made hospitals accessible to the vast majority. The electronic communication revolution at hand may be one of those potentially profound influences. Because of the 'information highway', it may no longer be possible for professional medicine to monopolise its special knowledge. The control of knowledge reinforces power, and power is something patients are beginning to demand for themselves. The Internet, for example, will increasingly pressure medical professionals to share their knowledge with the general public. One imagines a HarvardMedNet or MayoMedNet widely available to millions of Internet-linked patients.

When one combines the rapid growth of electronic communications with American individualism and distrust of authority, one can particularise speculations about the future. Are we now at the beginning of an era in which the sufferers from particular diseases, especially the esoteric and expensive ones, will find one another through the Internet and interact as mutual patient support groups? They will ask one another what treatments worked for them and how they located the services or products they used. The answers may be largely outside the confines of scientific medicine. The community of suffering will tend also to share horror stories of poor medical care, reinforcing the motivation to search ever more widely for solutions.

Long-term care

The term 'long-term care' is used to capture the image of functional maintenance for dependent older people. As used in the USA, the concept is the primary focus of health services for elderly people, which include preventive care, supportive services, treatment, rehabilitation and several levels of nursing care. This comprehensive, patient-orientated, collective term is difficult for biomedicine to handle; for example, supportive services, unless they are explicitly medical, would not be considered as health care. The key to understanding long-term care is the concept of functional ability. As functional ability declines, various levels of support and care are needed to offset this reduction, as well as to restore as much functioning as possible (Harel and Dunkle 1995).

The rapid growth of the older population in many affluent countries during the 2020s and 2030s will bring a similar increase of the long-term care population, and will challenge the biomedical model in a major way. Even long-term care, in its classic definition (Katz 1983), has been defined by the language of biomedicine as 'institutional and non-institutional services for people with chronic conditions that are marked by a pronounced deviation from a normal state of health and are manifested in discomforting abnormal physical or mental conditions' (p.722). In other words, chronic disease is defined as a departure from normal physiological functioning, from which substantial recovery is possible in the long run. Nonetheless, the current approach, of battling heroically to save lives after the consequences of chronic disease have reached a crisis state while ignoring all else, will be challenged by future demand.

In the US health care system, because much less is invested in the prevention and management of chronic disease in the community than in the UK, older people are pushed into higher levels of medical care than they actually need. Studies have shown that from 20 to 40 per cent of those in nursing homes could be served as effectively by appropriate community-based services (or in a nursing home at a lower level of intensity) (Dunlop 1993; Weissert 1979). In fact, older people prefer overwhelmingly to remain at home when possible, where they can maintain a greater sense of interdependence with family members, friends and neighbours, and a lesser sense of dependency (McAuley and Bliessner 1985). The relative paucity of community-based, long-term care services in the USA is due to the hegemony of the curative emphasis in the biomedical model. Yet it is in the older patient population where new approaches to health and medicine will be hammered out.

There are however some encouraging events on the horizon. First, the Robert Wood Johnson Foundation is currently funding some policy assessments. The purpose of this programme is to appraise the effectiveness of giving cash, along with some advice, directly to the consumer – that is, to older persons and family members. In this way, they can manage long-term care by purchasing the home care and health services that are needed on an open, competitive market. Obviously there are obstacles, such as minimising paperwork and yet maintaining some system of accountability. But the point here is that the future process of looking for solutions outside the confines of hospitals and nursing homes has already begun.

Second, it is important to note that there seems to have been a decline in disabilities due to chronic illnesses in the older population during the 1980s. There was a decline of 4.7 per cent in disability prevalence between 1984 and 1989 for all persons aged 65 years, and more community dwelling and institutionalised (Manton, Corder and Stallard 1993). These declines in chronic disability rates may be due to a gradual increase in education and economic status among older people, which will increase in future cohorts (Friedland and Summer 1999). Further declines would offset the expected burden of chronic disease, although it is difficult to say at this point how much pressure it would take off the health care system because that system will also be changing (Smith and Longino 1995).

Treating older patients provides the model

Treating older patients is forcing us into the larger domain of the person, beyond the body, in search of answers. Geriatric assessment teams already provide a model to broaden the process of diagnosis (Siu, Reuben and Moore 1994). In geriatric centres in nearly all university-based hospitals, treatment plans are routinely reviewed by interdisciplinary teams. These look beyond the body to the social and physical environments of the patient and the support that is available. In this way, geriatric medicine points the way to an emerging paradigm, one that is more inclusive and sensitive to context.

To accommodate the emerging paradigm, medical education in the future will be strikingly different in some fundamental ways. Imagine a case conference in a medical school. The case presented is that of a 78-year-old man found unconscious by a neighbour in his fifth-floor apartment. When the man reached the emergency department, a quick chest examination pointed to bacterial pneumonia. The patient was treated with penicillin. One of his knees was also swollen, the result of osteoarthritis. The patient responded well to drug therapy; his fever came down, his lungs cleared, and he was released.

The interns and resident physicians found the case uninteresting. The diagnosis was quick and straightforward, the treatment appropriate, and the patient got well without complications. 'But there is more,' said the professor. 'It is artificial to stop at the boundaries of the body. There is a story here, and none of you discovered it because you did not ask all of the right questions.' The man's grief at the loss of his wife caused him to be depressed. He was socially isolated, lived alone, and had kept to himself since his wife's death. The depression caused a loss of appetite. The swollen knee made it painful to negotiate the stairs, so he did not go out for groceries. He became malnourished, which weakened his immune system and made him vulnerable to bacterial infections. Pneumonia took hold.

This is only the first chapter of the story. Two weeks after the first episode, the grieving man became intoxicated one night, vomited, and aspirated the vomit into his lungs. Again, the students talked about diagnosis and treatment. The professor shook his head. 'Don't you get it?' he asked. 'By limiting your view to the disease state, you are missing the other factors in the story. Until you understand this, you may be able to get a patient out of the hospital, but you cannot keep him out for very long.' This hypothetical example, drawn largely from Eric Cassel's (1991) examination of human suffering and the goals of medicine, illustrates how the treatment of older patients calls attention to the ineffectiveness of the biomedical model and presses for a broader way of defining medicine.

In the illustration of the older patient, the links between grief, isolation, depression, appetite, immune suppression and infection demonstrate the mind–body connection essential in the medical care of older people. For the elderly man, an ideal treatment plan would if possible alter his social, emotional and housing context, as well as the disease outcome of those interactive factors, to achieve the goal of reduced hospitalisations. It is also appropriate for other life stages. Children whose bed-wetting has no apparent physical cause and adults with stress-induced ulcers are prime examples of patients who would benefit from a beyond-the-body viewpoint.

Four forces drive social change: population, organisation, environment and technology. Change happens faster when these forces work in tandem. Both technological and organisational change is pressing us to define health care more broadly and to use new strategies to keep down costs. The environment is moving toward an image of health and health care consistent with other elements of our convenience-oriented, personalised society. But ultimately there will be many more old people, and their growing number will exert the final push for a new and broader paradigm of what it means to practise medicine.

Challenges to geriatric medicine

American medicine is very status conscious, and geriatric medicine comes near the bottom of the scale. This is also true of internal medicine and rheumatology. These are the medical specialities whose patients have the heaviest loads of chronic illnesses. AIDS patients are most often treated by internists. These specialities have no lucrative procedures (such as knee or heart valve replacements) to recommend. They cannot cure most of their patients. Rehabilitation and long-term care has lower status than acute care for two reasons. First, it is unexciting in comparison to heroic medicine, for saving lives dramatically is rarely involved. Nor do physicians engaged in those enterprises have the diversions or prestige of expensive new technologies that come routinely to the clinics of many other specialists. When the rules reward cure rates rather than measures of improved functioning or slowing of decline, the service is plainly stacked toward curative medicine. Second, chronic care does not pay for itself in the managed care organisations that dominate health care in the USA. Such care is therefore, in a sense, subsidised. It is the revenue generated by acute and elective procedures and consultants that makes managed care organisations solvent. Thus, in the context of corporate medicine, the practice of care for those with chronic illnesses is a pariah. The gap between the incomes of physicians with family practice or geriatric specialities and those of most other specialists is greater in the USA than it is in Britain.

These are some of the challenges facing medical gerontology in the USA. In this chapter, I have argued that the growth of the older population will increase the levels of chronic illnesses to the point that the biomedical paradigm which forms the ideological framework of the country's health care will crack under the strain. The result will be new health policy initiatives that do not focus with such single-mindedness on curative medicine, as seen through the lens of the biomedical model. The high technology and oversupply of consultants in the USA will not bear the weight of this change in the patient population. Already health care consumes twice the share of the gross domestic product (15%) in the USA than in the UK. As the crisis mounts, there is the opportunity for geriatricians and others, who see the value in going beyond the body in their understanding of good medical practice, to offer something of value to the health care community at large. They can more easily work from within the emerging paradigm.

References

Cassel, E.J. (1991) *The Nature of Suffering and the Goals of Medicine.* New York: Oxford University Press.

Dubos, R. (1959) *Mirage of Health.* New York: Doubleday.

Dunlop, B.D. (1993) 'Need and Utilisation of Long-Term Care Among Elderly Americans.' *Journal of Chronic Disability 29,* 75–87.

Foss, L. and Rothenberg, K. (1987) *The Second Medical Revolution: From Biomedicine to Infomedicine.* Boston, MA: Shambhala.

Fox, D. (1993) *Power and Illness: The Failure and Future of American Health Care Policy.* Berkeley: University of California Press.

Freund, P.E.S. and McGuire, M.B. (1999) *Health, Illness, and the Social Body.* Upper Saddle River, NJ: Prentice Hall.

Friedland, R.B. (1999) *Challenges for the 21st Century: Chronic Conditions.* Washington DC: National Academy on an Aging Society.

Friedland, R.B. and Summer, L. (1999) *Demography is Not Destiny.* Washington DC: National Academy on an Aging Society.

Harel, Z. and Dunkle, R.E. (eds) (1995) *Matching People with Services in Long-Term Care.* New York: Springer.

Katz, S. (1983) 'Assessing Self-Maintenance: Activities of Daily Living, Mobility and Instrumental Activities of Daily Living.' *Journal of the American Geriatrics Society 31,* 721–727.

Kitwood, T. (1998) *Dementia Reconsidered: The Person Comes First.* Buckingham: Open University Press.

Longino, C.F., Jr. (1997) 'Pressure from Our Aging Population Will Broaden Our Understanding of Medicine.' *Academic Medicine 72,* 841–847.

Longino, C.F., Jr. and Murphy, J.W. (1995) *The Old Age Challenge to the Biomedical Model: Paradigm Strain and Health Policy.* Amityville, NY: Baywood.

McAuley, W.J. and Bliesner, R. (1985) 'Selection of Long-Term Care Arrangements by Older Community Residents.' *The Gerontologist 25,* 188–193.

Manton, K.G., Corder, L. and Stallard, E. (1993) 'Estimates of Change in Chronic Disability and Institutional Incidence and Prevalence Rates in the U.S. Elderly Population Form 1982, 1984, and 1989 National Long-Term Care Surveys.' *Journal of Gerontology: Social Sciences 48,* S153–S166.

Mittelmark, M.B. (1993) 'The Epidemiology of Ageing.' In W.R. Hazzard, E.L. Bierman, J.P. Blass, W.H. Ettinger, Jr. and J.B. Halter (eds) *Principles of Geriatric Medicine and Gerontology,* 3rd edn. New York: McGraw-Hill.

Siu, A.L., Reuben, D.B. and Moore, A.A. (1994) 'Comprehensive Geriatric Assessment.' In W.R. Hazzard, E.L. Bierman, J.P. Blass, W.H. Ettinger, Jr. and J.B. Halter (eds) *Principles of Geriatric Medicine and Gerontology,* 3rd edn. New York: McGraw-Hill.

Smith, M.H. and Longino, C.F., Jr. (1995) 'People Using Long-Term Care.' In Z. Harel and R.E. Dunkle (eds) *Matching People with Services in Long-Term Care.* New York: Springer.

Starr, P. (1982) *The Social Transformation of American Medicine.* New York: Basic Books.

Weissert, W.G. (1979) 'Rationale for Public Health Insurance Coverage of Geriatric Day Care: Issues, Options, and Impacts.' *Journal of Health Politics, Policy and Law 3,* 555–567.

Zanner, R. (1988) *Ethics and the Clinical Encounter.* Englewood Cliffs, NJ: Prentice Hall.

CHAPTER 3

Towards Person-Centred Care for Older People

Michael Nolan

Recent British government White Papers and subsequent service priorities for both the health and social services highlight a number of common themes intended to inform future policy and practice (DoH 1997, 1998a, 1998b). Prominent among these are the promotion of independence for users and the development of quality indicators which capture their 'experiences' of services. Although these trends apply to all client groups, they are particularly relevant to the needs of older people, as illustrated, for example, by the current emphasis on the compression of morbidity and preventative health interventions and the renewed interest in rehabilitation (Joseph Rowntree Foundation 1999; Nocon and Baldwin 1998; Prophet 1998; Sinclair and Dickinson 1998).

While such policies are seen to 'make sense' in both human and financial terms, critical analysis suggests that the primary motivation is economic, with the main aim being to reduce demand for acute and long-term care beds (Hanford, Easterbrook and Stevenson 1999). This raises significant tensions between the stated policy aims, which are often largely rhetorical, and the reality of services as conceived, delivered, evaluated and experienced. For example, it is now recognised that the health service has placed too much emphasis on 'counting numbers, on measuring activity, on logging what could be logged', largely ignoring the needs of patients (DoH 1998c), and that there has to be a reorientation of services so that they focus on what 'really counts' for patients (DoH 1997). Simultaneously, however, there are calls for the standardisation of outcome measures (Sinclair and Dickinson 1998) and the creation of structures such as the National Institute for Clinical Excellence (NICE) which overtly privileges objective, scientific knowledge and associated methodologies above lived experience. The detrimental effects of such trends are all too apparent on priorities in acute health care of older people, which has increasingly emphasised rapid throughput and discharge and neglected 'basic dignified care' (Audit Commission 1997; Health Advisory Service 1997; 'Health Advisory Service 2000' 1998). Consequently older people have been denied minimum standards of care in even personal hygiene, nutrition and continence. The degree of public concern occasioned by these deficiencies has been sufficient to cause a significant change in the emphases of such initiatives as the National Service Frameworks which, temporarily at least, have moved away from the original focus on 'patients with particular conditions' (DoH 1998c) and towards broader and more heterogeneous groups such as older people (see Chapter 5).

Similarly, if social services are genuinely to reflect the priorities of users, families and carers, then there is a need for considerable remedial work, especially in services for older people in which ageist attitudes remain prevalent and practitioners often have limited expectations of the willingness and capacity of older people to participate fully in planning and evaluating their care (DoH 1998a; Social Services Inspectorate 1997). This chapter argues that while empowerment, participation and person-centred care pervade the health and social service policy and practice literatures, the fragility of these concepts is evident in the way that services are currently delivered and the often implicit vested interests which promote and sustain professional hegemony. Using rehabilitation as an example, the relevance of promoting independence and its associated outcome measures is critically appraised, from which it is suggested that a reorientation of professional ideologies and practice is required to address the needs of older people.

Services for older people

Exploring the outcomes of care

Uncertainties about the intended outcomes of services for older people, particularly those who are frail, are long standing and apparent in both the health and social services. The few attempts that have been made to specify policy outcomes have often been either imprecise or adopted arbitrarily, and frequently reflect agency or professional priorities rather than the needs of older people. With reference to social care, Challis (1981) identified seven outcomes for community-based social services for older people: compensation for disability, maintenance of independence, nurturance, morale, social integration, improved family relations and community development. Despite many attempts to achieve greater clarity, few precise objectives for the community care of older people have however been identified and most contributions have been an expression of general principles (Henwood 1992). This is still apparent in the most recent White Paper on the social services which states that the aim of interventions is to promote 'independent and meaningful' lives (DoH 1998a). Little thought has however been given to what constitutes an independent and meaningful life, the implicit assumption being that it is best achieved by maintaining older people in their own homes.

Indeed there is a pervasive consensus that the main aim of support for older people should be to maintain them in their environment of choice (International Association of Gerontology 1998), which is universally and uncritically accepted as being their own homes (Victor 1997). In a recent comprehensive policy analysis, Rosalie Kane (1999) however laments that little thought has been given either to the intended outcomes of home care (beyond keeping an older person at home), or to what living at home might mean in terms of an older person's quality of life. She proposes ten objectives for the home care of older people, and argues that while policy makers subscribe in principle to such objectives, in reality the 'softer' outcomes, such as enhancing well-being and promoting a meaningful life, are rarely funded or prioritised. Although her reference is to the US welfare system, the analysis has wider relevance. Walker (1995), for example, considers that despite 'half a century of promises', UK community care policy has failed to address the needs of older people, because agencies actively seek to relinquish responsibility for providing services to the most vulnerable groups (Table 3.1).

Table 3.1 The potential goals of home care for older people

- Improving/maintaining health
- Providing comfort/freedom from pain
- Improving/slowing deterioration in function
- Meeting needs for assistance and care
- Improving knowledge/self-care abilities
- Improving psychological well-being
- Enhancing social well-being
- Promoting a meaningful life
- Maximising independence/autonomy
- Maintaining at home

Source: Kane 1999

Some commentators have also questioned the taken for granted belief that living at home invariably provides a better quality of life (Baldwin, Harris and Kelly 1993; Lawton, Moss and Dunamel 1995). Peace (1998, p.107) contends that community care 'has at its heart a basic philosophical principle that receiving care at home is infinitely better than in institutions'. This perception is sustained by the belief that domestic settings are intrinsically superior to institutional care, which is usually portrayed as poor. She suggests that this is not necessarily the case, as others assert (Baldwin *et al.* 1993). One study found that very frail older people living at home spend only about 7 per cent of their time in purposeful, enriching activity, and that a more stimulating environment could be provided elsewhere (Lawton *et al.* 1995). More empirical work in this area is required.

If the success of community care for older people is evaluated uncritically and simply by the maintenance of people at home, the independent ability to perform the 'activities of daily living' (ADL) has had a similar status in health care since the earliest days of geriatric medicine. The speciality's impetus in the UK was the desire of its pioneers, such as Marjorie Warren, to counter the nihilism that surrounded the care of older people and their belief that, with appropriate treatment, many could return to their homes. Early work was remarkably successful and many older people who for years had languished in long-term care were rehabilitated. Later, however, as geriatric medicine vied for status with general medicine and surgery, the inability to 'cure' many of the conditions of old age became an impediment (Wilkin and Hughes 1986). The consequence was that improvements in functional ability, as measured by ADL, were substituted as a measure of 'success' and as an indicator of when medical responsibility ceased. Similar developments occurred in the USA where Clark (1995) has charted the way in which the heroic (or curative) model of geriatric care was replaced by a focus on the quality of life. Finding that this concept is unusually elusive of definition or measurement, other indicators, mostly related to ADL, came to be used as proxies.

On both sides of the Atlantic, success in geriatric medicine has therefore come to be equated almost exclusively with improved functional ability and autonomy. It has been suggested that this reflects an aspect of the American way of life, which 'lionises' autonomy and independence (Kivnick and Murray 1997; Trieschmann 1988). Although ADL perspectives continue to predominate (Porter 1995), recently there has been a more sophisticated approach to evaluating services for older people, in which raising the quality of life becomes a principal aim (Martlew 1996; O'Boyle 1997). Among its problems are that when subjective elements are included in quality of life measures, they usually reflect the perceptions of researchers (Day and Jankey 1996; Farquhar 1995; Haas 1999; O'Boyle 1997). To compound matters there is frequently a 'youthful bias' with many scales containing items of questionable relevance to older people (Reed and Clarke 1999).

The ways in which services are defined and evaluated can often have a pernicious effect. Minkler (1996), for example, has been highly critical of the vogue concept of 'successful ageing', which is partly synonymous with independence, and argues that its elevation marginalises those who do not meet its criteria. She suggests that efforts to promote empowerment must focus on alternative concepts such as interdependence. Following a similar logic, Phillipson and Biggs (1998) contend that a current challenge is to build models of welfare that transcend dependency and help older people to maintain or construct a viable identity. According to Kivnick and Murray (1997), this implies thinking beyond remediation and compensation and setting the aim of gerontological practice as to identify and enhance older people's abilities and assets.

A telling illustration of the potentially deleterious effects on both older people and care staff of inappropriate service outcomes is in long-term care (LTC). In recent decades LTC has been primarily the responsibility of the health services, but because many older people in acute hospitals could not meet their criteria of success – for example, functional improvement and no better outcome indicator was identified – these individuals often became the subject of 'aimless residual care' (Evers 1991). In an effort to construct a legitimate outcome for their activity, staff substituted notions such as 'good geriatric care' (Reed and Bond 1991). Being difficult to specify in simple outcome terms, it was never accorded status or value, and the speciality's staff found it increasingly difficult to sustain motivation and morale. The transfer of responsibility for LTC since the early 1980s from the National Health Service (NHS) to the independent nursing home sector has done little to improve the situation, for there are still few clear or explicit goals and vague exhortations of dignity and autonomy prevail. Reacting to the elusive nature of such ideals, the sector has turned to more specific but less holistic performance indicators, such as the 'lounge-standard patient', one who is clean and presentable for visiting time (Lee-Treweek 1994). To reach this target, Lee-Treweek contends, staff often go to extreme measures and sometimes forcibly dress residents, which she terms 'bedroom abuse'.

Although this is an extreme example, as the cited recent reports from the Audit Commission, the Social Services Inspectorate and the Health Advisory Service clearly demonstrate, there is a gulf between the reality of service delivery and the fashionable rhetoric of empowerment and person-centred care. The gap is conceptual as well as practical and reflects the perceptual difference between professionally constructed service intent and the actual wishes and aspirations of older people (Livingston, Watkin and Manela 1998; O'Boyle 1997; Reed and Clarke 1999). The differences and contradictions are brought into sharp relief when rehabilitation is considered.

Contrasting models of rehabilitation

The current policy imperative of promoting independence among older people has focused considerable attention on the role of rehabilitation (DoH 1998a, 1998b). Hitherto rehabilitative services for older people were relatively underdeveloped but this is rapidly changing (Baker, Fardell and Jones 1997; Hanford *et al.* 1999; Sinclair and Dickinson 1998) and they now figure prominently in policy statements as well as non-governmental reports such as the Royal Commission on Long-Term Care (1999). Whether this results in more appropriate and sensitive services remains to be seen. The benefits will be determined largely by the way in which rehabilitation is defined and evaluated: it is argued here that the wider adoption of current methods of rehabilitation is likely to disadvantage older people.

The research evidence is not encouraging. Based on a longitudinal study of the rehabilitation of over 200 stroke patients over six years, Becker (1994) vividly portrayed the disadvantage and powerlessness that older people experience. She argued that models of rehabilitation are 'exclusionary' and ageist because staff decide which patients constitute 'good rehabilitation' candidates and use implicit criteria about their potential for functional improvement. The majority of the individuals deemed most likely to improve were relatively young and had suffered less severe strokes, while those not meeting staff criteria were consigned to 'geriatric care'. Once labelled, the treatment that patients received differed markedly. 'Good' candidates had more intensive therapy based on clear goals, and staff were more likely to advocate on their behalf. Conversely geriatric patients were often infantilised and asked to perform what they perceived as meaningless tasks without adequate explanation. If they complained this was taken as an indication of their lack of motivation, reinforcing and justifying staff appraisals of their poor rehabilitation potential.

Becker's analysis clearly reflects her sociological orientation but even the medical literature has criticised the way in which the rehabilitation of older people is practised, arguing that the views of patients are often ignored and that the focus is on the short-term goals of staff (Ebrahim 1994). Young (1996) voiced similar concerns and highlighted several common misconceptions about rehabilitation, including its finite nature and preoccupation with physical functioning. The therapy literature also reflects a growing discontent with a purely physical orientation, arguing that to be of value activity has to be both purposeful and meaningful from the patient's perspective (Mayers 1995; Trombly 1995).

Various commentators have advocated the need for a new approach to the rehabilitation of older people which places greater emphasis on its temporal dimensions and includes a more diverse set of outcomes that extend beyond physical functioning (Barolin 1996; Bond 1997; Ory and Williams 1989). Recent British publications suggest however that such calls are likely to go unheeded, with both the definition of rehabilitation and the outcome measures used still being dominated by professional perspectives. From their analyses of recent trends in rehabilitation policy, Nocon and Baldwin (1998) concluded that the primary characteristic of rehabilitation is its focus on the restoration of either function or role. They argue that rehabilitation is a time-limited intervention which must be distinguished clearly from services such as primary prevention and maintenance. It seems paradoxical at a time when government policy is explicitly that the needs of users should not be 'pigeon holed' by existing services, that the currently promoted types of care are predicated on just that (DoH 1998a).

A complementary review of the effectiveness of rehabilitation paid particular attention to the most commonly used outcome measures (Sinclair and Dickinson 1998). This highlighted several influences on contemporary rehabilitation, including the emphasis on capturing the views of users and carers, and the shift towards rehabilitation 'in the community'. The review found ironically that the commonly used outcome measures were conceptually and methodologically limited, because they relied on easily quantifiable indicators such as 'length of hospital stay' and 'improvements in physical functioning'. Furthermore, despite the high profile that family carers now enjoy in the policy arena, most studies included no outcome measures for carers. These conclusions have been corroborated by a meta-analysis which found that rehabilitation is usually evaluated by three criteria: survival, functional ability and discharge destination (Evans *et al.* 1995). Therefore, although current policy is to develop quality indicators which reflect the experiences and aspirations of service users, rehabilitation is deemed successful if someone survives a period of hospitalisation, returns home and is able to wash, dress and feed themselves.

In their comprehensive review of the rehabilitation literature, Nolan, Nolan and Booth (1997) compared professional accounts of rehabilitation with those of disabled people using five 'tracer' conditions which were chosen to reflect differing experiences of illness: stroke, myocardial infarction, spinal injury, multiple sclerosis and arthritis. Although the sampling design maximised the variation in important illness characteristics, such as onset, course, incapacity and outcome, the review revealed remarkable consistency across conditions and within informant groups along with considerable differences between the groups (Rolland 1994). In other words, disabled people identified similar themes largely irrespective of condition, but there were marked disparities between disabled people's and professionals' perceptions. Nolan *et al.* (1997) suggest that it is possible to conceptualise rehabilitation in terms of two 'ideal' types: the 'restricted isolated model' and the 'comprehensive integrative model' (Table 3.2). While these models are primarily heuristic and neither exists in its pure form, current approaches to rehabilitation approximate to the restricted isolated model, whereas the comprehensive integrative approach better reflects the views of disabled people and their carers (Nolan *et al.* 1997).

This is not to suggest that cure is never appropriate nor that, if achievable, a return to former function should be sidelined. Clearly, when cure is possible this would be everybody's preferred option. However, to limit definitions of success to cure or functional improvement, and to perpetuate an approach to rehabilitation based on a strictly finite input, is to ignore the biographical, temporal and existential challenges that people experience in the face of chronic illness and disability. Similar challenges confront many people as they age, for while the majority of older people are relatively fit and well and there are indications that it is possible to reduce dependency, advanced age provokes questions of identity and worth (Phillipson and Biggs 1998). Interestingly, several theorists in both psychology (Baltes and Carstensen 1996; Brändstädter and Greve 1994; Steverink, Lindeiberg

Table 3.2 Rehabilitation: contrasting models

Restricted isolated model	Comprehensive integrative model
• Physical orientation	• Incorporates biographical/existential elements
• Focus on impairment/functional aspects of disability	• Addresses handicap at individual, community, environmental and societal levels
• Finite, time-limited, emphasis on acute care, chronicity neglected	• Temporal/longitudinal emphasis, chronicity important
• Outcome/effectiveness driven, economic concerns predominate quantifiable, measurement orientation, static and a-contextual	• Expanded range of outcomes, incorporation of subjective indicators, includes process variables, dynamic and contextual
• Hospital orientated	• Includes all environments
• Mainly reactive, secondary prevention	• Proactive, primary prevention seen as important
• Individualistic focus on patients' functional ability	• Perspective of family unit seen as important
• Fragmented, ad hoc service provision and follow-up	• Co-ordinated, seamless provision
• Professional (medical) hegemony on expertise and power, interventions of little relevance to daily reality/personal meanings of disabled people/carers, disempowering	• Expertise/power vested with disabled people/carers, interventions high/relevant to daily reality/personal meanings, empowering
• Dominant, western cultural ethos, male orientated, problem-solving, personal autonomy	• Recognises issues of gender, culture, ethnicity, interdependence, community values
• Methodologically blinkered, theoretically restricted	• Methodologically and theoretically eclectic
• Experimentally and empirically driven	• Pluralistic models valued

Source: Nolan, Nolan and Booth 1997

and Ornel 1998) and sociology (Johnson and Barer 1997; Nilsson, Ekman and Sarvimäki 1998; Wenger 1997) advance remarkably similar accounts of adaptation in old age which highlight the importance of subjective and perceptual influences rather than objective circumstances. Although structural and environmental factors clearly play a part, a good quality of life is therefore still possible in adverse circumstances. Indeed personal meanings and values seem to play the most significant role in advanced age which implies that if health and social services are to work in genuine partnership with older people then it is important to realise the rhetoric of person-centred care.

Person-centred care

Several recent commentators have advocated new 'cultures' of care as in dementia (Kitwood 1997), rehabilitation (Nolan *et al.* 1997) and long-term care (Henderson and Vesperi 1995). Their common theme is the notion of person-centred care; an approach which recognises differing perspectives and values and requires that services reflect individual aspirations (Barker, Reynolds and Stevenson 1997; Clark 1995; Williams and Grant 1998). Realising such an approach means that practitioners must understand the experience of illness and disability, rather than simply be able to identify the symptoms and cause of disease, and learn to see the person behind the condition, which Minkler (1996) calls the 'human face'. This poses searching questions about the relationships between service providers and users, the types of knowledge each hold, and the relative power such knowledge confers.

The bases of professional expertise have been increasingly challenged in recent years, as has the often taken for granted superiority of theoretical knowledge (Eraut 1994; Schön 1987; Paley 1996). Even medicine now tacitly acknowledges the value of both science – managing the disease – and art – the care of patients as individuals (Cassell 1991). Simultaneously, far greater recognition has been given to the knowledge and expertise held by disabled people and family carers (Charmaz 1987; Nolan *et al.* 1996; Robinson 1988). Writers such as Barnard (1995) argue that practitioners must learn the skills of 'empathetic witnessing' in order to share understanding with disabled or ill people, so that each better appreciates the perception of the other.

Others have promoted similar ideas, although using different terms, such as 'therapeutic reciprocity' and 'inter-personal mutuality' (Kivnick and Murray 1997; Marck 1990; Nolan and Grant 1993). Williams and Grant (1998) suggest that to comprehend what it is like to live a particular kind of life, person-centred care requires knowledge of people as individuals as well as their beliefs, values and understandings.

Such a position undermines the notion of 'professional distance' and the belief that an 'outsider expert' can analyse a situation in a dispassionate and detached manner, applying objective knowledge to solve the problem. However, although welcoming more emancipatory models which view individuals as active agents and analysts of their own experience, Thorne and Paterson (1998) believe that the 'outsider expert' still has a critical role to play and caution against a headlong rush towards patterns of delivery in which professionals act simply as gatekeepers to services. Rather they call for a blending of professional and lay knowledge, in which neither is privileged over the other and with each being more prominent at different points in an extended relationship.

Clearly, therefore, while technical competence is a requirement for person-centred care, it is a necessary rather than a sufficient condition and other types of knowledge and skills are needed. These have been termed 'person-centred knowledge' (Liaschenko 1997) and 'inter-personal competence' (Fossbinder 1994). Although these frameworks derive largely from a nursing perspective they have wider application across health and social care. Liaschenko (1997) argued that there are three broad types of knowledge that can inform practice:

1. *Case knowledge*: this comprises biomedical and disembodied knowledge of a particular condition; for instance, stroke. The emphasis is 'on that part in need of fixing'.

2. *Patient knowledge*: this is best viewed as 'case in context' knowledge or, in other words, information about a person's social circumstances and level of support which provides a better understanding of the impact of the 'stroke' and the resources that can be mobilised.

3. *Person knowledge*: this is based on understanding 'biographical life' which for Liaschenko (1997) comprises three components:

- agency – a person's ability to engage in activity that is meaningful to them
- temporality – the person's normal routines and patterns of living and how illness interferes with and modifies them
- space – a person's social relationships and interactions.

These three elements help to structure identity and to create and sustain a sense of belonging.

Liaschenko (1997) suggests that while promoting the use of 'person knowledge', most practitioners rely primarily on 'patient knowledge'; that is, they collect personal information about the patient (user/client/older person) not in order to get to know them as an individual but rather to know how to respond to the 'case'. She sees nothing inherently wrong in this but it should not be masqueraded as 'person knowledge'. Indeed she believes that 'person knowledge' is neither possible or appropriate in all cases. In acute illness, for example, where cure and rapid treatment are the aims, 'person knowledge' may be unnecessarily intrusive. In long-term therapeutic relationships, however, Liaschenko (1997) sees 'person knowledge' as essential. She cautions that its implementation has political and financial consequences, and doubts whether there is either the will or the resources to support genuine person-centred care: '...the kind of attentiveness this [person] knowledge demands is increasingly being seen as fluff, not essential to a vision of health care in which people are cared for only on the basis of case and patient knowledge.' (*ibid.*, p.37)

Eliciting 'person knowledge' requires interpersonal skills of a high order and sufficient time and opportunity. The rapid throughput in acute settings gives too little time, while in long-term settings many staff are insufficiently trained or reimbursed to develop and maintain such skills. Halldorsdottir (1997) argues that modern health care has promoted a separation of technical competence from the affective elements of care, with the former being accorded greater status and value. Therefore the sort of interpersonal competence promoted by

Fossbinder (1994) is rarely fully acknowledged or valued (see Table 3.3).

Table 3.3 Dimensions of interpersonal competence

Dimensions	Examples
Translating	Informing, explaining, introducing, teaching
Getting to know you	Personal sharing, humour, being friendly, 'clicking'
Establishing trust	Creating confidence in ability to provide competent care
Being in charge	Knowing what to do
Anticipating need	
Being prompt	
Following through	Delivering care as promised
Enjoying the job	
Going the extra mile	

This is certainly the case when assessment, whether conducted by health or social care practitioners, is considered. Assessment is seen as

Source: Fossbinder 1994

the key to good health care for older people, with the collected information forming the basis for future care planning (Audit Commission 1997; Health Advisory Service 1997; 'Health Adivsory Service 2000' 1998). Yet this important activity is often left to the most junior medical or nursing staff who through inexperience may conduct a limited assessment. This frequently results in substandard care in important dimensions such as nutrition or continence and, in the case of swallowing assessment, can be life threatening. Less dramatic but no less important examples can be found in social care. For instance, the assessment of older people is often affected by ageist attitudes, with practitioners underestimating the ability of older people to play a full and active role and accepting depression and social isolation as inevitable consequences of ageing (Social Services Inspectorate 1997). Poor practice is also apparent in the assessment of carers' needs and when practitioners make implicit and ill-informed judgements about whether an assessment is required, with significant numbers of carers being unaware that their needs have actually been assessed (Fruin 1998).

Realising person-centred care

Without devaluing the importance of technically competent case and 'patient knowledge', it is clear that 'person knowledge' requires different but complementary skills and understanding. While these are largely interpersonal, other types of knowledge are also important. Griffin (1997), for example, argues that if individuals are to be empowered and enabled to use service systems to their best advantage then they need certain forms of understanding. Furthermore, if professionals are to facilitate such an understanding they too require a thorough grasp of four types of knowledge:

1. *Structural knowledge* of the way the health and social services work.

2. *Communicative knowledge* and the ability to interpret the language used by both patients and professionals.

3. *Cultural knowledge* and the influence of differing ethnic and racial beliefs on the way that health and illness are construed and the expectations individuals have of service systems.

4. *Social knowledge* of the individual, their resources and background. (after Griffin 1997)

The four types overlap with 'patient knowledge' (Liaschenko 1997). The latter's orientation differs, however, with its role being primarily to alert practitioners to the individual's response to illness, whereas Griffin suggests that practitioners utilise the listed four types to enable individuals to exert greater control over their situation. This latter approach is more emancipatory. As noted earlier, professional expertise, often in the form of 'case knowledge', needs to be blended with lay insights and understanding of the impact of illness and disability on a 'particular' life. Both contribute to the design and delivery of appropriate and sensitive person-centred care. It is therefore clear that person-centred care requires a reorientation of current practice and more fundamental changes, not least in defining what constitutes knowledge and 'evidence' in particular, and in the methodologies used to generate such evidence.

Conclusion

Analysts have long argued that UK policies for older people are based largely on 'general principles' (Henwood 1992) and that while a value-based approach is important, the cited values are frequently 'simple in their expression but highly complex in their translation into policy and practice' (Hughes 1995, p.45). Wistow (1995) contended that community care policy promotes conflicting aspirations, as with the simultaneous promotion of assessments based on individual need with resource efficiency and cost effectiveness. Such tensions are increasingly manifest in health care, with policy promoting the notion that quality evaluations should be based on the 'real experiences' of users (DoH 1997, 1998a). How such 'real experiences' are to be captured is patently missing and the quality infrastructures being developed are still primarily based on the logic of the randomised controlled trial.

This inevitably sustains the status quo, leading to the development of ever more sophisticated outcome measures, fuelled by the desire of the medical profession to have a 'test for every occasion' (Day and Jankey 1996). Fortunately counter-arguments are proliferating, with calls to move beyond 'statistical sophistication' (Bowling 1995) and towards approaches which capture the biographical and temporal dimensions of older age (Clark 1995; O'Boyle 1997).

A critical gaze also has to be applied to the 'values' driving recent policy initiatives, particularly the promotion of independence and the implicit assumption that this is an essential component of an acceptable quality of life. Such a stance overlooks the importance of collective values and interdependence (Clarke 1995; Kivnick and Murray 1997). According to Minkler (1996), the way forward is to apply the principles of critical gerontology, which aim not only to improve understanding of social ageing but also to change it for the better. Therefore realising person-centred care will mean debunking much accepted wisdom and that both academics and practitioners work in partnership with older people. The inherent danger of questioning current values and ideologies with arguments that are themselves articulations of general principles is that the prescriptions skirt the issues just as much. Certainly there is scope for the development of more relevant theories about what constitutes a meaningful life in advanced age, especially those which focus on the existential dimensions of frailty (Coleman 1997).

In the meantime there is a pressing need to improve the services which older people currently receive. What is required are practical and concrete examples that lay the foundations upon which more sensitive and appropriate outcomes can be built (see Davies *et al.* 1999). It is essential that work with older people is valued and promoted as a high status aspect of practice. This will certainly require a reorientation of professional training with recent studies in nursing, for example, showing that the needs of older people receive scant attention (Davies *et al.* 1996; Nolan *et al.* 1997). The National Service Framework for Older People (see Chapter 5) may well provide some of the necessary impetus, but will need to be accompanied by sustained action, inevitably raising questions about the funding available and what we are prepared to pay for. Resources by themselves will be insufficient, as the study by Davies *et al.* (1999) on promoting dignity for older people in acute hospitals demonstrated. It is also necessary for staff to value 'fundamental' care associated with personal needs such as washing, dressing, feeding and toileting. These often provide the context within which person-centred care is made manifest, particularly for very frail individuals, and as such should be valued as skilled and important activities.

References

Audit Commission (1997) *With Respect to Old Age.* London: Audit Commission.

Baker, M., Fardell, J. and Jones, B. (1997) *Disability and Rehabilitation: Survey of Education Needs of Health and Social Service Professionals – The Case for Action on Disability and Rehabilitation.* London: Open Learning Project.

Baldwin, N., Harris, J. and Kelly, D. (1993) 'Institutionalisation: Why Blame the Institutions?' *Ageing and Society 13,* 69–81.

Baltes, M. and Carstensen, L.L. (1996) 'The Process of Successful Ageing.' *Ageing and Society 16,* 4, 397–422.

Barker, P.J., Reynolds, W. and Stevenson, C. (1997) 'The Human Science Basis of Psychiatric Nursing: Theory and Practice.' *Journal of Advanced Nursing 25,* 4, 660–667.

Barnard, D. (1995) 'Chronic Illness and the Dynamics of Hoping.' In R. Toombs, D. Barnard and E.C. Barnard (eds) *Chronic Illness: From Experience to Policy.* Bloomington: Indiana University Press.

Barolin, G.S. (1996) 'Geriatric Rehabilitation ("Alters-Rehabilitation"): The New Challenge for Social Medicine and Science.' *International Journal of Rehabilitation Research 19, 3, 201–218.*

Becker, G. (1994) 'Age Bias in Stroke Rehabilitation: Effects on Adult Status.' *Journal of Aging Studies 8, 3, 271–290.*

Bond, J. (1997) 'Stroke.' In I. Philp (ed) *Outcomes Assessment for Healthcare in Elderly People.* London: Farrand.

Bowling, A. (1995) 'The Most Important Things in Life: Comparisons between Older and Younger Population Age Groups by Gender. Results from a National Survey of the Public's Judgements.' *International Journal of Health Sciences 6, 4, 169–175.*

Brändstädter, J. and Greve, W. (1994) 'The Aging Self: Stabilising and Protective Processes.' *Developmental Review 14, 52–80.*

Cassell, E.J. (1991) *The Nature of Suffering and the Goals of Medicine.* New York: Oxford University Press.

Challis, D. (1981) 'The Measurement of Outcome in Social Care of the Elderly.' *Journal of Social Policy 10, 2, 179–208.*

Charmaz, K. (1987) 'Struggling for Self: Identify Levels of the Chronically Ill.' *Research in the Sociology of Health Care 6, 283–321.*

Clark, P.G. (1995) 'Quality of Life, Values and Teamwork in Geriatric Care: Do We Communicate What We Mean?' *The Gerontologist 35, 3, 402–411.*

Clarke, C.L. (1995) 'Care of Elderly People Suffering from Dementia and Their Co-Resident Informal Carers.' In B. Heyman (ed) *Researching User Perspectives on Community Health Care.* London: Chapman and Hall.

Coleman, P. (1997) 'The Last Scene of All.' *Generations Review 7, 1, 2–5.*

Davies, S., Ellis, L., Laker, S., Philp, I., Brooker, C. and Warnes, A. (1996) *Evidence of Pre- and Post-Regulation Preparation for the Care of Older People.* Final Report to the English National Board. School of Nursing and Midwifery. Sheffield School of Nursing, University of Sheffield.

Davies, S., Nolan, M.R., Brown, J. and Wilson, F. (1999) *Dignity on the Ward: Providing Excellence in Care.* London: Help the Aged.

Day, H. and Jankey, S.G. (1996) 'Lessons from the Literature: Towards a Holistic Model of Quality for Life.' In R. Renwick, I. Brown and M. Nagler (eds) *Quality of Life in Health Promotion and Rehabilitation: Conceptual Approaches, Issues and Applications.* Thousand Oaks, CA: Sage.

Department of Health (DoH) (1997) *The New NHS, Modern Dependable.* Cm. 3807. London: The Stationery Office.

Department of Health (DoH) (1998a) *Modernising Social Services: Promoting Independence, Improving Protection, Reviewing Standards.* Cm. 4169. London: The Stationery Office.

Department of Health (DoH) (1998b) *Modernising Health and Social Services: National Priorities Guidance, 2001–2002.* London: DoH.

Department of Health (DoH) (1998c) *Quality in the New NHS.* London: DoH.

Ebrahim, S. (1994) 'The Goals of Rehabilitation for Older People.' *Reviews in Clinical Gerontology 4, 2, 93–96.*

Eraut, M. (1994) *Developing Professional Knowledge and Competence.* London: Falmer Press.

Evans, R.L., Connis, R.T., Hendricks, R.D. and Haselkorn, J.K. (1995) 'Multidisciplinary Rehabilitation versus Medical Care: A Meta-Analysis.' *Social Science and Medicine 40*, 12, 1699–1706.

Evers, H.K. (1991) 'Care of the Elderly Sick in the UK.' In S.J. Redfern (ed) *Nursing Elderly People*. Edinburgh: Churchill Livingstone.

Farquhar, M. (1995) 'Elderly People's Definitions of Quality of Life.' *Social Science and Medicine 41*, 10, 1439–1446.

Fossbinder, D. (1994) 'Patient Perceptions of Nursing Care.' *Journal of Advanced Nursing 20*, 1085–1093.

Fruin, D. (1998) *A Matter of Chance for Carers? Inspection of Local Authority Support for Carers*. Wetherby: Social Services Inspectorate/Department of Health.

Griffin, F.N.U. (1997) 'Discovering Knowledge in Practice Settings.' In S.E. Thorn and V.E. (eds) *Nursing Praxis: Knowledge and Action*. Thousand Oaks, CA: Sage.

Haas, B.K. (1999) 'Clarification and Integration of Similar Quality of Life Concepts.' *Image 31*, 3, 215–220.

Halldorsdottir, S. (1997) 'Implications of the Caring/Competence Dichotomy.' In S.E. Thorne and V.E. Hayes (eds) *Nursing Praxis: Knowledge and Action*. Thousand Oaks, CA: Sage.

Hanford, L., Easterbrook, L. and Stevenson, J. (1999) *Rehabilitation for Older People: The Emerging Policy Agenda*. London: King's Fund.

Health Advisory Service (1997) *Services for People Who Are Elderly: Addressing the Balance*. London: The Stationery Office.

Health Advisory Service 2000 (1998) *'Not Because They Are Old': An Independent Inquiry into the Care of Older People on Acute Wards in General Hospitals*. London: Health Advisory Service.

Henderson, J.N. and Vesperi, M.D. (eds) (1995) *The Culture of Long Term Care: Nursing Home Ethnography*. Westport, CT: Bergin and Garvey.

Henwood, M. (1992) *Through a Glass Darkly: Community Care and Elderly People*. London: King's Fund.

Hughes, B. (1995) *Older People and Community Care: Critical Theory and Practice*. Buckingham: Open University Press.

International Association of Gerontology (1998) 'Adelaide Declaration on Ageing.' *Australian Journal on Ageing 17*, 1, 3–4.

Johnson, C.L. and Barer, B.M. (1997) *Life Beyond 85 Years: The Aura of Survivorship*. New York: Springer.

Joseph Rowntree Foundation (1999) *Developing a Preventive Approach with Older People*. York: Joseph Rowntree Foundation.

Kane, R.A. (1999) 'Goals of Home Care: Therapeutic, Compensatory, Either or Both?' *Journal of Aging and Health 11*, 3, 299–321.

Kitwood, T. (1997) *Dementia Reconsidered: The Person Comes First*. Buckingham: Open University Press.

Kivnick, H.Q. and Murray, S.U. (1997) 'Vital Involvement: An Overlooked Source of Identity in Frail Elders.' *Journal of Aging and Identity 2*, 3, 205–225.

Lawton, M.P., Moss, M. and Dunamel, L.M. (1995) 'The Quality of Life among Elderly Care Receivers.' *Journal of Applied Gerontology 14*, 2, 150–171.

Lee-Treweek, G. (1994) 'Bedroom Abuse: The Hidden Work in a Nursing Home.' *Generations Review 4*, 2, 2–4.

Liaschenko, J. (1997) 'Knowing the Patient.' In S.E. Thorne and V.E. Hayes (eds) *Nursing Praxis: Knowledge and Action.* Thousand Oaks, CA: Sage.

Livingston, G., Watkin, V. and Manela, M. (1998) 'Quality of Life in Older People.' *Aging and Mental Health 2,* 1, 20–23.

Marck, P. (1990) 'Therapeutic Reciprocity: A Caring Phenomenon.' *Advances in Nursing Science 13,* 1, 49–59.

Martlew, B. (1996) 'What Do You Let the Patient Tell You?' *Physiotherapy 82,* 10, 558–565.

Mayers, C.A. (1995) 'Defining and Assessing Quality of Life.' *British Journal of Occupational Therapy 58,* 4, 146–150.

Minkler, M. (1996) 'Critical Perspectives on Ageing: New Challenges for Gerontology.' *Ageing and Society 16,* 4, 467–487.

Nilsson, M., Ekman, S. and Sarvimäki, A. (1998) 'Ageing with Joy or Resigning to Old Age: Older People's Experiences of the Quality of Life in Old Age.' *Health Care in Later Life 3,* 2, 94–110.

Nocon, A. and Baldwin, S. (1998) *Towards a Rehabilitation Policy: A Review of the Literature.* London: King's Fund.

Nolan, M.R. and Grant, G. (1993) 'Rust Out and Therapeutic Reciprocity: Concepts to Advance the Nursing Care of Older People.' *Journal of Advanced Nursing 18,* 1305–1314.

Nolan, M.R., Nolan, J. and Booth, A. (1997) *Preparation for Multi-Professional Multi-Agency Health Care Practice: The Nursing Contribution to Rehabilitation within the Multidisciplinary Team, Literature Review and Curriculum Analysis.* Final Report to the English National Board. London: ENB.

Nolan, M.R., Walker, G., Nolan, J., Williams, S., Poland, F., Curran, M. and Kent, B.C. (1996) 'Entry to Care: Positive Choice or *Fait Accompli?* Developing a More Proactive Nursing Response to the Needs of Older People and Their Carers.' *Journal of Advanced Nursing 24,* 265–274.

O'Boyle, C.A. (1997) 'Measuring the Quality of Later Life.' *Philosophical Transactions of the Royal Society of London, Series B: Biological Sciences 352,* 1363, 1871–1879.

Ory, M.G. and Williams, F. (1989) 'Rehabilitation – Small Goals, Sustained Interventions.' *Annals of the American Academy of Political and Social Science 503,* 60–71.

Paley, J. (1996) 'Intuition and Expertise: Comments on the Benner Debate.' *Journal of Advanced Nursing 23,* 4, 665–671.

Peace, S.M. (1998) 'Caring in Place.' In A. Brechin, J. Walmsley, J. Katz, and S. Peace, (eds) *Care Matters: Concepts, Practice and Research in Health and Social Care.* pp.107–125. London: Sage.

Phillipson, C. and Biggs, S. (1998) 'Modernity and Identity: Theories and Perspectives in the Study of Older Adults.' *Journal of Aging and Identity 3,* 1, 11–23.

Porter, E. (1995) 'A Phenomenological Alternative to the "ADL Research Tradition".' *Journal of Aging and Health 7,* 1, 24–45.

Prophet, H. (1998) 'Fit for the Future: The Prevention of Dependency in Later Life.' Paper Delivered at the Continuing Care Conference, London.

Reed, J. and Bond, S. (1991) 'Nurses' Assessment of Elderly Patients in Hospital.' *International Journal of Nursing Studies 28,* 1, 55–64.

Reed, J. and Clarke, C.L. (1999) 'Nursing Older People: Considering Need and Care.' *Nursing Inquiry 6,* 208–215.

Robinson, I. (1988) 'The Rehabilitation of Patients with Long Term Physical Impairments: The Social Context of Professional Roles.' *Clinical Rehabilitation 2,* 339–347.

Rolland, J.S. (1994) *Families, Illness and Disability: An Integrative Treatment Model.* New York: Basic Books.

Royal Commision on Long-Term Care (1999) *With Respect to Old Age: A Report by the Commission on Long-Term Care.* London: The Stationery Office

Schön, D. (1987) *Educating the Reflective Practitioner.* San Francisco: Jossey-Bass.

Sinclair, A. and Dickinson, E. (1998) *Effective Practice in Rehabilitation: The Evidence of Systematic Reviews.* London: King's Fund.

Social Services Inspectorate (1997) *The Cornerstone of Care: Inspection of Care Planning for Older People.* London: Department of Health.

Steverink, N., Lindeiberg, S. and Ornel, J. (1998) 'Towards Understanding Successful Ageing: Patterned Changes in Resources and Goals.' *Ageing and Society 18,* 4, 441–468.

Thorne, S. and Paterson, B. (1998) 'Shifting Images of Chronic Illness.' *Image 30,* 2, 173–178.

Trieschmann, R.B. (1988) *Spinal Cord Injury: Psychological, Social and Vocational Rehabilitation.* New York: Demus.

Trombly, C.A. (1995) 'Occupation: Purposefulness and Meaningfulness as Therapeutic Mechanisms.' *American Journal of Occupational Therapy 49,* 10, 960–972.

Victor, C.R. (1997) *Community Care and Older People.* Cheltenham: Stanley Thorne.

Walker, A. (1995) 'Integrating the Family in the Mixed Economy of Care.' In I. Allen and E. Perkins (eds) *The Future of Family Care for Older People.* London: HMSO.

Wenger, G.C. (1997) 'Reflections: Success and Disappointment – Octogenarians' Current and Retrospective Perceptions.' *Health Care in Later Life 2,* 4, 213–226.

Wilkin, D. and Hughes, B. (1986) 'The Elderly and the Health Services.' In C. Phillipson and A. Walker (eds) *Ageing and Social Policy: A Critical Assessment.* Aldershot: Gower.

Williams, B. and Grant, G. (1998) 'Defining "People-Conditions": Making the Implicit Explicit.' *Health and Social Care in the Community 6,* 2, 84–94.

Wistow, G. (1995) 'Aspirations and Realities: Community Care at the Crossroads.' *Health and Social Care in the Community 3,* 4, 227–240.

Young, J. (1996) 'Caring for Older People: Rehabilitation and Older People.' *British Medical Journal 313,* 7058, 677–681.

CHAPTER 4

Rationing Care

Alan Maynard

Introduction

The negative overtones associated with the word 'rationing' lead many to deny its existence in health and social care systems worldwide. This response is as foolish as it is inappropriate. It is obvious that professionals who control access to care routinely ration the available volume and quality of care. Rationing occurs when someone is denied (or simply not offered) an intervention that everyone agrees would do them some good and which they would like to have (Williams 1998). The criteria determining the practice of rationing by professionals in the health and social care systems are implicit and variable, with services being available in some areas and denied to similar patients in other areas. Thus there is evidence of older people being denied surgery – for example, coronary artery bypass procedures and cancer treatment – even though outcomes with good practice can be excellent. Often, of course, there is a risk that reported outcomes are poor, not because of an inferior capacity to benefit among older people, but because patients are offered poor quality care (for a discussion, see Maynard 1993).

The ubiquitous nature of rationing is self-evident, in the British National Health Service (NHS) as elsewhere. An older patient is denied surgical treatment of cancer of the oesophagus while an 80-year-old man severely injured in a road traffic accident in Greater Manchester is 'ferried' around the North of England to an intensive care bed in

Harrogate. Meanwhile, thousands of people in pain and discomfort are waiting for cheaper, cost-effective interventions which will restore mobility and reduce pain (hip and knee replacement) and give sight to the blind (cataract removal). How should these competing claims on NHS resources be managed? The absence of agreement about allocation criteria, and the problem of poor evidence about the cost effectiveness of competing interventions in health and social care, are indicative of the need to have a systematic approach to the issue of rationing. There are several interlinked issues which have to be dealt with in an integrated fashion if rationing is to achieve its social goals.

An integrated approach to rationing

Rationing (or what economists call the allocation of resources) involves a series of related steps consequent to the answering of the following questions:

1. What is the purpose of health and social care provision?
2. What criteria should determine access to health and social care?
3. What is need?
4. What is the trade-off between efficiency and equity?
5. Who should judge the need of competing patients?
6. How should the performance of those who ration health and social care be policed?

Let us explore each of these issues, remembering throughout that they are part of the integrated whole of an efficient system of rationing care.

What is the purpose of health and social care provision?

The answer to this question appears to be obvious, i.e. the purpose of the health and social care system is to improve health where possible and to manage its maintenance and decline where improvement is impossible. As this definition of purpose is uncontentious for most, it is remarkable that no existing health and social care system, public or private, measures its success explicitly and systematically. For instance, in Britain the NHS consumes about £45 billion each year. Much of the policy debate (and media hype) focuses on whether this expenditure is 'adequate' and whether the NHS is underfunded. When not focused on finance, the public debate involves the exchange between political groups of rhetoric and pledges that waiting lists and times will be improved under Labour or Conservative governments. Why is that debate and policy discussion focused on 'inputs' – for example, the 'adequacy' of funding and the number of doctors, nurses and beds – and processes or activities – for example, the number of general medical practitioner (GP) consultations, outpatient visits and inpatient procedures – rather than on the success or failure of using these 'ingredients' in the process of producing health improvements for patients?

Health gains are not easy to measure. The ideal is a sensitive mechanism which indicates improvements in the length and quality of life. No health care system has a measure of its success in producing health. In private health systems the focus of management data is activity and the prices paid for procedures. Thus the US system of managed care spends 20 cents in each health care dollar on administration and marketing. This large expenditure produces no indication of whether the care offered to patients improves their health. Recently this issue has been highlighted in a US Institute of Medicine report (Kohn, Corrigan and Donaldson 1999) whose authors, using limited local studies, estimated that between 44,000 and 98,800 people die each year as a result of medical errors.

The British NHS does no better. This system is cheap to manage as administrative costs are only 5 per cent of expenditure. This frugality ensures that clinicians and all other decision makers are ignorant of what they do in terms of cost, volume and success, and of producing health. It is remarkable that there is no demand for such data from clinicians, nurses and other managers so that they can demonstrate to patients that the care they offer is of good quality and effective. The tradition of western medicine is to trust the professionals to govern themselves to ensure quality. Unfortunately the professionals and their associations, the Royal Colleges, have failed to honour society's trust. Extreme consequences of this have recently been the high rate of mortality of young children undergoing paediatric cardiac care in

Bristol, and general medical practitioner Harold Shipman's protracted murderous abuse of his elderly patients. The post-Bristol trauma is leading to the establishment of elaborate procedures to improve quality and protect patients from deficient practice. After the Shipman case general practice will never be the same. Again it is remarkable how little of the previous policy debate has been concerned with the measurement of success and failure in producing health, i.e the quality of care. Clinical governance can only be effective if there are data about the comparative success of individuals, teams and organisations such as hospitals and general practices.

At present routine health outcome data are poor in the NHS. After collecting and hiding mortality data for four decades, the relative performance of English hospitals in killing their patients has been published in the last year; the Scots have been publishing similar data for nearly five years. Poor performance on such data may be the product of inaccurate data collection or case severity; for example, one surgeon may treat fit young people and another acutely sick older patients. Consequently such data have to be used with care. In the recent past, outcome data for NHS hospitals aggregated deaths and discharges and, as a consequence, it was impossible to distinguish between vertical (walking) and horizontal (dead) discharges. Such distinctions are now possible. However, there are still no data about whether 'survivors' are wheelchair bound or can dance the 'light fantastic'. In other words, no systematic measurement of functional status is used to illuminate the achievements of practitioners.

What is needed to supplement survival data is measurement of the quality of life. Thus, as an older person enters the system and is diagnosed as suitable for a hip replacement, their quality of life in terms of physical, social and psychological well-being and pain would be assessed and monitored through the period of hospital care and rehabilitation. There are routine validated and cheap methods of monitoring these outcome attributes, but little routine use is made of them in health care systems. For instance, two years ago the manufacturers of the 3M hip prosthesis admitted that it was deficient and offered to pay for their replacement. One-fifth of these patients have still not been identified, as routine NHS records are so poor that they fail to indicate who has got what spare part. This casual approach is complemented by the failure to follow up patients routinely to identify success and failure. This is a sad reflection on professional practice and the weakness of purchasers. The latter should contract not just for the procedure but also for follow-up: how else can they discriminate among alternative surgeons and withhold their business from those who do not produce good health care outcomes?

Although therefore everyone agrees that the business of the health care industry is the production of health, no one measures success or failure systematically in its terms. Success until recently has been taken on trust. Now it is evident that this trust has been badly used, and that a thorough measurement of health is an essential ingredient in the quality assurance and the rationing processes. But health care is only part of the caring process and social care is also very important. The quality of life (in terms of physical, psychological and social well-being and pain management) of an older person who has a hip replaced should be measured from the initial consultation in the GP's surgery, through the hospital and rehabilitation, and for years after the patient resumes everyday activities in the community (bacteria in hip cement may take ten years to appear and the durability of prostheses needs long-term evaluation, while operations may fail to remove pain).

An older person who has a stroke can gain considerably from rehabilitative care in the hospital and beyond. However, they may be unable to live independently and require support in the home or in institutions. Assessments can be made – for example, with the activities of everyday living scale or generic quality of life measures – to determine the effectiveness of care packages designed for such patients. Such evaluation has been slow to evolve in social care. A nice example of this is evaluative research on social work. Most of this literature is qualitative and the profession has been very reluctant to invest in randomised controlled trials even though every policy innovation they make is a social experiment which requires evaluation. When such methods are used to complement the qualitative approach, their results often disappoint the optimists who believe that activity is always beneficial (McDonald 1997). Without systematic evaluations of health and social care packages that emphasise the measurement of effects and the costs of achieving them, practice will be unproven and professionals may misuse resources which could be used to care for other clients.

What criteria should determine access to care?

There are three things which are certain in life: death, taxes and scarcity. Everywhere and always decision makers, be they individuals or societies, are confronted by the ubiquitous problem of scarcity. In health care systems choices have to be made which determine who will have access to what services and when. Older people in Britain are made to wait twelve months and more for procedures such as hip and knee replacements and cataract removals which are demonstrably cost effective and transform the life of beneficiaries. Older people in the USA can receive these procedures within days of their diagnosis if they have insurance or independent means to fund their care; and older people without private insurance can get access to care through the Medicare programme. The young American poor who need such procedures face greater uncertainty in accessing care but will be 'repaired' in due course. Different groups in different health care systems face differing financial and time barriers to care.

In Germany the drug viagra is regarded as a 'recreational' drug and is not reimbursed by the sickness funds. In Britain the drug is available only to a narrow range of patients and the rest of the population can access it by private prescription and payment of the full price. In the USA the managed care companies usually allow their beneficiaries three tablets per month; that is, they control their cost by rationing sex. Access to nursing and residential home care is variable and uncertain. Many stroke patients can be trapped in an expensive NHS bed because either there is no funding for community care or there are no places. When health and social care resources are rationed, 'cure and care' services should be allocated in integrated packages which deal with episodes of need, regardless of whether that demand falls on the NHS, local authority, social services or the family. Such care packages should be 'bundled' on the basis of effectiveness and cost of their ingredients, both of which should be measured thoroughly.

These examples demonstrate the various ways in which access to care can be rationed: time, money and bureaucratic rules in public and private systems limit access to care even when clinical and social need is demonstrable and the interventions are cost effective. The choice of the rationing methods is determined by goals and values. In most care systems there is a reluctance to rely on whether people are willing and able to pay. This is so even in the USA where 40 cents in the health care dollar is funded by government. In most of western Europe, in contrast, willingness and ability to pay have been discarded as the determinant of access to care, and there is a consensus that patients should be treated on the basis of their need. There is, however, a reluctance to clarify this concept.

What is need?

Need can be either a demand or a supply concept. Let us discuss this in the context of health care. A patient may demand health care because he or she feels unwell. The doctor may feel that no disease exists, that it is self-limiting, or that nothing can be done for this patient. Thus there is a patient need but a denial of the need by the doctor. If the concept of need adopted in a public health care system is the ability of the patient to benefit per unit of cost from care, the deployment of scarce resources on this basis can lead to the maximisation of health gains from a limited budget. Let us elaborate this simple benefit principle (noting that a Quality-Adjusted Life Year or QALY is one year of good quality life, with no physical, social or psychological impairments).

1. Assume that there is a group of patients with health problem B which can be treated with therapy X or therapy Y. The characteristics of these therapies are that X produces 7 QALYs and Y produces 20 QALYs. A clinician brought up in the Hippocratic tradition of doing the best for the patient in his care would choose therapy Y. This choice would also be preferred by the individual patient.

2. These choices are based on the evidence about clinical effectiveness, but the purchaser is interested in the maximisation of health gains from its limited budget. Let us assume that

therapy X costs £700 and therapy Y costs £10,000. Then therapy X produces each QALY at an average cost of £100, while therapy Y produces a QALY at an average cost of £500. Therapy Y produces 13 more QALYs (compared to therapy X) at an additional cost of £9,300 (£10,000 − £700), i.e. the marginal cost of an additional QALY by using therapy Y is £715.

The clinician concerned with the individual perspective of the patient in his care would choose the clinically superior intervention (Y) and in so doing would practise inefficiently. To practise inefficiently is to deprive other patients of care from which they would benefit more: all choices, including those which are inefficient, impose opportunity costs (the value of benefits forgone) on society. From a utilitarian perspective, i.e. the greatest happiness of the greatest number or maximisation of population health gains from a finite budget, inefficiency can be regarded as unethical. Thus the inefficient practitioner also works unethically. The efficient option is therapy X which produces a QALY at a lower cost. Thus if the total budget for this therapeutic area was £100,000, intervention X would produce 1000 QALYs while use of intervention Y would produce only 200 QALYs. The efficient intervention (X) generates more QALYs from the limited budget even though it is less clinically effective than therapy Y.

If the adopted definition of need is 'benefit per unit of cost', there are two immediate consequences. First, the clash between the individual perspective of clinicians and the social perspective of economists, public health physicians and purchasers has to be recognised and resolved. If the objective of policy is the maximisation of health gains from the finite NHS budget, then the social or 'population' perspective and the least cost per outcome criterion must be adopted. Second, the adoption of new technologies should be determined by economic effectiveness and not solely on the basis of clinical effectiveness: the latter is a necessary but not a sufficient condition for the use of a therapy. Similar arguments pertain in social care: the purchasers' concern is not merely effectiveness but cost effectiveness. As in health care, the measurement challenges are considerable but knowledge about 'what works' and at what cost is gradually increasing (Knapp 1984, 1995; McDonald

1997). Again there is potential conflict between providers' focus on effectiveness and purchasers' focus on cost effectiveness. If the objective of social care is to achieve maximum benefit at least cost for clients, the economic paradigm must, once again, dominate.

What is the trade-off between efficiency and equity?

The Thatcher and Blair reforms of the NHS continued the British tradition of large unevaluated social experiments. Their architects were hurried in their design and implementation of these reforms. As the then President of the Royal College of Physicians remarked at the time of the Thatcher reforms, 'instead of ready, take aim and fire, the government choose to get ready, fire and then take aim'. As ever, one of the characteristics of these reforms was the failure to clarify the policy goals. The implication of the Thatcher reforms and the complementary reforms of Blair is that the goal is to improve the efficiency with which resources are used. More recently the Blair government has emphasised equity but their definitions of this concept have been vague.

It is evident from the behaviour of decision makers in all health care systems that efficiency is not the sole objective of health care decision makers. For instance, interventions to save low birth weight babies result in the survival of infants whose quality of life is much impaired due to physical and intellectual disabilities. Such interventions are not efficient, but reflect social preferences for equity targets such as the high valuation of the lives of newborn children. A review of the many attempts by many administrators, as in New Zealand, Sweden, Norway, Finland, the Netherlands and the state of Oregon in the USA, reveals good intentions but a confused focus in the incorporation of equity issues into rationing criteria (Maynard and Bloor 1998). The Swedes offered a range of equity concepts and failed to develop and adopt any, although one of their ideas, the concept of life cycle equity in health, has been developed into the 'fair innings approach' (Williams 1997).

The antecedents of this approach are interesting. Anthony Trollope in his novel *The Fixed Term* developed the idea of all members of society being allocated a fixed period of life and then accepting death when their allocation expired. The American philosopher Daniel Callahan (1987) advocated the rationing of health care by age, precipitating a debate about at what age treatment should be withdrawn, whether there should be gender differences in that age, and whether it was more appropriate to focus on chronological or physiological age. Williams's approach is different and provocative. His argument is that older people who have had a fair innings should agree to the redistribution of care (even if its provision is efficient) to the young who may be chronically ill and have not had a 'fair innings'. Thus to achieve life cycle equity and give everyone a fair chance of a reasonable term of good quality life, resources would, for instance, be taken from the efficient treatment of older people with orthopaedic surgery for the hip or knee, and reallocated to a young person with, for instance, multiple sclerosis or some disability arising from low birth weight delivery, even if such treatment is inefficient.

The objective of such redistribution is self-evident: to reduce inequalities in healthy life spans. The opportunity costs are equally as obvious: such a policy would reduce the quantity of overall population health gain achievable from a limited budget. In essence efficiency gains would be given up to achieve greater equity. How much efficiency should be given up to achieve what type and level of equity? Who should decide these trade-offs and, if it is politicians, how will the public influence this exercise of power? These are some of the complex issues raised by being explicit about the equity goal. Such explicitness would make all decision makers more accountable and would avoid the continuing 'fudging' of the definition of equity and the trade-off, if any, that society desires between it and the single-minded pursuit of efficiency.

Effective rationing is needed of the considerable investment in the production of evidence about the costs and benefits of alternative health care interventions, be they diagnostic, therapeutic, rehabilitative or palliative. The purpose of the Cochrane Collaboration, an international network of research groups using common methodologies, is to produce meta-reviews by re-analysis of pooled experimental data (for an elaboration, see Maynard and Chalmers 1997). This is the start of an overdue and complex task, although the focus on economic rather than merely clinical aspects of care and cure needs emphasis (Maynard 1997). The results of this work will take many years to become available, let alone translate into practice. There is a risk that impatient politicians, looking for 'quick fixes' in the short term, will tire of awaiting such enlightenment. Such impetuosity will need to be restrained and politicians educated to ensure that policy is 'confused' with facts.

The Cochrane approach, of systematically reviewing existing data to highlight what is needed and what needs improved evaluation, is gradually being applied to other social policy areas but progress is uneven. What is the evidence base for social care, education and criminal policy? Not only should health care be evaluated in carefully designed trials, but there is also a need to investigate the work of social workers, teachers, judges and policemen. Systematic reviewing of the evidence base in such areas is more problematic than in health care because of the relative absence of well-designed prospective trials with comparators (randomised and controlled trials). The maturation of such processes will provide the material on which to ration more openly and efficiently. The principles under which such rationing will be implemented will include (Williams 1998):

- the treatment of equals equally and with due dignity, especially when near to death

- the meeting of people's needs as efficiently as possible (imposing the least sacrifice on others)

- the minimisation of inequalities in the lifetime health of the population.

Who should judge the need of competing patients?

Once the principles by which health and social care are to be rationed are accepted, the next issue is the implementation of the decision rules. How are the principles of rationing to be translated into practice? The social choice for this role has been made: the medical and other caring professions generally accept that they ration. They have to be trained to ration in the way society – their paymaster – wants, and they have to be seen to establish frameworks by which their activities will be monitored to ensure accountability. The professionals may not be neutral interpreters and users of the economic data which are used to establish practice guidelines and protocols. Often the medical evidence does not exist or is distorted by poor science. Medical and social work practice varies considerably between similar patients and clients. Sometimes the poor science is the product of commercial incentives offered by the purveyors of drugs and equipment (Freemantle and Maynard 1994; Gotzsche 1989).

A fundamental issue in the rationing process is the removal of the ethic of individual responsibility and its replacement by the social ethic. Doctors, social workers, nurses and other professionals have to deliver not on the basis of demonstrable effectiveness but in relation to cost effectiveness. The politics by which the managerial and purchaser ethic drives out the ancient Hippocratic ethic will challenge practitioners and the teachers in medical, nursing and other schools, all of whom still tend to ignore the importance of economics in the education of those who will ration care in the future.

How will the performance of the rationers be policed?

The establishment of rationing criteria and the improvement in the evidence base set the parameters for the rationing processes. With the practitioners as rationing agents, the final step is to create a policing system to ensure that these social agents perform in a manner consistent with the wishes of society. The creation of the National Institute for Clinical Excellence (NICE) and the Commission for Health Improvement (CHIMP) are an essential part of the policing process of medicine and nursing – provided they maintain high standards of academic rigour and independence. The system of clinical governance is vague, well intentioned and under-resourced as politicians appear to believe that quality and accountability can be purchased cheaply. Much of the policing of clinical practice is being handed over to the Royal Colleges, even though it is their poor performance which has created much public anxiety about their competence. The policing of nursing and social work practices must also be evidence based, rigorous and transparent.

There is a risk that such efforts will be inadequate, especially as they have scant resources with which to implement change and conservatism and complacency are still evident. For instance, the Royal Colleges have decided (at last) that all practitioners will be re-accredited every five years. This will involve not only testing their mental and physical health but also their competence to practise. How the latter will be determined is as yet unclear; for example, will it be related to education and training (process) and/or health outcomes for patients? Having made the decision to permit the Colleges to deal with these aspects of clinical governance, it is essential that government and the public monitor their performance closely. Re-accreditation in nursing and other social care professions will have to be developed further.

Overview

Rationing, or the denial or simply the failure to offer care which benefits the patient and which they would want, is ubiquitous in all health and social care systems. However, the principles which determine 'who gets access to what care and when' are usually implicit and implemented by professionals in arbitrary and unaccountable ways. Another consequence of this is 'postcode' rationing where access to care for similar patients on opposite sides of the street may differ. Such variations in medical and social care practices and provision are considerable and inequitable. Rationing should be practised according to explicit rules which encompass the preferences of society in relation to efficiency and equity. The rationing agents, usually professionals, should exercise their choices in relation to such criteria and be accountable for the efficient and equitable delivery of care to their patients and clients. Such an integrated system of rationing or resource allocation may disadvantage older people, especially if the fair innings approach is implemented. However, all choices involve winners and losers and if older people are not to lose some other group has to be disadvantaged. Such hard choices are made every day in all health and social care systems and should not remain implicit and arbitrary as they are now.

References

Callahan, D. (1987) *Setting Limits: Medical Goals in an Aging Society*. New York: Simon and Schuster.

Freemantle, N. and Maynard, A. (1994) 'Something Rotten in the State of Clinical and Economic Evaluation.' *Health Economics 3*, 2, 63–69.

Gotzsche, P.C. (1989) 'Methodology and Overt and Hidden Bias in Reports of 196 Double Blind Trials of Non-Steroidal Anti-Inflammatory Drugs in Rheumatoid Arthritis.' *Controlled Clinical Trials 10*, 31–56.

Knapp, M. (1984) *The Economics of Social Care*. Basingstoke: Macmillan.

Knapp, M. (1995) *The Economic Evaluation of Mental Health Care*. Aldershot: Ashgate.

Kohn, L.T. Corrigan, J.M. and Donaldson, M.S. (eds) (1999) *To Err is Human: Building a Safer Health Care System*. Washington DC: National Academy Press for Institute of Medicine.

McDonald, G. (1997) 'Social Work: Beyond Control.' In A. Maynard and I. Chalmers (eds) *Non-Random Reflections in Health Services Research: On the 25th Anniversary of Archie Cochrane's 'Efficiency and Effectiveness'*. London: British Medical Journal Publishing.

Maynard, A. (1993) 'Intergenerational Solidarity in Health Care: Principles and Practice.' In D. Hobman (ed) *Uniting Generations: Studies in Conflict and Cooperation*. London: Age Concern England.

Maynard, A. (1997) 'Evidence Based Medicine: An Incomplete Method For Informing Clinical Choices.' *Lancet 349*, 126–129.

Maynard, A. and Bloor, K. (1998) *Our Certain Fate: Rationing in Health Care*. London: Office of Health Economics.

Maynard, A. and Chalmers, I. (1997) *Non-Random Reflections in Health Services Research: On the 25th Anniversary of Archie Cochrane's 'Efficiency and Effectiveness'*. London: British Medical Journal Publishing.

Williams, A. (1997) 'Rationing Health Care by Age: The Case for.' *British Medical Journal 314*, 820–822.

Williams, A. (1998) Personal communication.

CHAPTER 5

Designing and Implementing a National Service Framework

Ian Philp, Anne Ashe and Kate Lothian

The opinions expressed in this chapter are those of the authors and are not necessarily the same as those of the Department of Health.

Introduction

In this chapter, we describe how a National Service Framework (NSF) was developed for the health care of older people in England. NSFs are part of a wider quality agenda for the National Health Service (NHS) in England, and were introduced by the Labour government following its election in 1997. An NSF is an innovative mechanism which is intended to produce a high and nationally uniform standard of care, to eliminate unacceptable practice, to reduce local variations and to drive up the quality of care. If successful (and they are still 'on trial'), they are likely to be adopted by other countries. Work on the initial NSFs for coronary heart disease and mental illness began in 1998 and were implemented in April 2000. The work for the health care of older people framework commenced in 1999, with implementation planned from April 2001. An NSF for diabetes is to follow a year later. Readers are referred to the Department of Health (DoH)[1] for additional information about the entire programme and content of the NSFs. The chapter has been organised around the following topics: the underpinning values of the

NSF for the Care of Older People and how it will contribute to the wider quality agenda; how the values have shaped the recommendations; how a professional consensus was sought; how users and carers were involved throughout the process; and how evidence was obtained and used to support the recommendations. It concludes with a discussion of the likely impact of the NSF if and when fully implemented.[2]

The policy context

Quality is at the heart of the British government's strategy for modernising both the NHS and statutory social care, and its agenda for health service quality improvement was outlined in *A First Class Service: Quality in the New NHS* (DoH 1998). Important elements of the policies include the establishment of the National Institute of Clinical Excellence (NICE), which will provide clear advice on clinical and cost effectiveness, and the setting of quality standards partly through the NSFs. The effective local delivery of these standards will be through a new system of clinical governance buttressed by strengthened lifelong learning for health professionals and modern systems of professional self-regulation. A statutory duty to ensure 'quality' will be effected by giving all NHS providers a responsibility for clinical governance, and by new legislation governing the regulation of the various health professions. There are to be strong monitoring mechanisms, including the establishment of a Commission for Health Improvement, the introduction of an NHS Performance Assessment Framework, and a National Patient Survey.

NSFs will set national standards and define service models, put in place programmes to support implementation, and establish milestones and performance indicators against which progress will be measured. The underpinning structures and 'factors of delivery' for an NSF are:

- research and development
- clinical decision support systems
- health technology information

- human resources
- operational funding and capital.

The local delivery mechanisms will be the Health Improvement Programmes, long-term service agreements, clinical governance, provider partnerships, communication and information technologies, and local development plans (for services, organisations and staff). Delivery of an NSF's ambitious but realistic programmes must recognise that substantial change requires time, a determined and effective approach to reshaping clinical and social work practice, and a commitment to leadership and improvement within and among agencies, local communities, patients, service users and their carers.

The criteria that are applied for a service or treatment area to be designated for an NSF are:

- relevance to the wider government health and welfare agenda
- importance of the health issue in terms of the absolute levels of mortality, morbidity, disability or resources (and the proportion of these that expert opinion believes or evidence demonstrates to be avoidable)
- an area of public concern
- evidence of a gap between actual and acceptable practice and of real opportunities for improvement
- complex care pathways
- a need for service improvement that may require significant reconfiguration
- organisational and clinical problems which require new or innovative approaches.

Given these criteria it is easy to see why NHS care services for older people were chosen as the government's third NSF.

The case for its commission was highlighted by a series of reports during 1999 about unacceptable practice in general hospital wards. A newspaper campaign about the lack of respect for the dignity of older patients in general hospital settings was followed up by a confirmatory report *'Not Because They Are Old': An Independent Inquiry into the Care of Older People on Acute Wards in General Hospitals* (Health Advisory Service 2000). Subsequent campaigns by Age Concern England (Gilchrist 1999) and Help the Aged (Davies *et al.* 1999) with continued press attention ensured that NHS care for older people remained in the public eye and became a high priority for the government. The NSF, formally titled the National Service Framework for National Health Service Care of Older People, is the largest and most complex of the NSFs to date. Older people (65 years or more) account for about 14 per cent of the UK population, but use around one-half of health and social care services and account for two-thirds of emergency medical admissions to hospitals. The framework has to cover NHS hospital and community health services, the health care components of residential and nursing home care, as well as the transitions between these settings. It also covers the care of all adults with stroke, dementia and injuries sustained through falls, as it is illogical to separate by age the management of these conditions which are not exclusive to older people.

The primary focus of the NSF is on frail older people, and therefore on the oldest old, but it is also concerned with the promotion of the health and well-being of all older people and with disease prevention in old age. The framework also deals with the palliative care of older people, including the relief of distressing symptoms and end of life care. Moreover, it would not make sense if the NSF did not recognise or take into account the key role that statutory social services play in the care of older people. Older people's needs do not fit neatly into health versus social, or medical versus nursing, pigeon holes. Many need treatment, care and support from more than one organisation. This NSF therefore covers the interface between health and social care.

It is recognised that there are many strengths in existing NHS care for older people, including well-developed multidisciplinary special-ities in geriatric medicine and old age psychiatry. By international standards there is also a strong system of primary health care in the UK. Other components of the care system have not, however, been uniformly excellent, and it is also important to recognise that the overall direction of UK health policy has shifted. Prior to 1997, the emphases in the delivery of care had been on the efficient use of hospital beds and professional self-regulation, but subsequently there have been important new directions: stronger external regulation of professional practice, and a closer examination of the effectiveness of services in meeting users' needs across as well as within service and organisation boundaries. A more person-centred health service is clearly one which would suit older people, whose health care needs are often multiple and require a multidisciplinary and multi-agency response, and whose voice is seldom heard in the health care 'marketplace'.

The role of the advisory group

To develop the NSF, an external reference group (ERG) was established. Membership was limited to two co-chairs, namely a clinical professor of health care for older people (the first author) and the chief inspector for social services, plus 12 opinion leaders from geriatric medicine, old age psychiatry, general practice, nursing, occupational therapy, speech and language therapy, physiotherapy, social services (2), health service management, Help the Aged (representing older people) and the National Carers' Association representing family carers. Several members of the ERG in turn chaired task groups which examined NHS care of older people from different perspectives; of which three were based on conditions (stroke, falls and mental illness), two on care settings (acute hospital services and primary with community care), one on transitions in care, and one on the processes of assessment and care planning. One member of the ERG chaired an older people's reference group, and another a focus group of family carers. The three remaining ERG members took responsibility for cross-cutting themes, such as age and race discrimination, cost effectiveness, and human resources.

Members of the task groups were drawn from a wide range of disciplines and backgrounds and all the groups included representatives of older people. The members of the ERG and the task groups were nominated by the Department of Health and approved by ministers and were not therefore acting as representatives of their professional bodies or organisations. The diverse backgrounds of the external advisers, users and carers were intended to ensure that the recommendations would reflect the complexity of NHS care of older people and be informed by the perspectives and concerns of both providers and users.

In addition, many key authorities and organisations were consulted, including: Age Concern England, Health Advisory Service, British Geriatrics Society, Royal College of General Practitioners, Royal College of Physicians, English National Board for Nursing, Midwifery and Health Visiting, and UK Central Council for Nursing.

Table 5.1 Organising values and principles of the National Service Framework

Underpinning value: *Person-centred care*	
Principle	*Purpose*
Promoting health and well-being Systematic assessment of needs Co-ordinated response to needs	Meeting needs
Fair access	Non-discriminatory practice
Preserving dignity Promoting autonomy Partnership with carers	Appropriate delivery of care
Staff competence (Evidence of) evidence-based practice	To a high standard of care

Table 5.2 Service models reviewed for the External Reference Group

- Primary care and health promotion
- Specialist care of frail older people (including falls)
- Specialist mental health services (including old age depression and dementia)
- Organised stroke care

The work of the task groups was structured around a set of values and principles developed by the ERG (Table 5.1). Two guiding tenets were

that these principles should apply irrespective of and across the various settings of care, and that the overall approach would promote person-centred care rather than organisational convenience. Generic standards were developed for each principle. These were to be monitored by newly developed indicators which could be specific to setting, stage-of-care or condition. Service models were developed to describe the main structural components and care pathways through the system of care (Table 5.2). The development of the standards, indicators and service models was undertaken by synthesising the advice from the task groups, the older people's reference group and the carers' focus group. Drafts of a synthesis report were discussed with each of the nine groups, identifying where their ideas had been taken on board, amended or omitted. Most omissions were because the ideas were outside the terms of reference of the ERG, but all the submitted recommendations were passed for consideration to the DoH (and on a few occasions to other departments of state). Feedback meetings helped to refine the synthesis report, which formed the basis of the ERG's final report and that was submitted in February 2000 to the government.

Supportive evidence

Objectives, scope and methodology

Two researchers were employed to help compile the evidence underlying the NSF report. This work was conducted in parallel with the drafting of the document, so did not act as a base for the report but rather as a framework for testing and validating ERG policy suggestions. It was anticipated that a thorough literature search would reveal whether any issues of patient care were being neglected in the report, whether all the recommendations could be substantiated, and whether any changes to the draft were needed. As such, the findings of the researchers provided supporting evidence for the final report's recommendations. It was also understood that the literature search might reveal areas for which there is lack of evidence and would therefore generate useful pointers for future research.

The coverage of the NSF on the care of older people was inevitably vast and demanded an extensive literature search. Pressure of time meant, however, that it was important to restrict its scope as well as the consulted sources. Task group chairs were therefore asked to list the specific topics which they believed needed an 'evidence base'. Searches were also conducted and evidence collated on several additional topics identified as important by the ERG. Altogether searches were carried out on 25 topics, from the spiritual and cultural dimensions of care in acute hospital wards, through the best methods of health promotion and preventive care for older people, the benefits of community-based and hospital-based rehabilitation, neuro-surgical management of subdural haematomas, the management of dementia and the methods of geriatric assessment, to training for geriatric care. Throughout the searching exercise, particular emphasis was placed on users' and carers' perspectives, as the ERG were keen that this should be a focus of the report.

Table 5.3 Categories of reviewed evidence

Category	Description of category
Evidence from research and other professional literature	
A1	Systematic reviews which include at least one randomised control trial
A2	Other systematic and high quality reviews
B1	Individual randomised control trials
B2	Non-randomised, experimental studies
B3	Well-designed non-experimental studies, controlled statistically if appropriate, including well-designed qualitative studies
C1	Descriptive and other research (e.g. convenience samples) (not in B)
C2	Case studies and examples of good practice
D	Summary articles and discussions of relevant literature (not in A)
Evidence from expert opinion	
P	Professional opinion based on clinical experience or reports of committees
U	User opinion from old people's reference group or similar
C	Carer opinion from carers' focus group or similar

The researchers sought advice on appropriate databases from a systematic review team at the School of Health and Related Research of the University of Sheffield. As well as the normal electronic databases of medical and social science literature, the researchers drew from less usual sources of evidence such as contacts suggested by task group members and evidence already known to the ERG. A total of 15 databases were searched.[3] Although they did not comply with all the criteria of formal systematic reviews, the searches were thoroughly conducted.[4] Outputs were saved from over 200 independent search strategies of varying complexity, and a detailed information management system was developed to allow ease of identification, access and retrieval. The accumulated files of references were sifted by the researchers to a core set of around 2000. Task group chairs then identified the items that they believed should be included in the ERG report, and added references which they had identified from their own sources. The resulting list of over 300 key references is the evidence base for the NSF report.

The researchers weighted these references using a system specifically developed for the NSF. Six established weighting systems were examined and a typology was developed drawing primarily on the systems used by the monthly listing of evidence-based medicine *Bandolier* (Moore 2000) and by the thematic occasional *Health Evidence Bulletins – Wales* (Barker, Weightman and Lancaster 1997). Although held in high regard, it was felt that these two systems did not adequately recognise the importance of good non-interventional research and the experiences of users and carers (Britton *et al.* 1998; Murphy *et al.* 1998). In view of the inconsistent conventions for research methodologies and semantic differences in terminologies, it was also considered important to develop a system which would integrate the NSF's medical and social service themes. The system thus finally developed for this NSF and used in the report is shown in Table 5.3. It incorporates systematic and other quality reviews, experimental research, non-interventional research and expert opinion from professionals, users and carers. Following the weighting process, the weighted evidence was incorporated into the ERG report.

Discussion: Building an evidence base

The extent and complexity of the literature search confirmed the breadth of this NSF and demonstrated that there is a wealth of evidence available on some aspects of its coverage but hardly any or none for others. For example, several hundred references were identified on the health prevention and promotion issues that are relevant to older people and on rehabilitation after falls, but few were found on either the commissioning of care for older people or the spiritual and cultural needs of older people in acute care. It is possible that some lacunae are covered in the 'grey literature', such as practice notes, policy documents and unpublished research reports. This material is not generally available and its dissemination depends on local networks and databases, conferences and word of mouth. Alternatively, the relevant evidence may not be generated by medical and particularly clinical research, but by studies in the fields of social services, public administration and financial management. The latter fields are less well covered by electronic databases, abstracts services and other literature search tools. But practitioners need to be aware of all of these sources of information if they are to develop policy and practice which makes the best use of the available evidence, particularly where a multi-sector, cross-professional approach is required.

One restriction of an evidence-based approach to the development of good practice in the NHS became evident from the NSF work. This is that the published evidence about best practice – for instance, on professional training – often deals with the status quo and rarely points to gaps or needed directions of change. While, for example, it is straightforward to identify articles and research about current practice or developments in training, not surprisingly it is less easy to find evidence of what is not happening. If therefore there are aspects of care for which training is inadequately developed, then, by definition, there can be no evidence on the most effective methods of training for that aspect of care.

This NSF has also raised questions about the weight to be given to different types of evidence and about the relative validity of experimental and non-experimental evidence. Aspects of health provision which focus on care rather than treatment, which aim to incorporate patients' (and carers') views or which draw from policy development in the social services are not always suitable for research which employs controlled trials or other 'gold standard' clinical and scientific methodologies. At a more mundane methodological level, the NSF work revealed several information management problems associated with gathering evidence. One was the overlap in coverage of various databases, which resulted in the duplicate retrieval of many references. Another was that the software which has been designed to collate references from several databases does not necessarily handle outputs from all relevant databases. The result is that information management is complex and time consuming. It was also found that different databases use different terminologies for similar issues, making practically impossible both the standardisation of information retrieved from different sources and the use with different databases of absolutely consistent search strategies.

Impact

The NSF will have seven key features (Table 5.4). The work to prepare the NSF has been of a greater order of magnitude than is usual for even large academic projects, and it was conducted in just 11 months (April 1999 to February 2000). The inquiries and the consultations have been very seriously undertaken, remarkably broad and exceptionally well informed by generous and strong consensual support. Given sufficient engagement from all health and social professionals, implementation of the framework is likely to bring great benefits. The culture of health care for older people should shift away from organisational convenience to person-centred care.

Table 5.4 Key features of the External Reference Group's report

• Philosophy of person-centred care
• Service models (see Table 5.2)
• General principles (see Table 5.1)
• Generic standards and specific indicators of quality in care
• Implementation plan
• Recommendations for future research and development
• Success criteria

Structural components will be reorganised accordingly, particularly in relation to the care of both older people who are frail or have mental health problems and people of all ages with stroke. This should lead to a reintegration of the hospital and community elements of specialist services for these patients.

Primary care will focus on promoting the health and well-being of all older people, disease prevention, case finding, and the co-ordination of care. Social services will work more closely with primary health care teams and specialist health care providers. Horror stories about older people in health care settings should become a thing of the past. Older people should have greater control over their health care contacts and raised expectations. Family carers should feel that they are true partners with the practitioners in the care of their relatives. The health and social care needs of older people and family carers will be systematically assessed and reviewed. Care will be better co-ordinated, and age discrimination will be rooted out of the health service. All generalist or specialist staff working with older patients will be able to take pride from working in a quality service. Basic and continuing professional training programmes will ensure that staff are competent (in knowledge, skills and attitudes) to care for older people and ready to innovate in ways consistent with the emerging evidence about best practice.

Postscript

The chapter was written before the publication of the Framework by the Department of Health. The following summary has been added at proof stage.

Implementation

The government accepted the report of the External Reference Group as the basis for the National Service Framework. It has commited funds for an additional investment of £1.4 billion per annum for health and social care services for older people by 2004. New investment will be used to eliminate age-based polies which deny older people access to services; for example, by extending breast screening to older women and removing means-tested funding for the nursing component of long-term care. Hospital services will be required to improve standards of care so that the dignity, privacy and autonomy of older people will be preserved. High quality palliative care services will be extended to meet the needs of older people, and there will be greater attention to meeting nutritional needs and tissue viability in hospitals and nursing homes. Organised services, for stroke, falls and mental health services based on best practice, will be estabilished in every health district. Community-based care will be improved with investment in domiciliary services, community rehabilitation services, home adaptations and rehabilitations aids.

Pro-active support for vulnerable older people will be improved through targeted health checks and the development of personal care plans. A new service, *Care Direct*, will provide information and advice about health, social care, housing, pensions and benifits by telephone and through the Internet, drop-in centres and outreach centres. The full NSF will be published late 2000 with implementation from 2001 under the leadership of the National Director for Services for Older People.

Notes

1   Department of Health, Wellington House, Whitehall, London SW1A 2NS (www.doh.gov.uk/nsf/nsfhome.htm).

2   The terms of reference for the ERG included 'to work within existing resources'. Spending on health care in the UK is proportionately less than comparable countries in the EU, while health care expenditure per head of population in England is the lowest of the four UK nations. Improving quality in health care for older people will require not only clear policies, explicit standards and monitoring systems, but also additional investment.

3   These were: *Ageinfo, British Nursing Index, Centre for Reviews and Dissemination, Cochrane Library of Systematic Reviews and Controlled Trials, Cumulative Index to Nursing and Allied Health Literature, Effective Health Care Bulletins, Effectiveness Matters, Health Evidence Bulletins: Wales, Health Management Information Consortium, Health Technology Assessment, Medline, National Research Register, PsychLit, Scottish Intercollegiate Guidelines Network*, and *Turning Research into Practice*.

4   Each search was focused on older people using keywords associated with geriatrics, while search indexes and thesauruses identified other keywords appropriate to the topics. Search tools were then used to combine, limit or explode the keywords.

References

Barker, J., Weightman, A.L. and Lancaster, J. (1997) *Health Evidence Bulletins, Wales, Project Methodology* (online). Cardiff: University of Wales College of Medicine. Available from http://ebw.uwcm.ac.uk/method/index.html (accessed 10 February 2000).

Britton, A., McKee, M., Black, N., McPherson, K., Sanderson, C. and Bain, C. (1998) 'Choosing between Randomised and Non-Randomised Studies: A Systematic Review.' *Health Technology Assessment 2*, 13.

Davies, S., Nolan, M., Brown, J. and Wilson, F. (1999) *Dignity on the Ward: Promoting Excellence in Care.* London: Help the Aged.

Department of Health (DoH) (1998) *A First Class Service: Quality in the New NHS.* London: DoH.

Gilchrist, C. (1999) *Turning Your Back on Us: Older People and the NHS.* London: Age Concern England.

Health Advisory Service (2000) *'Not Because They Are Old': An Independent Inquiry into the Care of Older People on Acute Wards in General Hospitals.* London: Health Advisory Service.

Moore, A. (ed) (2000) *Bandolier* (online). Monthly listing of evidence-based medicine. Headington, Oxford: Bandolier, Pain Relief. Available from http://www.ebando.com (accessed 10 February 2000).

Murphy, E., Dingwall, R., Greatbatch, D., Parker, S. and Watson, P. (1998) 'Qualitative Research Methods in Health Technology Assessment: A Review of the Literature.' *Health Technology Assessment 2*, 16.

CHAPTER 6

Defining Difference
Health and Social Care for Older People
Gillian Dalley

A version of this chapter has been published as an occasional paper by the Centre for Policy on Ageing.

The history of the British health and social services since 1948 shows that the drawing of boundaries, often followed by speedy attempts to nullify their impact, has long been a feature of public administration. Boundaries have been drawn between services, between client groups, between locations (community and hospital), between professions, and between agencies and sectors. It can be argued that those at the margins or on the cusps have always been the victims. This chapter looks at some of the more recent boundary disputes and considers some of their consequences – particularly as they affect the largest client group involved: older people.

Setting boundaries and marking out territory are characteristic features of group behaviour. In policy making and implementation several factors coalesce to reinforce this tendency: professional differences, agency solidarity, opportunistic group interest and competition for resources all play a part. In the confrontation between these competing forces, the interests of the client are often put at risk. Too often policy makers and professionals fail to recognise the dangers inherent in this interplay of forces when they try to introduce changes in policy or organisational structures and procedures. Instead they fall back on a favourite stratagem, namely exhorting professionals and practitioners to collaborate in developing a seamless web of care or 'joined up' services.

Health and social services have been subject to constant redefinition since 1948. The 1980s in particular saw a continuous revolution in the health service, with boundary changes, the introduction of general management and structural integration, all culminating in the National Health Service and Community Care Act 1990. The first decade of the twenty-first century is likely to see further change with mergers of health authorities and the establishment of primary health care trusts. Changes in primary care signify less another redrawing of administrative boundaries than the reconfiguration of professional and managerial boundaries. General medical practitioners (GPs), long considered the mavericks of the formal managerial system within the National Health Service (NHS) because of their unwillingness to cede their 'independent professional' status, in an ironic twist are now being expected to lead the new structures. Social services have gone through their own changes during the last decade. In the case of social work, the concept of care management has transformed the old style. Within the framework established under the 1993 community care provisions of the 1990 Act, social workers have become budget holders, needs assessors and bureaucrats. The idea of case work with individual older clients as central to the social work task appears to have disappeared.

It is ironic that the reason for many of the changes has been the intention to produce or ensure smoother inter-agency or intra-agency working. The theory-free nature of such policy changes has however been evident down the years. Little attention has been paid to research which has suggested that this may not be a problem-free road, and even less to examining the fundamental reasons why this should be so. A stream of policy documents (DHSS 1978, 1981; DoH 1998b) has demonstrated a simple faith in the ability of the system to transform itself. From *A Happier Old Age*, published in 1978, to *Partnership in Action*, published in 1998, the message has been the same –

service provision and the quality of life for users will only improve if professionals and their organisations work better together, as the following excepts show:

> The promotion of a satisfactory quality-of-life for elderly people and adequate provision for their care involve many different organisations and individuals. But the effectiveness of all the various efforts depends a great deal on the extent to which people work together and play their part in changing attitudes where these bar progress. (DHSS 1978, p.40)

> There is no single, simple solution. It is essential that health and social services authorities and Primary Care Groups/Trusts (which are being developed to enable GPs, community nurses and other health and social care professionals to improve delivery of care) regard it as part of their core business to work together towards shared objectives. There is action in hand to move towards that goal already. We want to remove any existing constraints in the system and help agencies commission and provide services across boundaries more effectively. (DoH 1998b, p.6)

Mere exhortation to achieve improved collaboration, however, does not mean it will happen. Sociologists of the professions and analysts of organisations and human behaviour in groups show how differences are generated by the very nature of boundary setting. Simply redrawing or redefining them does not work; neither does the reiteration of hopeful expectation. There are many reasons for this, including professional attitudes, different funding arrangements, lack of communication and variations in local policies and procedures.

In a study conducted in the 1980s into professional attitudes towards community care policy (Dalley 1991a), three sets of factors were identified as conditioning the views and responses of different groups of professionals. First there was professional ideology; that is, the shared belief systems which are created and maintained through the development and consolidation of common knowledge bases along with training processes to which entry was guarded and circumscribed. Second, there was the power of cultural allegiance, often associated with particular organisations and their ways of doing things, and frequently based on assumption, stereotype and long-term unquestioned custom and practice. Third, there was force of circumstance, the conditions under which professionals just had to get on with the work and do the best they could in trying situations. Cutting across these three sets of factors were what anthropologists have called the assumptive worlds of individual workers; the attitudes associated with individuals as social beings which cause them to hold certain beliefs about the respective roles of the state and the individual, of the private and the public spheres, and of family responsibility and obligation. The challenge for researchers is to identify when and under what circumstances these often competing allegiances (ideological, cultural, circumstantial and personal) achieve dominance and to what effect. The challenge for practitioners and managers is then to overcome them.

However widely accepted a policy may be – as is the case for community care – its interpretation may vary widely and in the end it may be circumvented either intentionally or unintentionally. Often this is because of the strength of the factors outlined above, yet policy makers and those charged with the implementation of policy as often fail to take them into account. The cleavage between professional views and user or carer views is well recognised and the provision of inappropriate and unacceptable services is often accounted for in these terms. Recent research has demonstrated the lack of fit between what users want and what professionals provide. But the differences of views among professionals and the consequences for service provision are rarely examined. There is a tendency for professions to grow and split as greater specialisation and technical expertise develop and for an accompanying proliferation of 'professional' views. The tendency is sufficiently strong and influential to justify close examination of the strength and impact of professional ideology.

The power of professional allegiance has fuelled many of the problems associated with the failure to co-ordinate services effectively. The 'medical model' is commonly given as an example of professional ideology, and other professions readily recognise the concept and the reality of medical dominance. But there is less acknowledgement that other professions too are influenced by comparable sets of attitudes and expectations. Their origins have been traced by some researchers to the

'apartheid' that has long characterised the training of the various professions which provide services across the community/institution
divide. This again tends to be relatively theory-free. On the face of it,
common education and training might be assumed to be the answer.
But Janet James (1997), prefacing a small study which examined how
far common education programmes overcome professional boundary
drawing, noted that rather than facilitating collaborative attitudes it
made things worse. The forces pulling groups apart were clearly
stronger than the good intentions to draw them together.

Aside from professional differences, other factors exacerbate
division: funding arrangements, spatial and administrative boundaries
and failures in communication. In the mid-1980s, the Audit
Commission (1986) report on community care drew attention to the
divisive impact of:

- the separation of responsibilities among various governmental
  departments and agencies: the NHS, Department of Social
  Security, and local government

- the lack of co-terminosity between district health and local
  authorities

- the patchwork of fragmented services delivered by agencies
  with different lines of accountability, and 'different priorities,
  styles, structures and budgets'.

Yet all were expected to co-operate effectively.

The Griffiths Report confirmed these findings and concluded that
'the gap between political rhetoric and policy on the one hand [and]
between policy and reality in the field on the other hand' was bigger in
the context of community care than in any other policy area (DHSS
1988). The proposed solution was to identify a lead agency – the local
government authority – to be responsible for community care
assessment, and second to clarify budgetary responsibilities among
social services, housing and health authorities. The last continue to be
responsible for health care, broadly defined as 'investigation, diagnosis,
treatment and rehabilitation undertaken by a doctor or by other professional staff to whom a doctor (sometimes a GP) has referred the patient'.

The third proposal was to establish the local authority as an enabler rather than the provider of services.

Recent studies in the North West NHS Region, however, confirm that boundary problems remain. Rather than the 'Berlin Wall' being dismantled as a result of a series of government initiatives to promote collaboration, as foreseen by the then Secretary of State for Health, Frank Dobson, the inter-professional and inter-agency divisions persisted (Hiscock and Pearson 1999). Other studies, while less pessimistic, have noted the extent of the challenge that has to be overcome to achieve effective collaboration (Hudson *et al.* 1997). It is important to remember that older people in receipt or in need of services suffer the consequences of these problems and failures. Broadly there are three areas for concern:

- the manner in which fragmentation undermines service quality
- the problem of the health/social care divide
- the tendency for older people to be excluded from the health system.

Older people are the predominant consumers of services which cross the inter-agency divide. They go into hospital more than other age groups and similarly they require more post-hospital services at home. Those who have not been into hospital recently are also more likely to receive community health services, from district nurses, specialist nurses and occupational therapy. They receive various services under the auspices of local authority social services, such as home care, meals on wheels and day centre services. According to the philosophy of the new community care, they were to receive a 'seamless service'. Although services are delivered by many different agencies and professionals, they should be received by the individual client as undifferentiated and smoothly co-ordinated. Research has shown that this rarely happens, and the common experience is of bewildered clients receiving visits from up to a dozen different professionals from several different agencies.

Many techniques for overcoming the problems of inter-agency working have been recommended and tried, such as patient-held records, common assessment tools, different professionals sharing the same offices, the pooling of information on a systematic computerised basis, the concept of the community care worker at the level of the individual patient, and, at an organisational level, joint commissioning, locality budgeting and decentralisation to localities (Dalley 1991b). Problems however abound. A confusing array of care workers provides different parts of the care package to a background of disputes which arise about who provides what. They may arise because one agency wants to shift responsibility for funding and/or providing the service, or because one group of workers claims it as their territory and struggles to maintain its grip. The problems have a long history but they still persist. Reports from the Social Services Inspectorate (1998) and from the Scottish Office (1998) show that inter-professional and inter-agency co-operation at the interface between the hospital and the community still remains problematic. The seamless service remains for many a pipe dream.

In an unpublished study of a single local authority social services department which the Centre for Policy on Ageing (1998) conducted, the case records of 200 clients moving into residential or nursing homes along with the notes of a further 100 clients receiving home care were examined. The object of the study was to investigate whether differences in decision-making patterns could be discerned among the local offices of the authority. Incidental to the main object of the study was the opportunity to build a profile of the care which people were receiving in their own homes and the sorts of circumstances which influenced the decision for them to go into residential care. It provided some illuminating insights. The 100 people at home were all receiving complex packages of care. A typical case might involve several different home-care workers from different agencies – local authority and private – visiting several times a day: for example, a care worker to help the individual get up, wash and have breakfast; a district nurse to tend clinical needs; the delivery of meals on wheels; another care worker to put the individual to bed; followed sometimes by a night sitter. The following two cases were not unusual:

> An 82-year-old woman with Alzheimer's disease who was physically and mentally very frail and lived at home with her

daughter received a mixed package of care: a local authority home carer seven mornings per week to help with personal hygiene; an agency nurse seven mornings a week to dress a sacral pressure sore and get the client out of bed; a district nurse from the local NHS trust in the evenings and during the night to change the lady's position; a care worker from a home-care agency paid for by local authority between 9 am and 4 pm on Fridays; and another care worker from the same agency, paid for by the daughter, daily from noon to 2 pm and from 5 to 7 pm.

A man aged 85 years had received 24-hour care since 1993 following a stroke. He was sight impaired, had difficulty swallowing, and had diabetes and ulcerated heels, and needed assistance to get in and out of bed and all personal care. He received a mix of care from a private care agency, district nursing, home care and night care, together with a rota of care provided by his daughters.

How seamless, on this evidence, is a service that comprises so many disparate elements? Although in some areas of the health service attempts have been made to ensure that the individual client is dealt with by a single professional or as few professionals as possible (for example, through the introduction of a named nurse and a key worker) such solutions are rarely found in community care for older people. While it may be unrealistic to expect 24-hour care to be provided by a tiny pool of carers specifically for every older client, the theory of care management, care packages and the appropriate matching of needs to services suggests something more than the fragmented services outlined above. The provision at different times of the day of short inputs measured and costed in minutes, by various workers from different agencies, typifies a service which is wholly task focused and mechanistic. The personal and humane qualities of service that are required and pledged are singularly absent.

It is a truism that as long as the service user does not experience the services as fragmented or disjointed then it does not matter who provides each element, as also that the difference between health and social care is a technical and bureaucratic irrelevance if the service is experienced and perceived as seamless. But there are two major reasons why it does matter: money and responsibility. The first reason is familiar to most older people. The issue of charging for social care in contrast to free at the point of use NHS care has been a matter of deep concern for many years. Older people feel betrayed when they find that they have to pay for social care. The official response to this concern is to say that this is nothing new, and that social care services provided by the local authority have always been subject to a means test. It is, however, a dishonest response. The rhetoric of community care claims to offer a seamless service designed to meet the needs of individuals solely on the basis that they need a particular type or mix of services. In assessing the individual, according to the rhetoric, the professional assessor is disinterested and mindful only of the health and social care needs of that individual. In reality, the assessment and which service(s) are deemed to be required have massive implications for the recipient. In recommending social care, a train of financial consequences is set in motion; in recommending health care, it is not. A failure to acknowledge this divide is disingenuous.

It also matters if under the cloak of seamlessness one of the partners is withdrawing from or shifting the extent of its responsibility. One of the most disturbing developments over recent years has been the way in which the NHS has been changing its definitions as to what constitutes health care. It is becoming more and more apparent that what the man or woman in the street would regard as a straightforward health service responsibility is increasingly being disavowed by the NHS. This was put succinctly in evidence from the British Geriatrics Society (BGS) to the House of Commons Health Committee's inquiry into long-term care in 1995, when it stated that until at least 1981 it had been relatively simple to define the difference between health and social care: the infirm and the sick were a health service responsibility, and the frail and the aged were the responsibility of the local authority. The BGS noted however that it is in the nature of frailty in old people that in many cases their social and health requirements are entwined and change over time (House of Commons Health Committee 1995). Thus to divide sharply between health care on the one hand and social care on the other is problematic.

But the dichotomy has become a challenge for more than assessment. The NHS has responded to the changes in community care by shifting its definitions, perhaps opportunistically in order to save money, but also in response to central government pressure. Indeed, the way in which the NHS has responded is an interesting case study of how different professional interests within the NHS have reacted to outside influence. The BGS, for example, according to its evidence just cited, regretted the way in which long-term care has been shifted out of the NHS. They suggest that it has been general managers and their finance directors who have followed government imperatives most readily, probably motivated as much by the opportunity to save money at a time of growing demand in other areas of the service as by any belief in the clinical appropriateness of their financial decisions. By 1993, the NHS had divested 33 per cent of its long-term care beds (Hudson 1998), and most of the would-be occupants were being cared for in the private residential and nursing home sector, redefined as social care patients and assessed by the newly responsible local authorities, or being maintained in their own homes by various means. It is these individuals on the cusp of the health–social care divide who most directly experience its definitional, allocation and organisational problems.

When the NHS's rush to divest itself of responsibility for long-term care became apparent, the government was forced to react. It issued a stern warning to health authorities and trusts which stressed the need to maintain long-term care provision – but within limits. Examination of the guidance shows how far the health service has moved from the simple distinction between health and social care that was previously employed. Among the stated eligibility criteria, for the first time a person had to require specialist treatment to qualify for NHS long-term (or continuing) care. The health service was required:

- to promote the effective recovery and rehabilitation of patients

- to arrange and fund palliative care, including inpatient palliative health care in hospitals and hospices and, in a few cases, in nursing homes capable of providing this level of care

- to provide specialist palliative health care to people already in nursing homes

- provide palliative health care support to people in their own homes or in residential care

- provide continuing inpatient care where the complexity or intensity of the medical, nursing or other clinical care, or the need for frequent and not easily predictable interventions, requires the regular (in the majority of cases at least weekly) supervision of a consultant, specialist nurse or other NHS member of the multidisciplinary team

- provide care for those who (a) require routinely the use of specialist health care equipment or treatments involving the supervision of specialist NHS staff; or (b) have a rapidly degenerating or unstable condition which means that they will require specialist medical or nursing supervision

- provide respite health care for people with complex or intense health care needs (under specified circumstances)

- provide access to specialist or intensive medical and nursing support for people placed in nursing homes, residential care homes or in the community

- provide community and primary care services for people at home or in residential care homes

- provide specialist transport. (DoH 1995)

Of course this specification hits hardest and is at its most restrictive for those people who have been denied access to hospitals and placed in or discharged to private (or voluntary sector) nursing homes. Many people who have been considered for and denied NHS-funded care under these eligibility criteria are in need of considerable care. By lay standards, at least, they are in need of health care by virtue of their admission to a nursing home. According to this perspective, not only is there a health–social care divide but also a health–health divide; that is, a distinction within the health care arena as well as one between health and social care. Elderly care specialists have registered a growing concern that there is a group of patients consigned to nursing homes who are outside the boundaries of their care. The specialists cannot normally enter the homes to assess the residents who may have a potential for rehabilitation or be in need of acute care (Black and Bowman 1997; Bowman 1997). While there may be instances of good practice where GPs and specialists collaborate to provide comprehensive care (Marshall 1998), too often it is lacking.

The consequence of hair-splitting definitions across a range of long-term care issues seems to be that nursing homes are becoming 'no-go areas' for NHS staff. The NHS has withdrawn from its funding and caring responsibilities. Elderly care specialists have been divested of responsibility for the patients discharged to them; GPs in many cases do not have expert knowledge to monitor and manage the residents' conditions; and NHS community health services do not normally have access.

The conflict over where responsibility for care lies has been highlighted in the recent 'Coughlan' case at the Court of Appeal (Royal College of Nursing and others 1999). The Court ruled that Ms Coughlan, a patient in an NHS nursing home, was entitled to long-term NHS nursing care even after she had been admitted to a private nursing home since her primary need for accommodation was because of her health needs. The ruling led the DoH (1999a) to issue interim guidance on the boundary distinctions but, to date, no conclusive guidance has been given and the problem remains. The recommendation by the Royal Commission on the Funding of Long Term Care (1999) that personal care (a more precise and generous definition than nursing care) be provided free at the point of use could help towards a solution, but the government's definitive response to the report has been delayed and so far there is no indication that the government will accept the recommendation.

Nonetheless the residents of nursing homes clearly have health care needs by any definition. Of the 200 people entering either residential or nursing homes, over half were admitted to nursing homes (CPA 1998). The following cases of admissions to nursing homes, either as self-funders or supported by the local authority, were not unusual:

- An 82-year-old man living alone; heart attack, stroke, cancer in the right eye, prostate and skin, arthritis, recent attack of shingles, depressed, requires 24-hour supervision.

- A 90-year-old man, living with a son who has learning difficulties, receiving an intensive package of care, requires 'high level of nursing care', 'totally dependent, requires to be fed', requires 24-hour nursing care.

- A 91-year-old woman with cancer of the gullet, dementia, leg ulcers, requires 24-hour nursing care.

- A 79-year-old woman with breast carcinoma, rheumatoid arthritis; broke both arms after a fall at home which have failed to heal because secondary carcinoma deposits found in bones; 'does not meet NHS continuing care criteria'.

It seems to be a strange world that suggests the NHS should not maintain its responsibility for such individuals. As David Price, a health services researcher, has said, 'within the reformed NHS, people who are ill and old are now treated differently from people who are just ill' (Price 1996, p.5).

Conclusions

Discrimination on the grounds of age has become accepted, acceptable and unexceptionable. The expectation that older people should pay for their long-term care if they can afford to is evidence of this generational discrimination (Dalley 1999). No other age group is treated in this way. At the other end of the generational scale, for example, maternity care is not means tested. Moreover, the diversion of the NHS away from long-term care can be seen as a symptom of another fundamental shift. Increasingly it is becoming apparent that the health service will focus its concerns on the one hand on the acute sector, in 'high tech' hospitals reserved for heroic interventions, speedy recovery and early discharge, and on the other hand on primary care treatment, assessment and referral and the promotion of healthy lifestyles. Alongside, the new public health will concentrate on improving the healthiness of schools, neighbourhoods and working environments, by setting targets to reduce avoidable deaths and setting up Health Action Zones to demonstrate how these aims can be achieved.

In all this little mention is made of the older population and the needs of the very old. Indeed the Green Paper *Our Healthier Nation* (DoH 1998a) seemed to be suggesting that by reducing premature deaths the problem is solved, and that reaching old age is a sufficient goal in itself. Upper age limits for many of the targets were set at 65 years, and there was little consideration of how to raise the quality of life and quality of care of older people. The succeeding White Paper *Saving Lives* (DoH 1999c), presumably responding to the ensuing criticism, raised the age limits for some of the targets to 75 years (for cancer, coronary heart disease and stroke). In terms of the health issues facing older people and their increasing numbers, it can be persuasively argued that the needs of those aged 75 years and over should be just as much a matter of public policy concern as those of younger age groups. The very old are in danger of being more and more excluded from mainstream policy making.

Even within the gerontological community, where the goals, aspirations and well-being of older people are to the fore, there is a tendency to focus only on the positive aspects of old age. It is one of gerontology's guiding precepts – perhaps a reaction to generations of negative images produced by the media, by people in everyday conversation and indeed in professional textbooks. Rehabilitation, the promotion of independence and autonomy are now the key words which guide gerontological discourse. Indeed the very terms 'old' and 'frail' are inadmissible in some circles. Of course there is strong evidence to suggest that rehabilitative interventions can be highly effective and the current strategic emphasis placed on it is welcome (DoH 1999b; Young *et al.* 1999). It is the dominance given ideologically to the idea that 'successful ageing' should be a universal goal and that those who do not achieve it are regarded (or regard themselves) as failures which is open to criticism (Rowe and Kahn 1997; Scheidt, Humpherys and Yorgason 1999). This emphasis has an unintended consequence, for, increasingly, the old and the frail are in danger of being rejected and ignored because they do not conform to the acceptable image of ageing. Colluding with these ideas, are gerontologists failing old people and deluding themselves? It seems that in promoting the concept of positive ageing to the exclusion of other aspects of ageing, gerontologists may be tolerating and even sanctioning those societal attitudes which consign people in advanced old age to the outer reaches of the welfare state.

References

Audit Commission (1986) *Making a Reality of Community Care.* London: Audit Commission.

Black, D. and Bowman, C. (1997) 'Community Institutional Care for Frail Elderly People.' *British Medical Journal 315,* 441–442.

Bowman, C. (1997) 'Institutional Care in the Community: From Chaos to Integration of Health and Social Care?' *Reviews in Clinical Gerontology 7,* 3, 189–191.

Centre for Policy on Ageing (CPA) (1998) 'Community Care Assessments of Older People Entering Residential and Nursing Homes.' Unpublished report.

Dalley, G. (1991a) 'Beliefs and Behavior: Professionals and the Policy Process.' *Journal of Aging Studies 5,* 2, 163–180.

Dalley, G. (1991b) 'Patterns of Management in Community Units.' In A. McNaught (ed) *Managing Community Health Services.* London: Chapman and Hall.

Dalley, G. (1999) 'Care, Costs and Containment: The Social Policy of Long-Term Care.' *Policy and Politics 27,* 4, 533–540.

Department of Health (DoH) (1989) *Caring for People: Community Care in the Next Decade and Beyond.* Cm. 849. London: HMSO.

Department of Health (DoH) (1995) *NHS Responsibility for Meeting Continuing Care Needs.* Circular HSG (95) 8. London: DoH.

Department of Health (DoH) (1998a) *Our Healthier Nation: A Contract for Health.* Cm. 3852. London: The Stationery Office.

Department of Health (DoH) (1998b) *Partnership in Action (New Opportunities for Joint Working between Health and Social Services): A Discussion Document.* London: DoH.

Department of Health (DoH) (1999a) *Ex Parte Coughlan: Follow Up Action.* Circular HSC 1999/180. London: DoH.

Department of Health (DoH) (1999b) *Modernising Health and Social Services: National Priorities Guidance 2000/01–2002/03.* London: DoH.

Department of Health (DoH) (1999c) *Saving Lives: Our Healthier Nation.* Cm. 4386. London: The Stationery Office.

Department of Health and Social Security (DHSS) (1978) *A Happier Old Age.* London: HMSO.

Department of Health and Social Security (DHSS) (1981) *Growing Older.* Cmnd. 8173. London: HMSO.

Department of Health and Social Security (DHSS) (1988) *Community Care: Agenda for Action.* The Griffiths Report. London: HMSO.

Hiscock, J. and Pearson, M. (1999) 'Looking Inwards, Looking Outwards: Dismantling the "Berlin Wall" Between Health and Social Services?' *Social Policy and Administration 33,* 2, 150–163.

House of Commons Health Committee (1995) *Long-Term Care: NHS Responsibilities for Meeting Continuing Care Needs.* First Report, Volume II. *Minutes of Evidence.* London: HMSO.

Hudson, B. (1998) 'Circumstances Change Cases: Local Government and the NHS.' *Social Policy and Administration 32,* 1, 71–86.

Hudson, B., Hardy, B., Henwood, M. and Wistow, G. (1997) 'Working Across Professional Boundaries: Primary Health Care and Social Care.' *Public Money and Management 17,* 4, 25–30.

James, J. (1997) 'Joint Working in the Care of Older People: Can Interprofessional Education Help?' *Health Care in Later Life 2,* 2, 121–128.

Marshall, M.N. (1998) 'How Well Do General Practitioners and Hospitals Work Together? A Qualitative Study of Cooperation and Conflict within the Medical Profession.' *British Journal of General Practice 48,* 1379–1382.

Price, D. (1996) *Continuing Care for Older People: The Responses to Circular HSG (95) 8.* Newcastle-upon-Tyne: University of Northumbria.

Royal College of Nursing and others (1999) *Who Should Fund Long-Term Care? Implications of the Court of Appeal Judgment.* London: Royal College of Nursing.

Royal Commission on the Funding of Long Term Care (1999) *With Respect to Old Age: Long Term Care – Rights and Responsibilities.* Chairman: Sir S. Sutherland. Cm. 4191-I. London: The Stationery Office.

Rowe, J.W. and Kahn, R.L. (1997) 'Successful Aging.' *The Gerontologist 37,* 4, 433–440.

Scheidt, R.J., Humpherys, D.R. and Yorgason, J.B. (1999) 'Successful Aging: What's Not to Like?' *Journal of Applied Gerontology 18,* 3, 277–282.

Scottish Office (1998) *Hospital Discharge for Frail Older People.* Edinburgh: The Stationery Office.

Social Services Inspectorate (1998) *Getting Better? Inspection of Hospital Discharge (Care Management) Arrangements for Older People.* London: DoH.

Young, J., Brown, A., Forster, A. and Clare, J. (1999) 'An Overview of Rehabilitation for Older People.' *Reviews in Clinical Gerontology 9,* 2, 183–196.

CHAPTER 7

The Medical–Social Boundary and the Location of Personal Care

Julia Twigg

Personal care increasingly lies at the heart of debates concerning the long-term care of older people. Who should provide such care? How should it be funded? Is it the responsibility of the health authority or of statutory social services? Should private individuals be expected to pay for such help? Personal care lies across the medical–social boundary and as such presents particular problems for welfare systems. But personal care also raises questions about its appropriate provision. Its intimate character places it ambiguously in the care system. The centrality of the issue was recognised in the recent Royal Commission on Long-Term Care. The report defines personal care as

> the care needs which give rise to the major additional costs of frailty or disability associated with old age. We deliberately do not use the term 'health care' or 'social care' because of the confusion that now surrounds those terms and their association with particular agencies or forms of funding. Personal care is care that directly involves touching a person's body (and therefore incorporates issues of intimacy, personal dignity and confidentiality), and is distinct both from treatment [or] therapy (a procedure deliberately intended to cure or ameliorate a pathological condition) and from indirect care

such as home help or the provision of meals. (Royal Commission 1999a, p.67)

It continues: 'This type of care is the main source of contention in the debate about the distinction between health care and social care.' The conclusion of the majority report was that personal care should be provided free to all those assessed as in need, and exempted from means testing. It was opposition to this recommendation that formed the basis for the minority report, the *Note of Dissent*, appended by two members. They argued that such provision would be enormously expensive (exceeding the estimates in the main report), would burden taxation and bring no new money into the long-term care sector, and would primarily benefit the better off who, under the current system, often have to fund their own personal care. The long silence of the Labour government, and the rumours that the minority report was a Treasury plant, presaged the eventual decision that the recommendations be largely ignored. Personal care remains in the charged, means tested sector.

It is clear that, from the perspective of the government, the issue is one of funding. Should personal care be treated like health care and be free at the point of use or, like social care, be funded by individuals with private resources? Where should the financial responsibility lie: with the collectivity in the form of the public purse, as the majority report suggested, or with individuals, with some residual help from the state for those without enough? This debate about funding and responsibility needs, however, to be set in the context of a network of other assumptions about the meaning and provision of various forms of help and assistance. Personal care has particular features that mean that its provision is not always straightforward. It also poses problems because it lies across the major 'fault line' of community care that divides the two great territories of health and social care. Across welfare systems, even of quite different types, we can observe various approximations to this division. The aim of this chapter is to explore how the boundary between these two systems is constructed, and then use that analysis to reflect on the specific position of personal care in welfare systems.

The medical–social boundary

The first thing to note is that no single criterion defines the boundary between medical and social care. Rather the boundary is specified by several sets of overlapping criteria – institutional, financial, professional, intellectual and ideological – that in combination define the character of the two sectors. Where the division falls according to these criteria can differ, so that the fault line is ragged. Though conceptually separate, the different institutional, financial and ideological attributes are connected and rest on and reinforce one another. Thus, at the level of ideology the privileged position that medicine occupies as a knowledge system underlies and reinforces the assumptions which underline the comparative extent and the mode of its funding. To emphasise the diversity and range of the two categories, that they overlap and extend beyond the customary usage of 'medicine' and 'social services', the terms 'medical care' and 'social care' are employed in this chapter.

The medical–social boundary is at its clearest and most significant at the institutional level (see Table 7.1). This is particularly the case in the UK where health care is organised and funded through the National Health Service (NHS) largely out of general taxation; and social care is organised and overseen by local authorities, with the additional involvement of the voluntary sector. The situation has not always been so clear cut. Up until 1973, local authorities were involved in providing health care through mother-and-baby clinics, family planning, domiciliary nursing for older people and, at an earlier stage, through Poor Law infirmaries and asylums (Means and Smith 1985). Such shifts illustrate the permeable nature of the boundary, particularly during the early twentieth-century development of the welfare state. Many local authority services developed historically out of a system of social assistance which tended to be organised, as in many European countries, at the level of the municipality (Swann 1988).

The institutional division between health and social care is also reflected in their governance by the ways in which power is brokered and decisions made. There is a common pattern across western welfare systems: social care tends to be discussed, determined and often organised at the level of municipalities, whereas medical care is nationally organised. This reflects a wider judgement about the nature of social care which, as we have noted, is customarily seen as a matter for local option and control. Though health, too, has its origins in the community, the post-war development of national schemes, whether in the form of national health services or nationally regulated health insurance, drew health care to the centre. This focus also reflects the social power of doctors who are able to resist incorporation into the local state and retain national influence and prestige. This is particularly clear in the British case, where the medical profession during the 1940s and the 1960s successfully fought off local authority control.

Table 7.1 The medical–social care boundary

Aspect of the service	Health care institutions	Social care institutions
Entitlement	Social right	Residual right
Level of governance	National	Municipal
Financial responsibility	Free at point of use	Individual or means tested
Professional orientation	Medicine and professions supplementary to medicine	Social work
Professional status	Accepted	Denied
Knowledge base	Biomedical and clinical science, i.e. 'hard' science	Social science/therapies, i.e. 'soft' science
Application of technology	High and esteemed	Low and not esteemed
Action	Direct, bodily and professional	Vague, psychosocial and lay
Legitimation and power	'Real' life and death needs, Necessary	Disputed 'needs', Optional

The third dimension is funding. Common to many welfare systems is a broad distinction between health care, which is provided on a universal or insurance basis and not paid for by the individual, and social care which falls into the territory of means testing and in which individuals are expected to fund themselves if they have the resources, and rely on the state only when they cannot. The exact pattern of provision is, of course, more varied than this simple account suggests, and the described financial arrangements for medical care best fit tax-based universalistic systems as in the UK and Sweden, where health care is provided on a citizenship basis, broadly free at the point of use, and regarded as an unquestioned social right. It applies also in countries like Germany and France with a social insurance model, whereby health care is funded by compulsory insurance contributions paid by employees and employers, and where the contributions reflect income but benefits are standard (Tester 1996; Wall 1996). In these systems, coverage has been extended historically to the entire population – again underlining the special status of health care as a public good, for a similar extension does not normally apply to income or social care benefits – and medical care is in general free at the point of use, with some variable charges.

The major exception among affluent countries is, of course, the USA, but even there the particular status of medical care is reflected in its funding arrangements. Medicare does provide medical cover for all older citizens regardless of income, though it is compromised in terms of coverage – no prescription drugs – and by co-payments and deductibles. The coverage of Medicare thus itself reduplicates the status system within medicine, in that it broadly meets acute medical need but not chronic and long-term care. American exceptionalism only really comes into play for those under pensionable age, where the responsibility for meeting health care costs falls upon the individual, to be met either by personal resources or covered by private insurance or employment-related benefits. Those unable to meet these face a pauperising test: they are required to spend down their assets in order to become eligible for the means-tested cover of Medicaid, which is a residual provision for the poor, covering both medical and social care costs.

If we turn to social care, it is clear that the sector is financially and institutionally more varied than medical care. Which forms of care are free and which charged for and at what rates varies across systems and over time has varied historically (Glendinning, Schunk and McLaughlin 1997; Royal Commission 1999b; Tester 1996). For example, home help in Sweden, the home of universalistic services, is charged for, but Swedish pensioners have high incomes. By contrast in Denmark, home help has recently at times been free and at other times charged for. Under both regimes levels of provision have remained very high (Rostgaard and Fridberg 1998). In Britain, local authorities were empowered under the 1948 National Assistance Act to charge for home help, though many, particularly in poorer areas, chose not to and preferred to make provision without charges on a citizenship basis. Rates of cost recovery were in general low during the early post-war years (Means and Smith 1985). The introduction of 'care management' and the growing privatisation of provision in the wake of the 1990 NHS and Community Care Act brought a revival of charges, and the majority of recipients of home care now have to contribute financially (73 per cent in a Personal Social Services Research Unit 1998 study). Though there is a means test, it is set at such a low level that even those whose incomes fall below the poverty level may still have to contribute. In Germany, by contrast, under the reforms of 1995 home care has been moved across the funding boundary and is not paid for by individuals but collectively through the extension of the health care insurance to cover care at home. Previously such care was available to individuals only by paying for it themselves or by seeking help from the means-tested social assistance system – a stigmatising procedure which required the older person to have a very low income. In the USA the picture is complex and varies among the states. In general, home care is either funded by individuals as the recipient or short term as an extension of Medicare (a strategy to reduce hospital costs), or on a means-tested basis by Medicaid as part of the long-term care of the poor (Benjamin 1993; Feldman, Sapienza and Kane 1990).

Broadly speaking, therefore, although variation abounds, there is also a common pattern for social care to be regarded as something that individuals should predominantly pay for themselves. It is regarded much like other day-to-day living or housing expenses – part of ordinary social life – and something therefore for which people are personally responsible, always with the proviso that those who cannot manage will be helped on a means-tested basis. The linking of social care to ordinary social life also appears to make it more subject to political judgements than is the case with medical care. This characteristic has been noted at the level of governance, but is also seen in the variation in levels of home care among European countries. The inference must be that social care provision is more driven by policy choices than medical care (Royal Commission 1999b).

The fourth criterion of division is that of professional orientation. All health care professionals, however distinct their practice, to some degree look to medicine for their authority and knowledge base. It provides the integrating focus not just for the subordinated profession of nursing, but also for groups like radiographers, physiotherapists and other speciality therapists: all termed in a telling phrase, 'professions supplementary to medicine'. Social care activities by contrast fall under the professional remit of social work. Even though the majority of workers in the sector have no formal social work qualifications, their practice is shaped organisationally by social work values (though these are increasingly subject to challenge from managerialist approaches), and they work under senior staff who customarily have a social work qualification. The professional status of social work is, however, less strongly established even within the profession itself than in medicine – that archetype of all that a profession means – and social work's ideo-logical control of the sector is less assured. The clash of the professional cultures of medicine and social work causes many of the recurrent problems that frustrate joint working across the divide. Social workers outposted to general medical practices, multidisciplinary teams in mental health care and disputes between hospital consultants and field social workers on the issue of bed blocking all provide examples of institutionalised inter-professional conflict across the medical–social divide (Huntingdon 1981).

The division is not simply one of professional orientation but has an epistemological root in the different knowledge bases of the two sectors. The biomedical model derives from and is legitimated by its close association with science, the dominant and most powerful mode of thought in modern western society, which endows it with an unques-tioned authority (Estes and Binney 1989). Social care by contrast is rooted in the 'soft' social sciences and the sometimes disputed thera-peutic tradition. Its knowledge base is not accorded the same status as 'hard' science.

The division is also reflected in the comparative orientation to technology. Modern medicine is increasingly marked by high levels of technology, whether machine or drug based. This is reflected within the status system of medicine for high-tech, science-based interventions occupy the prestigious heartland of 'scientific medicine'. Social care, by contrast, rarely involves complex technology. Indeed a 'technological fix' tends to be poorly regarded, and is often seen as an evasion of the essentially social or interpersonal character of people's needs.

Medical practice is characterised as involving skilled, physical interventions that act forcefully on the body and which could not be undertaken by another. Social care interventions by contrast are either more ethereal – counselling or other interpersonal work – or more mundane, providing day-to-day assistance of a practical sort. Today's dominant culture tends to deny the specialised character of the first and to downgrade the status of the second (discussed further in Chapter 2). In either case, they are seen as activities that many people do without training, and the professional status of social care is thus undermined. At times, medicine deals with life-threatening situations, and this dramatic quality endows it with additional importance, for in certain situations getting help is literally vital. The social care professions rarely impact on people in that way.

As epidemiological and social science research has shown, the social environment is far more significant than medicine in determining the pattern of life, survival and suffering. In the pervasive social perception, however, medicine remains the more significant, and this feeds into the belief that medicine is 'necessary' and social care in some sense 'optional'. As we noted earlier in relation to payment and social rights, there is a widespread acceptance that medical needs are 'real' needs and ones that should be met by society. Indeed to define a problem as medical is to locate it in a privileged policy discourse, which means that only those qualified to diagnose and prescribe have opinions that should be listened to.

The division reduplicated within health care

There are cleavages not only between medical and social care, but within medicine itself. Nursing clearly lies within the medical sphere; it is integral to the medical enterprise and it draws on the same biomedical knowledge base. But in many senses nursing shares the same structural position in relation to medicine as does social work, care work or other forms of social care. The skills it emphasises as unique to the profession derive from a wider 'holistic' view of the patient which encompasses their emotional and social being. Holistic traditions of nursing emphasise the person as an integrated being. Lawler (1997) argues that while medicine deals with the body as an object of science – anonymous, dependent, passive and reductionally reduced to the sum of its malfunctioning parts – nursing strives to integrate the lived body of personal experience. Such accounts of nursing are of course highly idealised: the reality of most modern nursing is one of time pressure and specialisation leading to skill mix and fragmentation. Nursing does however embody values that have affinities with the social care sector, and it shares at the structural, institutional and professional levels immense problems in establishing its professional status and the independence of its knowledge base. The predominant position is still that nurses are ancillary to doctors: on hand to carry out their orders and to provide the setting that makes medical practice possible (Lawler 1991).

These divisions are also gendered, in that most nurses are female and in the sense that the tasks they perform and the qualities they exhibit are traditionally associated with women (Davies 1995). Nurturance, care, emotional labour and intimate body care are all conventionally regarded as female tasks. Medicine by contrast is associated with a set of 'masculine' values and practices in which scientific mastery, technological dominance and professional authority underwrite the status of the occupation, even though its tasks are more and more performed by women. Gender thus operates not just at the level of the individual but also structures the nature of the organisation (Acker 1990). This gendered division of labour is widely diffused in the caring professions. The social work and social care sectors are predominantly staffed by women and their values of empathy, warmth, psychological discernment, practicality and hands-on help are those traditionally assigned to women (Balloch *et al.* 1995).

A division between medical and social care is also inherent in the distinction between cure and care. Both are properly part of medicine, but cure is pre-eminent. The relative standing of care versus cure is echoed in the comparative prestige of acute versus chronic care, which in turn conditions representation of the medical–social boundary. The result, with increasing pressure on resources, is that chronic care and support is increasingly designated as social care. These distinctions are mirrored in the ranking of medical specialisms. High-tech, science-based and cure-oriented specialisms have higher status than those with a large care component, such as learning disability, rehabilitative medicine, psychiatry and geriatrics. These either manage chronic conditions or deploy skills that approximate to those of the ordinary social world, and as such approach the requirements of social care. Such specialisms often attempt to take a more holistic view of the patient, and their practice is often in multidisciplinary teams. They are also specialisms that have relatively high proportions of women staff. While from the patients' perspective these wider sympathies are of value, from the viewpoint of medicine they carry little weight, for those specialisms are in general lowly regarded.

Lastly, the setting of treatment, care and support is significant. The defining setting of modern medicine is the hospital. It was not always so, but with the nineteenth-century rise of the infirmary and the development of drug-based and device-supported interventions in the twentieth, the hospital has become the epicentre of modern scientific medicine. It is also where path-breaking and Nobel prize-winning knowledge is generated, where the most complex work is undertaken, and where the leaders of the profession are located. Community-based medical work does not enjoy the same status, accolades or fascination (shifts in power relations around community purchasing by general practitioners are having only a minor effect on this). In a similar way, it is ward-based hospital work that has defined the nature of nursing, and provides the dominant source of its status and legitimacy. Community nursing, by contrast, has always had a lesser and marginal quality, for it takes place 'out there', in unmedical settings and hidden from the hospital gaze. Community nursing has also traditionally been more engaged with low status bed work and personal body care: until the 1980s this formed the main task of district nurses.

An asymmetrical relationship

As will have become clear, the relation between medical and social care is unequal in terms of professional status, power and political legitimacy. At a conceptual level, care is the defining sector and social care a residual category, representing 'all the rest'. Indeed the term 'social care' is itself problematic and lacks the coherence of 'medical care'. In various of the divisions outlined above, alternative terms such as 'society', 'social work' and 'social science' are more appropriate, demonstrating the unfocused nature of this side of the boundary.

Some influential commentators have represented the care complex as not two systems but one: that of medicine as a totalising system of knowledge and power that constructs all aspects of the social world (or those aspects it chooses to recognises) in its terms. This is the sense in which Foucault (1973) speaks of the medical gaze. By this account, all aspects of life – the social world, personal relations, habits and feelings – are potentially relevant to the medical enterprise and capable of becoming subject to it. They form the background to medical practice and are admitted to the territory of medicine by the judgement of doctors and according to their relevance. Medicine by this account is not so much a discrete part of the social world, as a form of knowledge that constitutes aspects of its entirety. By extension this representation suggests that social care is not a parallel or equal sphere but the setting in which medicine operates.

The dominance of 'medical care' has not gone unchallenged. We have already noted that a substantial and influential accumulation of research has established the significance of social and cultural factors in the origin of health and illness. Since the 1960s, there has been a persistent critique of the medicalisation of life and of the improper colonisation of sectors of it by the medical profession (Illich 1976). Within health and social care, the arguments have been most powerfully articulated in Britain by the disability movement, but they have also been influential from and among the constituencies concerned with learning disability, mental health problems, childbirth and terminal illness. In all these sectors attempts have been made to reassert the significance of ordinary social life and of the models of care that it requires (Brown and Smith 1992; Oliver 1990; Ward and Philpot 1995). With regard to older people, the debate has been less developed. This is partly because older people by virtue of their earlier lives are more strongly linked to the structures of ordinary life than people with learning difficulties or lifelong disability, so that ordinary life models require less articulation. But it is also a product of ageism and policy pessimism (promoted by the greater size of the planning population) which means that it is harder to debate and implement progressive approaches in care services for older people.

A shifting boundary

As we have noted at various points, the boundary between medical care and social care is not fixed but shifting, not least because it is subject to changing ideological and policy pressures. In recent years, there has been a marked tendency for the medical boundary to be drawn back, and for more and more care activities to be reclassified as 'social'. In part this has been driven by the ideological factors that have been described. Even within medicine there is now a broad consensus that hospitals and medical institutions are inappropriate settings for long-term care and that more domestic forms of provision, ideally in the person's own home, are preferable (Royal Commission 1999b). Such understanding has underpinned the growing emphasis on 'community care' which, although officially promoted since the 1960s, has only recently received full policy attention and funding.

The principal driver behind the transfer is however money. Community care is perceived to be cheaper than hospital care, partly because capital costs are lower (for to a large degree they are met by the users providing their own accommodation), and partly because levels of staffing and qualifications are lower in the community (unskilled low paid care workers substitute for nursing staff). At the institutional level, with the invention of the term 'continuing care' in the 1990s, chronic conditions, even those requiring nursing support, have increasingly been recategorised as social care, though the exact nature of the boundary has remained contentious and subject to changing legal judgements and government guidance (Hunter 1999). One consequential major shift has concerned the community nursing service, which no longer provides personal care in the form of washing and bathing except as part of a clearly medical intervention. 'Social baths', as they are now termed, must be provided in the social care sector.

Personal care: The medical body and the social body

We saw at the start of this chapter how the majority report of the recent Royal Commission recommended that personal care be a non-means-tested provision. The issue was primarily treated as one of finance, of costs to the individual as opposed to the state, and was located in a wider debate concerning the nature of the welfare state and the specification of the risks which it should protect. Personal care by this judgement belongs to the same territory as chronic health care needs: something that should be provided free at the point of use for all in need. The recommendation was not, however, a judgement as to who should provide such care; and the report implicitly accepted the relatively recent organisational changes which have separated the purchaser (payment) and provider roles.

The association of personal care with chronic health care needs reflects a changing approach to the body in the service system. In the past, the remit of social care stopped short of the body. That was the point at which medical care began. But the growing significance of personal care in the maintenance and support of older people at home has meant that new responses are required, which assert the co-existence of a 'social body' alongside the traditionally recognised 'medical body' (Table 7.2).

Personal care is constructed as those things that an adult would manage for him or herself – washing, dressing, eating and excreting. Domestic tasks by contrast – preparing food, washing clothes, cleaning the house – are commonly provided socially, either within the domestic economy as part of the traditional gendered division of family labour, or in the formal economy, either by paid domestic work or by retail services such as laundries and restaurants. Whichever way, their social production is customary and unproblematic. Personal care is, however, by its nature transgressive. It involves direct hands-on intimate contact. Such bodywork can entail observing, manipulating and evaluating the body, typically in a state of undress. It may involve dealing with human wastes, and thus with managing pollution and disgust (Miller 1997). Nurses have traditionally had a special sanction in these areas. Their symbolic purity, evinced in their habit-like uniforms, enables them to manage pollution in others (Littlewood 1991). Their training enables them to negotiate body access in ways that allow its transgressive character, though, as Lawler shows, this training has largely been implicit (Lawler 1991). There has therefore traditionally been an assumption that personal care is best undertaken by nurses, not for reasons of formal qualifications, but because nurses are culturally sanctioned to do this work.

Table 7.2 Medical–social distictions in health care

	Dominant tasks	
Attribute	Cure	Care
Condition	Acute	Chronic
Status of specialities	High	Low
Archetypal setting	Hospital ward	Patient's home, in the community
Archetypal professional	Doctor, male	Nurse, female
Prevailing care principle	Rationality	Emotion/nurturance
Funding per contact	High	Low

But the assumptions on which this rests may be mistaken. Increasingly this work is undertaken in the community by care workers; and personal care now forms a major part of the publicly funded home-care service. By and large these staff are untrained, and rely on personal sensitivity and gendered social skills to negotiate and undertake their work. Though the provision of such care is not unproblematic, evidence from a recent study suggested that most older people would rather receive such help from care workers than nurses (Twigg 2000). They perceived the care workers' style as more homely, and the social model of care better fitted to the day-to-day nature of their needs. Their views of nurses were sometimes negative. In relation to low-level needs such as bathing, they were perceived as being unreliable; and they too often reminded older people of bad experiences in hospital where their bodies had been pulled about during investigation and treatment. Managing and caring for the body is, thus, not necessarily a medical matter and can be provided appropriately within social care. Doing so however requires that the needs of the 'social body', not simply the 'medical body', are recognised and met by care.

Conclusion

As we have seen, the medical–social care boundary is a pervasive division across western welfare systems. Where exactly it lies is, however, subject to shifting social and policy definition, creating a grey area and a contentious zone. Personal care is located in the zone of contention because of the special significance of the body and its management. Traditionally in the welfare services the body has been regarded as the territory of medicine, but increasingly this assumption is subject to question. It may indeed be appropriate to locate body care firmly in social care. But this should not necessarily mean that individuals be required to fund it from their own resources. Personal care is important for the well-being of older people. We need to recognise this and uncouple the inherited link between the mode of care and how it is paid for.

References

Acker, J. (1990) 'Hierarchies, Jobs and Bodies: A Theory of Gendered Organisations.' *Gender and Society 4*, 2, 139–158.

Balloch, S., Andrew, T., Ginn, J., McLean, J., Pahl, J. and Williams, J. (1995) *Working in the Social Services*. London: National Institute of Social Work.

Benjamin, A.E. (1993) 'An Historical Perspective on Home Care Policy.' *Milbank Quarterly 71*, 1, 129–166.

Brown, H. and Smith, H. (eds) (1992) *Normalisation: A Reader for the Nineties*. London: Routledge.

Davies, C. (1995) *Gender and the Professional Predicament in Nursing.* Buckingham: Open University Press.

Estes, C.L. and Binney, E.A. (1989) 'The Biomedicalization of Aging.' *The Gerontologist 29,* 5, 587–596.

Feldman, P.H., Sapienza, A.M. and Kane, N.M. (1990*) Who Cares for Them: Workers in the Home Care Industry.* New York: Greenwood Press.

Foucault, M. (1973) *The Birth of the Clinic: An Archaeology of Medical Perception.* London: Routledge.

Glendinning, C., Schunk, M. and McLaughlin, E. (1997) 'Paying for Long-Term Domiciliary Care: A Comparative Perspective.' *Ageing and Society 17,* 123–140.

Hunter, M. (1999) 'Ruling Sows Confusion.' *Community Care,* 4–29 August, 10–11.

Huntingdon, J. (1981) *Social Work and General Medical Practice.* London: Allen and Unwin.

Illich, I. (1976) *Limits to Medicine, Medical Nemesis, the Expropriation of Health.* London: Boyars.

Lawler, J. (1991) *Behind the Screens: Nursing, Somology and the Problem of the Body.* Melbourne: Churchill Livingstone.

Lawler, J. (1997) 'Knowing the body and embodiment: methodologies, discourses and nursing.' In J. Lawler (ed) *The Body in Nursing.* Melbourne: Churchill Livingstone.

Littlewood, J. (1991) 'Care and Ambiguity: Towards a Concept of Nursing.' In P. Holden and J. Littlewood (eds) *Anthropology and Nursing.* London: Routledge.

Means, R. and Smith, R. (1985) *The Development of Welfare Services for Elderly People.* London: Croom Helm.

Miller, W.I. (1997) *The Anatomy of Disgust.* Cambridge, MA: Harvard University Press.

Oliver, M. (1990) *The Politics of Disablement.* Basingstoke: Macmillan.

Personal Social Services Research Unit (1998) 'Evaluating Community Care for Older People.' *ECCEP Bulletin 2.* Canterbury: Personal Social Services Research Unit.

Rostgaard, T. and Fridberg, T. (1998) *Caring for Children and Older People: A Comparison of European Policies and Practices.* Social Security in Europe 6. Copenhagen: Danish National Institute of Social Research.

Royal Commission on Long-Term Care (1999a) *With Respect to Old Age: A Report by the Royal Commission on Long-Term Care.* Cm. 4192-I. London: The Stationery Office.

Royal Commission on Long-Term Care (1999b) 'Lessons from International Experience.' In Royal Commission (1999) *With Respect to Old Age – Rights and Responsibilities: The Context of Long-Term Care Policy: Research Volume I.* Cm. 4192-II/1. London: The Stationery Office.

Swann, A. de (1988) *In Care of the State.* Cambridge: Polity Press.

Tester, S. (1996) *Community Care for Older People: A Comparative Perspective.* Basingstoke: Macmillan.

Twigg, J. (2000) *Bathing, the Body and Community Care.* London: Routledge.

Wall, A. (ed) (1996) *Health Care Systems in Liberal Democracies.* London: Routledge.

Ward, L. and Philpot, T. (eds) (1995) *Values and Visions: Changing Ideas in Services for People with Learning Difficulties.* Oxford: Butterworth-Heinemann.

CHAPTER 8

Older People, Citizenship and Collective Action

Marian Barnes and Sandra Shaw

Introduction

In the preface to an edited collection on inter-generational relations, Alan Walker quotes Maggie Kuhn, the founder of The Gray Panthers in the USA: 'I feel strongly that the old must not simply advocate on their own behalf. We must act as the elders of the tribe, looking out for the best interests of the future and preserving the precious compact between the generations' (Kuhn, p.x in Walker 1996). In suggesting that collective action among older people should not be solely in the interests of older people, Kuhn is asserting that the knowledge of elders can contribute to the well-being of all. The Gray Panthers organisation was founded in 1970, and was one of several social movements to emerge from the civil rights activity of the 1960s. The use of the term 'panthers' is an explicit reference to the 'Black Panthers' civil rights movement, and indicates a commitment to campaigning on policy issues not solely confined to the experience of ageing.

In the twenty-first century the welfare state is under pressure as a result of demographic change, ideological shifts and the impact of global economic restructuring (Walker 1996). In this context there is a danger that pluralism will lead to fragmentation as marginalised groups compete with each other for a share of increasingly residual services provided by the state sector. But action to raise the likelihood that a 'good old age' will be available to all seems a natural focus for solidarity. Most of us hope to survive to old age, and many of us will find ourselves taking on some responsibility for caring for older relatives. In this chapter we consider how older people can play a role as citizens in promoting collective well-being, as well as contributing to the development of services which are more responsive to their own needs. To locate collective action among older people within the contemporary debate on the nature of citizenship, we start with a brief discussion of its key themes.

The status and practice of citizenship

Barnes and Shardlow (1996) developed an analysis of citizenship to account for the nature and purposes of action being pursued by disabled people and mental health user groups. This analysis identified three dimensions of citizenship:

1. *Accountability*: are public services accountable to their citizen users?

2. *Rights*: are people receiving social justice in terms both of civil and political rights, and access to welfare services?

3. *Participation*: are people enabled to participate in the collective life of the community and thus to engage in the 'practice of citizenship'?

Much of the focus for discussion of citizenship in the context of the welfare state has focused on the second of these dimensions: the identity of the welfare citizen as a social rights bearer and the capacity of the welfare state to ensure the substantive realisation of these rights (Dean 1996). More recently, the citizenship debate has widened to embrace an analysis of the democratic deficit within welfare and in public services generally. This debate has emphasised the identity of the citizen not only as a recipient of public goods, but as an active participant in the governance of their affairs, and as a community member entitled to hold government to account (Ranson and Stewart 1994). In this analysis, citizenship is not only a status but also a practice (Prior, Stewart and Walsh 1995).

In her work on feminist perspectives on citizenship, Lister emphasises the sense of agency that is required when acting as a citizen. She suggests that 'the development of a conscious sense of agency, at both the personal and political level, is crucial to women's breaking of the chains of victimhood and their emergence as full and active citizens' (Lister 1998, p.38). Lister (and others) argue that casting women as victims of oppression damages the creation of opportunities for them to act politically. A similar argument can be advanced in relation to older people, the majority of whom are women.

Feminist writers have also pointed up the limitation of a notion of citizenship based solely in a rights-based 'ethic of justice', and have discussed the need to give new meanings to notions of equality and autonomy by viewing these also from the perspective of an 'ethics of care' (Sevenhuijsen 1998). At the core of such ethics are the values of attentiveness, compassion, relationality and commitment. Such virtues, it is argued, should not be confined to the private domain, but included in our understanding of what constitutes democratic citizenship.

Another theme of contemporary citizenship debates concerns the inter-generational dimension which is suggested in Kuhn's notion of tribal elders, and which would promote cross-generational learning and a sense of responsibility towards the future as well as the current generations. It is exemplified in Roche's (1992) discussion of the ecological dimension of citizenship, which incorporates the relationship between the human and the natural world and also requires consideration of the citizen's responsibilities to current and future generations.

The realisation of the social rights of citizenship remains important to the analysis of older people's experiences of the welfare state, especially the services they receive to enable them to maintain their desired level of health and well-being. However, this is only part of the story, for collective action among older people can also help to realise a broader conception of citizenship, one which gains strength by embracing notions of relationality and interdependence within and between generations. Not only is an ethic of care necessary for the development of welfare policies and practice which preserve the dignity of older citizens, but older people may also have skills in those aspects of social relations which can be a resource to other generations (see Bernard and Meade 1993). It is this broader conception which underpins the initiatives that are being developed through the Better Government for Older People Programme (BGOP) and through some Health Action Zone (HAZ) initiatives, and which acknowledge older people as contributors to, as well as recipients of, welfare.

Forms of collective action

The collective action through which older people express their citizenship and contribute to a vital civil society comprises various types of activity:

- *Political organisations:* including 'traditional' political action such as membership of political parties, 'single issue' politics such as involvement in environmental movements, and 'age-specific' politics such as pensioners' action groups.

- *Cultural groupings:* including activity based upon religious affiliation or ethnic identity.

- *Social or leisure groups:* including sports clubs, theatre clubs and arts and crafts groups.

- *Self-help activities:* which are often focused on general or particular health needs.

- *Voluntary action:* both age-specific, such as involvement in Age Concern groups, and participation in voluntary organisations generally.

- *Consumer groups:* based around people's identities as users of public services.

Age itself is only one factor which might provide the focus for collective action, for other identities or interests also prompt older people to organise collectively. Identities relating to gender, ethnicity, disability or sexuality may provide a shared experience which includes older people among groups not defined by age. Similarly, commitment to a cause, shared political beliefs and community groups centring on specific localities can result in older people participating in action which involves people of all ages. Voluntary action has long been a means through which older people fill valued roles alongside younger people: the Retired and Senior Volunteer Programme (RSVP) run by Community Services Volunteers estimates that over 10,000 people aged over 50 years are involved (online information at www.rsvpuk. freeserve.co.uk/rsvp.html).

Traditional notions of citizenship have related the concept almost exclusively to a political status and to action in the public sphere. More recently, however, feminist analyses of citizenship (e.g. Siim 1994) have challenged the distinction between the 'public' activities of, for example, political party membership and activism and the 'private' action of caring or involvement in carers' groups. Both define locations in which citizenship can be practised. The importance of action within 'civil society' – all those areas of society which are not included within the state or family life, including most voluntary associations – has been identified as necessary to build the 'social capital' which underpins social cohesion and economic success (Putnam 1993). Thus the contribution which older people can make to general social well-being can take place in various spheres.

There is an increasing diversity of organisations and community groups based around the shared experiences of older people and which have aims explicitly related to the social citizenship of older people. Some follow the long tradition of self-help, while others are overtly political and aim to provide a means through which older people can contribute to political and policy-making processes. Not all such action is new: as early as the 1930s in the USA, the Townsend movement demonstrated older people's collective action in pursuit of social citizenship (Amenta and Zylan 1995). In the UK, the National Pensioners' Convention provides a contemporary example of overt political organisation.

The significance of age-specific organisations is that they link politics with demography. Older people comprise an increasing proportion of the population; if they were to take up a united position on key issues, their electoral power would be considerable and they could be a significant lobby in conventional political processes.

Collective action among older people would be one of several new forms of political action which express the aspirations of a diverse society. Political objectives (in which we would include challenging ageist stereotypes) may also be pursued through cultural activities like Bealtaine, an annual festival of the arts organised by Age and Opportunity in Ireland.

Experiences of participation

To illustrate both the potential and the dilemmas of collective action among older people, the remainder of this chapter discusses examples of action of different types. We draw on research in which each of us has been involved: a study of three older people's organisations in Sheffield, and an evaluation of an Age Concern Scotland (ACS) project in Fife (Barnes and Bennett 1998, Cormie 1999 and Shaw 1996a describe the projects and the research).

In Sheffield the work compared the Sheffield Pensioners' Action Group (SPAG), an overtly political organisation which focuses on welfare rights issues, and AgeWell, an example of a project developed by Age Concern England with the aim of promoting health, well-being and the active involvement of older people as volunteers. The Fife User Panels adopted community development principles in working with frail older people who use community-based health and social care services. The objective, to increase the influence of frail older people over health and social care services, was pursued in two ways: by enhancing the capacity of older people to assert their individual needs through the personal empowerment that they gained from their participation in the panels; and by developing their collective influence through a representation role by which the panels acted as user consultation groups for statutory services. The objective was therefore to enable older people to assert their rights as social citizens and to establish a dialogue through which service providers could become more accountable to them.

The research projects had different designs and purposes. Here we draw from them to reflect on three important questions about the potential of collective action in enabling older people to express their citizenship. These reflections are offered as contributions to a developing debate, rather than as 'findings' from research expressly designed to address the particular questions:

- Why do older people participate in age-specific activity?
- What are the factors which tend to exclude older people from participation?
- How significant is an identity as an 'older person' in motivating participation?

Why participate?

There are many barriers to collective action among older people (see below). So what motivates those who take part to do so and are they unusual? By definition, the frail older people who were invited by ACS to become members of the Fife Panels had few opportunities for collective action because they were unable to leave their homes without assistance. At the time they were asked and agreed to join, half had no clear perception of the purpose of the panels. Some were prompted by the opportunity for social contact, some saw it as an opportunity for self-help, some saw it as a means of finding out more about services, while others were clearer that the main purpose was to talk about their experiences of services with a view to seeking improvements.

Other studies have found that older people who were invited to take part in focus groups in a primary care context, while unfamiliar with a user group, were very interested in the possibilities of 'having their say' and, perhaps more importantly, as a source of enjoyment and health promotion (Walsh *et al.* 1999). Curiosity motivated some of those who became involved in the Fife Panels. But while those who become active may be more 'adventurous' than those who decline the invitation, the Fife Panel members' health and social care needs were typical of many older people's (Barnes, Cormie and Crichton 1994). Participants also suggested that some people are more prepared than others to take risks:

> But you see my next door neighbour, she's not as old as I am, she's in her seventies and she's had a hip replacement; and another one has a

stroke and I'd like them to come, you see, but they'll not come because they don't want to take part in anything. They're frightened they have to speak; you know what I mean.

Positive experiences of being involved are important in sustaining motivation. Members enjoyed the social contact offered by panel meetings, the sense of being valued themselves, and being listened to by service providers, as well as the practical benefits of finding out about services that they had not known existed. Achieving specific service outcomes takes longer and is uncertain, although some members saw a potential for change which they had not previously thought possible. For example, panel members engaged in a dialogue with home-help managers about new models of domiciliary care and produced a 14-point 'Good Hospital Discharge' checklist. This became the focus of inter-agency work to improve the practice of hospital discharge. It was suggested that some members would be deterred if there was no evidence of change, while others would continue to attend meetings because of the intrinsic benefits they received from participation.

Other responses indicated that altruism motivated their involvement. There was a preparedness to accept that changes might be achieved for others, rather than themselves. These responses indicate an awareness among older people of the role which the panels could play in developing a 'conscious sense of agency' (Lister 1998). The experience of involvement is inadequately understood in terms of consumerist notions of empowerment as increasing choice (Barnes and Walker 1996). Rather it enables not only personal growth, but also a growth in collective consciousness and capacity for change (Thursz, Nusberg and Prather 1995).

What excludes older people from participating in collective action?

Warren (1999) has summarised the reasons why user groups in health and community care services have failed to draw their strength from older users:

- The colouring by ageism and stigma of general perceptions of the ability and willingness of older users to participate.

- A tendency among older people towards self-effacement or deference to professional and expert advice.

- Older individuals' fear of putting their pride and independence at stake by admitting to problems that signify dependence.

- An unwillingness to complain for fear of losing access to services.

We can add the practical difficulties faced by older people who are frail and need assistance to travel, and the fear that many older people feel in public spaces. By definition, participation in the Fife User Panels has to be enabled – members cannot travel to meetings without assistance. Some of the reasons given by nominees who did not join panels related to their physical incapacity. Some said they would not be able to cope with the travel, became tired easily or that they 'did not feel up to it'. Fear of being seen as a troublemaker can deter some people from becoming involved in groups which aim to change services. This may be a particular concern of older people who are dependent on services for many aspects of personal care, and who fear poor treatment if they complain. Low expectations have also been suggested as a reason why older people may be reluctant to express dissatisfaction with services (Wilson 1995).

Half of those who were invited to join the Fife Panels and who declined the invitation declared themselves uninterested or 'not keen' on group meetings (Barnes and Bennett-Emslie 1997). We can only speculate about the reasons for this reported lack of interest. Some individuals were discomforted at the thought of expressing views in a group, while others were reluctant to mix with people in a similar situation. But we wonder how much this may have to do with older people's low expectations that they will be taken seriously and be able to influence the services they receive. The apparent apathy which is often cited as a reason for not pursuing 'user involvement' may well reflect actual experiences of powerlessness in the face of professional control over services.

Another deterrent to participation is the perceived risk of becoming a victim of crime. Although statistically older people are less at risk than other age groups, they may perceive themselves to be at greater risk. This perception of increased risk is connected with media coverage of crimes against older people and the representation of older people as victims and was illustrated during a conversation between two members of SPAG:

William: They [older people] won't go out at night.

Mavis: It's over-done! [the fear]

William: It's there and it's sufficient to keep people indoors.

Mavis: I think it's a fear that's been built up and publicity's been given to that aspect. And I think it's a bit sad as well because it sets the generations against each other.

Media coverage of crime can create a unified identity of older people as victims, in contrast to younger people who are portrayed as the perpetrators of crime. Pain (1997, p.119) has suggested that the construction of old age as including 'victimhood' has a role 'in explaining patterns of crime and fear of crime'. The negative juxtaposition of old and young has the effect of making some older people too scared to participate fully in society. This indicates the importance of treating older people's citizenship as encompassing their inclusion as social participants and requiring their more active involvement in health and social care service arrangements.

One of the concerns which emerged from the Sheffield study was the image of organisations and the way this affected participation. For example, Age Concern Sheffield was seen as an organisation primarily for white, middle-class people. Those working in the organisation are seeking to change this, particularly with reference to ethnicity. It was suggested that initiatives which broadly address ethnic minority groups may not be able to take on board the issue of age in the way that Age Concern can. This sensitive area raises questions about whether ethnic background or age are the more significant in terms of disadvantage or individual identity.

AgeWell groups operate in various settings, such as sheltered or residential accommodation, so that older people who are often excluded from social participation are involved. At the time of the Sheffield research (1995), there were two Afro-Caribbean groups and one for male Asian elders, and a group for Asian women was being developed. This reflects the organisation's intention to include older people from different ethnic origins. Given the age distribution of the population, membership was potentially greater among women than men, and most white AgeWell members were single women. A different factor was seen to affect participation in SPAG. While not affiliated to any political party, it was seen by outsiders as a political organisation.

Some older people (as well as younger people) are reluctant to join explicitly political groups. In a study of disabled people's organisations, the political nature of such action was reported as a deterrent to some people taking part (Barnes *et al.* 1994). Such individual and communal perceptions of groups can determine whether or not someone chooses to join. This means that if groups or organisations wish to extend their membership, they may have to alter their image and present one that encourages people to join and become active participants. Below we address the question of whether 'age' per se is significant in motivating or deterring participation.

The significance of age in social identity

The Fife Panels deliberately sought to hear from those who are often not heard. As the criteria for membership included frailty, use of services and age, the participants were implicitly asked to accept the identity of 'frail older person'. Some local service providers were reluctant to accept that the panels' articulation of dissatisfaction with services was 'representative' of the passive majority of older service users (Barnes *et al.* 1994). An underlying objective of the project was to demonstrate that frailty in old age is not necessarily associated with an inability to speak out (Barnes and Bennett 1998).

At the first meetings of the Fife Panels, members talked about their experience of growing older and beginning to need support from informal carers or statutory service providers. This was not just a 'way in' to the discussion, but also a means of defining the changes which had taken place in people's lives, and of developing a collective awareness of shared and individual experiences. The members became aware of their contrasting expectations about the quality and standards of services which, in turn, challenged the normally low expectations of older people. Such consciousness-raising methods in women's groups have been well documented.

During the evaluation, the possibility of the panels meeting younger people was raised and prompted different views. Some members felt younger people would simply not be interested, while one emphasised the importance of the panels as an opportunity to hear older people's views. Some recognised the value of generating more understanding between the generations, and one panel member shared Maggie Kuhn's view about the need to develop solidarity with people:

> The younger people would understand the older people but also they bring better ideas because it's, as I say, it's their future as well as ours so therefore it will be up to them to take their positions in all departments of life. We're going to pass away anyway and we need the young ones to take over [and] change the world.

SPAG members also identified the importance of including younger members – not least because of self-interest: 'We should be able to get some younger people…to point out what their pensions are going to be like when they come to retirement age.' Many organisations for older people accept members at 55 years or more of age, but unsurprisingly people in their fifties and sixties do not think of themselves as old, see those in their seventies and eighties as old, but do not want to spend time with people of a different generation.

Self-identification as an 'older person' may result in non-participation. Some people regard themselves as 'too old' to become involved: this reasoning may have underlaid the comments of some in Fife who said they did not want to mix with others in a similar situation, or that they readily became too tired to take part in the panels. Siddell (1995) has explored the link between perceptions of age and perceptions of health and well-being. It is probably simplistic to consider age alone as determining whether people take part in collective action. A woman in her eighties, still active in the community in Sheffield, suggested that people living in residential care have 'little initiative left themselves', and may need older people who do not think of themselves as 'old' to speak for them. Some older people do accept increased dependency at the end of their lives – perhaps even enjoying younger people doing things for them. Shaw (1996b, 2000) suggests, however, that many older people in residential care still wish both to retain as much independence as possible and to participate socially. Hughes (1995, p.25) argues that older people are not just 'passive recipients, but also have the capacity to change themselves and their situations and to exercise their rights'. Murray (1997) demonstrates just how hard it can be for people who are not only old but also poor and in long-term care to become empowered.

Older people have to deal with many negative representations of old age. One interviewed in Sheffield expressed her frustration with the media in this respect: 'They [TV] have tremendous power to twist situations and represent older people as if they don't know what they're talking about; as if they're all needing care and always whining.' Often identity formation is not just a question of age but of how someone formerly lived their life. Continued independence in later life may be much more important to some than others:

> When you've been independent all your life, no matter what sort of work you've done, and you've got to go cap in hand, hold your hand out or whatever to ask for further benefits; because you can't do it on what is allowed through the law of the land. It's all wrong.

While there are advantages when older people work collectively with a shared identity and purpose, some of those interviewed for the Sheffield research resisted the idea of being separated in this way. They suggested that they hold many interests in common with younger people and that it was wrong to set 'old versus young'. For example, people on basic state pension are likely to face similar financial problems to young people on social security income support.

Groups of older people can have problems in sustaining their membership. Loss of members through death is a recurrent issue, as for both the Fife Panels and SPAG. During the first three years of the Fife Panels, 8 members died and 13 stopped attending because of illness, entry to residential care or other reasons. According to its original constitution, SPAG members were to be over the statutory retirement age.

In line with the National Pensioners' Convention, it was however concerned to attract new, younger members, and discussed reducing the qualifying age from 60 to 65 down to 55 years. As one member said, 'The trouble is we've reached the end of a generation and people are dying off now: the people who founded it.'

One problem in trying to move away from negative perceptions of old age is that we re-assess ourselves in relation to where we are in the life course, and make judgements about others in relation to ourselves. Once defined as 'old' solely by age, you stay old and get older. The status is not reversible like being divorced. Once you have 'gone public', by aligning yourself to a group for older people, you remain old until you die! One of the objectives of collective action is precisely to challenge stereotypes of what it means to be old – it may mean frailty, but it does not have to mean passivity. The evaluation of the Fife project demonstrated important ways in which older people changed as a result of taking part. They became more confident in their ability to speak out, but reserved their judgement about the extent of real change in services during the first three years. There were however important changes in the attitudes of the service officials who came into contact with the panels and a strong willingness to maintain a dialogue with the panel members. This held the promise of both service change and further developmental opportunities for the panel members. Thus what it means to be an 'old person' may be changed by the personal empowerment which comes through collective action.

Conclusion

Older people and the practice of citizenship

The Labour government elected in 1997 emphasises the active engagement of communities in several policy areas. Health Action Zones, the New Deal for Communities, community safety strategies and regeneration initiatives all require public bodies to demonstrate how they are working with local people and service users, in both defining and responding to the problems facing policy makers and service delivery agencies (Barnes and Prior 2000). At the same time, both locality and identity communities are developing their own organisations and strategies to support their members and to challenge the disadvantage and exclusion they experience.

Our argument in this chapter is that older people can and do play an active part in processes of community engagement and that such involvement has benefits not only for older people themselves, but for the health and well-being of the society as a whole. For example, Ivory (1998) reports evidence of older people making an impact not only on health and social services but also becoming a focal point for the community as a whole by taking up transport and mobility issues. Ginn (1993) discusses the role of older people from British ethnic minority groups, through the Standing Conference of Ethnic Minority Senior Citizens, in challenging the inequality experienced by black people. The Better Government for Older People initiative is not only concerned with enabling older people to have their say about services specifically for older people, but also with the contribution they can make to revitalising processes of governance. There are nevertheless significant factors which can get in the way of older people playing an active part: support and resources are necessary to make their participation possible. Beyond this, older people need to be convinced that politicians and the government have a genuine commitment to policies which respect their social rights as citizens.

The older people involved in the groups discussed here remember what it was like to be old and sick before the post-1945 welfare state. They may have a particular motivation to protect the gains that have been made. But it has been claimed that the increasing proportion of older people in the population is placing the welfare state under severe strain. Ageist stereotypes of passivity and dependency need to be challenged if the inter-generational contract is to be renewed. Collective action on the part of older people has an important part to play in achieving this objective, but there is also value in exploring the potential of alliances between older people's movements and those of disabled people and others with marginalised identities.

Acknowledgements

With acknowledgements to the Fife User Panel members for many positive experiences of active ageing, to Joyce Cormie and Maureen Crichton for making our involvement possible, and to Alan Walker for his commitment and collaboration on work in Sheffield and elsewhere. For the Sheffield research, the work of C.P.M Knipscheer, P.G. Klandermans and Th.N.M. Schuyt at the Free University of Amsterdam and other research partners is acknowledged.

References

Amenta, E. and Zylan, Y. (1995) 'It Happened Here: Political Opportunity, the New Institutionalism and the Townsend Movement.' In S.M. Lyman (ed) *Social Movements: Critiques, Concepts, Case-Studies.* Basingstoke: Macmillan.

Barnes, M. and Bennett, G. (1998) 'Frail Bodies, Courageous Voices: Older People Influencing Community Care.' *Health and Social Care in the Community 6*, 2, 102–111.

Barnes, M. and Bennett-Emslie, G. (1997) *'If They Would Listen': An Evaluation of the Fife User Panels.* Edinburgh: Age Concern Scotland.

Barnes, M. and Prior, P. (2000) *Private Lives as Public Policy.* Birmingham: Venture.

Barnes, M. and Shardlow, P. (1996) '"Effective Consumers and Active Citizens": Strategies for Users' Influence on Services and beyond.' *Research, Policy and Planning 14*, 1, 33–38.

Barnes, M. and Walker, A. (1996) 'Consumerism *Versus* Empowerment: A Principled Approach to the Involvement of Older Service Users.' *Policy and Politics 24*, 4, 375–393.

Barnes, M., Cormie, J. and Crichton, M. (1994) *Seeking Representative Views from Frail Older People.* Kirkcaldy: Age Concern Scotland.

Bernard, M. and Meade, K. (eds) (1993) *Women Come of Age.* London: Edward Arnold.

Cormie, J. (1999) 'The Fife User Panels Project: Empowering Older People.' In M. Barnes and L. Warren (eds) *Paths to Empowerment.* Bristol: Policy.

Dean, H. (1996) *Welfare, Law and Citizenship.* London: Prentice Hall.

Ginn, J. (1993) 'Grey Power: Age-Based Organisations' Response to Structured Inequality.' *Critical Social Policy 13*, 2, 23–47.

Hughes, B. (1995) *Older People and Community Care: Critical Theory and Practice.* Buckingham: Open University Press.

Ivory, M. (1998) 'Talking about a Revolution.' *Community Care*, 16–22 April, 14–15.

Lister, R. (1998) *Citizenship: Feminist Perspectives.* Basingstoke: Macmillan.

Murray, J. (1997) *Empowerment in Action: The Story of the Empowerment Project.* Edinburgh: Age Concern Scotland.

Pain, R.H. (1997), 'Old Age and Ageism in Urban Research: The Case of Fear of Crime.' *International Journal of Urban and Regional Research 21*, 1, 117–128.

Prior, D., Stewart, J. and Walsh, K. (1995) *Citizenship: Rights, Community and Participation.* London: Pitman.

Putnam, R. (1993) *Making Democracy Work: Civic Traditions in Modern Italy.* Princeton, NJ: Princeton University Press.

Ranson, S. and Stewart, J. (1994) *Management for the Public Domain.* Basingstoke: Macmillan.

Roche, M. (1992) *Rethinking Citizenship: Welfare, Ideology and Change in Modern Society.* Cambridge: Polity Press.

Sevenhuijsen, S. (1998) *Citizenship and the Ethics of Care: Feminist Considerations on Justice, Morality and Politics.* London: Routledge.

Shaw, S.M.I. (1996a) 'Increasing the Societal Participation of Older People.' Unpublished report on preliminary research. Sheffield: Department of Sociological Studies, University of Sheffield.

Shaw, S.M.I. (1996b) 'Evaluation of the Elderly Persons' Homes Review.' Unpublished report. Sheffield: Department of Sociological Studies, University of Sheffield.

Shaw, S.M.I. (2000) 'A "Home" in the Community.' Unpublished Paper.

Siddell, M. (1995) *Health in Old Age: Myth, Mystery and Management.* Buckingham: Open University Press.

Siim, B. (1994) 'Engendering Democracy: Social Citizenship and Political Participation for Women in Scandinavia.' *Social Politics 1,* 3, 286–305.

Thursz, D., Nusberg, C. and Prather, J. (eds) (1995) *Empowering Older People: An International Approach.* London: Cassell.

Walker, A. (ed) (1996) *The New Generational Contract: Inter-Generational Relations, Old Age and Welfare.* London: UCL Press.

Walsh, N., Allen, L., Baines, D. and Barnes, M. (1999) *Taking Off: A First Year Report of the Personal Medical Services (PMS) Pilots in England.* Birmingham: Health Services Management Centre, University of Birmingham.

Warren, L. (1999) 'Conclusion: Empowerment: The Path to Partnership?' In M. Barnes and L. Warren (eds) *Paths to Empowerment.* Bristol: Policy.

Wilson, G. (1995) 'Low Expectations Reinforced: Experiences of Health Services in Advanced Old Age.' In G. Wilson (ed) *Community Care: Asking the Users.* London: Chapman and Hall.

CHAPTER 9

The Entry to a Nursing Home

Residents' and Relatives' Experiences

Sue Davies, Jonas Sandberg and Ulla Lundh

Most studies of nursing home admission have focused on the experience of residents, while the needs of family carers at this time have been largely ignored. In particular, few studies have gathered qualitative data on relatives' experiences of helping a family member to move into a nursing home, and on the way in which they subsequently establish a new caring role. The temporal model of care-giving described by Nolan, Grant and Keady (1996) suggests that when carers assist an older person to move into a nursing home, they enter a new but still involved stage of their relationship, and that many require support to achieve a smooth transition. To date, however, there has been little research evidence to suggest the type of support which is most effective in these circumstances.

Our intention in this chapter is to report some preliminary findings from a study which aims to deepen the understanding of the needs of relatives and family carers of older people who move into a nursing home, partly to help nurses and other health care practitioners meet those needs. The research involves collaborators in the universities of Linköping in Sweden, Sheffield in England and Melbourne, Australia. In this chapter, we outline the background and methods for the study before comparing and contrasting some of the themes emerging from the British and Swedish data.

Background

Whereas the usual expectation would be that the entry of a frail or dependent relative into a nursing home would reduce the problems and responsibilities for carers, there is no doubt that many families find the event extremely stressful (Matthiesson 1989; Nay 1997). The experience is partly influenced by the general societal disapproval of any form of institutional care. In spite of recent improvements in the quality of the care environment, nursing homes continue to be seen as alienating places where individual rights are subsumed by institutional routines and regulations (Levine 1995).

Commentators have recently attempted to identify the processes and perceptions that shape and influence admission to residential or nursing home care, and suggested that it can be a positive choice (Nolan *et al.* 1996). Pearson *et al.* (1998) suggested that the tensions between an increasingly aged population (that probably imply an increase in nursing home use) and the negative public reactions towards institutional care could be resolved by examining the correspondence between the public discourse and actual experiences of nursing home admission. Misleading perceptions of nursing home care would then be challenged.

Several factors have been associated with helping relatives come to terms with nursing home entry, including a perception of control over the situation and the acceptability of the nursing home (Naleppa 1996). These factors point to the importance of adequate information to allow relatives to make informed choices. Several studies have considered the role of relatives in nursing homes and emphasised that nursing home staff should be aware of relatives' needs (Pillemer *et al.* 1998; Relatives' Association 1997) Family members experience loss, guilt and grief, and report that these emotions continue throughout the time that their older member is in the nursing home (Dellasega and Mastrian 1995; Johnson 1990; Tilse 1994). There are, however, few published reports of clinical interventions with families after an elderly relative moves into a residential institution. Conflicting role expectations may result in tensions between relatives and nursing home staff whose respective roles are rarely negotiated. Admission assessment normally focuses entirely upon the needs of the new resident. The difficulties that relatives experience are largely ignored (Duncan and Morgan 1994; Pearson *et al.* 1998). More generally there is some evidence that involvement with nursing home residents by relatives has a positive effect for both relatives and residents (Buckwalter *et al.* 1991; Relatives' Association 1997), although there are signs that it is not always welcomed by staff (Hasselkus 1988; Tickle and Hull 1995; Tilse 1994). Further research is needed to identify the types of involvement that result in positive outcomes.

Objectives and methods

The objectives of the research were common to all three national centres:

- to explore relatives' experiences of helping an older person to move into a nursing home

- to describe current practice within nursing homes in relation to supporting relatives, particularly around the time of admission

- to interpret the public discourse on nursing home care and the admission of new residents

- to integrate and critically analyse data from each phase of the study and identify consistencies and inconsistencies between these three discourses

- to generate understandings and insights to inform and assist people who have this experience in the future

- to generate publications and debate to inform and improve the practice of health professionals, particularly nurses working in nursing homes

- to disseminate the findings and stimulate debate to inform and influence policy makers.

There are three empirical phases to the continuing research. The first involves semi-structured interviews with people who have recently experienced a close relative's admission to a nursing home. Up to 60 carers in each country are being recruited using various methods including advertisements, contacts with nursing homes and carers' groups, and referrals from social services departments. Criteria for inclusion in the study are that the person identifies him or herself as a close relative, that he or she was personally involved in the relocation experience, and that the relocation to a nursing home took place within the previous five years. (In practice, relocation for all the Swedish participants took place within the previous year, and for almost all the English participants within the previous two years.) The samples in the two countries differed in that the Swedish included only spouses and the British mainly adult children. Nonetheless, both samples comprised the principal care-givers; they reflect differences in family care-giving relationships within the two countries.

The second phase will comprise detailed ethnographic case studies of up to three nursing homes in each country. The case studies will describe everyday life within the home through prolonged participant observation and interviews with staff, residents and relatives. The intention is to locate the admission of new residents within the work of the unit as a whole, contextualising the experiences that were explored in phase one. The third and final phase of the research will be a discourse analysis of public documents and other media which make reference to nursing home admission and which shape people's expectations of nursing home care.

Continuing care in the UK and Sweden

In order to interpret the findings from the Swedish and English interviews, it is important to appreciate the similarities and differences in both the cultural preferences and the health and social care systems of the two countries. In Sweden, for example, it is unusual for older people to live with their children whereas it is very common for husbands or wives to carry the major responsibility of caring for a dependent spouse. In England, family care-giving responsibilities are more likely to be shared between spouses and older children.

At present a very small proportion of care for older people in Sweden is provided by the private sector; for example, around 11 per cent of places in special housing (Socialstyrelsen 1998). Continuing care is provided in service houses (referred to as sheltered housing) and nursing homes, which are mainly run by the local municipalities and provide care for disabled persons whose care needs are from moderate to severe. As a result of the expansion of comprehensive public sector services for older people during the 1960s and 1970s, the demand for private sector accommodation has been very limited. This can be contrasted with the rapid expansion of private sector nursing home accommodation in the UK during the 1980s. For example, a national survey of nursing homes in 1996 suggested that 93 per cent were either privately owned or managed by large corporations (Davies *et al.* 1999). This situation has been widely attributed to the policy of funding private residential and nursing home care through the Department of Social Security. Some commentators have argued that this has resulted in many older people entering institutional care who might have remained in their own homes if alternative support services had been available (Challis 1993; Impallomeni and Starr 1995). By contrast in Sweden, home-help systems are well developed in accordance with the policy of enabling older people to remain in their own homes for as long as possible.

During the early 1990s, the health and social care systems of both countries were subject to major reform. In Sweden, responsibility for nursing home care was transferred from the county councils to the municipalities with the intention of clarifying lines of accountability. The municipalities became financially responsible for patients in hospitals once medical treatment was completed (Thorslund and Parker 1994), and they also assumed responsibility for arranging placement. Since these changes, the various institutions within the municipality – service houses, residential homes and nursing homes – have become more and more similar in relation to client group, surroundings, staff ratios and care routines. All types of provision are officially classified as special accommodation (Socialstyrelsen 1999).

In the UK, the NHS and Community Care Act (DoH 1990) introduced a contract culture to arrangements for continuing care. Services were to be provided through a system of 'community care' assessment and case management, with local authority social services departments purchasing 'packages of care' that might include home-care services and residential or nursing home care, provided by private, statutory and voluntary sector organisations. The emphasis on users and carers as consumers was intended to increase flexibility and consumer choice, but because the consumers have no direct purchasing power, this does not appear to have been achieved (Impallomeni and Starr 1995).

Interviews with relatives

By mid-1999, 56 interviews had been completed: 30 in Sheffield (involving 25 adult children and 5 spouses) and 26 in Jönkoping (all with spouses). All the interviews took place in participants' homes, lasted between 40 and 105 minutes, and were tape-recorded and fully transcribed. Data from the interviews have been coded and analysed using the QSR-NUDIST package (Qualitative Solutions and Research 1994) and a grounded theory approach to data analysis has facilitated the identification of categories and themes. Some of the themes represented in the common experiences of relatives in England and Sweden will be described before examining some of the more apparent differences which arise from the organisational arrangements and cultural influences of the two countries. In particular, we examine two processes: the decision about relocation, and establishing a role within the care home.

Making decisions about relocation

For many relatives in both countries, when helping someone move into a nursing home and supporting them in their new environment, the dominant perception is one of powerlessness. Prior to admission to the home, many participants had cared for their relatives for a long time, often with very little support from community services. In most cases, relocation took place following a crisis and after a hospital admission. At this stage most relatives had a vivid sense of a lack of control:

> They said they weren't putting any pressure on me but I felt pressured. I felt that if I didn't find somewhere very quickly they'd either find somewhere for me and give me somewhere that wasn't suitable or – I don't know – I'd have to leave her there. It wasn't – nothing was ideal. (a daughter, England)

Table 9.1 Ideal types of admission to a care home

The positive choice

Characterised by some consideration of when to enter care, and which home in which area is chosen. The older person is either a senior or equal partner or control is handed over following full discussion. Opportunities are available to explore: alternatives to care, feelings and perceptions about an admission, the type of home which is appropriate, and ways to maintain the continuity of care.

The rational alternative

Involves less anticipation, participation, exploration or information than the positive choice. The move is not regarded as desirable per se but the older person is able to create and sustain a perception that the admission is one or both legitimate and reversible. Older people sometimes turn the admission into an altruistic act on their behalf, rationalising that they have taken the decision for their carer's benefit. Alternatively, the older person may realise that they are too frail to manage at home and, particularly if the move has 'official sanction' (usually from a doctor), this allows a rational and reasonable justification for the move to be constructed.

The discredited option

The discredited option usually begins as either a 'positive choice' or a 'rational alternative' but shortly after admission the initial perceptions are damaged, e.g. the older person has been promised a single room and then has to share, or she or he was informed that other residents are lucid but actually a majority are cognitively impaired. In other cases, an older person entered care with false beliefs about the reversibility of the move or expecting a rigorous treatment regime which is not available. Such events sour initial expectations and create mistrust and resentment.

The fait accompli

The 'worst case scenario' occurs when most of the basic conditions for an acceptable move into care are absent. There is no anticipation, the decision is generally taken by others, and there is no opportunity to explore alternative arrangements, other homes, or emotional reactions to the move. There is a little good quality information. In such circumstances the move is usually perceived entirely negatively and there is no basis on which to create a positive or rational explanation.

Source: Adapted from Nolan *et al.* 1996

A similar concern about the lack of control of the decisions about a placement were also apparent among the Swedish participants. Several spouses described how they had to insist on getting a place in a care home for their relative. Two felt that their own views were ignored and said that they were offered more home-help hours instead of a placement. As one spouse explained, 'I said that I can't have her at home so they must help [and] support, and I got to talk to them down there, and we talked and they said that they would try to help you. "Try!" I said. "You have to do it."'

Many participants indicated that they felt that there was no 'ideal solution' and that admission to a nursing home was 'the only thing to do'. This reflects the 'discredited option' described by Nolan *et al.* (1996) (Table 9.1). The interview data from both countries provide little evidence that the possibility of admission to a care home had been anticipated, either by the older person or their relatives. On the contrary, several participants described how they had previously promised their relatives that they would never have to move into a nursing home. This produced overwhelming guilt when the decision was finally made. In a few notable exceptions, older people had made an active decision that they would move into a nursing home when the time was right and had planned for this eventuality:

> She recovered reasonably well from it [stroke], but she did say to me that she didn't want to go back home...she had obviously made that decision. In the past she had gone without to save for her old age and she had said, 'I want to go into a nursing home.' It was her decision. (a daughter, England)

Similarly, few older people were perceived to have been fully involved in the admission process. In some cases it had even been impossible for the older person to visit the home prior to moving in. In more than half the cases examined, the relative had made the final choice. Few relatives perceived that they had had the opportunity to discuss their feelings and explore alternatives to admission with health and social care personnel. After having suggested a home, professionals usually then played a minor role. In many cases, the family were left to work through the move themselves, both emotionally and practically. For spouses, in particular, feelings of powerlessness often coincided with emptiness at the perceived loss of a lifelong partner. It was not until the move itself that the experience of separation became a reality. The emotions were often heightened by self-accusation about not having done enough for their partner. As one of the informants in Sweden said, 'It is the deep loss...and the sense of community...that is so difficult...and one regrets what has been done and you ask yourself, "Maybe I have not worked enough with him to maintain his abilities."'

There were also examples in Sweden of poor communication between the caring spouse and the cared for person that were very stressful. Spouses usually felt that they had let their partner down, with some considering that this actually constituted a form of treachery, which understandably caused considerable distress. For example, one woman was too distressed to tell her husband about the decision; she experienced enormous guilt and was afraid that her husband would blame her:

> And then they started to tell me, 'You can't take him home.' I said, 'Well, what shall I do?' I didn't want him to...but the nurses were very nice and kind, I must say...I cried very much of course...very, very much...I tried to go out and not show him how I cried. 'I can't talk to him about this [the move], you will have to,' I said to the nurses. 'We will,' they said. (a spouse, Sweden)

There were, however, limited opportunities to explore such feelings, for the relatives generally experienced isolation and the professionals gave little attention to the emotional reactions. Overall, few of the requirements that would enable older people and their relatives to perceive admission to permanent nursing home care as a positive choice were present in the experiences of those interviewed.

Relatives' roles

In relation to establishing a role within the care home, the relatives in Britain frequently saw themselves as advocates, with a role to ensure an acceptable standard of care for the older person. More than half the relatives in both countries expressed dissatisfaction with the care received, with the majority finding it difficult to complain or to have any influence on care practice. Some described a fear of reprisal, and were anxious that to make any criticism would affect their relationships with the staff and the care of their relative. Many of those interviewed felt that staff in the care homes were unable to deliver care of the same standard as they had been providing at home. Some felt that many of the care assistants lacked the knowledge to provide proper care and that training was inadequate. On the whole, relatives experienced a reluctance on the part of nursing home staff to see them as partners in care and to recognise their expertise. As a daughter in England said, 'Because they think they're the trained ones with all the answers... You're not trained – the fact that you've been doing it doesn't count – you're not trained.'

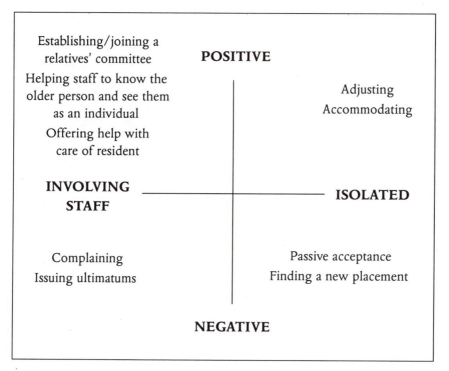

Figure 9.1 Coping strategies employed by relatives to develop and maintain relationships with nursing home staff

In the face of these difficulties, the relatives in the study used various strategies for coping and for establishing a role in the care home. These ranged from passive acceptance to providing the staff with ultimatums, but most relatives adopted an intermediate stance (Figure 9.1). More than half the British relatives interviewed said that they felt the need to 'fit in' with the routines of the nursing home and to 'avoid rocking the boat'. For some participants, this involved avoiding visits at mealtimes or while direct care was being given – this itself limited their participation in care-giving. Others expressed the fear that if they complained about the care, they would be asked to find an alternative home for their relative. One strategy which was commonly used to encourage staff to provide more appropriate care is to help them to get to know their relative's biography. A daughter in England explained, 'I try and leave photographs in her room. Her certificates for length of service with British Steel are on the wall, to let the carers know that she hasn't always been like this.'

During the interviews many participants expressed the wish to continue to be involved in their relative's care. None reported that this had been discussed with them at the time of admission. Conversely, relatives frequently described how they have had to take the initiative in order to retain some control and involvement in their relative's care. One woman who didn't want to be separated from her husband had brought an additional bed into his two-roomed flat at the nursing home. She visited her husband every other day and stayed overnight when she felt like it. Her caring burden had been eased but they were still together. For some relatives, however, such an initiative required a good deal of determination:

> I took all her stuff and arranged my mother's room. The staff at the home didn't want me to bring all the things that I was bringing in, because of fire regulations, but I knew my mother could get in and out so I over-rode them. They were just wanting to stamp their authority. If you're strong enough you can overcome it. Her room is a bit overcrowded but it's my mother's home and she's here for a few years yet. (a daughter, England)

Involving the family in furnishing the room before the move is common in Sweden and appears to help in making the home more familiar to residents, while also providing a legitimate reason for prior contact. In one case the whole family planned how the room was to be furnished and decorated, led by the partner being admitted to care:

> Because he was in hospital furnishing…and the nurses said, 'What
> has he done earlier in his life?' He has been lying here planning and
> planning [she laughs]…and I said that this is how he wants to have
> it in his new home. He has been selling furniture all his life…and I
> called our daughter and explained how dad wanted his new room.
> (a spouse, Sweden)

More than half the relatives interviewed made complaints about their
relatives' care. Staff responses were mixed, with some relatives reporting
reasonably swift resolution of the problems. Others found however that
any change was relatively short-lived, and that practice soon reverted to
the earlier pattern. If all else failed, some relatives issued an ultimatum. A
daughter in England said, 'I had a meeting with them to complain. I said
they would have to do something about it or I would do something.'
Many relatives in England, being unaware of the role of the local health
authority (the lowest administrative tier of the National Health Service)
in maintaining standards in nursing homes, did not know how to make
a complaint. Some Swedish relatives described how they had contacted
the local press and local politicians to highlight their concerns and
express their criticism of the care provided in the sheltered housing or
nursing home. One said:

> Yes, but I have tried you see…only in her interests…I really can't
> accept this…I hired two psychiatric doctors and one psychiatric
> nurse and I have been to the local authority social services
> department…I wanted to talk with the county commissioner
> during the election campaign. (a spouse, Sweden)

Not all participants found the admission of their relative into a nursing
home as a predominantly negative experience. A significant minority
perceived positive consequences both for the older person and for
themselves and were highly satisfied with the care that their relative was
receiving. Some reported an improved relationship with their relative.
Moreover, in the few cases where the admission had been anticipated
and carefully planned, both the older person and the relative adjusted
relatively well. As a daughter in England put it, 'One of the good things
about my mum being in the home is that the time we spend with her
now is quality time, because we don't have to do all the other jobs we

were doing for her before, like washing and cleaning. Now we can just be with her and talk to her.'

Differences between the English and Swedish experience

The main differences to emerge from the Swedish and English reports were about the experience of finding a placement. Many of those interviewed in England found the process of identifying and negotiating an appropriate placement for their relative extremely stressful and time consuming. Swedish participants, on the other hand, were generally offered a designated placement although, as noted earlier, this raised difficulties when the participants perceived the placement as inappropriate. The English informants said there was inadequate information to help them make decisions about the most suitable nursing home for their relative. Most were provided with only a list of homes and didn't know where to begin. Visiting homes was time consuming and expensive and most relatives didn't know what questions to ask. As a son in England said, 'The list he gave me, I didn't know which to start at. We looked at about eleven [homes].'

Many participants spoke of the need for a 'yardstick' or a 'grading system' which would enable them to compare homes against a specified standard. Relatives described inaccurate and conflicting information about the options open to them and, in many cases, experienced pressure to find a placement quickly. None of those interviewed were aware that they could access the inspection reports for individual homes produced by the health authority's registration and inspection unit. Financial worries were also a major concern. The system for funding long-term care in the UK is complex and was described by relatives as 'a nightmare' and 'a minefield'. Most relatives did not know what benefits they were entitled to nor how the nursing home fee would be calculated. As regards the shift of long-term care provision to the private sector, many participants perceived mainly negative consequences:

> Because it's a business now and people want to sell it to you. And people want to spend ages telling you every little thing about their home and why it's better than the one down the road. And then they'll come to the price, just as if they were selling double-glazing. (a daughter, England)

Some British relatives were surprised to find financial barriers to the selection of what they felt would be the most appropriate home, for high fees left a shortfall over the limit set by social services. Some found that their relative did not meet the nursing home's criteria for admission, as when they were visually or cognitively impaired. Others were astonished when they discovered that the 'trial period' following admission applied just as much to the management as to their relative or, in other words, that they might be asked to find an alternative placement for their relative if they were found 'unsuitable' for the home.

The factors which influenced the final selection of a home included: distance for travelling, familiar location, personal recommendations, and the 'feel' of the home. Once placement had taken place, however, most relatives perceive that to change would be almost impossible, even if they were unhappy about the standards of care. This is partly because publicly funded placements are perceived to be virtually unchangeable, but also because relatives perceived that relocation would be unsettling and stressful for the older person. This reinforces the importance of the initial placement decision. In Sweden, older people were not given a choice of nursing home: rather the home health care services team consider the client's needs in relation to the suitability of available vacancies and the older person is offered a place. A spouse explained, 'There were many who wanted to help. I wasn't allowed to decide anything about it [the move]: they [health care personnel] took care of everything.' If the home is not acceptable to the older person or their family, they have to wait for another to be identified by the home health care services. After accepting a placement, relatives often request a change of home if they are not satisfied.

Although the events surrounding the decision varied and were more positive for some than others, the move itself was described by most Swedish respondents in negative terms. The predominant experience was a feeling of powerlessness: the informants had made a decision about which they really weren't happy, but they had little ability to effect a change. To compound matters, they had no real choice as to which home their partner was to enter, as this was decided largely by local availability and the case manager. It took an assertive and persistent approach for an individual's choice to be achieved. Some respondents refused the first offer and decided to wait for a more attractive placement; others tried to change to a more appropriate home after admission. In one instance the wife of a man with dementia had to insist that he was moved three times before she found a home with which she was satisfied:

> Well, I was a little aggressive during that time...and they told me...that I was tiresome...but Gustav has worked here [in the area] for 40 years, so I believe that he has got some rights to get a good placement. 'You can't just stow him away,' I said. (a spouse, Sweden)

Discussion

Delivering quality care to frail older people represents one of the most significant challenges for health and welfare service providers in European countries, while the arrangements for 'community care' will continue to be one of the main policy challenges. Some form of collective care is likely to be needed by an increasing number of older people for at least several decades. In this chapter we have reported findings from the preliminary analysis of interviews with 56 close relatives of older people recently admitted to nursing homes in Sweden and England. The interviews provide firm evidence that the needs of relatives for information and support, both around and after the time of admission, are largely not met. Furthermore, despite provision being mainly by privately managed homes in Britain but predominantly by public organisations in Sweden, there are few differences between the countries.

The principal difference in the experience of nursing home admission was found to be the extent to which family members have the responsibility to find and negotiate a placement for their relative. The British arrangements are substantially a consequence of the purchaser–provider split in the health and social care services and the way in which placements are funded. The complexity of UK funding arrangements produces high levels of anxiety for older people and their families about whether they will be able to afford to move into and remain in the nursing home of their choice. Conversely, the lack of involvement in decision making about placements for relatives in Sweden results in feelings of powerlessness and heightened feelings of guilt. Given the market nature of the UK service, it is surprising that some relatives have low expectations of nursing home care. The reason is that direct spending power is in the hands of local authority social services departments, for they fund the majority of nursing home placements, and many older people and their relatives do not perceive themselves as consumers.

Most relatives find care staff friendly and acknowledge that they operate with limited resources, poor remuneration and inadequate education and training for their role. In some cases, this inhibited the participants from seeking support for themselves directly from care staff. In both countries, some relatives did have support from their families and friends, but many found that this created further tensions. A few participants confided to the interviewer that their conversation was the first opportunity they had had to talk about their feelings and emotions. Both the English and Swedish interviews made it apparent that relatives attach much importance to their continued involvement in promoting and ensuring the quality of life of their relative, but that such participation is rarely supported or facilitated and is sometimes blocked (Lundh, Sandberg and Nolan 1999). The staff rarely draw upon the expertise of family care-givers in planning and implementing care for residents and do little to enhance the experience of visiting.

With a few exceptions (see Raynes 1998; Reed, Cook and Stanley 1999), local and national initiatives to increase the participation of older people and their families in defining their needs and in planning care have largely passed by the residents of nursing homes and their families. In Sweden, shortfalls in the care provided for residents of some nursing homes were highlighted in 1999 by the media, which was followed by a government commitment to increase staff and to improve the standards of care and the specifications for accommodation and for communication between staff and relatives: 300 million Swedish kronor (£23 million) have been allocated to supporting these developments (Socialdepartmentet 1998).

Despite similar campaigns in the British media, the UK government has been slow to respond, at least in the allocation of additional resources. In 1997, the Labour government set up a Royal Commission on Long-Term Care to identify a sustainable system of funding the long-term care of elderly people, both in their own homes and in other settings. Its main recommendation is that nursing and personal care should be free at the point of delivery, while means testing is retained for accommodation and food (or hotel) costs. This would certainly help to reduce the anxiety which many older people and their families have about their ability to pay for long-term care. The report also proposed the setting up of a National Care Commission with a remit to monitor the implementation of the new funding arrangements, i.e. to generate evaluative information and monitor standards. The Centre for Policy on Ageing (1999) has drafted standards for care and accommodation in nursing and residential homes which, if fully implemented, would further increase confidence among the residents of nursing homes and their families.

While welcoming these developments, we believe that there is in addition an urgent need to examine the ways in which health and social care staff can better support relatives when they are helping an older person to relocate, and to enable them to establish a new complementary caring role. On the stress which in the UK is associated with nursing home admission, this could be reduced by making information about the options more readily available to older people and their families. In both countries, there is a need to develop service models which seek to involve older people and family members as equal partners in care rather than passive recipients. Such models must be applied at all stages of the transition to nursing home care, from assessment to placement and beyond. Drawing upon the expertise of family care-givers is likely to raise the quality of care and improve the quality of life for the residents and also to have positive benefits for staff and relatives. A recent review identified four interventions which might enable residents to maintain their relationships with close family and friends in mutually beneficial ways:

1. Creating a welcoming environment which encourages and supports visiting and working with carers to maximise their involvement and promote a sense of purpose.

2. Recognising and clarifying the roles and responsibilities of both groups.

3. Valuing and accessing the carers' knowledge and expertise, and drawing upon these as an important component of planned care.

4. Helping carers form a positive perception of the admission and acknowledging their entitlement to receive and to provide help; and dealing with their emotional reactions. (Nolan and Dellasega 1999)

Changing current practice to ensure that care staff are aware of the needs of relatives and of their potential role in meeting these needs will require close collaboration between researchers, educators and care providers. There is also likely to be an increasing role for service-user organisations such as the Relatives' and Residents' Association, which provides information and support to relatives and campaigns for improved standards of care. The research which we have reported provides compelling evidence that, as many older people and their relatives have learnt from direct experience, the way in which the transition to nursing home care is arranged significantly affects the quality of life of older people and the continuing relationship with their family carers. Current arrangements leave a great deal to be desired and can clearly be substantially improved.

References

Buckwalter, K., Cusack, D., Kruckeberg, T. and Shoemaker, A. (1991) 'Family Involvement with Communication-Impaired Residents in Long-Term Care Settings.' *Applied Nursing Research 4*, 2, 77–84.

Centre for Policy on Ageing (1999) *Fit for the Future?* London: Centre for Policy on Ageing.

Challis, D. (1993) 'Case Management in Social and Health Care: Lessons from a United Kingdom Programme.' *Journal of Case Management 2*, 3, 79–90.

Davies, S., Slack, R., Laker, S. and Philp, I. (1999) 'The Educational Preparation of Staff in Nursing Homes: Relationship with Resident Autonomy.' *Journal of Advanced Nursing 29*, 1, 208–217.

Dellasega, C. and Mastrian, K. (1995) 'The Processes and Consequences of Institutionalising an Elder.' *Western Journal of Nursing Research 17*, 2, 123–140.

Department of Health (DoH) (1990) *The NHS and Community Care Act.* London: HMSO.

Duncan, M.T. and Morgan, D.L. (1994) 'Sharing the Caring: Family Caregivers' Views of Their Relationships with Nursing Home Staff.' *The Gerontologist 34*, 2, 235–244.

Hasselkus, B. (1988) 'Meaning in Family Caregiving: Perspectives on Caregiver/Professional Relationships.' *The Gerontologist 28*, 5, 686–691.

Impallomeni, M. and Starr, J. (1995) 'The Changing Face of Community and Institutional Care for the Elderly.' *Journal of Public Health Medicine 17*, 2, 171–178.

Johnson, M.A. (1990) 'Nursing Home Placement: The Daughter's Perspective.' *Journal of Gerontological Nursing 16*, 11, 6–11.

Levine, D. (1995) 'Your Aging Parents: Choosing a Nursing Home.' *American Health: Fitness of Body and Mind 14*, 5, 82–85.

Lundh, U., Sandberg, J. and Nolan, M.R. (1999) 'Spouses' Experiences of Placing a Partner in Accommodation for Older People in Sweden.' Paper presented at the Vårdal Conference, 'Vårda och vårdas', Stockholm, March (in Swedish).

Matthiessen, V. (1989) 'Guilt and Grief: When Daughters Place Mothers in Nursing Homes.' *Journal of Gerontological Nursing 15*, 7, 11–15.

Naleppa, M.J. (1996) 'Families and the Institutionalised Elderly: A Review.' *Journal of Gerontological Social Work 27*, 1/2, 87–111.

Nay, R. (1997) 'Relatives' Experience of Nursing Home Life: Characterised by Tension.' *Australian Journal on Ageing 16*, 1, 24–29.

Nolan, M. and Dellasega, C. (1999) '"It's Not the Same as Him Being at Home." Creating Caring Partnerships Following Nursing Home Placement.' *Journal of Clinical Nursing 8*, 723–730.

Nolan, M., Grant, G. and Keady, J. (1996) *Understanding Family Care.* Buckingham: Open University Press.

Nolan, M., Walker, G., Nolan, J., Williams, S., Poland, F. and Curran, M. (1996) 'Entry to Care: Positive Choice or *Fait accompli*? Developing a More Proactive Nursing Response to the Needs of Older People and Their Carers.' *Journal of Advanced Nursing 24*, 2, 265–274.

Pearson, A., Nay, R., Taylor, B., Tucker, C., Angus, J., Griffith, V. and Ruler, A. (1998) *Relatives' Experiences of Nursing Home Entry: Meanings, Practices and Discourses.* School of Nursing, Research Monograph Series 4. Adelaide: University of Adelaide.

Pillemer, K., Hegeman, C.R., Albright, B. and Henderson, C. (1998) 'Building Bridges Between Families and Nursing Home Staff: The Partners in Caregiving Program.' *The Gerontologist 38*, 4, 499–503.

Qualitative Solutions and Research (1994) *Nudist Revision 3.0 for Windows.* Melbourne: Qualitative Solutions and Research.

Raynes, N.V. (1998) 'Involving Residents in Quality Specification.' *Ageing and Society 18*, 1, 65–77.

Reed, J., Cook, G. and Stanley, D. (1999) 'Promoting Partnership with Older People through Quality Assurance Systems: Issues Arising in Care Homes.' *NT Research 4*, 5, 257–267.

Relatives' Association (1997) *As Others See Us: A Study of Relationships in Homes for Older People.* London: Relatives' Association.

Socialdepartmentet (1998) *Nationell Handlingsplan för Äldrepolitiken: Mål, Inriktning och Förslag Till Åtgärder.* Prop. 1997/98: 113. Stockholm: Norsteds.

Socialstyrelsen (1998) *Statistics – Social Welfare: Activities in Community Care Services for Elderly and Disabled Persons 1998.* National Board of Health and Welfare. Stockholm: Norsteds.

Socialstyrelsen (1999) *Socialstyrelsens Meddelandeblad nr 2/99. 'ANHÖRIG 300' – 300 Miljoner för Utveckling av Stöd Till Anhöriga.* Stockholm: Socialstyrelsen.

Thorslund, M. and Parker, M. (1994) 'Care of the Elderly in the Changing Swedish Welfare State.' In D. Challis, B. Davies and K. Traske (eds) *Community Care: New Agendas and Challenges from the UK and Overseas.* Aldershot: Arena.

Tickle, E.H. and Hull, K.V. (1995) 'Family Members' Roles in Long-Term Care.' *MEDSURG Nursing 4*, 4, 300–304.

Tilse, C. (1994) 'Long Term Marriage and Long Term Care: "We Thought We'd Be Together till We Died."' *Australian Journal on Ageing 13*, 4, 172–174.

CHAPTER 10

Discharge from Hospital to Care Home

Professional Boundaries and Interfaces

Jan Reed and David Stanley

Introduction

A prevalent theme in the literature and policy debates about services for older people is the importance of multidisciplinary and multi-agency working. Older people are presented by some writers as having 'complex needs', whether medical descriptions of 'multiple pathology' or humanistic expressions of the need to provide holistic care and support. To these we can add the many views about the influence of physical, social, economic and environmental factors on well-being, all of which lead to the logical conclusion that to provide services which can deal with this complexity or to apply a holistic approach, then many different skills, resources, professional groups and services need to be co-ordinated. While the aspiration for co-ordinated care is laudable, its implementation usually brings a host of problems. Long-established institutional structures and professional boundaries are rigid and create different sets of goals and ways of working.

This chapter explores issues of multidisciplinary and inter-agency working by drawing on published models and the findings of two research projects which have explored practice at professional and service boundaries in care management and identified similar issues and problems. One project focused on the role of the nurse at the interface between health and social care in the discharge of older people from hospital; the other focused on the role of the social worker. For context we also explore the forces which create notions of professionalism and associated boundaries and some issues of definition in inter-professional practice.

Developing a sense of professionalism

We begin by examining the ways in which a personal sense of professionalism forms within the context of boundaries and develops with continued practice. Professional boundaries are determined in various ways and are never static. Trainees are initially socialised into a sense of professional identity in both academic and practice settings. Powerful value systems are internalised and a conception of one's own profession is developed, not only in its own right but also, importantly, in relation to the constellations of other professions with which the particular practice engages. Finally, views also form about how the multiple professions engage one with another and how their areas of expertise and operation overlap and complement.

Much has been written about inter-professional working but the term is rarely defined precisely and divergent understandings abound. Although the term 'inter-professional' is in everyday use, only rarely do we consider what it really means or what must happen to make its practice a reality. If a sense of professionalism first arises during initial training, at this time also the first notions of inter-professionalism develop. The capacity to appreciate how a boundary can blur must however follow a formed idea of the boundary of one's own professional tasks, and an understanding of the range and appropriateness of interdisciplinarity is realised from an understanding of, and confidence in, the individual's sense of their professional identity. By definition, mature professionalism can only develop over time.

We should be more precise in our use of the term 'inter-professional'. Does its use signify agreement that other professions have a contribution to make to our own work, that at a certain point someone else takes over or we take over from someone else, or that we work together with other professions? These differentiations might seem pedantic but they describe complex variations, as whether an individual works alone, with others from the same profession, or in a team that includes other professions. Another common term, the 'multi-professional team', also describes various working arrangements; for example, its members may all be based in the same location and work jointly, or alternatively a pool of expertise is dispersed but available. An additional emerging term is 'trans-professional', which has no clearly developed definition but its usage hints at core uni-professionalism crossing boundaries with other professions. What good inter-professional practice requires is challenging the boundaries that define our work, while taking care not to lose the special contribution of our own work.

Professionals commonly believe that no one else has the responsibilities which they fulfil, but occasionally sense that there is little difference between what they and others do (as most commonly with skills like communication), or that everyone is doing the same task despite their different professional origins. These varied and complex perceptions have been examined closely in our two studies of inter-professional practice in the care of older people – to which we now turn.

The nurse role in hospital discharge to care homes

The first study explores the practice implications of the discharge of older people from hospitals to care homes. The aims were to investigate older people's experiences of discharge from hospital to care home, and to identify the forms of support that might be needed (Reed, Morgan and Palmer 1998). The central role in decision making and organising the discharge process rests with social workers, but all staff can contribute to the support of older people through the move and we were particularly interested in the role of hospital nurses who have had sustained contact with the patients.

The data collection was carried out in two stages: through interviews with older people and family members, and in focus groups with staff. The interviews with older people were loosely structured and focused on their experience of the discharge processes, particularly any problematic or helpful aspects. The subjects were 48 patients who had recently been discharged from the study hospital to independent care homes. They were visited by the researcher within four weeks of their discharge and invited to participate in the study, and 20 were able and willing to participate. In addition, 17 relatives or 'significant others' were interviewed and asked to describe their experience of their relative's discharge. Patients' case notes were also examined for information about discharge arrangements and plans and to provide background material.

The focus groups with staff were to elicit opinions and ideas from the participants with a view to developing practice guidelines. The informants were colleagues, and the aim was to identify group perspectives in the context of their various professional roles and cultures (Reed and Payton 1997). Four focus groups involving fourteen independent sector care home staff (from nursing and dual-registered care homes), and three focus groups of hospital staff (one each of three nurses, three doctors and three social workers) were undertaken. Six written responses were received from NHS nursing staff and one individual interview was also undertaken.

Older people's experiences

The experience of moving into a care home was described as a profound change in their lives by many of the older people. Some had found the move distressing and that their subsequent lifestyle was uncomfortable or unpalatable, while others described the move as a relief from anxiety and uncertainty and life in the home as unexpectedly pleasant. Among these individual stories there was however one consistent theme: the passivity of older people in the process of moving. They did not expect support from staff and their coping strategies were characterised by stoicism. As one person told us, 'Well, you just have to get on with it, I mean there's no point in making a fuss'. Some older people expressed their concern to avoid being a burden to others, either staff or family members. As one man put it, 'they had better things to do', including looking after other people 'with more sickness' than himself. The judgement of many of our respondents, that other patients needed more staff time than they did themselves, appeared to be their own, but for a few the opinion most probably originated from the nursing staff. Nurses were reported as saying that 'it was time to move on' or 'they couldn't stay in the hospital for ever'. As one older person reported, 'They [the staff] said it was about time I was going, and they were right'.

It was also striking that the older patient informants did not think of themselves as people with any choices or control over care decisions. None voiced any objections to the verdicts of staff that they should move into a home, nor did they exercise much choice over the home to which they moved. The selection was delegated to family members or social workers, and accepted as being the only way such a choice could be made, given that they were too frail to visit homes themselves. As one person told us, 'My daughter sorted all that out – I couldn't go round those homes because I can't get about. I had to rely on her'. It did not seem that alternatives had been suggested, for example, in that transport could be arranged to visit a care home.

The older people also expected to fit in with care home regimes, and were surprised that they were allowed any choice or freedom. One lady, for example, was surprised to be 'allowed' to order a newspaper. Their ideas about care homes had been vague and were based on snippets of information from friends, acquaintances and the media. As one person told us, 'It was like taking a step in the dark. I didn't know what to expect'. Care home staff confirmed this by reporting that most older people had little idea about what life in the home would be like.

Family perspectives

The idea that discharged patients had insufficient need for medical care to be in hospital was shared by the staff and the older people. Family members, however, seemed less convinced and expressed concerns that the discharge had been rushed. These concerns stemmed from anxieties about the health of their relative, and because the process of choosing a home was more complex than they had expected. Some felt that they had not had enough time to choose carefully. As one family member told us, 'I had to go out and find a place quickly because she was coming out. I went to see a couple, but I didn't have time to work through the list'. The list referred to is that of the homes registered with the local authority and the health authority. It contains only addresses and numbers of beds which for most people was insufficient. They had very little guidance on what to look for in a home, or how to evaluate the care given. At the same time, family members felt a huge sense of responsibility to make the right decision.

The staff views

The hospital nurses' responses indicated that there was no standard approach to the discharge process. Any discussion with the patient was initiated by the older person, fragmented and ad hoc. The staff reported that they neither welcomed nor invited discussion and that it was rare. One nurse described older people as having 'made up their mind to accept their fate, and they don't see the point in discussing it [for] they only become distressed'. One nurse's written response did however indicate that older people rarely invited discussion and that sometimes nurses have to encourage them to talk: 'Sometimes patients don't openly ask for advice or support, but it's up to the nurse to spot the signs of anxiety and to approach the subject casually'. Where nurses did give examples of talking to older people about the impending move, the conversations took place while they were doing other things, such as helping the older person to dress. This approach avoided making a 'big thing' out of the move but also encouraged superficiality, for nurses described the purpose of these discussions as to 'cheer up' older people.

The nursing staff said that they knew little about care homes and could not offer much support. They were not clear, for example, about the difference between nursing and residential care, about inspection and registration, or about how care was financed. They also said that this was not part of their job to know these things, as other staff (for example, social workers) were in charge of the process. In addition, there was some hostility and suspicion towards private sector homes, which were described by one nurse as 'just in it for the money'. Some nurses had worked in private homes and reported low standards of care, and there was a reluctance to collaborate with staff from these homes. One nurse recounted a situation where a care home had asked for some information about a patient, but she had been reluctant to provide it: 'It seemed like laziness – shouldn't they be assessing them for themselves?

As their care will be completely different from on the wards, it seemed like a cop out'.

Social workers had more contact with care homes, and more knowledge of the systems of regulation and funding, but their expertise did not necessarily give them a sense of control over the process. They felt that they were responding primarily to pressures from medical staff to organise discharges and that they had insufficient time to spend with the patients to discuss their choices and preferences. They claimed that their professional skills in providing support were being eroded by their administrative roles in assessment and making arrangements for care. One social worker explained, 'I don't spend the time I used to…I just get a message from the medical staff, "this one's to go out", and just sort out the paperwork and maybe talk to the family. Sometimes I don't even get to see the client'.

Medical staff believe, however, that their role is mainly to make discharge decisions and decide the required level of medical care. Their concern was that the move should be made quickly and not governed by social service department finances. They talked of their concern for patients who were waiting to come into hospital, and that their needs override the needs of those who had received treatment and had no further need of acute care. When asked about older people moving into a care home, they reported an expectation that social workers and nurses would provide the necessary support and advice to patients. This was partly because they believed that treatment was their priority and this was not their role, and partly because of the way in which their time was managed and their contact with patients was organised. As one doctor put it, 'We see people on a round or at appointments and then we go away. Once we've told them where they're going to go, we disappear, and if they want to think about it later or discuss it…we're not there, but the nurses and social workers are'.

Comments on Study 1

Our findings suggest that the apparent stoicism of older people who are to move into a care home may mask feelings of loss and anxiety. If staff wish to support older people through the transition, they have to initiate discussions rather than waiting for older people to do so. More attention should also be paid to the responsibilities of the various members of the care team, particularly to who takes responsibility for managing the process or its elements. When everyone thinks someone else is talking issues through with older people, there is a strong possibility that no one is. The interviews clearly indicate that older people and their families need support, but also suggest that, despite the contributions of different disciplines in the hospital, support is neither co-ordinated nor consistent.

The care manager and the move into care homes

The second study explored the experiences of care management of older people moving into care homes (Stanley, Reed and Brown 1999). The aim was to conceptualise users' experience of and satisfaction with the care management process, and thereby to illustrate the interpersonal and, by association, inter-professional dynamics that affect their empowerment. A multi-method approach was used in studying eight older people who moved from hospital into a residential or nursing care home. Eligible subjects were identified by care managers according to criteria specified by the project team. The eight cases generated 45 interviews with older people, their family members and carers, the social services care manager, and care home and health care staff. The interviews for each case varied according to individual circumstances and social networks.

The findings confirmed that the process of care management was complex and revealed several tensions. There were many conflicting views among the informants, but here we concentrate on the extent to which the participants were able to identify and understand the role of the care manager. Given its statutory designation and its key role in co-ordination and providing support to older people, we anticipated that it would be widely understood. This was not however the case among any of the participant groups including, remarkably, some of the care managers themselves – among whom there was substantial confusion and dispute about what the role involved and what responsibilities and influence it carried.

Responses from older people

The responses from the older people revealed little if any understanding of care management. When asked who the care manager was, the respondents simply did not recognise the role, let alone who held it. When the interviewer identified the care manager by name, it became evident that the older person viewed this person as a 'friend', but was unable to explain how that friend had become involved in their circumstances. In other words, the role of the care manager was so informal as to appear non-instrumental to the older person. Not one response indicated that the older person knew that their care was being 'managed'.

Carers' responses

The Carers (Recognition and Services) Act 1995 requires that informal carers should be recognised explicitly. Care managers should therefore be involved with the carer and take their views and needs into consideration. As with the older people, however, carers were unable either to name the care manager or to recognise that he or she was involved with their relative. It was however recognised that the care manager had something to do with social services and might even be the social worker, although one carer believed the home care worker to be the care manager.

Staff responses

All of the care managers preferred the role descriptor 'social worker' and none used the specific functional title. It was evident from their responses that the professional job title was acceptable and meaningful, while the functional label was associated with bureaucracy and fiscal management and did not fit their professional self-image. With collaboration among health and social service staff being an essential requirement of the joint planning and provision of services, one would expect that health professionals would have a clear understanding of the care management role. While some did, they were also reluctant to identify positively social services personnel as formal holders of the role. One attributed the role to an occupational therapist and another to a consultant. Several said that either anyone could be the care manager or that the role did not have to be discharged by a specific person. A small minority thought that it might be the social worker.

Comments on Study 2

The interviews throw light on both inter-agency and intra-agency practice interfaces and reveal that staff have an ambiguous understanding of the care manager function while service users are generally unaware of the role. These lacunae point to problems in both user empowerment and professional liaison. None of the staff reported any training in inter-professional practice. Of equal concern was the clear evidence that the care interface was distorted by inter-professional manoeuvres; for example, the need to clear a hospital bed conflicted with other professionals' assessment that a move for the incumbent was premature.

Coupling our research findings with developments in professional practice and service delivery leads to conclusions which corroborate those of others before. Lewis and Glennerster (1996) asked whether care management is a new role or an old job in a new package and concluded that care management receives insufficient recognition in professional training. Similarly, a review of the future roles and training of mental health staff, which took into account the activities of nurses, social workers, occupational therapists, psychologists, general practitioners, psychiatrists and other support workers, identified a mismatch between training and practice leading to a lack of clarity in – and preparation for – their role in the multidisciplinary setting (Duggan 1997). This report also recommends the development of more explicit linkages between policy, services and training, as many others have before (see Lacey 1998; Øvretveit, Mathias and Thompson 1997). While it is axiomatic that national schemes of training can rarely keep pace with innovative practice, care management is no longer new. Given the abundant evidence that inadequate understanding of the role is widespread, there is a strong case for a fundamental review of current practice systems.

Conclusions

The findings from the two studies demonstrate well the rarity of a clear understanding of the multidisciplinary team. Best practice, in which various personnel discharge their different professional tasks to a common end and proactively facilitate each other in true inter-professional collaboration, is notable for its absence. The interview responses instead revealed more concern among staff with issues that were not the focus of the research; for example, status, job specifications, and individual interpretations of the roles.

A study by Hambleton *et al.* (1996) of inter-agency working in local authorities identified several influences on the effectiveness of collaborative working: incentives for joint working; leadership which was flexible enough not to become entrenched in internal perspectives; commitment to joint working as a primary objective rather than an optional add-on; inclusion of the voices of service users and other stakeholders, especially in the independent sector; and acknowledgement that effective collaboration requires an effective way of managing change. They also suggested that while inter-professional working could be developed in tandem with other responsibilities, collaborative working might best be developed by allocating the task to specific individuals, even to the extent of establishing separate multi-professional teams.

It is beyond the scope of this chapter to explore these management issues more fully, and there are many other matters that need to be considered. The tensions of working in a multidisciplinary team have to be documented; we need to know more about the influence of professional background on the conception of care management; and about the extent to which interdisciplinary training helps staff to understand other professional roles (Stanley *et al.* 1999). While however the development of current training models is an important short-term goal, the improvement which they can bring will be constrained by current staffing patterns. We support the Hambleton team's suggestion that a more radical approach is necessary, and specifically argue for a reappraisal of current professional models of practice, even to the extent of substantially rethinking the configuration of services. Discrete, separated services could evolve through several stages of multi- and inter-disciplinary working into a single integrated service. There is a clear willingness among professionals and policy makers to work in a more 'joined up' way (as the consequences of not doing so are apparent). The question is how far this can occur within existing service and professional structures with their different goals, training models, funding bases and working practices.

It may be that the pre-conditions for more collaborative working include joint training, shared budgets and non-hierarchical ways of working, but, more than all these, its achievement requires issues of power and control in the professions to be addressed. Several authors have drawn attention to the complex power relationships between professionals and service users and have highlighted the hierarchical relationships among professions (see Hudson *et al.* 1997; Hugman 1991). Power and authority associates with organisational and cultural positions, and power also varies among members of the same profession. It cannot be assumed that all members of a profession will speak with the same voice. Another dimension of power concerns the asymmetrical relationship between professionals and service users, for the control of resources usually rests with the former. If it is difficult for established professionals to negotiate these complexities, then it is even more problematic for service users. Arguments about the primacy of the needs of older people, which should override such considerations, may have rhetorical force but need to be translated into enabling and effective organisational and practice changes.

References

Duggan, M. (1997) *Pulling Together: The Future Roles and Training of Mental Health Staff.* London: Sainsbury Centre for Mental Health.

Hambleton, R., Essex, S., Mills, L. and Razzaque, K. (1996) *The Collaborative Council: A Study of Interagency Working in Practice.* York: Joseph Rowntree Foundation/LGC Communications.

Hudson, B., Hardy, B., Henwood, M. and Wistow, G. (1997) 'Working Across Professional Boundaries: Primary Health Care and Social Care.' *Journal of Public Money and Management 17*, 4, 25–30.

Hugman, R. (1991) *Power in Caring Professions.* Basingstoke: Macmillan.

Lacey, P. (1998) 'Interdisciplinary Training for Staff Working with People with Profound and Multiple Learning Disabilities.' *Journal of Inter-Professional Care 12*, 1, 43–52.

Lewis, J. and Glennerster, H. (1996) *Implementing the New Community Care.* Buckingham: Open University Press.

Øvretveit, J., Mathias, P. and Thompson, T. (1997) *Inter-Professional Working for Health and Social Care.* Basingstoke: Macmillan.

Reed, J. and Payton, V.R. (1997) 'Focus Groups: Issues of Analysis and Interpretation.' *Journal of Advanced Nursing 26,* 765–771.

Reed, J., Morgan, D. and Palmer, A. (1998) *Discharging Older People from Hospital to Care Homes: Implications for Nursing.* Centre for Care of Older People Occasional Paper. Newcastle-upon-Tyne: Faculty of Health, Social Work and Education, University of Northumbria.

Stanley, D., Reed, J. and Brown, S. (1999) 'Older People, Care-Management and Inter-Professional Practice.' *Journal of Inter-Professional Care 13,* 3, 229–237.

CHAPTER 11

The Quality of Home-Care Services in Sweden

Consumer Expectations and Changing Satisfaction

Gillis Samuelsson

Introduction

The current promotion of cost effectiveness and health reform in many western nations, coupled with population ageing, has led to a growing need for research into the provision of care for frail older people (Eliasson Lappalainen and Szebehely 1996; Health and Welfare Canada 1991; Kane and Kane 1985; Phillips, Applebaum and Atchley 1989). It is widely recognised that the availability and accessibility of home-care services contributes significantly to the well-being of and independent living among older people, and that the quality of home-help services is an important factor in their welfare. Although service providers are aware of the pressures to raise both the quality and quantity of formal support, they often have to compromise between the two to keep within spending limits while maintaining an acceptable delivery volume. For these reasons, quality assurance standards are usually applied (Samuelsson, Edebalk and Ingvad 1993). Measures of quality, rather than mere quantity, are therefore important when we evaluate and compare services. Since the problems of older people change, a well-functioning home-help service must adapt to the specific support needs of individuals.

A review of the literature on the quality of home care (Samuelsson, *et al.* 1993a) suggests that there are comparatively few studies from the home-care recipients' perspectives, while studies from the viewpoints of staff and organisations dominate. Several studies have described which quality characteristics are important to frail older people; for example, responsiveness to client needs, competence and attitudes of the staff, continuity, staff hours, accessibility, information and communication. No study was found however which strictly measured the relative importance of expectations attached to such attributes of quality. This perspective is one of the focuses of this chapter which explores the views of both carers and residents.

Home care in Sweden

To a greater extent than in other countries, in Sweden the care of older people is a public responsibility and private and voluntary organisations play a comparatively modest role (Daatland 1992; Johansson 1991). An important reason for this public pattern of support could be that about 80 per cent of women in Sweden are employed outside the home. The development of social home-help services in Sweden began towards the end of the 1940s, but it was not until the mid-1960s that direct state subsidies for home-help organisations were introduced. In general, the 1970s were characterised by a strong economy and the care of older people expanded rapidly. The number of home-help recipients increased rapidly up to the 1970s and then stabilised. During that period, the number of home-help hours per individual increased (Ds Fi 1987). By the 1980s, the quality of the home-help services was of increasing concern, for various problems concerned the provider organisations, such as decreasing resources, the rising number of high (or intensive) care recipients, high staff turnover and staff shortages (Gough 1987; Statens Offentliga Utredningar 1987, p.21; Sundström and Berg 1988).

Social services (home help, old age homes and long-term care) for older people in Sweden are mainly delivered by public non-profit organisations. There is a form of 'guaranteed' service controlled by regulations and laws for all people in need of support. The municipal social service departments have become the dominant providers and are responsible for the home-help service. They employ multidisciplinary teams to assess the services required by older people living in the community. Fees are charged for the different services according to income. The principal goal is to make it possible for older people to live as independently as possible. The Social Service Act states that the social service department must respect the needs, wishes and integrity of individuals. The main requirements here include client's involvement in the decisions, flexibility, availability, security, accessibility and opportunities for active participation in society.

The need for care and support is strongly correlated with age (Statistical Abstract of Sweden 1993). This means that the rising proportion of very old people will lead to an increase in care and support needs. A national cross-sectional survey of older people living at home in Sweden in 1988–89 showed that regular help and supervision (at least once a week) increased with age, from 20 per cent of the 75 to 79 years age group to 45 per cent among those aged 80 to 84 years. Men who lived alone received relatively more municipal help than women, whereas men who lived with another person received less help. In the group with subjective poor health 60 per cent received regular help, compared to 17 per cent with good subjective health. Social class differences in help patterns were small, as were the differences among educational groups.

In 1992 a comprehensive reform of the care of older people was introduced by which the municipalities were given the main responsibility for the care of older people and took responsibility for nursing homes. This reform was introduced at the same time as the cutbacks in welfare. Subsequently, a decreasing number of older people have received home care and the assistance has successively been concentrated on the oldest old and the most frail. Up to 1999 this policy continued and there are no plans to introduce a more preventative perspective in the allocation of home-help care. Reflecting this prioritisation, the eligibility criteria for home-care services have been raised, and interest in the quality of home care has increased (Eliasson Lappalainen and Szebehely 1996).

On the concept of expectations for care

The concept 'expectation' is widely used in theoretical economics, but little in other disciplines. Katona (1975) explained that expectations are formed on the basis of both past experiences and new information. When there is little new information, past experiences are highly influential, but when there is relevant new information, this tends to be the dominant influence on expectations. Wärneryd (1999) indicates that the mass media are an important factor in forming expectations, especially in representations of an impoverished future. Outside academic economics, the similar and partly related concept of 'social deprivation' is widely used. Rosenmayr (1979, pp.201–202) elucidates the term well: 'The internalisation of socio-economic disadvantages and the gradual acceptance of low standards blocks expectations and extinguishes aspirations. The individual becomes the cause of his or her own handicap, so that we may speak of self-incurred social deprivation.' This explanation directs attention to past experiences and to cohort differences. The expectations of the cohort born at the turn of the twentieth century might be quite different from that which grew up later and in a developed welfare society.

In the present study, all individuals were born prior to 1915 and many would have experienced relative social deprivation. Their cohort grew up when Swedish society was relatively poor and at a time when social welfare comprised the pauper system of poor-houses and poor-law relief. To receive assistance from these public sources was often considered a disgrace and was stigmatising. Many in the cohort who were participants in this study still remember the 'law of poor people' (Elmér 1963; Samuelsson 1981). A widely shared wish among them is 'to manage my life by myself as long as possible'. This desire for an independent lifestyle is a strong and dominant attitude among many older people in Sweden (Samuelsson 1981; Tornstam 1993). To receive support is also associated with a lowered social status, especially as reciprocity is a strong cultural norm (Tornstam 1993).

In a qualitative study of home-care recipients' service expectations, Sjöbeck (1992b) found that the assessment of quality in home care is very subjective and immensely variable among individuals. In her analysis, Sjöbeck found four different 'ideal types' of home-care recipients, which she called the 'displacers', the 'purchasers', the 'consumers' and the 'holders on'. The 'displacers' primarily sought good interpersonal relations with the home helper. 'Purchasers' were not concerned with personal relations but wanted a home-care helper who could be easily managed, was hard working, service oriented and did not try to be too informal. The expectations of 'consumers' were task oriented. They wanted the maximum service and tended to be passive. The 'holders on' wanted to stick to their own customs and routines. This group was also relationship oriented and sometimes they wanted the household tasks to be skipped in order to socialise with the care giver. They also experienced the most loneliness, wanted more care hours and were most concerned about continuity among the staff. Sjöbeck concluded that it was very important when planning, designing and providing home care to adjust the services to the specific needs of these four home-care recipient types. Her qualitative study could not however determine the relative frequencies and importance of the four ideal types of recipients.

Definitions of quality in home care

Quality attributes in home care are difficult to study for several reasons. Many dimensions of this concept need to be incorporated into a composite measure and, as stated, quality attributes are subjective. Thus it is difficult to find standardised methods that are valid and reliable. We must investigate the relative importance attached to various aspects of service quality as well as the relationships between these domains and levels of satisfaction or dissatisfaction.

What then is 'quality' in home care? The Swedish Standardisation Commission has defined quality in general as 'all characteristics of a product (or service), taken together, which contribute to its capacity to satisfy expressed or implicit needs' (Samuelsson *et al.* 1993b). As applied to home care, quality has been defined as 'the characteristics of the home-help process which provide more or less satisfactory solutions to the problems of the home-care recipient' (Edebalk, Samuelsson and Ingvad 1995).

Material and methodology

The population of interest comprised people aged 65 years and over who received home-help services (two hours per week or more) and lived in a large town (233,000 inhabitants), a small town (16,000 inhabitants) or a rural municipality (13,000 inhabitants). In each area, 60 informants were selected through stratified, unbounded random sampling, the stratification being by gender and age. The first study was completed between 1990 and 1992 and a follow-up took place in the large town (only) in 1997. Comparing the main and follow-up samples, there were no significant differences in the age or gender distributions (Samuelsson 1998). The follow-up was made after the comprehensive reform of the Swedish system for care of older people.

The interview concerning the informants' expectations of quality in home care was introduced as follows: 'We want to find out what you value in a home-help service, and how you would rate the quality of the help you are presently receiving. We will ask questions about both your ideas of an *ideal* home-help service, and also your satisfaction with the service you currently receive.' The Multi-Attribute Utility (MAUT) method was used to study the relative importance of quality attributes perceived to be important to consumers. This method was developed by Edwards and Newman (1982) and Hunt and Ross (1990) to measure the relative importance that respondents assign to various aspects of their home environment. The MAUT scaling technique was specifically adapted for the study of home-care services in Sweden (Edebalk *et al.* 1995). The attributes used in this study were identified in a qualitative study of clients' views about ideal home-care qualities (Sjöbeck 1992a, 1992b) and through earlier research on home-care services (Edebalk *et al.* 1989).

The procedure organises the quality attributes into a 'tree diagram' of ranked attributes (Figure 11.1). Our study identified three levels of attributes which focus on the interaction between the home helper and the care recipient. There were five primary or level one quality domains: continuity, suitability, availability, influence and personal relations. As shown in Figure 11.1, three of the level one domains subdivide into specific attributes at a second level ('personal relations' and 'influence' do not). For example, the 'suitability' of the home carer divides at the second level into 'personal qualities' and 'professional competence' and these, exceptionally, disaggregate into a third level. Further details of the method, the calculations of the rank values and the reasons why two level one attributes were not subdivided have been published (Edebalk *et al.* 1995; Samuelsson *et al.* 1993a). The MAUT scaling procedure allows additional levels and categories (Edwards and Newman 1982),

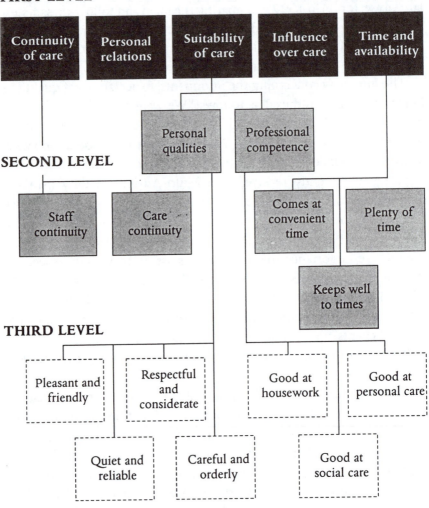

Figure 11.1 The tree hierarchy of quality attributes in home care

but a pilot study made clear that the informant interview should not be too complicated or long as many in the sample were very frail. Each quality attribute was defined by a specific statement, as illustrated in Table 11.1. The informant was asked to rank order the different quality attributes according to their importance; that is, which attribute was most important, second most important, and so on.

Table 11.1 Level one attributes of 'quality' in home care: Determining questions and ratings of importance by informants

Level one attribute	Statements to identify quality attributes	Mean	Standard deviation
Continuity	There is continuity in the staff and the care that I receive	0.220	0.040
Suitability	The carer is professionally competent	0.214	0.039
Personal relations	There is a personal relationship between you and the home help	0.212	0.046*
Time, timing and availability	I know when the home carer is coming, and there is plenty of time	0.193	0.042
Influence	I can influence the home carer's work	0.161	0.053

Note: Level of significance of difference in centrality: * $p < 0.001$.

The following background and contextual information was also collected: subjective health (poor, average or good); number of home-help hours per week (1–2, 3–7 or 8+ hours); employment status (workers, managers or self-employed); age group (65–74, 75–84 or 85+ years); urban–rural location; and type of household (single or co-habiting). From earlier studies, these are known to be significant background variables. The degree of functional disability, as measured by 'activities of daily living', has not been included in the analysis since it is known to be highly correlated with the number of home-help service hours.

Relative importance of quality attribute expectations

The rank ordering of the level one quality attributes is shown in Table 11.1. 'Continuity' together with 'suitability' and 'personal relations' were given the highest values. On the other hand, 'influence' and 'availability/time' received comparatively low evaluations ($p < 0.001$). When the scores were compared pairwise among the informants, neither of the last two quality attributes differed significantly to the other three level one attributes. There were no pairwise statistical differences among the informants' scores for 'continuity', 'suitability' and 'personal relations'.

The rank ordering of the seven quality characteristics at the second level showed that 'staff continuity' was ranked significantly higher than the others ($p < 0.001$). Medium importance were assigned to 'care continuity' and 'keeps well to times'. The quality attribute 'comes at convenient times' was rated significantly lower than all the other attributes except 'keeps well to times'. The five attributes aside from 'staff continuity' and 'comes at convenient times' did not differ significantly in the pairwise comparisons.

In the rank ordering of the seven quality characteristics at the third level, the highest ranking attribute was being 'good at housework' (cleaning, cooking, etc.) together with such personal qualities as being 'pleasant and friendly'. There were no significant pairwise differences among these three variables. The lowest ratings were given to 'competent in giving personal care' and 'respectful and considerate', and the scores on these variables differed significantly from those of the three highest ranked quality attributes. The scores for 'good at social care' and 'quiet and reliable' differed significantly to those for both 'good at housework' and 'pleasant and friendly' ($p < 0.001$).

The five main quality attributes related to different background variables

'Continuity' was established as overall the most important category at level one. Its scores significantly ($p < 0.05$) correlated with age but not with the other background variables that describe the characteristics of the informants: increased age associated with a higher value being placed on 'continuity'. The attribute 'suitability' was valued significantly more in the small town than in either the rural area or the large town. The relative importance ascribed to the level two attributes of 'availability/time' in descending rank order were: 'plenty of time', 'timekeeping', and 'when help was given'. This ordering, moreover, was stable for all categories of the background variables. Older people with few home-help hours valued 'influence' significantly higher than those having many hours of home help. Concerning the value attached to 'personal relations', no statistically significant differences were found in association with the background variables.

To summarise, expectations about the continuity of the service, especially staff continuity, were found to be the most important quality attributes followed by the suitability of the service and the carer's adeptness in personal relations. The least important quality attributes were found to be timing, availability and the informant's influence on their provision.

Satisfaction with the receipt of home care in 1992 and 1997

In the second part of the interview, respondents stated their satisfaction with the services they received using the same attributes that they had rated for importance. An identical questionnaire was administered in 1992 and in a 1997 follow-up in the city of Malmö in southern Sweden. A seven-point scale (7 = very satisfied) was used to measure the satisfaction level. Comparing the levels of satisfaction in 1992 with 1997, there was a significant decrease for 6 of the 17 attributes (Table 11.2). The strongest decreases in satisfaction were produced by the statements, 'The home helper gets on well with me', and 'I have an influence over the home carer's work'. There were also significant decreases in satisfaction for, 'The home helper follows the same routine in my home', 'The times at which I receive help', 'There is plenty of time to do the work', and 'The home helper is good at giving personal care such as bathing and dressing'. There were no significant changes in satisfaction with the five sub-attributes of the 'personal qualities' of the carer. The mean values for these five main quality attributes signify that the informants were between 'fairly' and 'very' satisfied.

Table 11.2 Satisfaction with home help received in Malmö, 1992 and 1997

Attribute of the home-help service	Satisfaction level	
	1992	1997
Continuity indicators		
The home help follows a consistent routine in my home	6.3	5.7*
The home help and I meet so often that we have got to know each other	6.1	6.0
Availability and time allocation indicators		
The times at which I receive help	6.4	5.9*
The allotted times are kept	6.1	5.8
There is plenty of time to do the work	5.9	5.0*
Personal qualities of the staff		
The home help is cheerful	6.5	6.4
The home help is respectful and considerate	6.4	6.3
The home help is quiet and reliable	6.5	6.3
The home help is careful and orderly	6.0	6.0
The home help is honest and reliable	6.7	6.9
Professional competence		
The home help is good at household tasks (cleaning, shopping, cooking)	6.0	5.9
The home help is good in personal care such as bathing and dressing	6.7	6.3*
The home help takes care of me well	6.5	5.0***
Influence on the care received		
I have influence upon the home help's work	6.3	5.5**
Relationship with the home help		
I have a good personal relationship with the home help	6.6	6.4
Aggregate assessments		
Of the home-help worker	6.2	5.9
Of all home-care services	6.0	5.6
NUMBER OF INFORMANTS	60	49

Notes: Levels of significance: * $p<0.05$, ** $p<0.01$, *** $p<0.001$.

When all 17 attributes are examined, the mean satisfaction in 1997 was slightly lower than in 1992. The respondents were also asked in 1997 if they received the help that they wished for and needed: 75 per cent said they did, 8 per cent were uncertain and 17 per cent said they did not.

An open-ended prompt was placed at the beginning of the 1997 interview: 'Please tell me how you think your home care is working for you'. A second question was: 'Have you any suggestions about how to improve your home-help services?' The replies were noted in detail by the interviewer, and the answers to the initial prompt were content analysed and grouped into three categories: primarily positive, both positive and critical, and primarily critical. In the positive answers, statements concerning the carer's personal qualities were most frequent (15 of 25 answers). The next most frequent references were to 'competence' followed by 'continuity' of the services. Among the positive and critical answers, the home-care helper's 'competence' and 'continuity' were the most frequently mentioned attributes. Third, among the critical comments, statements about timing and availability dominated and, to a lesser extent, about 'continuity' and 'how the help was organised'.

To summarise the findings from the open-ended prompt, a majority of the respondents were consistently positive about their home care. A quarter had both positive and critical comments and the remaining quarter were primarily critical. The most frequent positive answers concerned the home-care helper's personal qualities and competence. The most frequent critical comments concerned the availability of the services and, to a lower extent, the continuity of the home care. Some 43 per cent did not have any suggestions for improvements in the home-help service they received, while the others made several suggestions for improvements and changes, mainly concerning the home carer's performance, availability and continuity of the care service.

Discussion

The quality of home care is an important factor in the welfare of older people. When planning and implementing services it is of great value to have information concerning the preferences and expectations of home-care recipients. They should inform priority decisions, especially during cutbacks in the public services. It is important to describe and analyse the attributes of home-help services as precisely as possible in terms of both the recipients' actual contacts and their expectations. Several components of the fundamental task of specifying and evaluating the salient qualitative attributes have been defined (Edebalk *et al.* 1995). Accordingly our study began with a qualitative study of the recipients' expectations and their views about 'ideal' home care (Sjöbeck 1992a). Another component of the fundamental task is the operationalisation of the concept of home-care quality. This raises basic taxonomic problems, of correctly differentiating the most important quality attributes and preventing their confusion in subsequent questions and response categories (Edebalk *et al.* 1995). Similarly, it was necessary to check whether the importance that the informants ascribed to a care attribute was affected by their satisfaction or dissatis-faction with that aspect. An analysis of all the quality attributes showed that there were few correlations between the clients' ratings of their importance and their satisfaction with the home care received (Samuelsson *et al.* 1993b).

Overall this study of client expectations has indicated that 'continu-ity' in home-help services is one of the most important attributes of its quality. A number of earlier studies have noted this relationship between continuity and high quality service (Edebalk *et al.* 1989; Edebalk *et al.* 1995; Lund 1992; Ström 1990). In this study, 'staff continuity' was the most highly assessed dimension of home care. It appears in turn to be a necessary precondition for the home helper and the care recipient to develop a relationship built on trust. In general, assured continuity is also necessary for older people to feel secure. Continuity in care reduces the time spent on negotiating and discussing what should be done. Those who valued 'continuity' least were the younger age groups. They also enjoyed reasonably good health, needed few home-care hours and lived with others. The younger group considered 'suitability' of the personnel and their 'personal relations' to be the most important attributes of home care. Older people certainly valued continuity more highly than young old persons. This may be either because the younger informants had less severe problems or because they were more flexible.

'Personal relations' in formal care have received attention in several studies (Oldby 1989; Ström 1990). This study confirms that the personal relationship between the older person and the home-care helper is an important factor in older people's perceptions of the quality of the service. Among various subgroups of the informants, we found no statistically significant differences in the ranking of the importance of personal relationships, in contrast to Brun *et al.* (1984) who demonstrated, for example, that older people with working-class backgrounds wanted a personal relationship with home helpers unlike those from higher socio-economic groups.

It is well established, and has been confirmed in this study, that the qualifications and 'professional competence' of home-care staff strongly influence assessments of the quality of home-help services (Applebaum and Phillips 1990; Edebalk *et al.* 1989; Edebalk *et al.* 1995; Phillips *et al.* 1989). On the other hand, 'younger' older people, those in reasonably good health and those requiring fewer home-help service hours regarded 'suitability' as the most important quality characteristic. Competence in specific home services, such as house cleaning, laundry and shopping, were the most important quality attributes within the 'suitability' category. In the domain of 'personal care', there was a clear indication that women and the older age groups desired most home-care hours and ranked this characteristic highly. The only significant gender difference in the rank ordering of attribute importance was for 'personal care'.

The 'availability/time quality' attribute of care has been remarked upon in earlier research (Edebalk *et al.* 1989; Oldby 1989). The strong expectation that there should be 'plenty of time' can be interpreted as a surrogate for several other 'wants': that care-giving could be done more carefully; that the home helper has time to get to know the clients and their special needs; that stress is avoided; and that a trusting relationship is built (Thulin 1986). It could also be that the perception of a low capacity to influence the work of home helpers is explained by short contact time. The 'availability' of help attribute, on the other hand, refers to the time frame within which home help is given. This included such matters as the home helper coming at the scheduled time and staying for the allotted period, as previous studies have examined (Ds Fi

1987; Lundberg 1986; Thomas 1986). The present findings indicate however that the importance attached to the 'time' attribute was generally low. The older age groups assigned a significantly higher ranking than the younger to the characteristic 'when help is given'.

Until the late 1980s the home-help service was progressively expanding in Sweden. The expansion was inevitably expensive and has produced a reaction: the service has been successively cut back and targeted towards those with the highest needs for care. Concurrently, problems of staff turnover and recruitment have multiplied. The 'continuity' of care was compromised, as probably were other quality attributes such as 'suitability' and 'personal relations' (Edebalk *et al.* 1995). The Swedish population projections to year 2000 were for an increase of up to 18 per cent in the old-old group (80+ years). In the next few years it might be difficult to find additional funding to meet the increased demands for home-care services, even though the Swedish economy is presently robust. The government is considering substantial grants to the municipalities so that they can raise standards in the health and social care sector.

The ability of the client to influence their home-help service has often been regarded as an important feature of its quality (Statens Offentliga Utredningar 1987, p.21; Edebalk *et al.* 1989). In this study, however, 'influence upon the home helper' emerged as the least valued attribute by all groups. This finding does not in itself negate the importance of influence, but rather indicates that other quality indicators are even more important to frail older home-care recipients. Inadequate contact time and 'staff continuity' may give rise to the desire for greater influence on the provided service. Recipients of few home-help hours however rated 'influence' as more important than those who received many hours. The group who received least home care were mainly 'younger' older people who are less dependent upon home-help services; they also were born into a later, better educated and more demanding cohort. Older people who received most home-help hours also received most intimate personal care, over which the capacity to exercise 'influence' is probably not high. Taking into consideration that the Swedish home-help services increasingly concentrate upon the oldest old, it might be that 'influence' will continue to be a minor dimension of clients' quality assessments. On the other hand, the attributes of continuity, the suitability of personnel and aspects of availability and time are likely to be of increasing importance. These findings should be carefully noted in the future organisation and delivery of home care for older people.

Regarding satisfaction with home-care services, several studies using broad-based subjective assessments have shown generally high levels (Martin-Matthews 1995; Samuelsson, Edebalk and Ingvad 1994). The present study used a multi-method approach to explore quality attributes of home care received by older adults and confirmed a generally high degree of satisfaction with the service (Samuelsson *et al.* 1994). The follow-up study found no significant differences between 1992 and 1997 in satisfaction with 11 of the 17 quality indicators of home care. In spite of the reorganisation of the home-care service, cutbacks and the concentration upon those in most need in Sweden, client satisfaction did not decrease as drastically as one might have expected, even in the face of intense mass media criticism of 'elderly care' when the follow-up study took place. Wärneryd (1999) argued that this may have influenced the clients' answers negatively. On the other hand, their replies may have been influenced positively because the informants belong to a relatively deprived generation and were keenly aware of the country's economic difficulties, as well as able to recollect the spectre of the pauper system and poor-law relief. If such awareness lowered expectations, the result may have been more positive evaluations of current provision. Low satisfaction with the 'plenty of time' attribute was also evident in the qualitative interviews and may be associated with cutbacks in the time allowance for recipients.

The lower satisfaction with the home helper's 'personal care' might be because the clients in 1997 were more difficult to manage and in greater need of more qualified care than the group studied in 1992. Also, it is possible that the training of the home-care helpers had been neglected or that the qualifications of the staff did not correspond to the increased demand for care. The greatest satisfaction levels in both 1992 and 1997 were with the personal qualities of the staff. Thus, the problems of the home-care service are less at the individual level than with organisational priorities.

Our analyses of the satisfaction ratings by the background variables showed that people with low subjective health ratings were significantly more dissatisfied with their care than those with good subjective health. One explanation may be that poor health in itself negatively affects attitudes to home care. The analysis also showed that the clients who received many home-help hours consistently expressed low satisfaction. These results indicate the special difficulties that the home-help providers face in meeting the needs of the frailest clients. This problem may be resolved with increased staff time and improved training and organisation which, in turn, call for more funds. If these are not forthcoming, the service will increasingly focus on the frailest clients. Such prioritisation is inimical to home care having a role in prevention, so that people with low support needs can receive home help to maintain their independence and to delay or prevent the onset of additional problems and limitations. The lowest levels of satisfaction were related to the time and availability attributes of the home-care service. During cutbacks in welfare provision, this domain seems to be most affected, for it results in shorter allotted times for each care recipient and mounting difficulties in maintaining the quality of the service.

The quality of home-care services has a strong influence on the welfare of older people, and our findings must be taken into account when planning, implementing and evaluating the service. It is often necessary to make policy choices between the quality and quantity of home care. Due to rising care costs, the trade-off between costs and quality has to be managed ever more carefully. The present findings indicate that there are several key quality attributes that are particularly valuable to maintain. Most particularly, a high level of continuity and unquestionable professional competence are critical. Since per capita personnel costs are likely to rise, improved training and administrative efficiency gains must increasingly be used to maintain the current quality of the home-care services and to meet client expectations.

The principal goal of services for older people in Sweden is to help them live as independently as possible. The Social Service Act states that the municipal social service department must respect the needs, wishes and integrity of their clients. This requires attention to such factors as the opportunities to influence decisions, the flexibility, availability, security and accessibility of the service, and the promotion of active participation in society. In comparing these goals with the findings from our study, important discrepancies are revealed: for example, the clients' expectations of influence were ranked low in our study, but have a high priority in the legislation. Conversely, continuity did not figure prominently in the Social Service Act but had a high priority among our informants. Such discrepancies might be explained partly by differences in perspective, for policy is driven by a general political perspective over which the interpersonal relationships between home-help carers and their clients exert little influence.

According to Keating *et al.* (1997), care should be client centred and client and family involvement is important. Clients and their relatives ought to be seen as partners and primary decision makers in care-giving. Caring partnerships, in which services are provided by people with various informal and formal relationships, might be an appropriate way to respond to trends in Swedish society such as the rapid growth of the oldest old, higher divorce rates, lower fertility rates and increased female labour force participation. The combination of these trends is likely to reduce further the capacity of informal support networks to meet the growing demand for care (Keating *et al.* 1997). To 'pull down the walls' between professional and informal care-givers will be difficult, but this may be an essential first step if a general improvement of the quality of home care for older people is to be achieved.

Acknowledgements

This study was made possible by a grant from the Swedish Commission for Social Research (DSF) and was also supported by The Ribbing Foundations.

References

Applebaum, R. and Phillips, P. (1990) 'Assuring the Quality of In-Home-Care: The Other Challenge for Long-Term Care.' *The Gerontologist 30*, 4, 444–450.

Brun, C., Fagerstedt, B., Sternberg, J. and Eliasson, R. (1984) *Att Arbeta Inom Äldreomsorgen, att Vara Pensionär och att Möta Varandra.* Stockholm: Socialförvaltning, FoU-Byrån.

Daatland, S.O. (1992) 'Ideals Lost? Current Trends in Scandinavian Welfare Policies on Ageing.' *Journal of European Social Policy 2*, 1, 33–47.

Ds Fi (1987) *Kvalitetsutvecklingen inom den kommunala Äldreomsorgen 1970–1980. Rapport till Expertgruppen för Studier i Offentlig Ekonomi.* Stockholm: Liber.

Edebalk, P.G., Ingvad, B., Samuelsson, G. and Lannerheim, L. (1989) *Kvalitetsegenskaper in Hemtjänsten och Deras Relativa Betydelse – En Pilot Studies.* B-rapport, pp.1-12, Gerontologiskt Centrum, Lund.

Edebalk, P.G., Samuelsson, G. and Ingvad, B. (1995) 'How Elderly Rank Order the Quality Characteristics of Home Services.' *Ageing and Society 15*, 83–102.

Edwards, W. and Newman, J.R. (1982) *Multiattribute Evaluation.* Methodology paper, Series 07-26. Beverly Hills: Sage.

Eliasson Lappalainen, R. and Szebehely, M. (1996) 'Äldreomsorg, Kvalitetssäkring och Välfärdspolitik.' In W. Palme (ed) *Generell Välfärd. Hot och Möjlighet.* Stockholm: Nordstedts.

Elmér, Å. (1963) *Från Fattigsverige till Välfärdsstaten.* Stockholm: Aldus/Bonniers.

Gough, R. (1987) *Hemhjälp till Gamla.* Forskningsrapport no. 54. Stockholm: Arbetslivscentrum.

Health and Welfare Canada (1991) *Description of Long-Term Care Services in Provinces and Territories of Canada.* Ottawa: Health and Welfare Canada.

Hunt, M.E. and Ross, L.E. (1990) 'Naturally Occurring Retirement Communities: A Multiattribute Examination of Desirability Factors.' *The Gerontologist 30*, 5, 667–674.

Johansson, L. (1991) 'Caring for the Next of Kin: On Informal Care of Elderly in Sweden.' Doctoral thesis. Uppsala: Department of Social Medicine, University of Uppsala.

Kane, R.L. and Kane, R.A. (1985) *A Will and a Way: What the United States Can Learn from Canada about Caring for Older People.* New York: Columbia University Press.

Katona, G. (1975) *Psychological Economics.* New York: Elsevier.

Keating, N.C., Fast, J.E., Connidis, I.A., Penning, M. and Keefe, J. (1997) 'Bridging Policy and Research in Elder Care.' *Canadian Journal on Ageing 16*, 22–42.

Lund, U. (1992) 'Vård och Omsorg i Eget Boende på Äldre Dar.' Dissertation. Linköping: University of Linköping.

Lundberg, L. (1986) *Livet Inom Hemtjänsten.* Uppsala: Uppsala Kommun.

Martin-Matthews, A. (1995) *Homemaker Services to the Elderly: Provider Characteristics and Client Benefit.* Lund: Gerontology Research Centre.

Oldby, B. (1989) *Vårdkvalitet i Vårdsamverkan.* Forskningsrapport no. 45. Stockholm: Pedagogiska institutionen vid Stockholms universitet.

Phillips, P., Applebaum, R. and Atchley, S. (1989) 'Assuring the Quality of Home-Delivered Longterm Care: The Ohio Quality Assurance Project.' *Home Health Care Services Quarterly 1*, 38–46.

Rosenmayr, L. (1979) 'Progress and Unresolved Problems in Socio-Gerontological Theory.' *Aktuelle Gerontologie 9*, 4–21.

Samuelsson, G. (1981) 'Dagens Pensionärer – Sekelskiftets Barn.' Dissertation. Lund: Studentlitteratur, University of Lund.

Samuelsson, G. (1998) *Brukarnas Tillfredsställelse med Kvaliteten i Hemtjänsten i en Storstadskommun 1992 och 1997 – En Uppföljningsstudie.* B-rapport XII: 2. Lund: Gerontology Research Centre.

Samuelsson, G., Edebalk, P.G. and Ingvad, B. (1993a) 'Quality Attributes of Swedish Home-Help Services: A Consumer Perspective.' *Zeitschrift für Gerontologie 26*, 3, 202–207.

Samuelsson, G., Ingvad, B. and Edebalk, P.G. (1993) *A Method of Ranking Different Quality Attributes in Home-Help Services: 'Multiattribute Utility Technology'.* B-rapport VII: 4. Lund: Gerontology Research Centre.

Samuelsson, G., Edebalk, P.G. and Ingvad, B. (1994) 'Kvalitet i Hemtjänsten – En Studie i tre Olika Kommuntyper.' *Aldring och Eldre 3*, 20–25.

Sjöbeck, B. (1992a) 'Kvalitet i den Sociala Hemtjänsten ur Brukarperspektiv.' *Gerontologia 5*, 173–182.

Sjöbeck, B. (1992b) 'Pensionärers Förväntningar på och Bedömningar av Hemtjänst: Kvalitet i Brukarperspektiv.' *Aldring og Eldre 3*, 24-27.

Statistical Abstract of Sweden (1993) *Levnadsförhållanden, Pensionärer 1980–1989.* Rapport 81. Stockholm: Statistiska Centralbyrån.

Statens Offentliga Utredningar (1987) *Äldreomsorg i Utveckling.* Stockholm: Socialstyrelsen.

Ström, P. (1990) *Kontinuitet och Kvalitet i Hemtjänsten.* SoS-rapport 1990: 29. Stockholm: Socialstyrelsen.

Sundström, G. and Berg, S. (1988) *Vad har Egentligen Hänt inom Äldreomsorgen – Har Vård i Hemmet Ersatt Institutionsvård? Erfarenheter 1965–1985.* Rapport 69. Jönköping, Sweden: Institutet för Gerontologi.

Thomas, A. (1986) *Vardagsvanor och Ritualer: Om Några Gamla Människors Möte med Hemservice.* Stockholm: FoU-Bryån, Stockholms Socialförvaltning.

Thulin, A. B. (1986) *Vasastan-Projektet – En Studie av Personalomsättningen Bland Vårdbiträden i Socialdistrikt 1.* Stockholm: FoU-Bryån, Stockholms Socialförvaltning.

Tornstam, L. (1993) 'Formal and Informal Support for Older People.' *Impact of Science on Society 153*, 57–63.

Wärneryd, K-E. (1999) 'The Role of Macroeconomic Psychology.' *Applied Psychology 48*, 3, 273–296.

CHAPTER 12

Death and Dying
Changing the Culture of Care
Amanda Clarke and Elizabeth Hanson

Introduction

Palliative care has attracted increasing attention and support in recent years, but although older people have been at the centre of many policy initiatives and debates in the health and social services, they remain largely excluded from this branch of care (Field 1996; Seale 1998). In any discussion of the role of services in promoting the welfare of older people, it is necessary to examine the gaps as well as prominent innovations. This chapter argues that older people tend to be denied access to palliative care largely because of negative attitudes towards death and dying, and indeed, old age. Neuberger (1996) questions how we can have any sense of what older people want in life, if we refuse to discuss death and dying with them which, she argues, should not only take place when they are terminally ill, as is now usually the case. Smith (1996, p.1) believes that 'for many older people, attitudes to their own death, whether expressed or implicit, form an essential element in the quality of their lives', and asks how they can achieve participation and empowerment in their everyday lives if they are not provided with opportunities to talk about their fears and concerns about death and dying.

   To this end, the chapter discusses the attitudes towards death and dying of older people, policy makers, service providers, practitioners and researchers. The two authors have carried out separate studies of older people's perceptions of death and dying, and found that most of their informants were willing to talk about their concerns and anxieties about death and, further, that they wanted to be consulted about their health and social needs in later life. Given the tensions that arise from the contrasting attitudes to death and dying which are held by older people and service providers, the need to change the 'culture of care' becomes obvious. This chapter makes a case for the expansion and strengthening of palliative care for older people, and argues that such a change would valuably instil more empathetic and responsive care.

End-of-life and palliative care

Good practice in end-of-life care implies no more than excellence in medicine and nursing during the terminal phase of an illness. Palliative care, by contrast, can be defined as

> the active total care of patients whose disease is not responsive to curative treatment. Control of pain, of other symptoms, and of psychological, social and spiritual problems is paramount. The goal of palliative care is achievement of the best possible quality-of-life for patients and their families. Many aspects of palliative care are also applicable earlier in the course of illness, in conjunction with anti-cancer treatment. (WHO 1990, p.4)

The aims and approaches combine in the 'palliative care model', which can be applied to quite different levels of care. The palliative care approach places the patient and his or her family at the centre of care decisions and aims to sustain the best possible quality of life. It is increasingly accepted as a core clinical skill and a key component of clinical practice whatever the illness or its stage, which means that it should be applied not only at the terminal or end stage of an illness. Specialist palliative care services include hospice care and multidisciplinary palliative care teams, which provide advice and support, especially for the transition from hospital to home. Another key role is the education and training of other health care professionals in the palliative care approach (Clark and Seymour 1999, p.86).

Field (1994, 1996) believes that the medicalisation of death, primarily through the dominant role of the doctor in shaping the experience of those who are dying, has resulted in considerable psychological harm and suffering for both patients and their loved ones. Indeed, Bamford (1994) notes that during the twentieth century death had become rare and elusive in most people's experience, and that this may have fostered a belief that it is hard to die which, in turn, may have added to people's fears of growing old. This sequence of cause and effect is evident in John Hoyland's (1997, p.6) account of his stepfather's death on an NHS hospital orthopaedic ward. He died in pain and distress, for the doctors refused to administer morphine. Hoyland commented that 'the inability to deal appropriately with the needs of old people in our hospitals is compounded by what appears to be an almost total inability on the part of the NHS to deal with the fact that patients die'. He argued that older people who are not dying of 'a classically fatal condition' are denied the specialist care offered by hospices. If palliative principles had been applied care at an earlier stage of his stepfather's illness, there would have been more attention to his needs and to raising his own and his family's quality of life.

Hoyland's argument is substantiated by the findings of two authoritative surveys of the last year of life which contrasted people with and without cancer (Addington-Hall and McCarthy 1995; Addington-Hall et al. 1998a; Addington-Hall, Fakhoury and McCarthy 1998; Seale and Cartwright 1994). These showed that hospice care is primarily directed towards cancer patients who, on average, were younger than those with non-cancer conditions and therefore more likely to have family support. They also were more likely to have a well-defined course of illness which facilitated diagnosis and prognosis.

The assumption is widespread that in old age death comes naturally and easily, and that therefore hospice care is superfluous (Howarth 1998). But hospice and palliative care aim to help the individual to be in control of his or her dying process, on the assumption that a 'good death' is attainable (Field 1996; McNamara 1997). Since the majority of older people with chronic illnesses are not offered palliative care, whether in their own homes, institutions or hospices, they are denied opportunities to take control of the dying process (Addington-Hall 1998; Seale and Cartwright 1994; Sidell, Katz and Komaromy 1998).

Societal attitudes towards death

The ways in which we consider the care of dying people cannot be separated from society's general beliefs and assumptions about older people and their roles. Hazan (1994) posits that we are all influenced by deeply ingrained social attitudes, values and structures which affect the way in which old age (and death in old age) is constructed. The influences include, for example, the level of economic development, standards of living, family structures, social policy goals, the growth of life-saving technology and the expansion of the hospice movement. Field (1996) concurs, pointing out that in western societies death is not only a physical event, but that its character, pattern and meaning are shaped by societal factors, structures and beliefs (for further discussion see Clark and Seymour 1999).

Barriers against death are constructed and sustained by taboos, codes and customs, which include the avoidance of contamination by the corpse, the territorial segregation of cemeteries and avoidance of the dying (Hazan 1994, p.68). There are elements of contrived avoidance in the progressive displacement of older and dying people out of their homes and into acute and long-term care institutions (Seale and Cartwright 1994). Some sociologists, however, dispute the representation of death as a societal taboo (Clark 1993; Mellor 1993; Walter 1993). For Mellor, death is less a forbidden subject than an event which is generally sequestrated from the public arena. In Gidden's (1991) view, death is hidden from sight primarily because individuals cannot perceive the process of dying as anything other than the incipient loss of control. Death only becomes problematic when it is premature; when a person has not lived out his or her life expectancy. We cannot, however, avoid the inevitability that one day we all die; older people are 'reminders of our mortality' (Tallis 1999, p.23). Becoming old is therefore perceived as dangerous and older people pictured as between life and death, in a continual limbo (Hazan 1994).

Several British medical sociologists have made substantial contributions to the study of the dying process (Clark 1993; Field 1994, 1996; Seale and Cartwright 1994). They tend to argue that until recently there has been a reluctance to explore death and particularly the experience of dying in old age (Howarth 1998; Sidell 1996). While Hazan argues that this is to do with the fear of confronting death, Walter suggests that the neglect of the sociology of death in old age may be associated with 'gerontology being driven by the old as a problem for society, rather than by death as a problem for the elderly' (Walter 1993, p.280). The dearth of literature and research on ageing and death has colluded with the general reluctance to discuss death. This, together with the assumption that death in older age is 'natural' and therefore 'easy', leaves older people without the help they might need as they face either or both their own deaths and the deaths of those to whom they are close (Sidell 1995). It can also be argued that if older people are seen collectively as a burden when the majority are living relatively independently in their own homes, they may be seen as even more of a burden if they are in need of specialist and expensive end-of-life care (Warnes 1993).

Older people's attitudes towards death and dying

Our account now draws on the authors' recent studies (with pseudonyms to protect the identities of the research participants). One study, the 'Advancing Gerontological Education in Nursing' (AGEIN) project, explored the nature and experience of the last years of life for older people and their families through a single, semi-structured, in-depth interview with nine participants in their own homes (Seymour and Hanson 2001). Most interviews were with the older person and their spousal carer. All the primary informants were chronically ill and heavily dependent on their family carers and the health and social care services. Because of their chronic health status and dependency on family carers, they were thought likely to be approaching their last years of life. They were asked about their daily lives, their health needs and about the services they received.

The other study, Clarke's doctoral research, explored the experience of later life using a biographical approach and through two or three open-ended, in-depth interviews with 23 participants, most of whom were not receiving health or social care services. The first interview collected the life story and current circumstances, and the subsequent interviews compiled personal accounts of people's views and experiences of growing older, during which the themes of death and dying were sometimes raised. Neither study asked the participants questions which referred directly to death. Despite some clear differences between the two studies, there was a common response from the two sets of informants: older people are willing to and do talk about death.

Unruh (1983) argued that as people grow older, perceptions of 'living' begin to be supplanted by perceptions of dying. Both studies found that although people did talk about death, there was little evidence of older people becoming preoccupied with death, as Unruh implies. This was true even for the participants in the AGEIN study who were thought to be approaching their last years. Participants in both studies sometimes alluded to death with phrases such as 'living on borrowed time', 'we're all born to die', 'if we live longer' and 'there's nothing to look forward to except cremation'. A few participants did not refer directly or indirectly to death. This is not to say, however, that when given the opportunity, older people do not want to talk about death. As Smith (1996, p.1) points out, older people may want to think about death and, when given the opportunity by 'their more squeamish younger friends and relatives', to talk about the experience. The few opportunities that health and social service professionals give their patients and clients to talk about death can probably be associated with the absence of the required skills and appropriate training.

Religious faith and the acceptance of death

It is important to acknowledge the diversity of older people's attitudes. Some participants accepted death as a 'natural' part of life, while others worried about dying or being left alone after their partner had died. Williams's (1990) study of attitudes to death and illness among older Aberdonians found that many participants with residual Calvinist beliefs 'accepted' the inevitability of death. Among Clarke's participants, too, this acceptance and rationale was widely apparent. The participants with a belief in an afterlife talked more directly and with more acceptance about death (see also Bury and Holme 1991).

Josephine Buxton, a retired nursing auxiliary, felt that she was fortunate to have lived until the age of 61 years and said, 'I'm extremely lucky to be my age because I've nursed a lot of young people who have passed on and they've not enjoyed life to the full as I have.' Doreen Thomas, aged 96 years, seemed to accept the inevitability of death in saying, 'I'm looking forward to reaching heaven. I'm not frightened about death. If it comes tonight, I am ready.' Another participant, Maureen Williams, said that her Christian faith sustained her. She had been widowed 18 months before her interview and looked forward to meeting her husband again when she died. She said, 'Knowing that I'll meet him again, I think that has helped me. In the beginning, it doesn't come to you as clearly as that because the mist is so great that you don't go beyond the actual physical miss of the person, not for a while, and then that comes into your mind and it helps.'

Clearly, practitioners need to be sensitive to such beliefs since they may substantially influence a person's attitude to their own death and their expectations, behaviour and mental state during the dying process. Josephine Buxton thought that her experience as a nursing auxiliary and her religious beliefs helped her accept death. She said, 'A year of corn has to die before you can get another field of corn. To all the people that I cared for over the years, when they said to me, "Am I going to die?" I've always said, "Well, we all have to die one day." But you don't dwell on it because dying is as sure as being born; death is assured.'

From the AGEIN study too, most participants did not skirt around the inevitability of death. One man in his early eighties with a severe right-sided weakness from several strokes candidly said, 'Well, it's where we all end, isn't it? We all end up in the same place, don't we?' Even if death is accepted as inevitable it does not mean however that there is a 'right' time to die (Howarth 1998). The increase in longevity in modern society has led people to expect to live long. While Maureen Williams said, 'You look forward to heaven. I can say I am either here or I am not. I have peace and contentment.' She added that she did not 'want to go from this world yet' and wished to see her grandchildren grow up. For Brian Jenner, aged 61 years (Clarke's study), there was no future to look forward to and no afterlife. He said, 'All that awaits us in the end is death.' But to him death was still some way off since he equated death with 'being *really* old'.

Older people's anxieties about death and dying

It is sometimes assumed that since older age is the last stage before death, the older one becomes, the less frightening the prospect (Howarth 1998). Although as we have seen some people accept the inevitability of death, Sidell (1995) pointed out that, however aware people might be of their finitude, many are anxious about the process of dying. Both of our studies revealed that people may want, or at least to be given the opportunity, to discuss their plans and fears regarding death and dying. Josephine Buxton recognised that not everyone shares her acceptance of death and that attitudes vary: '[During] my experience as a health worker, I've seen some people die who are terrified of dying and try to escape from [it], and I've seen people who die in a serene sort of way, people who are comforted, who have someone holding their hands.'

Unruh (1983), Buckman (1993) and Marshall (1996) argued that it is usually personal illness, declining abilities or the deaths of relatives and friends that bring thoughts of death into people's minds. This was reflected in both studies. Among Clarke's informants, Alice Kendrick, in her early nineties, described the death of a friend who had died after falling down the stairs. Alice said that she had stopped attending funerals because she would be going to 'so many' and, 'the older you get, the nearer to the front of the church you get'. From the AGEIN study, Violet Cassidy, a spousal carer of a man with a severe stroke, confided:

> A fortnight ago I saw a death in the newspaper and it was a girl I'd started school with, and I thought, 'Oh dear, there used to be four of us and now I'm the only one left.' And that worried me for a day or two. I thought, 'That could have been me.' It does worry you

sometimes, because I'm the youngest of a family and they're gradually going.

For Maureen Williams, it was the death of her husband that caused her to reflect upon her mortality: 'It brings it home to you, that you are getting older and that you haven't got as much in front of you as you've lived: you know, the years will be so much fewer than they have been.'

Among Clarke's participants, George and Anne Daley, a couple in their late seventies, expressed concern about one of them dying before the other. George said, 'Eventually…one of us is going to die and leave the other. And I know it happens to so many people, but it doesn't alter the fact that for the person concerned it raises problems.' Similarly, several spousal carers in the AGEIN study expressed a concern about dying first and what the consequences would be for their partner. Mary Cowlishaw said, 'I worry about what would happen to William if anything happened to me, because I think that social services would run circles round him – he hasn't got the speech to defend himself.' One carer, whose husband required significant assistance in most activities of daily living and was prone to frequent fits, admitted that her husband had been worried when she had recently been unwell. He had said, 'Nobody will want me.'

Several participants in Clarke's study confided that they were anxious that they might die alone. Alice Kendrick said, 'I do sometimes wonder, if I don't feel well in the middle of the night, "Oh dear, what would happen if they couldn't get into me?" When it boils down, you don't want to go. It's not a case of when, it's you wonder how.' Maureen Williams expressed a similar concern when saying, 'I think, "Nobody would know if I was dead or not… Oh how terrible to die all by yourself."' When told that another participant had expressed a similar worry, with some reassurance she said, 'Have they? It's nice to know because you think you're being funny.' Another participant who expressed anxiety about dying alone, Lillian Grayson, commented, 'The only fear I've got is if I'm left alone when I die and nobody finds me. You read about that, but otherwise I'm all right.'

Abbey (1999) suggested that when older people say, 'Please help me to die' or 'I'm no use to anyone any more', such comments may arise from depression, loss or grief and are attempts to open a conversation about the process of dying. Several participants in the AGEIN study admitted that it was when they felt 'down' that their thoughts turned to death and dying. Philip Lott said, 'I watch telly and I count the bricks on the wall – that's all I do. Sit here. I think about snuffing it.' Similarly, a family carer turned to his wife and said, 'What do you keep saying? You're fed up at times, aren't you?' The wife's mother, who was aged 83 years and had suffered a severe stroke, replied, 'Yes, and I ask God if he'd take me.'

Attitudes towards service provision

Comments from participants in the AGEIN study highlighted the importance of person-centred care as an influence on the quality of their lives (Nolan, Grant and Keady 1996). Although not receiving specialist palliative care, its principles were seen as very important by all participants. All but one were supported by home-care workers who visited on average twice daily to help the spouse carer with the activities of daily living. Participants spoke of the importance of the personal qualities of the care worker and the development of a trusting relationship. For example, Lucy Green, a carer, said, 'It's his attitude toward Harry. He knows exactly what to do, he doesn't hassle him, he just lets him take his time. We've got to be more like friends now.'

Contrasting examples were given of care workers' practice. Some reported that the carer clearly demonstrated respect for the cared for person through the appropriate use of touch during intimate care, while others described a carer that communicated their lack of respect for the client through gesture. Suzanne Field, a family carer, commented, 'She's gentle with him, she knows what he wants generally. Her attitude is more a concern for the patient than getting a job done and getting out as quick as she can.' Conversely, Juliet Weaton said, 'They want to be here and gone: they're in too much of a rush and pull him off balance, and then he gets irritable because he's not in control.'

Carers who enjoyed a trusting relationship with a care worker explained that they would turn to them for help if they needed and also felt they could talk with them about the future. Jim Clegg explained,

'We've spoke with Ann (the care worker) mainly. I've said, "If anything happens to me, you'll see to her won't you?" Straight away she said "Yes".' Several participants spoke of their frustrations with the poor continuity of care which in some cases led to distrust. One family carer, Gillian Collins, said, 'This is the problem, you get somebody different every night.' Her husband added, 'Because when it's one that's never been, she's got a lot of explaining to do.' Gillian continued, 'I have to start all over again [to explain] what he needs doing for him and how to do it.' Similarly, another carer, Freda Griffen, said, 'It might be any of a dozen that have been. One dropped him in the bath and broke my bath rack – [with] complete indifference as to how much work [he] created for me.'

For most participants the inputs of nursing and medical help were not high. In most cases, it was the responsibility of the family carer to contact the professional carer if they had any problems. Lydia Abbott, a family carer, said, 'They don't get in contact with me unless I ring.' There was a notable absence of regular assessment and monitoring. Phillip Wright spoke of the lack of co-ordination among the formal services and described the absence of person-centred care: 'Each of the professionals assume I'm being taken care of somewhere else – everyone sees to a very little bit. There's no one who just looks after the people.'

These views and experiences of service provision indicate their end-of-life care needs and the value of day-to-day, person-centred care for people with chronic illnesses. The common wish is that the practitioners get to know them personally in order to understand their everyday needs and, in the process, build a trusting relationship in which fears and aspirations for the future might be discussed. The palliative care approach embodies these person-centred principles. The majority of the primary participants also had unrelieved symptoms such as pain and frequent fits. Such conditions are invariably improved by specialist palliative care services, as shown by the surveys of non-cancer patients during the last year of life (Addington-Hall *et al.* 1995, 1998a, 1998b).

Recommendations for practice

Our findings and other research suggest several ways in which the situation of older people who are dying might be improved. Most are integral to the palliative care approach which actively encourages the participation of the dying person and puts them at the centre of the formal care process (Bosanquet 1997). They are given opportunities, for example, to talk about death and dying, as our findings show most older people wish to do when given appropriate and sensitive opportunities. We have also found that most older people and their family carers want to be involved as far as possible in decisions regarding end-of-life care.

There is a need to create more suitable settings in which to enable a dialogue about death and dying. Providing a personal context in which people feel comfortable to talk about planning their dying takes time, for a relationship of trust and intimacy has to be built up between the service user and practitioner. Moreover, it requires a radical attitudinal change, given the reluctance of practitioners and others to consult older people about any aspects of their lives, but particularly to discuss and confront the issues of death and dying. It also requires great skill, for, as Abbey (1999) points out, people's diverse needs and wishes need careful differentiation.

A biographical approach is particularly appropriate to elicit older people's views on their end-of-life care needs. In the context of talking about their past and present lives, people's anxieties and needs, including any concerns about death, can be raised. The biographical approach does not fracture life experiences, but provides the framework and means to evaluate the present, re-evaluate the past and anticipate the future (Cotterill and Letherby 1993). People should not be obliged to talk about death, as by a direct question, but given the opportunity to talk about whatever they want. The approach may inform assessment, planning and evaluation by helping practitioners to see people as they once were, not only as they are now (Bornat 1994). This promotes 'a therapeutic relationship which is directed at gaining an effective outcome from care that is centred on the person's needs and life per-spectives' (McCormack 1996).

Moreover, whether in a community setting or institution, a supportive environment needs to be provided for the staff, to allow them to express, reflect upon and confront their own fears regarding death and dying (Abbey 1999). This is especially important if the care worker develops a close and trusting relationship with a client and his or her family. Adopting a palliative care approach does therefore have many implications for resources; not least in the requirement for additional staff, for each person to have a key support worker, and to release staff for training in communication skills and in caring for people dying from all conditions (Katz, Komaromy and Sidell 1999).

Older people also see the need for better co-ordination between health and social care services, between non-specialist and specialist services, and between home and hospital. For this to happen, changes in the education and training of practitioners are required, perhaps to encourage carers of older people to work and learn alongside specialists in palliative care (Buckman 1993; Katz *et al.* 1999). We have also found that older people are willing to discuss their concerns and anxieties about death and, further, that they want to be consulted regarding their health and social needs at the end of life. We conclude, therefore, that there is an imperative need to change the way in which we all think of death and older age, for this is a prerequisite for a change in the culture of end-of-life care.

Acknowledgements

The AGEIN study was funded by the English National Board for Nursing and Midwifery. The grantholders are Mike Nolan, Sue Davies, Jane Brown and Gordon Grant at the University of Sheffield.

References

Abbey, J. (1999) 'Palliative Care.' In R. Noy and S. Garratt (eds) *Nursing Older People.* Sydney: MacLennon and Petty.

Addington-Hall, J.M. (1998) *Reaching Out: Specialist Palliative Care for Adults with Non-Malignant Diseases.* Occasional Paper 14. London: National Council for Hospice and Specialist Palliative Care and Scottish Partnership Agency for Palliative and Cancer Care.

Addington-Hall, J.M. and McCarthy, M. (1995) 'Regional Study of Care for the Dying: Methods and Sample Characteristics.' *Palliative Medicine 9,* 27–35.

Addington-Hall, J.M., Lay, M., Altmann, D. and McCarthy, M. (1995) 'Symptom Control, Communication with Health Professionals and Hospital Care of Stroke

Patients in the Last Year of Life, as Reported by Surviving Family, Friends and Carers.' *Stroke 26*, 2242–2248.

Addington-Hall, J.M., Lay, M., Altmann, D. and McCarthy, M. (1998a) 'Community Care for Stroke Patients in the Last Year of Life: Results of National Retrospective Survey of Surviving Family, Friends and Officials.' *Health and Social Care in the Community 6*, 112–119.

Addington-Hall, J.M., Fakhoury, W. and McCarthy, M. (1998b) 'Specialist Palliative Care in Non-Malignant Disease.' *Palliative Medicine 12*, 417–427.

Bamford, C. (1994) *Grandparents' Lives: Men and Women in Later Life.* Edinburgh: Age Concern Scotland.

Bornat, J. (ed) (1994) *Reminiscence Reviewed.* Buckingham: Open University Press.

Bosanquet, N. (1997) 'New Challenge for Palliative Care: To Share Its Special Mission with a Wider Audience.' *British Medical Journal 314*, 1294.

Buckman, R. (1993) 'Breaking Bad News: Why Is It Still So Difficult?' In D. Dickinson and M. Johnson (eds) *Death, Dying and Bereavement.* London: Sage.

Bury, M. and Holme, A. (1991) *Life after Ninety.* London: Routledge.

Clark, D. (ed) (1993) *The Sociology of Death.* Oxford: Blackwell.

Clark, D. and Seymour, J. (1999) *Reflections on Palliative Care.* Buckingham: Open University Press.

Cotterill, P. and Letherby, G. (1993) 'Weaving Stories: Personal Auto/Biographies in Feminist Research.' *Sociology 27*, 1, 67–79.

Field, D. (1994) 'Palliative Medicine and the Medicalization of Death.' *European Journal of Cancer Care 3*, 58–62.

Field, D. (1996) 'Awareness and Modern Dying.' *Mortality 1*, 3, 255–265.

Giddens, A. (1991) *Modernity and Self-Identity.* Cambridge: Polity Press.

Hazan, H. (1994) *Old Age Constructions and Deconstructions.* Cambridge: Cambridge University Press.

Howarth, G. (1998) '"Just Live for Today": Living, Caring, Ageing and Dying.' *Ageing and Society 18*, 6, 673–689.

Hoyland, J. (1997) 'Thanks, NHS, for a Rotten Way to Die.' *The Independent Tabloid*, 22 April.

Katz, J., Komaromy, C. and Sidell, M. (1999) 'Understanding Palliative Care in Residential and Nursing Homes.' *International Journal of Palliative Nursing 5*, 2, 58–62.

McCormack, B. (1996) 'Life Transitions.' In P. Ford and H. Heath (eds) *Older People and Nursing: Issues of Living in a Care Home.* Oxford: Butterworth Heinemann.

McNamara, B. (1997) 'A Good Enough Death?' Paper presented at the 3rd International Conference on the Social Context of Death, Dying and Disposal, University of Wales, Cardiff, April.

Marshall, V.W. (1996) 'Death, Bereavement and the Social Psychology of Ageing and Dying.' In J.D. Morgan (ed) *Ethical Issues in the Care of the Dying and Bereaved Aged.* New York: Baywood.

Mellor, P. (1993) 'Death in High Modernity: The Contemporary Presence and Absence of Death.' In D. Clark (ed) *The Sociology of Death.* Oxford: Blackwell.

Neuberger, J. (1996) *The End or Merely the Beginning.* London: Counsel and Care.

Nolan, M., Grant, G. and Keady, J. (1996) *Understanding Family Care.* Buckingham: Open University Press.

Seale, C. (1998) *Constructing Death: The Sociology of Dying and Bereavement.* Cambridge: Cambridge University Press.

Seale, C. and Cartwright, A. (1994) *The Year before Death*. Aldershot: Avebury.

Seymour, J. and Hanson, E. (2001) 'Palliative Care and Older People.' In M. Nolan, S. Davies and G. Grant (eds) *Working with Older People*. Buckingham: Open University Press.

Sidell, M. (1995) *Health in Old Age: Myth, Mystery and Management*. Buckingham: Open University Press.

Sidell, M. (1996) 'Ageing and Death.' In J. Neuberger (ed) *The End or Merely the Beginning*. London: Counsel and Care.

Sidell, M., Katz, J.T. and Komaromy, C. (1998) 'Death and Dying in Residential and Nursing Homes for Older People.' Unpublished report to the Department of Health. Milton Keynes: School of Health and Welfare, The Open University.

Smith, J. (1996) 'Introduction.' In J. Neuberger (ed) *The End or Merely the Beginning*. London: Counsel and Care.

Tallis, R. (1999) 'Old Faces, New Lives.' *Times Higher Educational Supplement*, 9 July, 23.

Unruh, D. (1983) *Invisible Lives: Social Worlds of the Aged*. London: Sage.

Walter, T. (1993) 'Sociologists Never Die: British Sociology and Death.' In D. Clark (ed) *The Sociology of Death*. Oxford: Blackwell.

Warnes, A.M. (1993) 'Being Old, Old People and the Burdens of Burden.' *Ageing and Society 13*, 3, 297–338.

Williams, R. (1990) *A Protestant Legacy: Attitudes to Death and Illness among Older Aberdonians*. Oxford: Clarendon Press.

World Health Organisation (WHO) (1990) *Cancer Pain Relief and Palliative Care*. Technical Report, Series B04. Geneva: WHO.

CHAPTER 13

Design for Later Life
Beyond a Problem Orientation
Roger Coleman

Overview

In this chapter it is argued that considerable benefits will flow from a shift in the positioning of products and care services targeted at older people, away from an emphasis on deficit, decline, disability and dependency, to an emphasis on well-being, activity and independence. From this perspective, the seemingly intractable problems of population ageing with increasing dependency can be tackled by developing products and services that support independence, enable activity and allow older people to take an active role in maintaining their well-being. 'Inclusive design' and 'enabling' products and care services can deliver successful solutions in a way that aids and adaptations cannot, and commercial opportunities will open up to those manufacturers and care providers which are prepared to make the necessary investment in design.

In this chapter some of the reasons why inclusive, age-aware design is not as prevalent as one would wish are explored, and examples and case studies are presented as pointers to a future in which this approach becomes the norm. In addition, the challenges of population ageing which face both the public and the private sectors are examined, and the benefits are identified of moving beyond a problem orientation to meet more effectively the needs and aspirations of older people. It will be shown that to deliver these benefits requires both changes in the attitudes of designers and product developers and revised assumptions about ageing and care provision. The design and the care professions must embrace an activity-based, user-centric approach to the promotion of both independent living and a more domestic approach to institutional care.

Special needs versus mainstream design

In the past, the needs of older people have customarily been perceived as 'special'. As a consequence attention has focused on aids and adaptations rather than the enabling potential of improved mainstream design. Models of ageing which emphasise declines in capabilities have reinforced the association of ageing with disability (think how often the term 'the disabled and elderly' appears in research reports and public statements), and encouraged a widespread, problem-oriented response to population ageing.[1] Our lives are being shaped by various new technologies and are pervasively affected by the design of products, services and environments: the extent to which all these develop with or without consideration for the needs and aspirations of older people will have a profound effect on their activities and quality of life (Brouwer-Janse *et al.* 1997). There is presently an opportunity to design and develop a new generation of products and services that are life enhancing for people of all ages, and which also address the particular needs of older people – for independence, employment, care, welfare, education, and social contact – without the stigma presently attached to aids, adaptations and institutionalised care.[2]

By ensuring that older people can live in their own homes, travel, socialise and take care of themselves for as long as possible, we can extend their independence and life quality and help them, in Tom Kirkwood's terms, successfully to meet the challenges of ageing: 'For society, the challenge of successful ageing is a paramount issue touching on all aspects of life – social, economic, medical and spiritual. For the individual, the challenge is to reach old age in optimum health and to develop the resources and attitudes to preserve independence and quality of life for as long as possible' (Kirkwood 1999, p.11).

We live in a world which is designed, engineered and manufactured; a constructed world of products, technologies and infrastructures which extend our capabilities in quite astonishing ways, and which collectively have contributed substantially to our new-found longevity. The pressing task now is to make that world age friendly and supportive of us as we grow older, not just of our ageing bodies but also our changing expectations, aspirations and lifestyles. In so doing we can make it possible to approach the concept of 'care' from the perspective of extending older people's capacity, in effect, to care for both themselves and each other, by providing a more considerate environment in which old age is not problematised, and by offering care services which more effectively support independence in old age.

A built-in bias

Designers tend to be young and marketing and advertising executives younger still, while company directors, although more aware of the impact of changing demography on the marketplace, are likely to have grown up with consumerism and to associate it more with youth than with age. This amounts to a built-in age bias in much of industry and retailing, which regards the older customer as less important than the young, and shies away from associating its products and services with the older consumer. As a consequence it is not usual for older people's needs to be taken into consideration, even ergonomically – the video recorder with its plethora of tiny buttons and complicated interface is widely recognised to epitomise the problem (Figure 13.1). However, if older people find products and services difficult to use or access, they are deemed to be the problem, not the video recorder. This undermines older people's sense of competence and ultimately their independence, by rendering them irrelevant and helpless in the face of change.

Designers are not the only culprits, for the representations of ageing that are most frequently presented to designers are predominantly negative, focusing on illness and the decline of capabilities. Moreover, most voluntary sector organisations emphasise the negative rather than

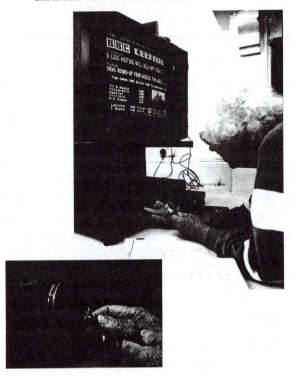

Figure 13.1 Programming the video recorder

positive aspects of old age, as their income depends on the general public's empathy for older people. Unfortunately, this emphasis on decline rather than change in capabilities leads to the association of ageing with disability and dependency. In other words, as Peter Laslett puts it, there is a tendency among experts on ageing to 'problematise the subjects of their study' through 'portrayal of their incapacities and their uselessness'. Older people tend to accept this representation 'without reference to what is objectively known about the decline of persons in their later years' (Laslett 2000, p.2). This in turn contributes to the most common problems that older people face: loss of control over one's life, loss of independence and the associated decline in self-esteem. These changes are not an inevitable consequence of old age and can happen at any age.

Both professionals and older people tend to interpret an impairment or illness fatalistically as a consequence of age, which is then 'solved' by prescribing care, an aid or an adaptation. Unfortunately, just as care is not necessarily welcomed by older people, so aids and adaptations are likely to be rejected, due to what designers call their 'product semantics' – the subtle, or in this case brazen, messages and social meanings that products carry with them and which stigmatise. A problem is not fully solved by a treatment or an aid that emphasises the illness or an incapacity. Such 'solutions' only reinforce the sense that the 'problem' originates with the person. A better approach is to address the inadequacies of their environment through alternative designs and care strategies.

A personal experience

My interest in this subject area was sparked when a friend contracted multiple sclerosis in her early thirties. After a period of decline during which she became wheelchair bound, and then relative stability, a decision was made by the local social services that she could no longer look after herself independently and should enter institutional care. She was about to lose control over her own life because of her condition, when it was her flat, and in particular the kitchen, that was the real problem. It was apparent to me that this situation could be successfully addressed by appropriate design, and that there was no reason why she should not continue to live in her own home.

This happened some two decades ago when attitudes were a little different and home modifications rarely carried out, but after some persuasion it was agreed that if the kitchen could be suitably improved then she could stay at home. With a colleague, I designed, built and installed a new kitchen and my friend subsequently lived at home for many years. However, for her, the aesthetics of the new kitchen were just as important as the ergonomics and her measure of success was that the neighbours should be jealous. She did not want a 'wheelchair' kitchen, but a stylish and functional cooking space with clever appliances, neat storage ideas and personal touches. She was not thinking about her 'disability', but about herself as an independent woman with a desirable modern kitchen.

In today's world, design is as much about desire and aspirations – things that drive purchasing decisions – as about function and price. Offering someone a 'disabled' kitchen rather than an 'enabled' kitchen presses all the wrong buttons. This is not just a question of language, but a matter of aesthetics and the subtle psychological factors that motivate and demotivate us. The situation is further complicated by notions of illness and incompetence. Just as most people over the age of 50 years have some long-sightedness and benefit from wearing glasses, so most older people have some form of arthritis, rheumatism or stiffness which affects their ability to bend, move about, grip, lift and otherwise use their bodies. If we accept, fatalistically, that this is due solely to age, and that with it comes an inevitable progression into illness, disability and dependency, then we can only be depressed by the prognosis. However, if we are offered strategies for compensation, ways of considering how best to live in the presence of that future self, then we might consider taking steps to change our lifestyles – lose some weight, take more exercise, live a more active life – and consider future-proofing our home in ways that will make it easier to use as we grow older (Fisk 1993).

My eyesight has changed considerably since I was in my twenties, but I am not appreciably hindered by those changes. Now 56 years old, I wear varifocal glasses and have done so for nine years. Being visually oriented by nature, my eyesight is very important to me. So I ensure that my glasses are properly prescribed, that they function at all distances and, as far as possible, under all conditions. I have additional glasses for working at the computer and at the drawing board, where my requirements are different. Compensatory equipment is today readily available, of high quality and likely to continue to improve. I am therefore dismayed when my friends refuse to wear glasses and generally fail to accept what is happening to them. Many do not want to admit to themselves or other people that their eyesight is changing, which they see as a sign of progressive decline, and so collude in making a problem of their sensory decrement. If my friends have problems with glasses which are marketed as fashion items, then imagine just how difficult it is for people to accept the aids and adaptive devices they are offered as a solution to 'their' problem of becoming old.

Responding to the challenge

It is important that designers understand the changes which accompany the ageing of the eye, but it is equally important that they recognise ageing as a variable, natural process and an integral part of our biological nature; and that they recognise and understand the potential for intervention through good, age-aware design, both at a personal level in improving life quality, and in the more general terms of creating an age-friendly environment. The more we understand and embrace these matters both personally and professionally, the better we will manage the transition from a young to an old society.

In *Time of Our Lives*, Tom Kirkwood reminds us, 'There is an unfortunate tendency to see the greying of the world's population as a disaster in the making instead of the twofold triumph that it really is.' He concludes: 'If it turns out now that we lack the will and strategies to accommodate the elderly people that result from these successes, and to realise their potential as a benefit not a burden, then perhaps we should seriously question whether as a species we can justly continue to conduct our affairs under the grandiose title of *Homo sapiens*' (Kirkwood 1999, p.8). Here we have the core of the case for moving beyond a problem-oriented approach to ageing at the personal, professional and political levels. If, instead of a prognosis of progressive illness, reinforced by inappropriately designed products and environments, we can offer people practical ways to promote their future well-being and support those choices with appropriately designed and attractive products and environments, then we might turn generalised alarm into manageable issues and optimistic outcomes. These are the challenges for commerce and industry, for politicians and for professionals from several disciplines.

By making it possible for people to take responsibility now for their future physical and mental condition and quality of life, we can more accurately identify the real problem as dependency, not old age, and counter that by developing strategies for maintaining and extending wellness. In addition, by reconsidering the design and management of care environments, particularly in institutional settings, we can shift the emphasis from illness to well-being and the ambience, if not the actual setting, from that of the institution to that of the private house, thereby making care and rehabilitation more welcome and more effective.

Over the past 20 years, concepts like 'inclusive design', 'universal design', 'design for all', 'trans-generational design', 'gerontechnology' and 'new design for old' have emerged on both sides of the Atlantic to include the needs of older and differently abled people in mainstream design (Coleman 1993; Kose 1999; Ostroff and Preiser 2001; Reents 1997). Such design approaches are now taking root in Japan and Australia and, in conjunction with a growing interest in wellness among both health care professionals and older people themselves, constitute a positive and life-enhancing response to population ageing. All these approaches are essentially inclusive and challenge the prevailing idea that older people have 'special' needs which require 'special' aids and adaptations. To date, the major achievement of these new design approaches, particularly in the USA, has been to reinforce the anti-discrimination legislation concerning the access of disabled people to the built environment with changed planning and building codes and the spread of 'access audits'. These are having a profound effect on the design of public buildings and spaces, recreational areas and leisure facilities. Legislation and design practice can develop hand in hand to remove progressively more obstacles to people's freedom of movement, and through the adoption of international standards can diffuse the benefits to more and more parts of the world – to the great benefit of older people.

Such legislation will not however deliver equivalent changes in mainstream products and services. Without unacceptably coercive legislation, in these fields the driving force for desirable change has to be the market and the mechanism a myriad of compelling business cases selecting commercially viable opportunities. At present many of the market forces are working in the opposite direction: one might say that there is a vicious circle obstructing the development of a healthy market for life-enhancing products and services. The foremost problem, I believe, is that people are insufficiently informed as consumers. Under the current model, as suggested above, we tend to wait until an individual has a problem (for example, their arthritis makes it no longer possible for them to cook for themselves), at which point a care professional recommends kitchen aids and adaptive devices available through specialist catalogues, advice centres or suppliers. Not only does this reinforce the user's sense of incapacity, but the market volume is minimised, and hence the profitability of such products is small. Were people more fully informed of what is available and what might be suitable for them, were that advice readily accessible before rather than after the event, and were those products on the open market, then the pressures would work in the opposite direction; to reduce the price while increasing quality, turnover and profitability. This would encourage greater investment in design and innovation.

So long as supportive products are obliged to fit within the specific niches created by welfare legislation and statutory provision, then the achieved market volume will be inevitably small. The net result is low investment in design (as this has to be paid for out of sales revenue), a downward pressure on prices, which with small turnovers can only be achieved by cutting quality, and a stigmatising of the user by association with the way the device is described and distributed. Even such technicalities of a product as whether or not a professional carer must advise or assist, whether or not it is supplied through the health or welfare system, and whether or not a sales (value-added) tax is charged, can have more influence than its function on how it is described, marketed, used and perceived. Once a product becomes associated with being sick or disabled, its presence is seen and experienced as stigmatising (Mandelstam 1997).

Another factor, of which I have personal experience, is that manufacturers can become comfortable with working in specialist prosthetic niches, as they enable business with a limited number of well-known and secure clients and reduce exposure to competition. They then have little incentive to expand into other markets, not least export markets with their immense variation in the ways that products are sold and distributed. Some years ago my own company developed and licensed a component-based product for the education sector. This was of particular value to children with various disablements, but was attractive, highly functional and also suitable for children who were not disabled. It was considerably cheaper than similar products because it was highly adaptable and it replaced imported products that were more specific in application. The product had considerable export potential, but the company producing it had neither experience nor aspirations that extended much beyond its small but captive British niche. The fault lay not in the company but in a system of supply and distribution which could not deliver products to the people who would benefit from them. These will become more important issues as a single European market evolves, because greater sales and changing manufacturing processes will mean that products once treated as 'special' will be mass produced. Person-specific versions could also be produced at a reasonable price, given adequate investment in production technology.[3]

Reaping the rewards

Harmonising on a European scale the provision of 'technical aids' and 'assistive devices' and exploring new opportunities for life-enhancing products and services could stimulate a true consumer market in 'enabling' products that achieve levels of turnover and profitability sufficient to encourage further innovation and investment in good design. I believe these opportunities can be broken down into three categories or 'product sectors', which I have described elsewhere but which it is useful to recount (Coleman 1999a). The first set of opportunities lies in 'mainstream' markets, all those goods and services that are marketed to the population as a whole by all manner of outlets from retail chains to restaurants and magazines: cars, air travel, home and garden products, leisure activities, entertainment and holidays. 'User-aware' design can remove environmental obstacles and encourage the participation of people of all ages and abilities in everyday activities, while 'inclusive design' has a similar role to play in making everyday objects age-friendly – for example, packaging that can be opened without using a knife; chairs that are easy to get in and out of; clothing that is light, warm, easy to put on and clean, while elegant and good looking; signage and information graphics that are clear and readable; and controls that are simple to understand and operate. These features broaden the appeal of such goods and make life better for all who use them, not just older people.

The second opportunity lies in 'niche' products and services for older people that are positive and non-patronising: insurance policies for those aged 50 plus, activity holidays, adaptable housing and internet services. As an example, the bulk of the do-it-yourself and interior decor markets are targeted at young householders, when many older people would be well advised to make changes to their homes that will help them live independently. There are already some excellent household products on the market and there is considerable scope for developing more and better products that can make a positive contribution to active lifestyles and independence. Unfortunately, most people are unaware of what products are available and do not realise how they could improve and 'future-proof' their homes with good, age-friendly interior design.

Third, there is a growing market for 'enabling' products and services that address the needs of older people who are disabled or require regular or full-time care, such as information technology interfaces and communication systems for all manner of applications, from home-delivered services to institutional care. At present, this market sector is seriously underdeveloped, but the manufacturers which succeed in the expanding European market will do very well. In particular, those that invest in good design and seek to break the prevailing institutional mould will find that their products and services have a broader appeal and higher sales.

Inclusive design

None of these three product sectors has been fully developed, and considerable commercial opportunities exist for those companies that offer the required goods and services. That this challenge is approachable through good design can be readily demonstrated in each of the sectors. First, among 'mainstream' products there have recently been considerable advances in packaging design. Among other innovations, there is the flip-top toothpaste tube which, with the electric toothbrush, makes effective dental hygiene possible for a much wider group of people than the traditional designs (Figure 13.2). Such design is 'inclusive' because it obviates the need for special products. A further example is the cordless kettle, which is useable by those who find unplugging and reconnecting a corded kettle difficult or impossible.

Figure 13.2 Flip-top toothpaste tube

A good example of the potential of skilful design to shift a product from the specialist 'enabling' to the 'mainstream' category is the Good Grips™ range of kitchen ware, developed and distributed by Sam Farber (Coleman 1999b). Sam's wife, Betsy, suffered from arthritis and was having difficulty cooking, which she enjoyed. Sam had made money from his previous kitchen equipment business, COPCO, and felt that he of all people could and should do something about Betsy's frustrating condition. Sam's sales and marketing skills and experience had taught him that good design adds value to a product, so he briefed a leading New York design company, Smart Design, to produce a high quality, mass market product range that works well and would appeal to people of all ages and abilities. The result of that collaboration is now widely on sale in high street kitchen shops, supermarkets and from kitchenware catalogues (Figure 13.3).

A key feature of the products is the large diameter Santoprene® rubber handle. These handles are non-slip, easy to hold and soft to the hand. The shape of the handle maximises the gripping surface and so minimises the effort and joint flexing required. Top chefs and television cooks use Good Grips™. They are modestly priced, available to all and

Figure 13.3 Good Grips^{TM} grater

come not with stigma but with style built in. The rapid sales growth in the UK and Europe confirms the substantial market for age- and ability-friendly products if the design is of high quality, and if the special features are skilfully promoted for all. More and more of such products are seen by retailers as items that sell well. In a recent kitchenware catalogue, not only is the Good Grips™ potato peeler 'back by popular demand', but many reputable manufacturers' products emphasise ease-of-use features such as 'comfort grips' or 'comfortable soft touch handles'. There is even a copycat handle on one of the featured new products, demonstrating how great is the demand for appropriate, non-stigmatising cooking equipment (Figure 13.4).

In terms of age-friendly 'niche' products and services, the financial services and holiday sectors have been most successfully developed. Saga Holidays have the lead, but there are many other business opportunities in helping older people identify appropriate goods and services, tracking them down, vetting and offering them with supportive and non-patronising advice. In the past such services if available at all have been provided by the health and social services and voluntary organisations, but usually after the support need has arisen, with all the negative connotations which have been described. What is required is advice and promotion before the need arises and which helps people 'future-proof' their homes and environments.

Figure 13.4 Good Grips™ gardening tools

Education and information

Young designers tend to design for themselves rather than the population as a whole and it is difficult to interest them in older people. At the Royal College of Art (RCA) in London, we use the concept of 'designing for our future selves' as a way of encouraging students to think of their own future needs, to design for the entire lifespan, and to recognise older people as simply themselves in the future rather than another species. This approach is based on Peter Laslett's concept of thinking 'processionally', or of 'living in the presence of all our future selves' (Laslett 1996 pp.ix and 7).

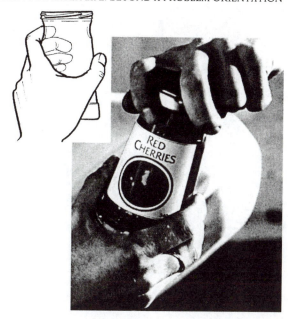

Figure 13.5 RSA student design award winner: Gavin Pryke – a jar we can open

The results of the last five annual DesignAge competitions held at the RCA, and of the New Design for Old section in the Royal Society of Arts student design awards (Figure 13.5), demonstrate the range of opportunities for business and design that emerge from an age-aware approach (Coleman 1996; Myerson 1999). At the RCA, with support from The Lifespan Trust, we have been exploring home 'improvement' for older people as an alternative to 'adaptation'. It involves interviewing older people, surveying their kitchens and bathrooms to identify potential problems and hazards, discussing how they would like to see them improved and offering age- and ability-friendly product options and design advice (Figure 13.6). The results have featured in *Goodtimes* (February–March and April–May 1999), a magazine targeted at retired people, in the BBC's *Good Homes* magazine (July 1999, March 2000) and on the BBC2 'Home Front' programme (9 June 1999, 10 November 1999), thereby capturing an audience of over four million people. The response has been sufficiently positive to convince us that there is a potentially substantial home improvement market, equivalent to the young adult market targeted by many interior design, home improvement and do-it-yourself magazines and retailers.

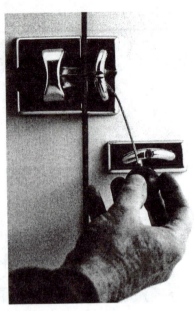

Figure 13.6 RSA student design award: Sally Muddell – finger-friendly door security

Expanding this market could go a long way to extending people's independence in later life, but part of the problem is the lack of appropriate
advice and information about existing products. The Consumers' Association has moved in this direction, by involving the Research Institute
for Consumer Affairs (now RICAbility) and its panel of older and
disabled people in usability testing of household and consumer
products, and by publishing the results in *Which?* magazine. Still
lacking is a ready source of information for older people about positive
lifestyle products like holidays and financial services, and those that
deal with the more private and hitherto stigmatised aspects of growing
older – the stairlifts and incontinence pads. Many of the titles now
aimed at the retired population carry 'aids' advertisements, but do so
reluctantly because, while income generating and useful to some
readers, they are a turn-off for others. This ambivalence is due to the
magazine format and the fact that such titles are aimed at a very broad
age range.

Electronic magazines can avoid this sort of conflict by tailoring their
pages to the individual reader, and so offer information and advice

about niche lifestyle and personal products. ThirdAge.com in the USA has made considerable progress in this direction in little more than a few months and is already a very valuable business (Friedman and Langlinais 1999). A similar Internet site has recently been launched in Britain and there are likely to be more, driven by the move to digital TV and its convergence with the Internet. If these developments genuinely help older people manage their lives and remain in control, then their impact should be significant, especially if they feed back consumer needs to suppliers in ways that help improve quality and availability while keeping prices under control. This would create a virtuous circle of raised consumer awareness and increased sales.

A domestic aesthetic

In the care or 'enabling' sector, two products encouragingly exemplify a shift from institutional to domestic references, not just in styling but in 'product semantics'. John Miller designed and now manufactures the Comfacto bed (Figure 13.7), which combines electronically controlled functionality with add-on elements including a ladder-like attachment that allows people with limited strength in their lower limbs to lift their legs progressively into bed (Coleman 1997, pp.124–125). The use of timber and attention to detail effectively conceals the working parts of the bed and offers high functionality combined with a domestic aesthetic.

This same combination is displayed by a range of bedroom and living room furniture produced originally by the German company Bisterfeld und Weiss (B+W), which is now owned by the leading Dutch care-sector furniture manufacturer, Kembo. Recognising that there was very little attractive yet ergonomically functional furniture available for physically impaired older people, B+W identified market opportunities in both private homes and institutions. The company first developed an easychair, with a footrest, arms that fold down to make it easier to get in and out of, and a side-panel-cum-pocket for personal items (Figure 13.8). This chair preserved the high quality detailing of their contract furniture range and included features to improve comfort, especially for people who spend most of their day sitting in the same place, making it ideal for institutional settings.

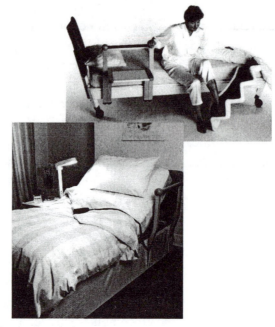

Figure 13.7 The Comfacto bed

The designer, Arno Votteler, wanted to develop a range of furniture which functions well for older people and which, by having thoroughly domestic appearance and styling, conveys no hint of the stigma of furniture specifically for 'the elderly and disabled' (Figure 13.9). The

Figure 13.8 B+W easychair

overall concept was to produce all the elements – tables, chairs, cupboards – to create an attractive personal environment, especially for people who live predominantly in one room, and to bring the warmth and taste of the home into institutional settings and sheltered housing. Design and development were carried out over two years with professional ergonomic advice and all items were given practical tests in

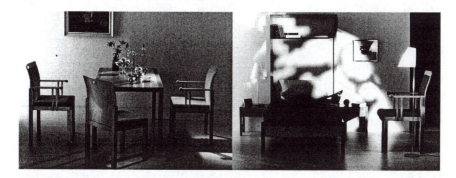

Figure 13.9 B+W range of 'domestic' style furniture

hospitals and comparable settings and user tested for functionality and acceptability. The appearance of the furniture is restful and careful attention has been given to the hygiene issues which are important for care managers (Figure 13.10). Styling and detailing are co-ordinated to offer in combination durability, functionality, appearance and value, the preconditions for volume production and a good market share (Coleman 1999b).

Figure 13.10 B+W chairs from the 'domestic' range

In conclusion

To respond to the growing number of older people, the research and design communities have an alternative: either to focus on declines and deficits in people's performance and capabilities on the presumption that societal ageing leads inexorably to more dependency and an escalation of the associated social and economic costs; or to work from a model which promises the possibility of extended activity and independence through a constructive focus on capabilities, adaptability and enhancing performance. Choosing the latter would make a valuable contribution to the containment of the social and economic costs of a growing number of older people. There is a developing consensus that the independence model is preferable, but its pursuit raises the problem of how to promote, on the one hand, supportive, life-enhancing and non-stigmatising design for the mass market – the inclusive design approach – and, on the other hand, how to deliver the more specialised and customised goods and services that will enable independence well into old age and displace institutional care into the domestic setting.

The current shift in consumer markets from 'products' to 'services' offers potential for implementing the independence model. For example, mobile phones are increasingly sold as part of a package which offers mobile communication on demand (that is, a service rather than a product). Targeted products and services are being developed that offer style and status to young people, flexibility and functionality to the business community and confidence and contact to older people and their families and carers. Vibrating phones are available that are both unobtrusive in business meetings and a boon to people with hearing loss, and we can look forward to other products which offer personalised functionality and interfaces to a wider and wider range of services (Brouwer-Janse et al. 1997). In addition, built-in intelligence in products and the built environment offers such possibilities as packaging that warns if the contents are out of date, cookers that switch off a ring left on by accident, and lights that turn on when someone gets out of bed at night. Health care insurers could exploit these developments through innovative services that help and encourage people to take advantage of the heightened capabilities they bring, thereby extending independence and reducing the likelihood and cost of institutional care.

The obstacles can be surmounted, given the will, appropriate information and commercial incentives. We must first overcome the lack of accurate information about the nature and range of capabilities and impairments in the population as a whole, for its absence means that design managers in large companies are unable to present to their directors a convincing case for an inclusive design approach. Second, the fact that design teams and individual designers lack an understanding of the impact of disease and age-related impairments on substantial sectors of the population must be counteracted. Third, we must correct the bias in ergonomic data which was initially gathered primarily for military applications and then extended to around 90 per cent of the population but does not adequately represent the older age groups or disabled people.[4]

There is therefore an urgent need to gather data on age-related disease, impairment and associated changes in capabilities, and to interpret these in ways that are accessible to commercial decision makers and the design profession. There is also a need to bring that knowledge and an understanding of appropriate design responses into design education and training. The vision is to establish a virtuous circle which leads better informed companies to identify opportunities to extend their markets; encourages design teams to understand the needs and capabilities of older people and to create better products; promotes greater independence among older people; stimulates competition within the market; and leads to better designed and more affordable goods and services. By replacing the stigmatising aids and adaptations of the past with attractive and 'inclusive' products, we can normalise or de-problematise situations and conditions previously associated with dependency.

As the professional field of service design opens up, particularly in telecommunications, multidisciplinary teams are working in a seamless way on concepts for services that integrate products and interactions with and between users. One can envisage the provision of health and social care in a similar way, both in the community and in traditional hospital and nursing home settings. More positive enabling approaches will make it possible to reconstruct care as a range of services that is designed with attention to the users' needs and perspectives. Here there are exciting opportunities for new collaborations between industry, designers, gerontologists and other researchers, as they explore alternatives to current models of care, and develop the innovative products and services to deliver them (Figure 13.11).

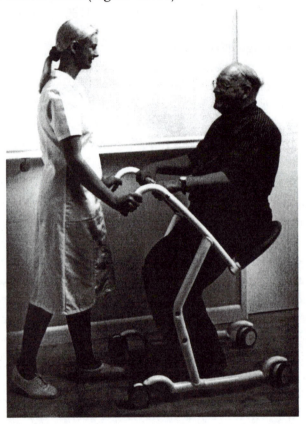

Figure 13.11 The 'Stedy', by RCA Industrial Design Engineering (IDE) student Etienne Iliffe-Moon, now in production by Arjo Ltd of Gloucester

As an example of what can be achieved, at the Helen Hamlyn Research Centre based at the RCA, Dan Plant, a recent masters graduate in industrial design engineering, has been working on protective clothing by integrating fabrics with a polymer that hardens rapidly on impact. To be successful this programme will require the involvement of specialists from several disciplines, including gerontology. It aims to deliver body protection for various users including those engaged in sports and recreational activities, the security services and others exposed to violent attack, and to open up new possibilities for the care of older people (and others) vulnerable to falls. By enabling independence and improving life quality, 'inclusive' design has the potential to serve as a care and support service for older people and makes it possible for them to take control of and contribute to their personal well-being. In addition, giving more attention to the 'design' of services raises the potential for extending independence and de-institutionalising the context of care, for it will enhance the quality and acceptability of care provision in many contexts, from community support, through sheltered housing, to the specialist fields of rehabilitation and dementia.

Notes

1. Over the past ten years there has been a marked and welcome shift in the terms used in book titles, e.g. from *Designing Kitchens for the Elderly and Disabled* (Fleetwood 1990), through *Design Guidelines for Elderly and Disabled Persons* (Juul-Andersen and Jensen 1997), to the non-stigmatising *The Design of Home Appliances for Young and Old Consumers* (Freudenthal 1999).

2. British and European responses are gathering pace, as exemplified by the establishment of the Design for Living Taskforce which reports to the UK Office of Science and Technology's Foresight 'Ageing Population' Panel; and the cross-platform theme, 'Design for all for an inclusive information society', of the European Union's Fifth Framework for research and development.

3. In the USA there is evidence of a growing awareness of the market potential of products targeted at older and disabled people, including home modifications loans (see 'People with Disabilities are Next Consumer Niche', *Wall Street Journal*, 15 December 1999).

4. This situation is being addressed through a series of Department of Trade and Industry (DTI) publications that considerably extend the range of population groups for whom up-to-date ergonomic data are available (Norris and Peebles 1998, 2000).

References

Brouwer-Janse, M.D., Coleman, R., Fulton-Suri, J.L., Fozard, J., de Vries, G. and Yawitz, M. (1997) 'User Interfaces for Young and Old.' *Interactions 4*, 2, 34–46.

Coleman, R. (1993) *Designing for Our Future Selves*. London: Royal College of Art.

Coleman, R. (ed) (1996) *10 years of RSA New Design for Old*. London: Royal Society for the Encouragement of Arts, Manufactures and Commerce.

Coleman, R. (ed) (1997) *Design für die Zukunft*. Cologne: DuMont Buchverlag.

Coleman, R. (1999a) 'Ageing Populations: Challenges and Opportunities for Design and Industry.' In W.S. Green and P.W. Jordan (eds) *Human Factors in Product Design: Current Practice and Future Trends*. London: Taylor & Francis.

Coleman, R. (1999b) 'What Design Can Do.' In J. Peto (ed) *Design Process: Progress Practice*. London: Design Museum.

Fisk, J. (1993) 'Design for the Elderly: A Biological Perspective.' *Applied Ergonomics 24*, 2, 47–50.

Fleetwood, H. (1990) *Designing Kitchens for the Elderly and Disabled*. Ormskirk: Thomas Lyster.

Freudenthal, A. (1999) *The Design of Home Applicances for Young and Old Consumers*. Ageing and Ergonomics Series no. 2. Delft: Delft University Press.

Friedman, J.P. and Langlinais, T.C. (1999) 'Best Intentions: A Business Model for the Economy.' *Outlook 1*, 34–41.

Juul-Andersen, K. and Jensen, E.M. (1997) *Design Guidelines for Elderly and Disabled Persons*. Taastrup: Danish Centre for Technical Aids for Rehabilitation and Education.

Kirkwood, T. (1999) *Time of Our Lives: The Science of Human Ageing*. London: Weidenfeld & Nicolson.

Kose, S. (ed) (1999) *Design for the 21st Century: An International Conference on Universal Design*. Tokyo: Toshi Bunka Sha. (In Japanese.)

Laslett, P. (1996) *A Fresh Map of Life: The Emergence of the Third Age*, 2nd edn. London: Weidenfeld & Nicolson.

Laslett, P. (2000) 'The "Problem of Old Age": Let Older People Speak for Themselves.' Unpublished manifesto.

Mandelstam, M. (1997) 'What's in a Name? Disability Aids and Assistive Equipment.' In R. Coleman (ed) *Design für die Zukunft*. Cologne: DuMont Buchverlag. (In German.)

Myerson, J. (ed) (1999) *Design for Our Future Selves*. London: Helen Hamlyn Research Centre.

Norris, B. and Peebles, L. (1998) *Adult Data: The Handbook of Adult Anthropometric and Strength Measurements – Data for Design Safety*. London: Department of Trade and Industry.

Norris, B. and Peebles, L. (2000) *Older Adult Data: The Handbook of Measurements and Capabilities of Older Adults – Data for Design Safety*. London: Department of Trade and Industry.

Ostroff, E. and Preiser, W. (eds) (2001) *Universal Design Handbook*. New York: McGraw-Hill.

Reents, H. (1997) *Handbuch der Gerontechnik*, 2nd edn. Landsberg: Ecomed-Verlagsgesellschaft.

CHAPTER 14

Older People, Telematics and Care

Josephine Tetley, Elizabeth Hanson and Amanda Clarke

Technological innovation and the caring services

As the number of health and social care professionals working in the care services reduces across Europe and the USA, interest in the use of innovations such as telemedicine and telecare has increased (Shortliffe 1998; Strode, Gustke and Allen 1999; Wootton *et al.* 1998). While the use of technology within society and health care is increasing, the notion of providing support and advice using technology in place of, or even in conjunction with, 'hands-on' contact remains controversial, with concerns being expressed that the quality of care delivered may be reduced. At the same time, the increased use of personal computers in the home and at work has improved the lay person's access to health care information which, in turn, has led to concerns that technology may increase people's expectations to a level that care providers are unable to meet. This chapter therefore explores to what extent new technology can be used to improve the quality of life and everyday experiences of frail older people and their family carers taking into account the following issues:

- the pressures for technological development within care

- the role of patients and clients in the development of new technology

- user acceptance of new technology
- the extent to which technology affects the quality of life
- the role of technology in improving access to services and information
- access to new technology and the cost of equipment.

Over the last twenty years health care has seen the rapid adoption of new technologies not only in biomedical applications but also in computerised information systems for care planning and records, routine data collection, and the transmission of laboratory test results to practitioners. There can be little doubt that scientists and practitioners have driven much of this development. While there may be benefits for patients, the development of expensive technology for diagnoses and treatment, rather than for prevention and management, is arguably not always the best solution for improving the health of individuals or society (Le Fanu 1999). Moreover, there are concerns that new developments such as telemedicine and telecare will also be developed more by professionals to drive forward biomedical boundaries, rather than to inform, educate and support individuals (Shortliffe 1998). The last few years have, however, seen increased calls for new and familiar technology to be used to improve public access to education, information and support, not least to avert hospital admissions and reduce the use of other high cost medical interventions (DoH 1998, 1999; Hanson, Tetley and Clarke 1999; Rogers, Entwistle and Pencheon 1998; Rogers, Flowers and Pencheon 1999).

The ACTION project

Considering the value and limitations of technology in everyday caring contexts, this chapter draws on examples from a multi-centre European gerontechnology project, 'Assisting carers using telematics interventions to meet older persons' needs', known for short as ACTION. This is a 36-month project funded by the European Union (EU) programme, Telematics for the Integration of Disabled and Elderly People (TIDE). This is the largest nurse-led project to have received funding from the EU and involves partners from England, Northern Ireland, Republic of

Ireland, Sweden and Portugal. It should be noted that the primary aim of the project was to explore to what extent the autonomy, independence and quality of life of frail older and disabled people and their family carers could be maintained or enhanced with the combined use of new and familiar technology (Magnusson *et al.* 1998). The ACTION project examined responses to a particular combination of devices: a video-phone, a television and remote control connected to a video-conferencing system and a networked computer. The video-phone enabled the carers and frail older people who took part in the project to have face-to-face contact with other family carers and older people and with health and social care workers. The system also provided access to various multimedia programmes that were created by the project partners. The chapter draws mainly from the authors' own research conducted in Sheffield but where appropriate draws on data generated by our European partners.

A clear preliminary finding from phase one of the ACTION project was the need for improved access to information. Family carers said that they often received information from other family carers, but that this was not always up to date and its availability and receipt were uncertain. It was often only 'in an emergency' that carers found out about useful services such as respite care, and that 'some carers [were] unknown to professionals until a crisis occur[red]'. In response to such vagaries, the British government has recognised the role of telephone helplines by introducing NHS Direct and is promoting the use of the Internet. Moreover, the National Health Service Information for Health Strategy argues that a well-informed public, by having increased autonomy and control over their lives and more choice, will make more appropriate and selective use of services and that this will lead to a reduction in the burden of inappropriate calls on the service (Burns 1998, p.81). The strategy further proclaims:

> The latest information technology presents huge opportunities to improve the quality and accessibility of health services to patients. The government is determined that new information strategies should be a vehicle for improving the way NHS services are delivered, making them more responsive to patients' needs. Improving the quality and range of information available to patients

and the public about health and health services will be equally important. (Burns 1998, p.79)

In addition to the use of technology in health and social care, it is increasingly used for everyday tasks such as paying bills, banking transactions and food shopping (Ballabio and Moran 1998; Czaja and Sharit 1998). It can therefore be argued that the use of the new information technologies is becoming essential and that the non-inclusion of older people, whether at the design stage, in training or product promotions, will limit their ability to be fully participative citizens. Cowan and Turner-Smith (1999) stress the importance of consultation and partnership and argue that if health sector technology is to address quality of life issues, it must take on board much more than health care applications. The ACTION project therefore consulted with carers and older people about their perceived needs for support and services and involved them in the development of the ACTION system and its multimedia programmes.

Development of new technology

During the first phase of the study, in the five participating European countries focus group discussions were conducted with: family carers (most of whom were aged over 65 years); professional carers from various health and social care services; and individuals who work with the users of private and voluntary organisation services. The aim of the focus groups was to identify the key issues that affected the carers of frail older people. After the focus groups, questionnaires were distributed to the family carers and local user groups were established to continue the consultation process as well as to research and develop the technological applications. Throughout the project, carers and older people were consulted. The family carers, older people and user representatives were recruited in Sheffield through the Alzheimer's Disease Society, the local carers' centre, two sitting services for family carers, an NHS hospital trust, a family doctors' practice and social service providers. We endeavoured to recruit recently engaged and long-established carers and carers from ethnic minority communities. The professional carers included nurses, doctors, physiotherapists, social workers and welfare rights officers. We acknowledge that in this initial stage we did not identify 'hidden' carers unknown to service providers.

During the development and evaluation of the technology and multimedia programmes, the consultation process followed a user-centred iterative approach which requires the designers of technology to recognise that:

- product specification is not an abstract exercise and many requirements emerge out of the direct experience of using prototypes

- in many cases developers may have to enter iterative cycles of development and evaluation before a satisfactory solution is achieved

- it is important to obtain good feedback about product performance in actual use. (Poulson, Ashby and Richardson 1996)

The aspiration of this user-centred approach was for enhanced access to education, information and support in a format that could easily be used by family carers and older people in diverse community and institutional settings (Berthold 1997; Clarke *et al.* 1999; Tetley and Bradshaw 1998). To test this premise, the ACTION system was installed in several locations in Sheffield. Site one was a social services neighbourhood centre that provides day care and support for carers and older people. Site two was a hospital-based unit for older people, most being physically and cognitively frail and waiting transfer to a continuing care placement such as a nursing or residential home. The third site was a medical centre. At all three the intention was that family carers and older people could 'drop in'. In addition, three family carers who were registered at the medical centre agreed to have the ACTION system in their home. Using high-speed telephone lines it was possible for family and professional carers to link to any of the sites through the video-phone.

User acceptance of new technology in care

At the start of the project, we were aware of a widespread presumption that older people would not use a system of the kind proposed simply because it was new technology. Our early findings did indeed show that family carers across Europe were worried about the use of modern technology, and that many had no previous experience of using a personal computer (Tetley *et al.* 1997). On the other hand, most carers were familiar with other electronic innovations such as compact disc players and microwaves and most had used television remote controls. To enable older people and carers with limited experience of the new information technologies to have the confidence to learn the required new skills, using the television (the most familiar technology) as the information interface was seen as the best way of easing the transition between established and new technology. During the development of the ACTION system, usability was tested at the university by carers and older people (Clarke *et al.* 1999). Feedback from the user trials indicated that there were ways in which the system and the information content could be improved. Some users felt that the remote control handset was too small; while others wanted more information about the financial benefits or costs of services. Some also felt that a few of the terms needed to be simplified or explained; for example, palliative care and reminiscence therapy. Although the usability trials indicated areas for improvement, we were encouraged to find that our informants could easily use the equipment and operate the programmes.

At one stage, four family carers aged from 45 to 85 years took part in conference video-phone links with project partners in Barcelona. Their successful participation supports the argument of Thursz, Nusberg and Prather (1995) that older people have witnessed and adapted to many new technologies throughout their lifetimes and therefore no intrinsic incompatibility exists between advanced age and learning to use new devices. It must, however, be recognised that the ACTION project was not open-endedly exploring the use of technology by carers and older people but specifically its application to care. It could not be assumed that a generally positive attitude to technology would prevail in the caring situation. Indeed, during the first phase of testing, one carer requested that the equipment be removed from her home as it provided a constant reminder of the intimate caring tasks which she performed. She found the system an eyesore and its presence in her home distasteful (Hanson and Clarke 2000). By contrast, another informant carer invited the neighbours in to admire the system, suggesting a positive attitude and possibly even pride as a pioneer innovator – analogous to being the first person in a neighbourhood to possess a car or television set.

The Royal Commission on Funding Long-Term Care recognised that 'users (and their carers) will most readily use technology that is desirable because it enhances their social status as well as enabling them to do things or making them feel better' (Cowan and Turner-Smith 1999, p.335). In sum there are diverse influences upon and reactions to new technology. While our primary research interest was in the response of older people and family carers, we were aware of the need to explore the attitudes and experiences of professional care workers in using new technology and that, because professional carers act as 'gate-keepers' to services and resources, it is important to recognise that they must have a positive attitude to technology if they are to encourage older people to adopt the innovation (Barnes 1997; Barron 1996; Rogers and Elliot 1997).

As the project developed and the prototype multimedia programmes were tested, there was considerable positive feedback. Some 347 professional carers from the five participating European countries completed usability questionnaires and filled in log-diaries. These enabled users to write down what they had found helpful or unhelpful about the programmes, the remote control and the video-phone. The professional carers generally felt that the videos were beneficial. One said, 'I think that having the videos and photos is excellent. They would be good for patients to watch when choosing nursing homes'. Another said that she liked the videos and felt that they were suitable for people who could not read well. The ACTION system comprises eight multimedia programmes and a video-phone. The professional carers suggested that a different coloured background for each of the programmes would make it easier for users to navigate through the system. Nevertheless, negative attitudes persisted and in the later phase of the study some professional carers in Sheffield were still concerned that older people would not use the system because it was computer operated. One commented that, 'Older people...tend to say, "Oh no! I'm not going to use it. I know you've simplified it, but it's still difficult for us that haven't used a computer before to take it on board"'.

This was not, however, borne out by our tests of the system. In the first phase of field testing at the five centres, 217 evaluations were completed by family carers and older people. The ages of the older people using the system ranged from 56 to 101 years, while the carers and relatives were aged 19 to 88 years. The majority of the participants reported that using the system was easy. The two oldest users, aged 91 and 101 years, reported that using the system was difficult. Both were visually impaired and one had difficulty with fine motor skills. Although from a relatively small number of informants, these findings indicate that the prototype system could be developed to enhance its usability for frail older people. We are now looking for remote controls with larger buttons and are making 'voice-overs' of the text on each page.

The field testing produced other evidence of the value of the system to the end users. In the hospital setting, neighbourhood centre and the medical centre the use of the system was casual. Older people involved in this way said that the programmes were 'good for providing informa-tion' – they found the information about the shopping service particu-larly useful. One family carer described the system as being 'very user friendly'. He said that it 'certainly, save[d] time rather than endless visits and phone calls to agencies. The actual in-depth information about the homes [was] very useful.'

Technology, individual needs and quality of life

A case study

It is important to recognise that a good quality of life encompasses many things and not solely aspects of health. Thus any initiative that aims to address the quality of life should consider ways of exploring and meeting needs holistically (Cowan and Turner-Smith 1999). The potential value of the ACTION system for enhancing the quality of life can be illustrated by the case of John and Olive, who had the system in their home for several months.

John, an older man with several physical health problems, cared for his wife Olive who had dementia. He had thought about the possibility of arranging respite care for his wife before looking at the programmes on the system. John had tried to encourage Olive to view a video entitled *A Short Break in a Nursing Home*. Unfortunately Olive become angry and said, 'I'm not going into one of those.' John reported in his log-diary that he had again encouraged his wife to look at the respite care videos. John was surprised to find that they then captured her interest and that afterwards she said that she would like to go into a nursing or residential home for respite. They used the programme to find a nursing home that they both liked and was near to their home (Hanson and Clarke 2000).

Pescosolido and Boyer (1996) make the point that use of a service is never a single 'yes/no' decision, rather one based on patterns and pathways. In this instance the ACTION system enabled John and Olive to access the information on more than one occasion. They were able to reconsider the merits of a service as their caring situation changed. The flexible timing of the decision to access respite care was of particular advantage to John, Olive and their family because during the field testing John had to go into hospital for a minor operation. Olive used the respite care service while he was away. Her family doctor later told the research team that he had spoken to Olive and she had thoroughly enjoyed her stay. This prevented a crisis in care for all concerned. The video-phone was also helpful to John and Olive. John used it to consult a welfare rights officer who was able to assess the home situation and answer John's questions regarding council tax benefit. When subsequently John had his rentbook to hand, he was able to supply the officer with the information he sought. The welfare rights officer was also able to observe John and Olive helping one another, so confirming their mutual caring situation. Following the video-phone consultation, a home visit was arranged to process the paperwork. The result was that the couple were £62 per week better off. The welfare rights officer was surprised to find that John and Olive were underclaiming to such an extent (and added that the circumstances were untypical of most welfare rights assessments).

Several aspects of this caring situation case suggest, however, that John and Olive represent many similar couples. Their case illustrates the strengths of technological innovations in supporting older carers and care recipients. While many fear that technology will replace face-to-face contacts, in this case the welfare rights officer stated that the video-conference was more appropriate than a telephone consultation or an appointment at the welfare rights office because it enabled a better assessment of John and Olive's situation. For John, who was unable to leave Olive alone in the house, it was the only way in which he could access this information. Other factors may have contributed to John not having sought welfare rights advice earlier. Their family doctor had previously advised the couple on welfare rights and thought that they were claiming the full range of benefits to which they were entitled. Parallels can be drawn with the work of Rogers, Hassell and Nicolass (1999), who found that primary health care staff often act as gatekeepers to secondary services. The assessing officer further acknowledged that John and Olive had 'fallen through the net', as they were unknown to social services. If John and Olive had ever sought help, part of the assessment would have included a welfare rights assessment.

The case study of John and Olive demonstrates how technology can contribute to the empowerment of older people as well as improve their quality of life. With the back-payment of the previously unclaimed benefits, they were able to go on holiday. We recognise that quality of life is a broad concept and that ACTION has largely focused on the health domains. Feedback from carers to date reveals that in order to enhance other aspects of the quality of life we need to develop the system by including information and guidance on housing, leisure, culture and transport, services and opportunities.

Information, technology and empowerment

Reforms in the provision of community care services during the 1990s emphasised providing people with services that meet their individual needs (Barnes 1997; Tinker 1997). It has been argued, however, that many carers and older people are actually disempowered in the assessment process for they have little knowledge of the full range of available services, of the financial contribution they may have to make, or the ways in which they can influence the services they receive (DoH 1998; Tinker 1997). Moreover, improving access to local services is not straightforward. During the development of the ACTION system, concerns were expressed by formal care providers that increased knowledge can cause difficulties as the demands for services and people's expectations may be raised to levels which they are unable to meet.

Barnes (1997) observes that those undertaking community care assessments are often caught between calls for the provision of needs-led services and their responsibilities 'as a gatekeeper to public resources'. Rogers and Elliot (1997) also suggest that many primary care professionals are concerned about growing workloads and patients' rising expectations, and tend to see 'demand' and 'need' as dissociated. While we are sensitive to concerns voiced during the consultation process (particularly about raising expectations and user acceptance of new technology), we also recognise that a failure to improve access to information and services for carers and older people inhibits their abilities to judge which services are most appropriate for their situation. This view is supported by Rogers *et al.* (1998), who argue that information has an important role in helping people consider how best to help themselves. Rogers and Elliot (1997) further propound the idea that the provision of information is essential if patients are to become both active participants in their care and able to make informed decisions.

The ACTION system has offered information about services using video, text and photographs with the intention of supplying a full picture of what is available. This does not necessarily lead to increased demand, but rather the aim is to provide a tool for carers and older people to think more clearly about their needs and how best to meet them. Thus, ACTION can begin to help people have more say about what they do and do not want in their caring situation. It is emphasised that the ACTION system provides information about the services offered by many statutory, voluntary and independent health and social care providers. The value of an integrated information system has been emphasised by Rogers *et al.* (1999a), who found that it enables people to help themselves and manage their progress through health and social care systems without putting overwhelming strains on those services. For example, most carers and older people in the hospital used the system to help them manage the transition between home, hospital and the entry into long-term care facilities such as nursing homes.

The programmes enhanced the hospital's discharge procedures by providing patients and their carers with photographs, videos and maps, as well as written descriptions of nursing homes. One family carer found a home on the programme that he thought would meet his aunt's needs and decided to make a visit. He had felt helpless since he did not know where to start and said that the system helped him. A second family carer said that the system was 'useful', as she was able to look at all the potentially appropriate nursing homes for her mother. The carer was pleased that they had been able to choose homes in the area where her mother had lived for most of her life, and that she had been able to get information from the ACTION system at the right time. Professional carers also appreciated the value of 'having all the information together in one system'.

Access to equipment and meeting the cost of new technology

The principal barrier to the use of new technology within health and social care is cost. As shown by the ACTION demonstration project, the main costs are:

- equipment – computers, video-phone, security locks and, for some clients, a new television that can connect to a computer

- installation, line rental and use of fast telephone lines

- making and reproduction of videos
- programming and updating the programmes.

It is difficult for local health and social care providers to invest in new technologies when there are already cost pressures in maintaining existing levels of service provision. The situation is compounded in community care resource allocation by the tension between support for carers and support for the clients in greatest need (Warren 1999). The cost of new technology is reducing all the time and there is the possibility that an information system such as ACTION could be offered through the use of digital television, making it more accessible to a greater number. As Evandrou (1998, p.282) has argued, we must be concerned that the connected and the not connected will be the 'haves' and 'have nots' of the future. This danger is clearly reiterated in the NHS Information for Health Strategy where it is recognised that 'the opportunities of the information age must be open to all' and that 'strategies for providing public information on health and health services take account of the "information poor" in society' (Burns 1998, p.82).

Conclusion

Given that 60 per cent of carers do not receive care or services from mainstream health and social care services (DoH 1999), it is important that a system such as ACTION should be available without going through professional care agencies. However, carers who used the system in their own homes and those who accessed the system easily or regularly appeared more likely to benefit than those who accessed the system once only. If we are to progress beyond crisis-orientated care, it is therefore important that carers and older people are enabled to access education and information before or when they need support (Burns 1998; Nolan, Grant and Keady 1996; Rogers *et al.* 1999a). We need to recognise both that the Internet and local digital television services will provide a radically improved guide to services which may prove unusually socially inclusive and that there is an important continuing role for professional staff (Burns 1998). As both our study and the literature show, when others are positive it is more likely that older people will take up new technology, which underlines the importance in product development of user consultation. Cowan and Turner-Smith (1999) stipulated that for technology to be used by older and disabled people they must be able to influence its design to ensure that it meets what they want and not what others assume they need.

This chapter has described the positive ways in which technology has enhanced the quality of life for some of the carers and older people with whom we worked, but also made clear that for some carers the new technology does not provide the answers to their care problems. We do not therefore advocate new technology as a panacea for all the problems facing carers and older people, but rather see electronic information systems as potentially useful in helping carers and older people make more informed decisions (Cullen and Moran 1992). We have found that carers (family and professional) and older people have been cautious about using new technology but that, once they used the system, their confidence increased. These early findings from the ACTION project corroborate the view that older people, because of their lifelong experiences of change, are more willing to utilise new technology than is widely thought (Cullen and Moran 1992). The findings help to dispel the myth that older people and new technologies are incompatible.

References

Ballabio, E. and Moran, R. (1998) *Addressing the Needs and Potential of Older People and People with Disabilities in the Information Society: An RTD Approach for the European Union.* Brussels: European Commission DGXIII, Telecommunications, Information Market and Exploitation of Research.

Barnes, M. (1997) *Care, Communities and Citizens.* London: Longman.

Barron, A. (1996) 'Health over the Phone.' *Nursing Standard 10*, 41, 25–27.

Berthold, H. (ed) (1997) *Report on the Literature Survey and Users' Expressed Needs and Priorities.* Deliverable D04.1. Assisting Carers using Telematic Interventions to meet Older Person's Needs (ACTION) Project DE 3001: European Commission DGXIII Telematics Application Programme, Disabled and Elderly Sector. Borås: University College of Borås, School of Health Sciences, Sweden.

Burns, F. (1998) *Information for Health: An Information Strategy for the Modern NHS 1998–2005. A National Strategy for Local Implementation.* Wetherby: Department of Health Publications.

Clarke, A., Hanson, E., Shewan, J., Tetley, J. and Macaualy, V. (1999) *Verification Report: Break from Caring and Planning Ahead.* Deliverable D10.4. Assisting Carers using Telematic Interventions to meet Older Person's Needs (ACTION) Project DE 3001: European Commission DGXIII Telematics Application Programme, Disabled and Elderly Sector. Sheffield: University of Sheffield, School of Nursing and Midwifery.

Cowan, D. and Turner-Smith, A. (1999) *The Role of Assistive Technology in Alternative Models of Health Care for Older People*. Appendix 4. Research Volume 2. *With Respect to Old Age: Long Term Care – Rights and Responsibilites*. Cm. 4192-I. London: The Stationery Office.

Cullen, K. and Moran, R. (1992) *Technology and the Elderly: The Role of Technology in Prolonging the Independence of the Elderly in the Community Care Context*. FAST research report EUR 14419 EN. Brussels: European Commission.

Czaja, S.J. and Sharit, J. (1998) 'Age Differences in Attitudes towards Computers.' *Journal of Gerontology: Psychological Sciences 53B*, 5, 329–340.

Department of Health (DoH) (1998) *Modernising Social Services*. London: The Stationery Office.

Department of Health (DoH) (1999) *Caring about Carers*. London: The Stationery Office.

Evandrou. M. (1998) 'Great Expectations: Social Policy and the New Millennium Elders.' In M. Bernard and J. Phillips (eds) *The Social Policy of Old Age*. London: Centre for Policy on Ageing.

Hanson, E. and Clarke, A. (2000) 'Something to Benefit Both of Us: Can Telematics Assist Family Carers and Frail Older People at Home?' *Health and Social Care in the Community 8*, 2, 129–137.

Hanson, E., Tetley, J. and Clarke, A. (1999) 'Respite Care for Frail Older People and Their Family Carers: Concept Analysis and User Focus Group Findings of a Pan-European Nursing Research Project.' *Journal of Advanced Nursing 30*, 6, 1396–1407.

Le Fanu, J. (1999) *The Rise and Fall of Modern Medicine*. London: Little, Brown.

Magnusson, L., Berthold, H., Chambers, M., Brito, L., Emery, D. and Daly, T. (1998) 'Using Telematics with Older People: The ACTION Project.' *Nursing Standard 13*, 5, 36–40.

Nolan, M., Grant, G. and Keady, J. (1996) *Understanding Family Care*. Buckingham: Open University Press.

Pescosolido, B. and Boyer, C. (1996) 'From the Community into the Treatment System – How People Use Health Services.' In A. Horovitz and T. Schied (eds) *The Sociology of Mental Illness*. New York: Oxford University Press.

Poulson, D., Ashby, M. and Richardson, S. (eds) (1996) *USERfit: A Practical Handbook on User-Centred Design for Assistive Technology*. Brussels–Luxembourg: ECSC–EC–EAEC.

Rogers, A. and Elliot, H. (1997) *Primary Care: Understanding Health Need and Demand*. Oxford: Radcliffe Medical.

Rogers, A., Entwistle, V. and Pencheon, D. (1998) 'Managing Demand: A Patient Led NHS: Managing Demand at the Interface between Lay and Primary Care.' *British Medical Journal 316*, 7147, 1816–1819.

Rogers, A., Flowers, J. and Pencheon, D. (1999a) 'Improving Access Needs a Whole Systems Approach.' *British Medical Journal 319*, 7214, 866–867.

Rogers, A., Hassell, K. and Nicolass, G. (1999b) *Demanding Patients? Analysing the Use of Primary Care*. Buckingham: Open University Press.

Shortliffe, E.H. (1998) 'Health Care and the Next Generation Internet.' *Annals of Internal Medicine 129*, 2, 138–140.

Strode, S., Gustke, S. and Allen, A. (1999) 'Technical and Clinical Progress in Telemedicine.' *Journal of the American Medical Association 281*, 12, 1066–1068.

Tetley, J. and Bradshaw, A. (1998) *A Functional Specification for Programmes for Respite Care Choice and Long Term Planning*. Deliverable D07.2. Assisting Carers using Telematic Interventions to meet Older Person's Needs (ACTION) Project DE 3001: European

Commission DGXIII Telematics Application Programme, Disabled and Elderly Sector. Sheffield: University of Sheffield, School of Nursing and Midwifery.

Tetley, J., Berthold, H., Sundin, O., Chambers, M., Brito, L. and O'Reilly, A. (1997) 'Assisting Carers Using Telematic Interventions to Meet Older Persons' Needs.' In G. Anagianakis, C. Buhler and M. Soede (eds) *Advancement of Assistive Technology.* Amsterdam: IOS Press.

Thursz, D., Nusberg, C. and Prather, J. (eds) (1995) *Empowering Older People: An International Approach.* London: Cassell.

Tinker, A. (1997) *Older People in Modern Society,* 4th edn. London: Longman.

Warren, L. (1999) 'Empowerment: The Path to Partnership.' In M. Barnes and L. Warren (eds) *Paths to Empowerment.* Bristol: Policy Press.

Wootton, R., Loane, M., Maire, F., Moutray, M., Harrison, S., Sivananthan, S., Allen, A., Doolittle, G. and McLernan, A. (1998) 'The Potential for Telemedicine in Home Care.' *Journal of Telemedicine and Telecare 4,* 4, 214–218.

CHAPTER 15

Chinese Older People in Britain

Double Attachment
to Double Detachment

Ruby C.M. Chau and Sam W.K. Yu

Introduction

This chapter is concerned with the social exclusion of Chinese-origin older people in Britain and how social and other care services could make a contribution to promoting their social inclusion and well-being. With the increasing currency of the concept of social exclusion, the focus of study has been widened from distributional to relational issues (Room 1997). There are growing concerns, not only as to whether marginal groups have sufficient material resources to maintain a decent standard of living, but also whether they are able to participate fully in society (Abrahamson 1997). In this chapter social exclusion is defined as detachment from society and social inclusion as an attachment to society. Since ethnic minority groups organise their life in relation to both mainstream society and their own community, their social exclusion may be manifested by detachment from either or both.

There are several ways to cope with social exclusion, such as by strengthening access to education and employment. For example, an European Community (1994) policy paper sees unfavourable economic and social conditions as the main factors which create social exclusion, and suggests that social integration can be promoted through paid work and an increase in the employability of deprived groups. Since, however, most older people are retired and little interested in further education, initiatives by social and care services are more likely to help them secure social inclusion. Whether these services can fulfil this function depends largely on whether their resources are allocated fairly (or in relation to needs) and whether they can develop the capacity to meet minority groups' distinctive needs.

Because of language barriers, the lack of understanding of social rights or the experience of growing up in non-welfare or less developed welfare states, many members of the ethnic minority groups, including older people, are unable to gain sufficient access to social and care services. These problems are severe in the Chinese community. A report by the House of Commons Home Affairs Committee (1985) recorded that of the £30 million expected to go to ethnic minority projects under the Urban Programme during 1984–5, only £90,000 was allocated to projects connected with Chinese-origin people. In 1995, there were only two local authority social service departments with Chinese social work teams. The underprovision of social services for the Chinese-origin population suggests that they neither articulate their social needs effectively, nor exercise sufficiently their social rights to receive support when in need (Chinese Action Group 1985).

The provision of social and care services is much more than a technical or objective exercise: it is a locus of politics. In fact, the provision process always sees participants competing with each other, whether in defining caring needs, constructing and reconstructing caring relationships, or interpreting and reinterpreting the caring goals. With their different cultural backgrounds, older people from ethnic minorities have distinctive needs for and expectations of social care. 'Welfare', as seen by service providers, may be seen by older people as 'ill fare' and vice versa. It is therefore not surprising that there are endless debates on ways of promoting social inclusion through the care services. These debates reflect different ideologies and assumptions about ethnic minority populations: for example, whether or not they are willing or able to integrate into mainstream services (Jones 1979); or whether or not they prefer to confine their life to their own community. Recently, there have been growing debates about both culturally specific perspectives on need and the effectiveness of the minority groups' attempts to improve their quality of life through transnational contacts and the complementary use of both traditional and western medicine (Chau and Yu 1999; Lau 1991; Onyejiako 1991). Ethnic minorities should be able to choose how to cope with social exclusion, but it should be noted that the way they make decisions is subject to political, economic and social constraints. Norman (1985) pointed out that many older people in the ethnic minorities are vulnerable to a triple jeopardy of being old, finding social services inaccessible, and living in a hostile environment. Lister (1997) argues that in a capitalist society which emphasises economic independence, dependence on social welfare reduces self-esteem.

This chapter reports action research which aimed to help older people from ethnic minorities reduce their social exclusion and retain control over their own lives. It has followed a 'start where they start' approach which, instead of imposing readymade solutions, begins with the task of understanding whether and how the group has tried to deal with their social exclusion, and then examines the difficulties that their chosen methods encountered. This approach, we believe, not only develops our understanding of how they cope with social exclusion but also facilitates effective action to promote social inclusion. Before examining the approach in greater detail, three issues require clarification:

- the concept of social inclusion
- why and how Chinese-origin people engage with both mainstream society and their own community
- the experiences of older people in sustaining this 'double attachment' or adapting to its breakdown.

Evidence will be drawn from interviews during 1998 with 20 Chinese-origin older people in Rotherham, Doncaster and Sheffield, South Yorkshire, as part of a research project supported by the Joseph Rowntree Foundation.

Attachment to society

Three characteristics associate with people's attachment to society. Foremost is participation in the principal social institutions such as schools, family and the consumer market. In modern society it is difficult to integrate with 'the mainstream' if one is denied rights to education, employment and training. Social and occupational institutions play an important role in determining how people attach to the social order. They both impose social norms and help individuals to challenge and modify the existing social order.

Second, people's attachment to society has public and private dimensions. Certainly it is possible for people to live in isolation – hermits are found in all societies. If, however, people want to live their lives in mainstream society with ontological security, they need to share with others a common understanding of their self-identity and social reality. Hence people usually behave not only according to what they desire but also in relation to what is expected of them. While the mainstream society may not be morally infallible, those whose thoughts deviate from commonly held public belief face severe challenges. As a strategy to minimise anxiety and uncertainty, people commonly follow mainstream norms and rules in the ways they organise their life and develop their self-identity.

Third, to be attached or detached from society is seldom an 'all or nothing' choice. Attachment is often partial rather than encompassing. Moreover, it is one thing to advocate ideal norms and rules but quite another to follow them diligently in daily life. Gaps between what is believed and what is actually done are normal, but this does not mean that ideal norms and rules have no practical relevance, for they are often used to construct the 'ideal' way of life and to assess actuality.

Chinese people's attachment to mainstream society

According to the 1991 population census, 157,000 people self-declared as members of the Chinese ethnic group in Great Britain, just 0.3 per cent of the total population (Owen 1996). About 3 per cent of Chinese men (2400 aged 65+ years) and 6 per cent of women (4800 aged 60+ years) were of pensionable age (Warnes 1996, Table 6.1). The

British population of Chinese origin is attached to mainstream society in three ways, most evidently through their contributions to commerce and production, for the Chinese community is marked by a high participation rate. The 1991 census indicated that 70 per cent of men and 50 per cent of women were economically active, and of these that 88 per cent of men and 90 per cent of women were in paid jobs. Chan and Chan (1997) note that the rate of unemployment among Chinese-origin people is lower than the national average. Berthoud (1998) shows that the average earnings of Chinese-origin family households with at least one employed person is higher than in any other group including white people.

The findings in our study are in line with these observations. None of the interviewees were born in the UK. Seventeen had worked in the UK before their retirement, all in either restaurants or take-away food shops. Five had run their own Chinese 'take-aways'. They mentioned several advantages of the catering industry: the opportunities to meet other Chinese people, higher earnings than in their place of origin (when they first came) and being able financially to support the family. The high employment participation rate can be associated with not only the demand for their labour and skills but also their determination to gain an economic foothold even at a high personal cost. Employment in restaurants and take-aways is characterised by poor working conditions, heavy workloads, long and unsocial hours, insecure earnings and occupational hazards. An article in *Herald Europe* (Anon 1998) estimated that 20 per cent of Chinese catering businesses did not attract sufficient customers to cover their costs. Business failures force many to move out of their community and to another town where they start again and, together with occupational hazards and sickness, they make it common for Chinese-origin people to take early retirement. One study has shown that their health deteriorates much faster than in the similar aged white group (Owen 1994). Furthermore, because of the necessity of living near their take-aways and restaurants, many Chinese-origin people set up home above their shops, which explains the low rate of home ownership compared to other ethnic groups (Jones 1998).

The second characteristic of Chinese-origin people's attachment to mainstream society is the 'enclosure' of their participation in the catering industries in both private and public dimensions. It is a widespread stereotype that the Chinese community is close-knit, undemonstrative and 'keeps to itself'. Despite the low profile, the members are far from isolated, not least because most of their customers are British, and if their business is to thrive they must establish a workable relationship with local people. Even though many Chinese-origin people are not proficient in English, they can function effectively as waiters, waitresses and proprietors. Although many cannot grasp the complexities of the British legal system, they are able to follow the laws and regulations that apply to their businesses. Moreover, in cities like Liverpool, London and Manchester, 'Chinatown' is an important tourist attraction and income generator for the local economy, giving the community some standing in commercial and political associations.

The third characteristic of Chinese-origin people's attachment to the mainstream society is its specialised nature. Very often the contacts between Chinese-origin people and the rest of society are limited to the commercial relationship. While their cooking and catering skills are well known and highly recognised, their personal and social needs receive far less attention. The Chinese community is under-studied and many projects for meeting their social needs are underfunded (Chiu 1991; House of Commons 1985; Jones 1998). Besides lack of attention, the Chinese are also subject to mockery and suspicion. Parker (1994, p.627) gives an example of a customer in the television documentary 'Take-Away Lives' who remarked, 'I hate the Chinese: they're dirty, the kitchens are dirty. They never show you the kitchens and the inside, do they?'

Attachment to their own community

To meet their social needs, most Chinese-origin people turn to their own families. According to Wong (1985), the community stresses self-reliance and avoids asking for help from the government. The House of Commons Home Affairs Committee (1985) similarly argued that Chinese-origin people tend to keep their problems within the family. A recent study in Sheffield shows that many Chinese-origin women choose to rely on family members, friends and relatives to solve both minor and major problems. Only 4.7 per cent of the respondents sought help from government organisations or non-Chinese community organisations (Chau and Yu 1999).

As in other ethnic minority groups, women are the main negotiators with the social welfare and health institutions. To cope with the difficulties in contacting the professionals and to enhance their understanding of the social welfare and health systems, voluntary associations have formed groups to represent their interests and to share their problems. An example is the Lai Yin Association in Sheffield. It was established by a few volunteers in 1986 to promote the well-being of Chinese-origin women and their families, and subsequently developed into a formal organisation with its own constitution, a management committee and an average membership of 120. Despite its formal structure, the members regard each other as friends more than instrumental associates; a number come from the same extended families and formality is kept to a minimum. Members interact outside the organisation's activities, reflecting a preference to enhance their quality of life and solve their problems through informal means.

Working in Chinese restaurants and family-based take-aways sustains the ethnic Chinese population's attachment to their own community. This is not to say that their working conditions are better than elsewhere, for conflicts between employers and employees are not uncommon. When there are disagreements about working practices, however, by sharing language and culture they can usually understand the rationale behind the rules and demands. The Chinese Action Group (1985) discovered that some managers of Chinese restaurants regard running the business as similar to running a traditional extended family system. They treat their subordinates as family members and meet needs beyond those related to employment. Compared to restaurants, family-based take-aways are even more effective in enhancing Chinese family values, by providing opportunities for its members to take care of each other and, through working together, by nurturing their commitment to the family (Song 1995). In summary, Chinese-origin people are neither wholly isolated nor totally attached to mainstream society. Rather they maintain dual attachments to the host society and to their own community: to the former mainly by participating in retail catering; to the latter mainly for mutual help and support.

Retirement: From dual attachment to double detachment

Retirement to Chinese-origin men and women implies not only the loss of work but also disruption of their dual attachment to their own community and the host society. After retirement, they lose both the opportunity to meet local people as customers and the wages which enable them to be active consumers. Among the 20 Chinese-origin older people interviewed in South Yorkshire, their detachment from the labour market was obvious. Over half had had to retire on the grounds of ill-health before reaching 60 years of age, and their health problems were often work related, the commonest being arthritis, varicosity and phlebitis.

The interviews shed light on the ways in which Chinese-origin older people coped with the disruption of their dual attachments. Three strategies were identified, the first being to maintain the double attachment by using social services as an alternative contact with mainstream society. The second is to strengthen their attachment to the Chinese community through their family. The third is to withdraw altogether and return to their place of origin. The following paragraphs examine the difficulties associated with each of these strategies.

Social services as a link to mainstream society

Only three interviewees were users of mainstream social services: two lived in an older people's home and one used the home-help service. Eight were members of Chinese luncheon clubs and three had taken part in activities organised by Chinese community organisations. Most interviewees, including the active users, had ambivalent attitudes to social services and their rights as users. On the one hand, they thought that using social services could enhance their quality of life and solve some problems; on the other hand, they had to overcome several difficulties before they could benefit from social services, including language barriers and their ignorance of the system. Moreover, their working age practice of meeting needs through exchange relationships in both labour and consumer markets made them less prepared to receive services based on citizens' rights and altruism. Furthermore, several interviewees believed that social services were generally for mainstream society and would not meet needs specific to their culture and habits. Ambivalent attitudes are revealed in the following quotes from four informants:

> They, the British, are the hosts, we are guests. It is doubtless that social services are provided mainly for them, not for us.

> I don't know even a single English word, how could I use the services? I will use only what they give us.

> The government didn't look after me in the past. I don't believe that it will now come to take care of me. I am old and not valuable. There is no point giving attention to useless persons. The government provides services only for symbolic purposes. We are only a dot. But I still use the services because I paid tax and stamps before.

> Of course, the more services the better, but I hate to fill in forms. I hate asking people to fill in forms for me. If you ask people for help, you will become their burden.

The interviews demonstrated that using social services in some cases compromised the recipient's attachment to their family, for seven interviewees worried that the use of social services might deprive them of the opportunity to stay in their own community. They were especially afraid of living in hospitals and older people's homes where they would be seen as outsiders. This would not only isolate them from their own community but also require adjustment to a new environment for which they lacked the resources and experience to cope. One older woman told us about her friend who spent her final years in a nursing home where, she said, her life had been sad, lonely, insecure and 'disgraceful'. Our informant did not want to end up in a similar situation.

Another woman in her eighties told us about her experience of living in an older people's home where she had stayed for a year. The home had been converted from an old church building. She moved in because her son's family had started a business in another city. She said the corridors were so quiet that sometimes she suspected she was the only person in the massive building. Occasionally she went for afternoon tea in the common room; it was almost the only time to see other people. She was however the only non-English speaker and her interaction with the other residents was limited to general greetings.

Strengthening the attachment to the Chinese community through the family

As mentioned, many Chinese-origin people have a strong commitment and emotional ties to their families. However, many interviewees found it difficult to rely on their families to meet their physical and emotional needs. Although all had married and raised children, only half of the interviewees lived with their relatives. Nine lived alone and one lived next door to her daughter. The reasons for living alone included: death of spouse (8); poor relationship with children (5); children living in other cities (2); children living outside the country (2); marital problems (2); spouse in nursing home (1); to avoid the inspection of VAT officers (1). In some cases, a combination of these reasons applied. Although most of these older people were capable of looking after themselves in daily matters, there was a general worry about the unavailability of immediate help if an accident occurred.

One woman in her late seventies said that to cope with living alone she limited her activities to two ground-floor rooms. She had become blind after suffering from eye disease ten years earlier. Her husband had died six months before the interview. She had two daughters, both married and living with their families, one in London and one in Canada. This interviewee spent most of her time sitting next to the telephone waiting for her daughters to call. She was visited by an English-speaking home helper twice a day but did not find the service very useful. She could not communicate with the helper, who could not cook Chinese meals or competently buy Chinese groceries. When asked if she had considered moving to live with her daughters or to an older people's home, she said that she did not want to leave the house in which she and her husband had raised their family; nor was she sure whether she would be a burden to her daughters.

Not all of the interviewees received regular financial support from their children. Four said they received money at least monthly, six on special occasions (such as festivals and birthdays) and three irregularly. Four interviewees mentioned that they did not spend any quality time with their children and seldom shared their worries, although they were living under the same roof. Five interviewees were not clear whether they were the host or the guest in the family. In traditional Chinese families, the hosts were expected to be the breadwinners and took charge of the family decision-making processes. But older people in our interviews no longer played these roles and increasingly felt that they were 'peripheral' family members. Thirteen interviewees felt that they were no longer useful and said their lives were boring. These findings suggest that the capacity of Chinese families in meeting the needs of older people is declining or not as great as is generally assumed.

Complete detachment – Returning to the place of origin

Given the difficulties of enjoying a decent retirement in Britain, some interviewees had considered returning to their place of origin. Some had visited Hong Kong and mainland China to explore this possibility, but found that to live in their homeland would not be as easy as they had first imagined. One older woman said, 'The traffic in Hong Kong was so busy that I couldn't cross the road, even my son was scared'. An older man said, 'Every time I go to see my elderly mother in mainland China, I ask my doctor for some vaccinations. The hygiene there is poor. I don't even know where to find a doctor if I get ill'.

Another interviewee who was in her early eighties had been housebound following operations on both knees a year earlier, and she had heart problems and diabetes. She lived with her son and daughter-in-law who spent most of their time in their food-processing factory and take-away. Her mobility problem meant that she could not go out on her own. If she wanted to have a Chinese meal outside or visit friends, she had to wait until her son could take her. She felt that her life in Britain was meaningless. She had once moved back to Hong Kong, but after six months there she changed her mind. As she said, 'Nobody in Hong Kong will take care of me. I have been in Britain for more than forty years. Over these years, my friends and relatives in Hong Kong have established their own families, some have died already and I have lost touch with the others'. Added to such deterrents to a return move, the cost of living in Hong Kong has increased sharply in recent decades – its living costs were the third highest in the world in 1999. The money that Chinese older people have earned in Britain is normally insufficient for them to lead a decent life in Hong Kong. Finally, their immediate families are in Britain. Some of their children were born in Britain and have fully established themselves here, so a return to their origins would mean that they receive even less support from their families.

Conclusions

We have shown that many ethnic Chinese people in Britain, especially older people, actively attach to both mainstream society and their own community, but that their social inclusion is compromised by various barriers which impeded their access to health and social services, by pressures on the caring capacity of their families and by the difficulties of returning to their homeland. Measures which would improve their social inclusion and the support they receive from services include:

- more widespread interpreters

- ways of establishing a more equal relationship with health and social service professionals and of sharing views on needs and the service response

- more family support services to help sustain relationships between the generations

- more support to enable older people to use advanced technologies such as the Internet to facilitate contacts with their relatives in Britain and beyond.

It is however very important to let Chinese older people influence which measures should be implemented to strengthen their social inclusion, 'to start where they would start'. In response to the growing demands for user involvement in the provision of welfare services and the policy-making process, social scientists have argued that older people should be involved in deciding their destiny (McFee and Rowley 1996; Tout 1995). But even to achieve the influence now exerted by

Britain's larger but more youthful ethnic minority groups, Chinese older people should have more opportunities to define their needs in care-giving and receiving. One way this could be done would be to enable and encourage their participation in research and evaluation.

Minichiello and Walker (1996, p.6) point out that unlike research on 'other less dominant groups in society, e.g. women, black people and the gay community, [that] in the ageing field continues to be conducted by others – often younger people for and on behalf of the aged'. This raises the question of how to encourage Chinese older people to organise and to articulate both their needs and their views about solutions to social exclusion. Few older people are active in research on their own problems: a valuable experiment would be to support Chinese-origin older people's involvement in the study of their double detachment. This would create for them more opportunities to specify their problems, and no better way is apparent by which to establish either priorities or the acceptability and likely effects of service change.

References

Abrahamson, P. (1997) 'Combating Poverty and Social Exclusion in Europe.' In W. Beck, L. Maesen and A. Walker (eds) *The Social Quality of Europe*. London: Kluwer Law International.

Anon (1998) *Herald Europe 2*, 4, July.

Berthoud, R. (1998) *The Incomes of Ethnic Minorities*. ISER Report 98-1. Colchester: University of Essex, Institute for Social and Economic Research.

Chan, Y.M. and Chan, C. (1997) 'The Chinese in Britain.' *New Community 23*. 1, 123–131.

Chau, C.M. and Yu, W.K. (1999) *Report on Social and Health Needs of Chinese Women in Sheffield*. Sheffield: Lai Yin Association.

Chinese Action Group (1985) 'Memorandum Submitted by the Chinese Action Group.' In *Chinese Community in Britain: Second Report*. House of Commons, Home Affairs Committee, Session 1984–5, Vol. II. London: HMSO.

Chiu, S. (1991) 'The Family Care of Chinese Old People: A Study of the Chinese Communities in London and Hong Kong.' Unpublished PhD thesis. Sheffield: University of Sheffield.

European Community (1994) *Growth, Competitiveness, Employment*. Brussels: European Commission.

House of Commons Home Affairs Committee (1985) *The Chinese Community in Britain: Second Report*. Home Affairs Committee, Session 1984–5, Vol. II. London: HMSO.

Jones, A. (1998) *The Invisible Minority: The Housing Needs of Chinese Older People in England*. Occasional Paper 16. Birmingham: University of Birmingham.

Jones, D. (1979) 'The Chinese in Britain: Origins and Development of a Community.' *New Community 7*, 13, 397-402.

Lau, B. (1991) 'Meeting Health Needs by Traditional Medicine.' In A. Squires (ed) *Multicultural Health Centre and Rehabilitation of Older People.* London: Edward Arnold.

Lister, R. (1997) *Citizenship: Feminist Perspectives.* New York: New York University Press.

McFee, G. and Rowley, N. (1996) 'Developing a Positive Aging Agenda.' In V. Minichiello, N. Chappell, H. Kendig and A. Walker (eds) *Sociology of Aging: International Perspectives.* Melbourne: International Sociological Association Research Committee on Aging.

Minichiello, V. and Walker, A. (1996) 'Emerging Issues in Sociological Thinking, Research and Teaching.' In V. Minichiello, N. Chappell, H. Kendig and A. Walker (eds) *Sociology of Aging: International Perspectives.* Melbourne: International Sociological Association Research Committee on Aging.

Norman, A. (1985) *Triple Jeopardy: Growing Old in a Second Homeland.* London: Centre for Policy on Ageing.

Onyejiako, S. (1991) 'Out of Africa: A Cross-Cultural View of Stroke.' In A. Squires (ed) *Multicultural Health Centre and Rehabilitation of Older People.* London: Edward Arnold.

Owen, D. (1994) *Chinese People and 'Other' Ethnic Minorities in Great Britain: Social and Economic Circumstances.* Coventry: Centre for Research in Ethnic Relations, University of Warwick.

Owen, D. (1996) 'Size, Structure and Growth of the Ethnic Minority Populations.' In D. Coleman and J. Salt (eds) *Ethnicity in the 1991 Census, Vol.1 Demographic Characteristics.* London: HMSO, pp.80–123.

Parker, D. (1994) 'Encounters across the Counter: Young Chinese People in Britain.' *New Community 20*, 4, 621–634.

Room, G. (1997) 'Social Quality in Europe: Perspectives on Social Exclusion.' In W. Beck, L. Maesen and A. Walker (eds) *The Social Quality of Europe.* London: Kluwer Law International.

Song, M. (1995) 'Between "the Front" and "the Back": Chinese Women's Work in Family Businesses.' *Women's Studies International Forum 18*, 3, 285–298.

Tout, K. (1995) 'An Aging Perspective on Empowerment.' In D. Thursz, C. Nusberg and J. Prather (eds) *Empowering Older People: An International Approach.* London: Cassell.

Warnes, A.M. (1996) 'The Age Structure and Ageing of the Ethnic Groups.' In D. Coleman and J. Salt (eds) *Ethnicity in the 1991 Census, Vol.1 Demographic Characteristics.* London: HMSO, pp.151–177.

Wong, D. (1985) 'Chinese Community in Britain.' Memorandum submitted by D. Wong. In Home Affairs Committee, Session 1984–5, *The Chinese Community in Britain: Second Report*, Vol. II. London: HMSO

Bangladeshi Families
in Bethnal Green, London

Older People, Ethnicity and Social Exclusion

Chris Phillipson, Emadad Alhaq, Saheed Ullah and Jim Ogg

Introduction

Developing services for older people from ethnic minority groups is now a major priority within the health and social care system. Several studies during the 1990s highlighted problems relating to the under-utilisation of services, inappropriate care, racism and discrimination in service delivery (Blakemore and Boneham 1994; Askham, Henshaw and Tarpey 1995; Pharoah 1995). Ahmad (1993) conceptualised the issues in terms of the operation of traditional stereotypes relating to extended caring families and notions that the elderly will retire to their countries of origin. These and similar ideas resulted in the neglect of black and Asian elders, in both the academic and the policy literature.

To explore these themes, this chapter reports on a selection of findings from a larger study which has examined family and inter-generational change over the past 50 years (Ogg *et al.* 1996; Phillipson *et al.* 1998, 2001). The focus will be on the experiences of daily living among one ethnic group – Bangladeshi men and women living in the East End of London. The chapter reviews several interviews with this group and draws together some implications for the organisation and delivery of care in the community. The research discussed in this chapter was in three localities – the London suburbs of Bethnal Green and Woodford and the Midlands industrial town of Wolverhampton – which had all been the subject of social research in the 1940s and 1950s.

Townsend's (1957) influential study of Bethnal Green, *The Family Life of Older People*, concluded that, despite the development of a welfare state, family relationships in the decade after World War II appeared to be as strong as ever. By the 1990s, Bethnal Green had altered considerably, through 'comprehensive redevelopment' schemes during the 1950s and 1960s which displaced a proportion of the population to the outer suburbs and beyond (Porter 1994). By the 1980s and 1990s, several significant socio-demographic changes had occurred. Tower Hamlets (which contains the bulk of the former London County Council borough of Bethnal Green) was one of the few Greater London Council (GLC) boroughs to experience an increase in population between 1981 and 1991 (by 7.5%). The increase in very young children was especially important and by 1991 the share aged under 5 years in Tower Hamlets was the highest in London at 9.1 per cent (double the national average). This has much to do with the low average age and the relatively high fertility of the Bangladeshi ethnic minority population. The proportion of older people in Tower Hamlets is consequently below the national average (15.2% against 18.2). Within the old Bethnal Green boundary, the proportion is slightly higher (16%).[1]

Increased ethnic diversity has been another major social change, for nearly 40 per cent of those living in Bethnal Green are now members of ethnic minority groups, with Bangladeshis the dominant group (by 2001 they will be one-third of the resident population). This change has been highly significant, for in Bethnal Green the population has traditionally been more homogeneous than in many other East End boroughs (Phillipson *et al.* 1999). Finally, an important change in Bethnal Green is that the share of the population aged 85 or more years has increased from 2.5 per cent in 1951 to 7.5 per cent in 1991, mainly through the ageing *in situ* of the older, indigenous and predominantly white population (Warnes 1994).

Our research in Bethnal Green was carried out in three phases. The first phase consisted of an interview survey of a random sample of 195 people of pensionable age (women 60 years and over; men 65 and over), drawn from the age-sex registers of general practitioners. The response rate was 63 per cent. The second phase comprised qualitative interviews with sub-samples of white respondents aged 75 years and over and of 13 Bangladeshi respondents aged 60 or more years. The third phase was a focus group of nine Bangladeshi female carers in their forties and fifties, which explored issues of household support for younger as well as older members.[2]

Bangladeshi families in Bethnal Green

The main sample included 23 respondents originating from Bangladesh, of whom 21 had at least one child living at home. Fifteen (65%) Bangladeshi households had five or more people (a similar proportion to that reported for all Bangladeshi households in the 1991 Census). Only two of the 23 households were solo or spouses only, the rest included married as well as single children (nine of our respondents were living with married children and grandchildren or a combination in a three-generation household). Their circumstances are well illustrated by specific cases:

> Mr Hussein is aged 70 and lives in a four-bedroomed flat on the third floor of a council block in Bethnal Green. Mr Hussein came to Britain from Bangladesh in the late 1950s, living first in Birmingham and moving to London in the mid-1980s. Ten people live in his flat: Mr Hussein (the tenant), his wife, mother-in-law, four sons, two daughters and a granddaughter. Mr Hussein also has a nephew living in the same block, and three sisters and one brother living in East London. The granddaughter had been married in Bangladesh twelve months prior to the interview and was waiting for her husband to join her from Bangladesh.
>
> Another informant, Mrs Naser, aged 74, lives in a four-bedroomed flat and is in poor health with a combination of physical and mental health problems. A third, Mrs Khanum, is blind and has limited hearing. She lives with and shares a bedroom with her widowed daughter and her daughter's two sons, one daughter-in-law and two great grandchildren.

The daughter-in-law is the carer for both Mrs Khanum and her widowed daughter who also has psychiatric problems.

A fourth, Mr Miah, is aged 69 years and lives with his wife and seven of his eight children (all at school) in a ground-floor flat with five bedrooms. He arrived in London from Bangladesh in 1957 and has since been living in various parts of the East End. Their other child (a daughter) lives in a flat above them with her family. Mr Miah's flat is a converted laundry which once served the housing estate. He has three brothers who live in Leeds, Bradford and Birmingham.

Some of the sample's housing characteristics reflect the findings of the 1991 Census which showed that Bangladeshis have very poor living conditions and much overcrowding. Eade, Vamplew and Peach (1996) reported that nearly one-fifth (19%) of Bangladeshi households lived at the highest tabulated density category (over 1.5 persons per room), compared with less than 0.5 per cent of the total resident population and 8 per cent of Pakistani households. The situation of the Bangladeshis is reminiscent of the 1940s and 1950s 'family groups' described by Sheldon (1948) and Young and Willmott (1957). This level of overcrowding in the home raises the possibility of tensions between the generations, an issue explored later.

Migration history and background

A few Bangladeshis settled in Britain after World War I, working as articled seamen from British ports, and many lived in the East End of London.[3] The majority came from one district, Sylhet and, through a process of chain migration, many from particular rural settlements within it. They speak various dialects and the first generation had low literacy in standard Bengali. The majority are Sunni Muslims. In *The Roots and Tales of the Bangladeshi Settlers,* Choudhury (1993) records around 400 Bangladeshis from Sylhet living in London during the 1940s. He notes that these early job seekers often found it difficult to find jobs and some moved to the Midlands and further north to work in heavy industry and textiles. He describes their life during the 1950s:

> In the early days, the ex-Sylheti seaman settlers were middle-aged, fathers or grandfathers themselves, or in that age group. They usually did heavy industrial work. While at home they used to do

shopping, washing, cooking and thus spent time in housework. The weekdays, if there was any time in hand, they sat with their praying mats and prayed or sat with friends and enjoyed talking while rolling paper cigarettes. At the weekend if they were not working, they used to visit friends or play cards [and] they went to bed early to make up their lost sleep of the weekdays. (Choudhury 1993, p.137)

The history of this cohort of Bangladeshis is, then, one of complex attachments to various English industrial towns such as Coventry, Birmingham, Leeds and Luton, to East London and to their own villages in Bangladesh. As virtually no Bangladeshis aged over 50 years spoke English as their main language, they were an isolated community, often lodging with other migrants. By the 1980s many had reached pensionable age, but in circumstances which contrasted in significant respects with those of white elderly people in their locality. For some at least, their fragmented life course meant that their family life was more characteristic of men in their thirties and forties than of their own ages, the sixties and seventies. Their migration histories had influenced their family structures as well as the type of support available and produced major problems in their old age.

Household and family structure

Bangladeshis in Britain are typically described as having 'complex households'. This imprecise term clearly refers to the size of the household and, more especially, to generational depth. But Bangladeshi families and households are distinctive in more subtle ways, which only qualitative observations reveal. Given that being surrounded by kin of different generations is seen as desirable, does it pose disadvantages along with some advantages? Are there costs as well as benefits with regard to support? To start to answer these questions, we describe some features of the 13 households and their family structures and relationships.

Mr Ahmed lives in a three-bedroomed, ground-floor flat that was purchased from the local authority some seven years previously. The household of three generations comprises Mr Ahmed and his wife, four sons, two daughters-in-law and three grandchildren. Mr Ahmed brought his family to Britain in the early 1980s and described his early experiences in securing accommodation and his contacts with other relatives:

Interviewer: When you came back with your family did you live in the present flat?

Mr Ahmed: No, no. I lived in four flats in four months. I moved around wherever I could find suitable accommodation. I took private flats at first but did not find them suitable, sometimes because of the landlords. Then I applied to the council, it was the GLC then.

Interviewer: Do you have any other close relatives in England?

Mr Ahmed: I do not have any… The relatives I do have are distant… One lives nearby but that's about it. My daughters-in-law's families live nearby, in Tower Hamlets.

Interviewer: Are there any other relatives, close or distant, that you have regular contact with?

Mr Ahmed: No, not really. There are a couple of people from [my] village in Bangladesh that live close by with whom I have occasional contact.

Mr Hoque, in contrast, has many siblings and other relations living locally. He lives on the third floor of a council-owned block of flats in a multi-generation household comprising Mr Hoque and his wife, Mrs Hoque's mother, four sons (the eldest aged 19), and two daughters (one married with her own child). Mr Hoque also has three other married daughters, all of whom have children, whom he sees frequently. He explained that he had a large family including three sisters all living in East London. His brothers have now died but he is in regular contact with his nephews (one living in the same block of flats). He described his contact with his nephews as follows:

Interviewer: Among your nephews and your sisters, who would you say you felt closest to?

Mr Hoque: I am closest to my nephews. My nephews' fathers have all died so they come to me for help and advice.

> My sisters are busy with their families but they still
> think about me and I for them. Whenever I need to
> see my nephews at least one of them will come. If my
> nephews cannot come to see me then one of their
> wives will get a taxi and come round.

Most of Mr Hoque's close relatives are now in England, with the
exception of one brother. He does, however, have a son-in-law in
Bangladesh. One of his daughters was married in Bangladesh (some 12
months before the interview), and she is waiting for her husband to join
her. Her situation exemplifies an issue that to a greater or lesser degree
was important for many of those interviewed, the division of the family
between two continents. In some cases, most of the children were in
England but most siblings and extended relatives were still in
Bangladesh. In others, however, sons and daughters from an earlier or
the existing marriage had been unable or unwilling to join them in
London.

Such a case is 68-year-old Mr Bakht, who has been in England for
40 years and lives in a new house on an estate managed by a housing
association. He is married with two sons (one married) and two
daughters (both at school). An older married daughter lives in East
London. Mr Bakht also has important family ties still in Bangladesh. He
is severely incapacitated with a stroke and parts of the interview were
conducted with his wife:

Interviewer: Do you keep in contact with anyone in Bangladesh?

Mrs Bakht: His eldest son is in Bangladesh. You see he has
married twice… He married my cousin's sister and
had two sons and two daughters. Then he married me
after my cousin died and I came to England with my
five children. His eldest son from his first marriage is
here and has children.

Interviewer: Does he have contact with the eldest son from the
first marriage?

Mrs Bakht: Oh yes, they came round the other day to see him.

Children still living in Bangladesh was also important for Mr Miah, a
69-year-old married man. He lives on the third floor of a

three-bedroomed council flat with his wife and four children (aged 11, 8, 5 and 3 years). Mr Miah is in poor health and has had several heart attacks; he also suffers from diabetes. He has seven children from a previous marriage, three in Bangladesh and four in England (three in London). The eldest son in Bangladesh is now aged 40 years. Mrs Miah described the contact she has with her stepsons: 'They telephone occasionally, and we also phone. They try to keep informed about their father's health. They want him to go back to Bangladesh so that they can care for him, but I won't send him in this condition.' Mr Miah had strong emotional ties to Bangladesh and when the subject of returning to Bangladesh was raised he became distressed.

In the majority of cases, the older men who were interviewed had lived in Britain for at least thirty years. On the other hand, the women had invariably come much later (usually in the 1980s or early 1990s). Their situation was illustrated by Mrs Naser, a widow who lives in a three-bedroomed house with her daughter (also a widow). The daughter has two sons living with her, one daughter-in-law and two grandchildren. She also has a married daughter living elsewhere in London and another daughter in Bangladesh. Mrs Naser is extremely frail and suffers from a severe psychiatric condition. Her daughter described her mother's arrival in England and contact with relatives:

Interviewer. So you are the closest relative to your mother? How about your father?

Daughter. He died when I was young.

Interviewer. Who else does you mother have in the UK?

Daughter. Just me. My eldest son brought my mother here from Bangladesh by providing a sponsorship.

Interviewer. When did she arrive in the UK?

Daughter. About 5 or 6 years ago.

Interviewer. Before coming to the UK who lived with your mother in Bangladesh?

Daughter. My other daughter in Bangladesh.

Interviewer. Does your mother have any close relatives in the UK?

Daughter: My mother has one stepbrother who lives in Oldham. There are no other close relatives.

Most of these older people live, then, in households which are very different from those of white older people. They are multi-generational and several respondents had dependants still at school. For this and other reasons, family support raised several complex issues. While most of the respondents were surrounded by relations from younger genera-tions, it would be erroneous to conclude that family support was auto-matically available or provided without undue strain, for, as we shall see, the group faced considerable difficulties.

Care and support in the household

Many of those interviewed were experiencing poor health, notably with strokes, heart problems and diabetes.[4] Mr Bakht, referred to earlier, had had two strokes and was confined to bed at the time of the interview. His wife, who came to England seven years previously, was the main carer but she also supported her two school-age daughters and a son who had recently started college. She said that she gets some help from her children, her married daughter and her son-in-law:

Interviewer: What are the main things that your son-in-law helps you with?

Mrs Bakht: He comes round and spends time with his father-in-law or might help feed him a little, lifting him out of bed, into bed, into the chair, just generally being here at times.

Interviewer: How do you feel about the help that you get from your sons and daughters?

Mrs Bakht: They do what they can.

Interviewer: How do you think your husband feels about his care?

Mrs Bakht: He started to choke on some food the other night [and] my son rushed to help him and settle him down. I can't do all these things all the times.

Interviewer: Do you feel that you could do with more help in caring for your husband?

Mrs Bakht: I have been saying recently that if I had someone just to spend time with him while I was doing other things that would be really useful, whether it was for two or three hours it does not matter. The eldest son has gone to work, my son and daughters are at school and college and they'll be back late at 7 o'clock. What should I do in an emergency? He is not eating or toileting properly.

Mrs Bakht's situation raises the issue of the pressures of being responsible for the care of younger as well as older relatives. She gets some help, in that her husband goes one day each week to a day centre, but still feels under considerable pressure:

Interviewer: How does Mr Miah spend his day?

Mrs Bakht: He sits mainly in bed... One minute he wants to sit up, then lie down, then move to the other side, that is all. So I have to do all that.

Interviewer: Does he have any particular routine to his day?

Mrs Bakht: No, he will eat when he says. I keep asking him what he wants to do or eat. Before the last stroke he used to read the Koran, but now he can't.

Interviewer: How often does he go to the day centre?

Mrs Bakht: They come and take him every Thursday. They wanted to take him three times a week but now they can't.

Interviewer: Do you wash him?

Mrs Bakht: Yes, every Thursday before he goes to the centre. Then I clean him every other day.

Interviewer: How often do you change his clothes?

Mrs Bakht: About four times a day. Sometimes he spoils his clothes so I have to change him more [often].

Mr Miah was another of our respondents with a young family and in a poor state of health with a severe heart condition. We noted that he had been married before and has four children in Britain. Mrs Miah says she gets help when needed from her eldest stepson and the husband of her eldest stepdaughter. She talked about their role and described some of the things she does for her husband (whom she calls by the customary naming system Mr Ali):

Interviewer: Do any of your stepchildren visit in person?

Mrs Miah: Yes, at least one will come once a week… As you can see I cannot get out of the flat because of Mr Ali and he cannot go out because of his health – as there are no lifts. [Sometimes] when I have to leave the flat, for instance when my children have to get to school, [I] have to depend on my stepsons to help with things.

Mrs Miah: I have to bath him, take him to his bed and get him out [and] feed him.

Interviewer: Does anybody come in to help you?

Mrs Miah: No, but somebody did come to [help me receive] additional welfare benefit for caring for Mr Ali.

Interviewer: Have you ever applied for such a service?

Mrs Miah: Yes, I did once when I had an operation. I was confined to bed and I could not look after Mr Ali. My daughter phoned the local health clinic…but they did not send anyone round…then my stepdaughter and stepson-in-law helped out until I was better.

Mrs Khan, who was interviewed with her husband, also has intricate care responsibilities. They live in a three-bedroomed, ground-floor flat and both are in very poor health – Mr Khan is confined to a wheelchair. They live with three sons and one daughter, a daughter-in-law and one grandchild. The eldest son is married and currently unemployed, while the two younger sons are twins in their late twenties and both have learning disabilities. There is a fourth son (also with a learning disability) in Bangladesh who has been refused entry into the UK. Mr Khan became distressed during the interview when talking about him who, he said, has no one to look after him. Given the ill-health of Mr and Mrs Khan, the daughter-in-law and the eldest son were the main carers. When asked if Mr Khan had problems with bathing, Mrs Khan replied, 'Yes. I need help [and] my son cannot always help me. My daughter-in-law has to help.'

Support from within the extended family was also important for Mrs Naser, the widow whose household circumstances were outlined earlier. Her daughter, Mrs Bibi, said of her mother's health: 'She is unwell in the head. Before she used to speak constantly, almost too much. Now with medication she speaks very little. [At] the hospital the doctor gave her medication and she now speaks less... My mother cannot see, hear, speak or go to the toilet herself. One time she spent six nights in a hospital and I had to stay with her all the time.' The daughter also has health problems and is unable to provide support for her mother. Mrs Bibi reported: 'My own health is very poor. I take a lot of medication [and] am unable to do any caring. I take tablets at night and at times my head aches for the whole day.' Mrs Bibi's daughter-in-law, Mrs Begum, has become the key person supporting Mrs Naser. Mrs Begum, who is 25 years of age and has two children, came into the interview during a discussion about the value of day centre help and, in contrast with the views of her mother-in-law, suggested that it might be a good idea:

Interviewer: We heard from [your mother-in-law] that you are the main carer for your mother-in-law, her mother and your own two children. Is this a lot of work for you?

Mrs Begum: Yes it is but I have to do it.

Interviewer: What do you think might help you?

Mrs Begum: A day centre for my mother-in-law and grandmother sounds a good idea.

Other respondents who were in better health raised concerns about who would look after them if they became ill. One example is Mr Bokth who is 70 years of age and lives with his wife in a council flat. He has two daughters and a son, all still in Bangladesh. On several occasions they have tried to bring their son to England. They expressed their concerns for their future without any of their children close by:

Interviewer: Is your son married?

Mr Bokth: We went back and arranged his marriage two years ago.

Mrs Bokth: We tried to bring our son over but failed. But if one of my son's children could come over that would at least be something. We are old: who is going to look after us?

Interviewer: Do you have much contact with your daughters?

Mr Bokth: Not really. They are with their husbands and they have many children. The eldest daughter has seven children. They have no responsibility to care for us... They have to care for their husbands and children.

Interviewer: As you get older who will you turn to for care?

Mrs Bokth: We are already old, we have no one else. Other than our children, who else could look after us?

Interviewer: If you were ill who might you go to?

Mrs Bokth: Then we would be in great difficulty. How would we get by? No one would take us like your own child would.

Informal care in the Bangladeshi community

These accounts demonstrate the important role of women as carers for different generations within the family, as for an elderly husband (often 20 or more years senior), for children still at school or college and in some cases for grandchildren. Corrobative evidence of the pressure on carers is provided by the Tower Hamlets Bengali Carers Development Worker Project, which compiled profiles of 235 such carers. Three-quarters were women and nearly half aged 31 to 50 years. The majority were caring for people aged 50 years or more and around half reported illnesses as a result of the pressure of caring – stress and depression was a feature of these women's lives. The most prevalent illnesses among those being cared for were stroke, diabetes and heart problems. To gain insight into these issues, a focus group discussion was held with nine women carers, part of a carers' group based at a day centre for the Bangladeshi community. One focus of the discussion was the physical tasks associated with caring for someone with a disability:

Facilitator: What problems do you have in providing care?

Carer A: Lifting and carrying all day. Of course it is difficult.

Carer B: We get problems with our back, shoulders and other parts.

Carers C/D: We have to lift, push the wheelchair, feed and give medicine: we have to do the lot.

Facilitator: You told me you do everything by yourselves. Would any help from social services help you in your caring role?

Carer B: I do get help from social services but only for an hour. Sometimes in that one hour he does not need anything, no toileting or anything. So the helper comes and goes. One hour goes by very quickly.

But perhaps the most revealing aspect of these women's experiences concerned their vulnerability to threats of abuse and violence by their husbands. One carer described her husband's condition following a number of strokes: 'After his second stroke he could do nothing for himself. I had to do everything. Tower Hamlets Council [social services] did help.' In her account, however, she began to raise other concerns:

What happened was that the hospital informed my [general practitioner] and he spoke to the housing office who sent someone round to measure everything up. When they first fixed the rails my husband did not have the strength to use the rails. I had to lift him to do all the things he wanted to do but now, thanks to God, he can use the rails… But [after] my husband's first stroke my eldest son moved out. My husband would get very angry and would hit or push me… Eventually my eldest son got married [and] his wife could help me care for my husband. At the moment only my second son lives with me. Sometimes when it becomes very unbearable I phone [the community centre] to send someone round to help me which they do. I think the fact he cannot do anything for himself and that he is sitting all day has affected him mentally and therefore he becomes angry more frequently. Now things have not got better but worse… His temper has got worse and he becomes angry more frequently.

Later in the discussion, a women who had not previously spoken was encouraged to speak by the others:

Carer E: What can I tell you? He does not do anything for himself, he won't eat, sleep or change his clothes, he will just sit there in the same clothes. He will just bother me. Sometimes at 12 o'clock at night he will want to go out.

Carer B: You do not have any children with you?

Carer E: He won't sleep. He won't let me sleep and he will just bother me. Even when I'm tired and want to sleep he will bother me, and it is getting too much for me. He will eat at 8 o'clock and then want to eat at 10 o'clock, sometimes even interrupts me eating… I have to hide and eat.

Later the anxieties of the group were expressed in the following way:

Facilitator: [It] is beginning to come out that you all feel very tense or frightened, that you do not know what will happen next.

Carer B: Yes, they have a worse temper now than before; it is as if they could kill you sometimes.

Carer F: Yes, they are still quite strong, and he has a walking stick and threatens to hit me with it.

Another carer described her situation as follows:

Carer G: I don't know what he will do next. I never sleep comfortably, sometimes I feel he might kill me. I want to know how I can make him less bad-tempered with me. If anything ever happens to me he will have no one to care for him other than social services.

There is a sense of great vulnerability among these female carers (most of whom are non-English speaking). Many convey a sense of isolation, even those who are members of large extended families. For these women, the extended family provides some support, but much of the work and the pressure falls upon them as wives, daughters or parents. One woman spoke out towards the end of the discussion in a way which would be echoed in various ethnic groups and in many different societies: 'I want to say that within a whole family whenever someone falls ill it is up to us to care for that person, but when we fall ill there will be no one to care for us. But also he is only bad tempered with me, not to any other member of his family. Why is this so?'

Conclusion

It should be emphasised that in this chapter we have concentrated on problematic caring situations which are not necessarily the norm in Bangladeshi households, even if large three-generation households are relatively common. The expressions related in this chapter raise several important issues for the delivery of care services to ethnic minority groups. First, informal carers in this population may be under particular pressure. Caring is complex even when carried out in favourable circumstances, but for the women in our study conditions were far from ideal. Among the problems were overcrowding and inadequate facilities within the home. The extended family was the norm, but increased rather than reduced the range of needs. Language barriers to the wider population mean that many women carers face distinctive forms of isolation and marginalisation.

Second, scant knowledge and under-utilisation of services – particularly community health and social care – are widespread among Bangladeshi and other ethnic minority carers. The problems are compounded by the scarcity of resources in inner city areas, but some aspects of need urgently need a response. Access to interpreters is crucial. Askham et al. (1995) noted that nearly all their interviewees said it was important that those looking after them spoke their first language, but found that only 40 per cent of Asians had ever been asked in hospital whether they needed help with interpreting, and only 34 per cent in outpatient clinics. Communication problems when negotiating with health and welfare staff were certainly a major issue for our respondents and resulted in considerable additional pressures for informal carers. This is a major challenge for local authorities in the development of local strategies for carers, which aim to identify carers and their needs and to provide appropriate support and services. Clearly, a major test for this work will be the extent to which it reaches populations who have traditionally been isolated from mainstream provision.

Third, while recognising the problems facing our respondents, their strengths as a carer group should also be acknowledged by service providers. On the one hand, they have successfully built a network of community groups in response to a variety of needs. Women, for example, have developed their own organisations in seeking to overcome isolation within the home. Religious organisations have also been important in contributing to the welfare of the community. Such groups represent substantial forms of social capital which can be built upon and engaged with by those seeking to promote service innovation. On the other hand, a successful response will require more sensitive understanding of the distinctive histories of particular ethnic minority groups, as well as improved mechanisms for incorporating views about improving the delivery of community care. A critical task in this century will be to respond to the diversity of care needs among multi-cultural and multi-ethnic populations. In this context, moving ethnic minority elders from the margins of service provision will be a central part of the challenge.

Acknowledgements

A full report on the survey relating to the work discussed in this chapter may be found in Phillipson *et al.* (2001). The research was supported by the Economic and Social Research Council (grant L315253021). The authors would like to express their thanks to the men and women who were interviewed for the research. In the case of the qualitative interviews, pseudonyms have been used throughout.

Notes

1. See Warnes (1996) for a review of the age structure of British ethnic minority groups, and for the Bangladeshis specifically, Eade, Vamplew and Peach (1996).

2. For a fuller discussion of the methodology behind the survey phase of the study, see Ogg *et al.* (1996).

3. For a brief history of migration from Sylhet, see Gardner (1995).

4. For a review of the health of Bangladeshis in comparison with other ethnic groups, see Nazroo (1997).

References

Ahmad W.I.U. (1993) *'Race' and Health in Contemporary Britain.* Buckingham: Open University Press.

Askham, J., Henshaw, L. and Tarpey, M. (1995) *Social and Health Authority Services for Elderly People from Black and Minority Ethnic Groups.* London: HMSO.

Blakemore, K. and Boneham, K. (1994) *Age, Race and Ethnicity.* Buckingham: Open University Press.

Choudhury, Y. (1993) *The Roots and Tales of the Bangladeshi Settlers.* Birmingham: Sylhet Social History Group.

Eade, J., Vamplew, T. and Peach, C. (1996) 'The Bangladeshis: The Encapsulated Community.' In C. Peach (ed) *Ethnicity in the 1991 Census. Volume 2: The Ethnic Minority Populations of Britain.* London: HMSO.

Gardner, K. (1995) *Global Migrants: Local Lives.* Oxford: Clarendon Press.

Nazroo, J. (1997) *The Health of Britain's Ethnic Minorities.* London: Policy Studies Institute.

Ogg, J., Bernard, M., Phillips, J. and Phillipson, C. (1996) *Patterns of Kinship in the Urban Environment: Methodology of the 1995 Survey Phase.* Keele: Centre for Social Gerontology, University of Keele.

Pharoah, C. (1995) *Primary Care for Elderly People in Ethnic Minorities.* London: HMSO.

Phillipson, C., Bernard, M., Phillips, J. and Ogg, J. (1998) 'The Family and Community Life of Older People: Household Composition and Social Networks in Three Urban Areas.' *Ageing and Society 18,* 259–290.

Phillipson, C., Bernard, M., Phillips, J. and Ogg, J. (1999) 'Older People's Experiences of Community Life: Patterns of Neighbouring in Three Urban Areas.' *Sociological Review 47,* 4, 716–743.

Phillipson, C., Bernard, M., Phillips, J. and Ogg, J. (2001) *The Family and Community Life of Older People: Social Support and Social Networks in Three Urban Areas.* London: Routledge.

Porter, R. (1994) *London: A Social History.* London: Hamish Hamilton.

Sheldon, S.H. (1948) *The Social Medicine of Old Age.* Oxford: Oxford University Press.

Townsend, P. (1957) *The Family Life of Old People.* London: Routledge and Kegan Paul.

Warnes, A.M. (1994) 'Cities and Elderly People: Recent Population and Distributional Trends.' *Urban Studies 31,* 4/5, 799–816.

Warnes, A.M. (1996) 'The Age Structure and Ageing of the Ethnic Groups.' In D.C. Coleman and J. Salt (eds) *General Demographic Characteristics of the Ethnic Minority Populations. Volume 1. Demographic Characteristics.* London: HMSO, pp.151–177.

Young, M. and Willmott, P. (1957) *Family and Kinship in East London.* London: Routledge and Kegan Paul.

CHAPTER 17

Averil Osborn and Participatory Research
Involving Older People in Change
Lorna Warren and Tony Maltby

Introduction

At the 1998 British Society of Gerontology (BSG) Annual Conference in Sheffield, a special symposium was held to present the findings of participatory projects supported by the Averil Osborn Fund. Osborn was a social gerontologist, famed for her collaborative work with people in the public services, academic world and voluntary sector. Her commitment to change led her to highlight what she regarded as disturbing gaps between research, policy and practice. It also under-pinned her firm belief in action research, in which older people were involved alongside researchers, professionals and practitioners.

This chapter expands on that symposium. Through a review and reflection on the ideas and work of Averil Osborn, we explore the role of research in changing services for older people, focusing specifically on the involvement of older individuals in that process. Several initiatives, our own included, supported wholly or in part with grants from the Averil Osborn Fund, are discussed. They are linked by their encouragement of and support for development work as key ingredients in improving the quality of life and citizenship of older people. But, as

Osborn argued, the energy and money invested in social research is only well spent if its results are 'useful and usable' (Osborn and Willcocks 1990): that is, if they are widely disseminated, inform public debate and catalyse policy change. We consider the strengths and limitations of participatory research with older people in achieving these goals, taking into account its position in the wider research and policy arena. It is clear that this form of involving older individuals is still in its infancy, with its definition as yet limited and still generally agency led, and assessment of its impact on care service change rare. However, the Averil Osborn projects offer a starting point for exploring activities which look like providing 'more fertile opportunities for involvement' (Carter and Beresford 2000, p.22).

Averil Osborn

Averil Osborn was an exceptionally active and effective campaigner for the welfare of older people. She began her career in social gerontology in the mid-1970s, as a research officer in the Lothian Region Social Work Department. In the early 1980s, she moved to Age Concern Scotland as Assistant Director for Training and Development, at the same time holding a position as Honorary Research Fellow at the Nuffield Institute for Health in Leeds. In the 1990s, she joined the Joseph Rowntree Foundation in York.

Osborn was a prime mover in projects concerned with 'enabling' and 'empowering' older people in community development and in advocacy and information dissemination. On the cover of *Small and Beautiful* (Osborn 1990), one of the leaflets which she produced for Age Concern Scotland, the petals of a flower spell out the ideal qualities of day centres for older people: local, involvement, caring, activity, sharing, friendship, fun and warmth. These were effectively the principles which underpinned Osborn's work. A local identity fosters confidence and trust among older people and their carers. Local projects correspondingly should follow models of policy making and service delivery where older people are in control. Older service users 'may seek or be encouraged to contribute to' decisions affecting services. Efforts need to be made to reach the poorest and most isolated older people, the 'isolated loners'. There is much 'scope for greater experimentation in participation and self-government' (Osborn 1985a, p.11) and 'local experience' can be used to 'lobby local councillors, health board committees and MPs' (Jacques *et al.* 1986, p.1). Osborn's commitment was, therefore, not to champion 'major findings' and their 'dramatic and immediate implementation' – apocalypses are rare – but the 'slow cumulative impact of research' which, she argued, created a 'climate for change'.

Yet Osborn's (1985b) experiences suggested that efforts to encourage such experimentation and to gather together knowledge of such experience attracted little attention. Why, she asked, did 'the application of research to promote change in policy, practice and attitudes' (1984, p.239) have relatively low status within the social research community, and why did potential users underexploit research? Osborn recognised that the research process itself needed to be given attention in attempts to shift this situation. She believed it had the potential to be an 'extremely powerful development tool' and flagged action research as an option for researchers employed in service-providing agencies. She was aware that inhouse researchers were sometimes accused of 'going native', with its associated implications of reduced investigative rigour, interpretive honesty and fairness of reporting (Osborn and Willcocks 1990). But this did not mean that researchers could not have 'empathy' for the subjects (1985b, p.193). Research was, concomitantly, 'eased' by 'good contact with users and some degree of shared commitment' (1984, p.241), which boosted its chances of being put to use.

The part of social research linked most directly with social change, Osborn claimed, was dissemination. It could enable those who were otherwise less well placed to participate in improving life chances for themselves and for others. To this end, Osborn and her colleague Dianne Willcocks (1990) offered a *Good Practice Guide* to achieve the best route from producer to end user. Attention needed to be given to the 'them and us' relationship between gerontologists and older people, dissemination skills, the types and form of the information made available to different audiences, and the differential impact of findings on potential users. Dissemination, they concluded, was not an 'optional extra' but should be part of the research contract.

Osborn was, however, very aware of the effects of economic retrenchment. During the 1980s, funding for services and their delivery was typically short term. Programmes were seldom focused specifically upon the needs of older people and resources, especially time, for disseminating examples of good practice were simply not available. The consequences included disproportionate effort being expended on projects relative to their size, diverting inhouse researchers and their organisations from other essential albeit routine work. Funding programmes were, therefore, often declared as 'inefficient and wasteful of resources' (1985b, p.133). In fact, in this climate, there was little likelihood of research being carried out at all. Service agencies were reluctant to evaluate and review the impact of projects when they saw no adequate alternative source of funds and feared to 'rock the boat'.

At the same time the objectives of projects and the basis of their assessment centred on the concept of quality of life which, though enticing in its promise, was frustratingly ambiguous and difficult to define or operationalise (Robertson and Osborn 1985). Separating 'objective' features of people's life situation from the subjective perceptions and judgements made by those same individuals about their lives created an artificial divide. However, if subjective feelings about satisfaction were accepted as being an important component of quality of life, it was inevitable that the receivers of services should 'in some way be involved in decisions about the future organisation and development of those services.' (p.1) To that end, we needed to know more about what Osborn and her colleague Robertson referred to as forms of 'participation' in decisions that affect services:

> Is our traditional western assumption of participation through representation still adequate, or do we need to introduce more direct forms of participation in the decisions that affect the social services? What questions should be asked; who should be asking; of whom should answers be sought; and who should be responding to them? (Robertson and Osborn 1985, p.2)

The statutory duty of local authorities and NHS trusts to consult with users and their carers, mandated by the 1990 National Health Service and Community Care Act, was a spur for Osborn some five years later to produce a set of guideline pamphlets which proposed answers to some of these questions (Osborn 1991). 'Consultation' was the word being used officially, but in *Taking Part in Community Care Planning* Osborn stated that *involvement* (Osborn's emphasis) was what groups should seek:

> Being involved implies being active participants *involved in* community care planning, instead of passive respondents merely consulted about it…influencing the shape and choice of services leading to better, more user sensitive services. ('Why Consult?' pamphlet, p.2, in Osborn 1991)

Osborn recognised that the words 'participation', 'involvement' and 'consultation' were often used interchangeably but meant different things to different people, and so it was important to clarify their definitions. She also identified the term 'empowerment' as lying 'at the heart of placing users and carers at the centre of community care' ('Finding Out' pamphlet, p.7, in Osborn 1991). Since critics of community care were using it, Osborn was sceptical about the possibility of a sea change. However, efforts needed to be made to establish how key actors planned to change the balance of power. Ways of achieving it included both the commissioning of research – not just surveys – which sought out those hard-to-reach users or those with special needs, including ethnic minority groups, and support for community development work to find out what people want by 'involving and doing' (*ibid.*, p.10).

In sum, Osborn believed that access to relevant research could be used to 'help older people to participate in social change' by giving force and credibility to their voices as 'consumers', empowering them to secure the maximum benefit from the changes around them, and helping them to become actively involved in social change, rather than adopting the residual role of bystander or social victim (Osborn and Willcocks 1990, p.190). Although when discussing putting research into practice Osborn appeared to define 'users' primarily as policy makers and practitioners, current usage offers the potential to extend those arguments in ways which are consistent with her call for both 're-search-minded users and user-minded researchers' (Osborn 1984, p.239).

Older people and participatory research

Until recently, few commentators had directly tackled the issue of the participation of service users as researchers, despite the many different models of involvement (Carter and Beresford 2000). During the period in which Osborn was writing, however, user groups were organising and beginning to question research practice, particularly the ways in which it might reinforce top-down perspectives within welfare services (Beresford 1992; Nocon and Qureshi 1996). Researchers who are themselves either disabled or users of services now critique academic research and the research process as potentially disempowering (Barnes and Mercer 1996; Morris 1991; Thomas 1997). The disabled people's and social care service users' movements have developed their own research methods and methodologies and their own knowledge (Beresford 1997). Older people have been involved in these processes in various ways:

- in steering groups and as research advisers
- as originators of research questions
- in the collection and analysis of data
- in writing up and disseminating research findings.[1]

The UK policy arena

Since Osborn's death, new policy overviews or forums on the needs of older people have been developed. The government has declared a commitment to improving older people's participation in public policy making, and a new 'learning network' will help the sharing of ideas and encourage local authorities and central government departments to prepare for an ageing population (Department of Social Security 1998). In June 1998 the Better Government for Older People Programme (BGOP 1999) was launched with the aim of improving public services for older people through local authority-led inter-agency strategies and partnership with older people themselves. Recent additional possibilities for the participation of older people in the national policy-making process include the establishment of:

- an Inter-Ministerial Group for Older People to develop a co-ordinated strategy on older people. It is running 'listening events' which engage with 'ordinary' older people on consultation and involvement.

- an Older People's Reference Group to advise on the development of the DoH National Service Frameworks

- the BGOP national action research programme Older People's Advisory Group to begin to 'join up' the lessons from the above, government-led and other national initiatives and to determine how the voice of older people can influence the direction of BGOP. (Dunning 1999)

The research arena

The BGOP programme emphasises the importance of *consultation* (authors' emphasis) with local people to shape local services (Boaz 2000). The extent to which consultation exercises in the 28 BGOP pilots have focused on older people or whether specific initiatives have been implemented by authorities is not yet clear. However, a potential additional prong to the government's modernisation aims (Cabinet Office 1999) lies in the increase of funding to the Economic and Social Research Council (ESRC) to encourage the use of data and research (Walker 2000).[2] The director of the new ESRC Growing Older research programme (which includes among its six topic areas 'participation and activity in later life') has promised to raise the impact of findings on policy and practice (Walker 1999). Other existing research programmes on ageing, funded by the Nuffield and Joseph Rowntree Foundations, offer the possibility of a boost to UK research on services for older people.

These major funders of policy research are also incorporating a change of emphasis towards a programme of work with, as well as about, older people (Carter and Beresford 2000). Researchers are increasingly required to show how and to what extent service users have been involved in the drawing up of research proposals and/or subsequent plans for the design and execution of the research (Warren 1999). On the other hand, the incorporation of users' needs into various aspects of the research process is still driven as much by an emphasis on 'best value' in public services as concern with quality of life or local democracy. In many instances, requiring the inclusion of service users may be little more than a cosmetic exercise (Rappert 1997).

The Averil Osborn Fund

The aims of the Averil Osborn Fund,[3] in contrast, are centred primarily on the participation of older people in change. The BSG established the fund in 1994, following the sudden death of Averil Osborn.[4] Its goal is to encourage and support development work that will 'improve the quality of life and citizenship of older people and, of equal importance, to promote the involvement of older people in the design and practice of sound research' (Warnes 1999, p.21). The fund therefore represents a practical memorial by sustaining the research principles which Osborn espoused: 'creative' and 'appropriate' responses to an ageing population (Osborn 1985b). Its objectives provide the potential to promote the open flow of material or ideas which Osborn believed to be more generally characteristic of the service-based research community 'less widely available in published form' compared to academic findings (Osborn 1984, p.241). To this end, the prospectus welcomes 'various methodologies and approaches' and 'applications from a wide range of disciplines, professions and vocations', though projects are expected to have the support of experienced researchers or have access to such experience and advice through a supporting institution.

Between 1995 and 1999, there were five rounds of awards,[5] which offered grants to 16 projects, of which nine have been completed. Recent projects supported by the fund and include studies of the needs of older people in Upper Deeside and Tyrone, and of older Asian-origin citizens in Edinburgh. In some cases awards have represented a partial contribution to the costs of a larger project, or have enabled the extension or supplementation of an existing project. Otherwise they have been the main source of finances for pilot or developmental studies. Some of the funding has supported the dissemination of good practice and findings. Although few of the project reports have been commercially published, dissemination has been achieved through tra-

community centres, photographic displays, conferences, pamphlets, 'inhouse' reports, short articles, postcards and a video, as well as the special BSG symposium mentioned earlier.[6] An edited collection of the project's reports is planned.

Averil Osborn funded projects

The seven projects reported on below are all examples of change-oriented research with a focus on participatory methods to achieve their goals. Those methods have been diverse and the involvement of older people in disseminating their findings has varied. Some reports have been for academic audiences, but most have been for older people and the organisations with which they are involved (not that the two are mutually exclusive). In all cases, research has been at the local level where there is a possibility of taking forward findings.

One of the first grants was to Yvonne Craig to extend the work of the Elder Mediation Project (EMP), which aims to enable 'older persons to deal with their problems and conflicts constructively in ways that extend, rather than diminish, their human rights' (Craig 1992, p.4). The practical goal of EMP has been to help older people enhance their own decision-making capacities, even if they are not in abusive situations. Based on the experience of elder mediation in other countries, chiefly the USA, the UK project was developed by the national voluntary organisation Mediation UK, most of whose workers are older and from minority cultural backgrounds. The model has been one of 'diffusion' rather than 'empire building'. Social groups working with and for older people have been given information, training and resources to develop their own EMPs to suit organisational and local needs and the project has been steered by a group of older partners (Craig 1995). The Averil Osborn grant helped the scheme in its work with older people from Britain's ethnic minority groups, particularly in their dealings with 'officialdom'.

A second project with a 'self-help' or, in Craig's (1997) words, 'co-production of community care' approach was the Age Concern Cookstown initiative, reported on by David Savage. A team of 15 older volunteers and locals was recruited to carry out a questionnaire survey of the needs of close to 700 older people in the rural district west of Lough Neagh in Northern Ireland. The intention was to use the findings, on housing amenities, social contacts, services received and unmet needs, to inform the development of new initiatives. Those identified included outreach services, community transport, luncheon clubs and drop-in services (Age Concern Cookstown 1997). Just as important were the enhancement of life skills and increased sense of satisfaction experienced by the volunteer interviewees whose training, based on role play and covering issues of confidentiality, helped to promote their communication skills. Not only did their individual feedback inform the final report, but many have gone on to help organise a carers' group.

The recently completed initiative which focuses on ethnic minority older people and their carers in Edinburgh and Lothian (Bhatnagar and Munro 1999) demonstrated the importance of informing older people about available services before involving them in discussions on the adequacy of provision and ways of better meeting their needs. The Pilmeny Development Project, working with Milan (Senior Welfare Council), set up a five-week training course (an 'extended learning experience') for a group of 40 older people and their carers from Indian, Pakistani and Bangladeshi communities, in which both service providers and users were treated as 'educators'. The findings were supplemented by in-depth interviews with eight older Asian men and women and a focus group discussion. They effectively confirmed the failure of providers to respond appropriately to the wide-ranging needs of ethnic minority elders, who notably were defined as aged 50 years or more by ethnic minority participants. They highlighted policy gaps and issues that have been flagged by numerous commentators (see Butt and Mirza 1996). In terms of research processes, the project demonstrated the great importance of interpreting and translation to levels of participation. The need for adequate time to prepare written documents and accurately to explain 'jargon' and specialist terms was particularly important. Ethnic minority older people helped in the production of appropriate written materials, as well as being involved in meetings with service providers to report their findings. Significantly, some of the older users felt young Asian people were unable or ashamed to speak their respective languages and unappreciative of the situation of older Asian people. Their observations raised questions about the promotion of positive discrimination in community service sector employment as a simple solution to meeting the needs of ethnic minority elders.

Our own study shared the concern of the Lothian project to find out more about the needs of older people from ethnic minority groups. We focused specifically on older women, recognising their relative neglect in research and the inextricable intertwining of gender and ageing (Warren and Maltby 1998). This 'pilot' study involved 12 older women from different ethnic backgrounds living in Sheffield and Birmingham. We used a life story approach to establish key topics which might be effective as a starting point in exploring the way in which older women perceive and promote their well-being. Another aim was to consider the usefulness of such methods in illuminating cultural and socio-economic aspects of older women's well-being, and we also sought to give them a voice in the definition of their needs.

The findings highlighted linkages between social integration and well-being, revealed through the older women's discussion of education, employment, marriage, housing, health, activities and attitudes to ageing and older people. While these were common themes in the participants' life stories, there were also clear differences within the group in terms of their experiences. For example, the Pakistani and Chinese women talked of particular problems in accessing health and social services which, moreover, were often limited in terms of meeting certain cultural needs. They nevertheless felt gratitude for services they received as a reflection of growing up in countries which lacked systems of formal support for older people.

Reflection on our chosen approach centred on practical aspects relating to the setting up of the project, as well as the power context in which informants' views may be expressed. We noted, for example, the limitations of 'traditional' methods of recruitment to reach frail older women from ethnic minority groups, some of whom experience considerable isolation and exclusion. More committed and intensive efforts need to be made by researchers to establish contacts and demonstrate their trustworthiness and credibility as researchers. Like Anita Bhatnagar and Anne Munro (1999), we realised the important role of translators and the necessity of adequate briefing about the aims and methods employed. We also considered how differences in gender and age between researchers and interviewees may or may not be of significance to action research with older women, as well as the importance of sharing experiences of and attitudes towards ageing.

Other Averil Osborn Fund projects have used a mix of traditional and less conventional approaches to elicit older people's views on services and to disseminate findings. The Greater Manchester Centre for Voluntary Organisation (GMCVO) Older People's Initiative, co-ordinated by Carol Toffaleti, involved local consultation with voluntary organisations and older people's groups in four districts of the county about their housing concerns (Toffaleti 1997a). The findings were taken forward in innovatory ways. Older people were encouraged to press their political representatives for investment in housing, long-term and community care. They were informed of ways to do this in a user-friendly report (Toffaleti 1997b), which set the findings of a survey of older people's views on housing alongside examples of good practice.

The main aim, however, was to engage older people literally in voicing their needs. This 'action' phase took two paths:

- district-level meetings and a county-wide event, bringing together older people, providers and policy makers to share information and discuss concerns, and to promote further local action

- a community drama project, which demonstrated a creative alternative for engaging older people in expressing their views about housing.

The play centred on the impact of 1950s housing developments and was created, written and performed by and to audiences of older people. It was recorded on a video, *Changing Services* (Ordsall Local History and Drama Group 1998), and targeted at diverse service providers. In parallel, the priorities for local action identified within the county-wide seminar were incorporated into a four-page summary, 'Acting Locally to Improve Housing Choices for Older People'.

The products of older people's views were also collected and disseminated by the Homes and Housing Project, evaluated by Ruth Hecht (1997). In this case, older people living in rural Wiltshire were provided with the opportunity to use photography and image making (videos and computers) to explore ideas about housing issues. The initiators of the project, health promotion professionals from Bristol and Bath, recruited individuals from day centres and residential homes. They learnt and worked together as a group, acquiring new creative skills and an increased sense of confidence, self-esteem and control. An exhibition of their work was set up as an example of good practice at an Ageing Safely health promotion conference and a touring exhibition of the project planned. Members of the steering committee appear to have been the main participants in project presentations. Yet a clear strength of the project, in which images played a central role, was its potential to 'include' frail and isolated older people in the dissemination of findings through other means. In addition, the evaluation report of the project offered valuable reflections on practical, ethical and training issues relating to participatory working with a heterogeneous group of older people.

An innovative alternative to surveys, consultations and arts-based approaches was explored in the developmental project run by *ConsultAGE*, Richard Hollingbery's independent consultancy in ageing, and the Centre for Applied Gerontology (CAG) at the University of Birmingham (Hollingbery 1998, 1999). The grant was used to run a discussion group and two focus group sessions with volunteer participants drawn from CAG's standing panel, the Thousand Elders, to explore the feasibility of extending the centre's distinctive 'mystery (or secret) shopper' work from the commercial to the public services sector. Here the idea was to use 'mystery patients' to monitor and evaluate support received from health or social services.

What emerged from the group meetings was a focus on the common experience of hospital visits and a range of associated aspects (good and bad), including transport, the admissions process, information, facilities, attitudes of staff and nature of the visit. Of particular interest in relation to the development of the project, however, were the attitudes of older people themselves. The title of Hollingbery's (1999) report, *You Can't Ring the Bell!*, captures the older patients' perception of being a 'sitting target' and their concern for repercussions if they speak up for themselves. The outcome of the exercise was a recommendation that trained 'mystery visitors' be used instead of mystery patients and that they should be tasked to report back on specific matters rather than looking for general problems. The benefits of such a system are that it would not depend on make-believe complaints and would, for example, provide a formal system surrounding the activity, along the lines of arm's-length assessments of residential homes. It would also be less vulnerable to accusations of patient or researcher subjectivity (though it may be feasible for individuals undergoing elective surgery to participate). Older people would be involved centrally as observers, researchers and information and data providers, encouraging them to take a more assertive and proactive approach to getting the best out of services.

Conclusions: Involving older people in research

Commentators have described the practices of public and user involvement as 'technologies of legitimation': by which managerial legitimacy is maintained in an increasingly pluralistic policy arena (Harrison and Mort 1998; Williams, Popay and Oakley 1999). Where attention has been given to the 'crisis' in local democracy, it has been concentrated largely on evaluating the impact of initiatives on the lives of young people, ethnic minority groups and poor people. Although older people are aware that they have a lot of knowledge and experience to share, their views have seldom been sought or valued by government (Boaz, Hayden and Bernard 1999). Public and private sector bodies have recently made collaborative efforts to encourage the engagement of the general public in change.[7] Nevertheless, we are still some way from the full involvement of older people in the research process, especially as the actual initiators of research.

Of course not all voices are 'quiet' (Barnes and Bennett 1998). The next generation of older people – those who grew up in the 1940s and 1950s – may well have higher expectations, be more demanding and vocal about what they will and will not expect, and researchers are making efforts to research and work with older people, as the projects above clearly demonstrate. Notwithstanding the shifting philosophies of welfare research (Williams *et al.* 1999), there is still little commentary on or analysis of the effect of user involvement on research itself and of broader collaboration. Key concerns include the potential conflicts of interest among researchers, users, service providers and other relevant participants. The potential to exploit or exclude participants needs to be recognised and the ultimate ownership of findings made clear. Adequate resources are necessary to prepare for research projects which secure the involvement of service users. Researchers must be skilled in working with users. They must recognise the existence of generational differences as much as language differences and their responsibility to include those with impairments or learning disabilities. There is also the question of 'how to move from participation [in the research process] to [participation in the] implementation of findings' (Peace 1999, p.27). Crucially, participatory projects need to demonstrate how their results have fed into or influenced policy or practice (Carter and Beresford 2000).

The Averil Osborn funded projects have illuminated several of these issues as well as other important concerns, not all of which follow from limited funding. Few, for example, have discussed how outcomes are to be monitored and evaluated post-dissemination. Neither have they addressed the issue of the impact of the withdrawal of project workers on the lives of older participants and the sustainability of initiatives. The implications of the fact that not all older people want to be involved in participatory projects, or, where they are, to be involved to the same degree, has seldom been discussed. Like other examples of action research, initiatives are vulnerable to charges of being unrepresentative or subjective (Peace 1999). Indeed, in Craig's research (1997), did reliance on the judgements of the mediators, albeit older people themselves, allow older individuals involved in conflicts fully to 'name their reality' (p.56) or guarantee reliable and 'objective' reports of abuse and distress, even though observations were cross-checked? The accessibility of the more academic accounts of research findings, our own included, has also been thrown into question (Penhale 1998), with implications for their use by practitioners.

On the other hand, several positive developments have followed as a result of the award of Averil Osborn funding. The public confession from service providers in the Manchester project that they thought they knew what older people needed, but realised that they may not (Toffaleti 1997a, p.14), suggests that a new understanding was attained. Among the older participants, many learnt both that research skills 'are not a mysterious set of tasks that only highly trained academics can apply' (Peace 1999, p.23) and that they can bring a new language to and have a voice in conveying the findings. Many have experienced an increase in self-confidence as a result. A wide range of different models of participation targeting different topics has been supported and continues to be expanded. For example, we are fortunate in being able to develop our own research with support from the ESRC's Growing Older programme.

In general, however, it is still the case, as Osborn warned (1984), that academics may be subject to organisational expectations and con- straints, preventing them from taking part in research utilisation directly or from seeing it as a major or legitimate role. Under pressure to produce 'quick-fix' policy recommendations with limited and temporary funding, their efforts to encourage the participation of users within research may be subject to the same criticism of consultations more broadly: that is, they typically give another voice to those whose voices are already heard rather than to those who are isolated or hard to reach (Mabileau 1989; Warren 1999).

The Averil Osborn Fund can do little to overcome these hurdles directly. Its most important role in supporting processes of involvement in provision and change is acting as a channel for 'the sharing of experience on how to do it, how *not* to do it [author's emphasis], and the sharing of successes' ('Taking It On: Issues' pamphlet, p.9, in Osborn 1991). Moreover, the projects which it funds offer a potential model for the way forward in the 'user-friendly' presentation of research findings (Osborn and Willcocks 1990, p.196) currently sought by government ministers who desire clarity to be substituted for jargon (Major 2000). Dissemination will not only be 'about older people and for older people' (Osborn 1990, p.201) but also by older people. An additional benefit to arise from involving older people in research is the demystifying of the research process itself, which will be open to user critique (Warren 1999). Knowledge becomes owned by users and professionals alike, and control over its analysis and interpretation shifts from the hands of academics and policy makers. Finally, if the fund does become permanent it will provide a welcome test to Osborn's belief in the slow steady impact on assumptions and attitudes that is probably the major contribution of research. Despite their weaknesses, each of the Averil Osborn projects described above is, then, a small yellow brick in the research funding path to empowerment. They are helping to transform research utilisation from its status as 'another Cinderella' (Osborn 1984) to being a Dorothy on the road to self-help, but with the collective support from her friends.

Notes

1   For reviews and examples of different models of older people's involvement, see Barnes (1999); Cooper, Sidell and Lewisham, Older Women's Health Project (1994); Dodd, Mooney and Williams (1999); Fisk (1997); Goodman and Outram (1999); Mosse and Thornton (1999); Thornton and Tozer (1994, 1995); Tozer and Thornton (1995).

2.   In 2000 the ESRC is to receive 3 per cent more funding in real terms than last year, with another 2.5 per cent promised for 2000–01 (Walker 2000).

3   The latest report on the Averil Osborn Fund, written by Tony Warnes (1999), can be found in *Generations Review 9*, 3, 21–23. Details of how to apply for funding can be found at the British Society of Gerontology website (www.soc.surrey.ac.uk/bsg) or in writing from Prof. Tony Warnes, SISA, University of Sheffield, Community Science Building, Northern General Hospital, Sheffield S5 7AU.

4   Following her death, Averil Osborn's husband, Bob Peacock, donated her books, reports and papers on planning and voluntary groups to the Centre for Policy on Ageing. These have now been catalogued with its main library and resource collections.

5.   The Fund depends on charitable donations and income is small scale. Awards are therefore in the range of £500 to £1500.

6.   The symposium included a presentation by one of the older participants in the Cookstown project, Margaret Gilbert.

7.   On 23 February 2000, *The Guardian* and the Institute for Public Policy Research launched the Public Involvement Awards to be granted to 'the best and most innovative public involvement in the UK'. The scheme has been set up with support from Asda. Organisations which apply will be required to demonstrate that their policies or processes have been significantly improved as a result (see www.pip.org.uk).

References

Age Concern Cookstown (1997) *An Analysis of the Needs and Services Required by Senior Citizens in the Cookstown Area.* Cookstown, Tyrone: Age Concern Cookstown.

Barnes, C. and Mercer, G. (eds) (1996) *Exploring the Divide: Illness and Disability.* Leeds: Disability Press.

Barnes, M. (1999) 'Users as Citizens: Collective Action and the Local Governance of Welfare.' *Social Policy and Administration 33,* 1, 73–90.

Barnes, M. and Bennett, G. (1998) 'Frail Bodies, Courageous Voices: Older People Influencing Community Care.' *Health and Social Care in the Community 6,* 2, 102–111.

Beresford, P. (1992) 'Researching Citizen Involvement: A Collaborative or Colonising Exercise?' In M. Barnes and G. Wistow (eds) *Researching User Involvement.* Leeds: Nuffield Institute for Health, University of Leeds.

Beresford, P. (1997) 'The Last Social Division? Revisiting the Relationship Between Social Policy, Its Producers and Consumers.' In M. May, E. Brunsdon and G. Craig (eds) *Social Policy Review 9.* London: Social Policy Association.

Better Government for Older People Programme (BGOP) (1999) *Making It Happen: Report of the First Year of the Programme 1998–99.* London: Cabinet Office. Available from www.bettergovernmentforolderpeople.gov.uk (accessed 9 April 2000).

Bhatnagar, A. and Munro, A. (1999) *Understanding Community Care: Needs of Minority Ethnic Older People and Their Carers in Edinburgh.* Edinburgh: Pilmeny Development Project.

Boaz, A. (2000) *Listening to Local Older People: Progress on Consultation in the 28 Better Government for Older People Pilots.* Warwick: Warwick Business School, University of Warwick.

Boaz, A., Hayden, A. and Bernard, M. (1999) *Attitudes and Aspirations of Older People: A Review of the Literature.* Leeds: Corporate Document Services, Leeds City Council.

Butt, J. and Mirza, K. (1996) *Social Care and Black Communities.* London: HMSO.

Cabinet Office (1999) *Modernising Government.* London: Cabinet Office.

Carter, T. and Beresford, P. (2000) *Models of Involvement for Older People.* Briefing Report for the Steering Group, Older People's Programme. York: Joseph Rowntree Foundation. Available from www.jrf.org.uk/funding/priorities/scdc.htm#models (accessed 7 April 2000).

Cooper, M., Sidell, M. and the Lewisham Older Women's Health Survey Project (1994) *Lewisham Older Women's Health Survey.* London: EdROP, The City Lit Institute.

Craig, Y. (1992) 'Elder Mediation.' *Generations Review 2,* 3, 4–5.

Craig, Y. (1995) 'EMPowerment Not EMPire-Building.' *Generations Review 5,* 1, 7–9.

Craig, Y. (1997) *Elder Abuse and Mediation: Exploratory Studies in America, Britain and Europe.* Aldershot: Avebury.

Department of Social Security for the Ministerial Group on Older People (1998) *Building a Better Britain for Older People.* Hayes: Welfare Reform.

Dodd, H., Mooney, R. and Williams, C. (1999) 'Lewisham Older Women's Network: The Health Survey.' In S. Peace (ed) *Involving Older People in Research: 'An Amateur Doing the Work of a Professional'.* London: Centre for Policy on Ageing.

Dunning, A. (1999) 'The Participation of Older People in Policy Making.' *Generations Review 9,* 4, 19.

Fisk, M. (1997) 'Older People as Researchers.' In R. Sykes (ed) *Putting Older People in the Picture.* Kidlington, Oxfordshire: Anchor Trust.

Goodman, D. and Outram, S. (1999) 'Life on the Margins: Hidden Poverty and the "Real" Cost of Living for Pensions.' In S. Peace (ed) *Involving Older People in Research: 'An Amateur Doing the Work of a Professional'*. London: Centre for Policy on Ageing.

Harrison, S. and Mort, M. (1998) 'Which Champions, Which People? Public and User Involvement in Health Care as a Technology of Legitimation.' *Social Policy and Administration 32*, 1, 60–70.

Hecht, R. (1997) *Empowerment of Older People through the Arts: Evaluation Report*. Bristol: Bristol Area Specialist Health Promotion Service and Bath Health Promotion.

Hollingbery, R. (1998) *'You Can't Ring the Bell!' A Proposal to Develop 'Mystery Visitors' as a Quality Audit System Using the Experience of Older People Who Use Health and Social Services*. Petersfield: ConsultAGE in association with the Centre for Applied Gerontology, University of Birmingham.

Hollingbery, R. (1999) 'You Can't Ring the Bell!' *Generations Review 9*, 1, 17.

Jacques, A., Forster, A., Mein, H. and Osborn, A. (eds) (1986) *Reaching Out to Dementia Sufferers and Their Carers*. Edinburgh: Age Concern Scotland.

Mabileau, A. (1989) *Local Politics and Participation in Britain and France*. Cambridge: Cambridge University Press.

Major, L.E. (2000) 'Simply impossible.' *The Guardian*, 1 January.

Morris, J. (1991) '"Us" and "them"? Feminist Research, Community Care and Disability.' *Critical Social Policy 33*, 22–39.

Mosse, E. and Thornton, P. (1999) 'A Meeting of Minds: Older People as Research Advisors.' In S. Peace (ed) *Involving Older People in Research: 'An Amateur Doing the Work of a Professional'*. London: Centre for Policy on Ageing.

Nocon, A. and Qureshi, H. (1996) *Outcomes of Community Care for Users and Carers*. Buckingham: Open University Press.

Ordsall Local History and Drama Group (1998) *Changing Places*. Video film recording. Manchester: Community Arts North West in association with the Housing Corporation (North West Office) and Greater Manchester Centre for Voluntary Organisation.

Osborn, A. (1984) 'Research Utilisation: Another Cinderella?' In D.B. Bromley (ed) *Gerontology: Social and Behavioural Perspectives*. London: Croom Helm.

Osborn, A. (1985a) *Day Care for Older People in Day Centres: A Discussion Paper*. Edinburgh: Age Concern Scotland.

Osborn, A. (1985b) 'Short-Term Funded Projects: A Creative Response to an Ageing Population?' In A. Butler (ed) *Ageing: Recent Advances and Creative Responses*. London: Croom Helm.

Osborn, A. (1990) *Small and Beautiful*. Edinburgh: Age Concern Scotland.

Osborn, A. (1991) *Taking Part in Community Care Planning: The Involvement of User Groups, Carer Groups and Voluntary Groups*. Leeds: Nuffield Institute for Health Service Studies and Age Concern Scotland. (A guidelines pack with several separately titled and numbered pamphlets.)

Osborn, A. and Willcocks, D. (1990) 'Making Research Useful and Usable.' In S. Peace (ed) *Researching Social Gerontology*. London: Sage.

Peace, S. (ed) (1999) *Involving Older People in Research: 'An Amateur Doing the Work of a Professional'*. London: Centre for Policy on Ageing.

Penhale, B. (1998) 'Review of Yvonne Joan Craig's *Elder Abuse and Mediation*.' *Ageing and Society 18*, 3, 382–384.

Rappert, B. (1997) 'Users and Social Science Research: Policy, Problems and Possibilities.' *Sociological Research Online* 2, 3. Available from www.socresonline.org.uk/socresonline/2//3/3.html (accessed 7 April 2000).

Robertson, A. and Osborn, A. (1985) 'Introduction.' In A. Robertson and A. Osborn (eds) *Planning to Care: Social Policy and the Quality of Life*. Aldershot: Gower.

Thomas, C. (1997) 'The Baby and the Bath Water: Disabled Women and Motherhood in Social Context.' *Sociology of Health and Illness 19*, 5, 622–643.

Thornton, P. and Tozer, R. (1994) *Involving Older People in Planning and Evaluating Community Care: A Review of Initiatives*. York: Social Policy Research Unit, University of York.

Thornton, P. and Tozer, R. (1995) *Having a Say in Change: Older People and Community Care*. York: Joseph Rowntree Foundation in association with *Community Care* magazine.

Toffaleti, C. (1997a) *The Older People's Initiative. Giving Older People a Say. Acting Locally to Improve Housing Choices*. Manchester: Greater Manchester Centre for Voluntary Organisation.

Toffaleti, C. (1997b) *Voices for Choices. What Older People Say about Their Housing. Examples of Good Practice in Housing and Linked Services*. Manchester: Greater Manchester Centre for Voluntary Organisation.

Tozer, R. and Thornton, P. (1995) *A Meeting of Minds: Older People as Research Advisers*. York: Social Policy Research Unit, University of York.

Walker, A. (1999) 'The ESRC Growing Older Programme.' *Generations Review 9*, 4, 6.

Walker, D. (2000) 'Looking for Evidence.' *The Guardian*, 24 February.

Warnes, A.M. (1999) 'Stimulating Joined-Up Research – A Report of the First Four Years Work of the Averil Osborn Memorial Research Fund.' *Generations Review 9*, 3, 21–23.

Warren, L. (1999) 'Empowerment: The Path to Partnership?' In M. Barnes and L. Warren (eds) *Paths to Empowerment*. Bristol: Policy Press.

Warren, L. and Maltby, T. (1998) 'Researching Older Women's Lives and Voices. Older Women in the United Kingdom: Lives and Voices.' Paper delivered to the 14th World Congress of Sociology, Montreal, July–August.

Williams, F., Popay, J. and Oakley, A. (1999) 'Changing Paradigms of Welfare.' In F. Williams, J. Popay and A. Oakley (eds) *Welfare Research: A Critical Review*. London: UCL Press.

CHAPTER 18

Care Services
for Older People
The Forward Agenda

Anthony M. Warnes, Lorna Warren and Michael Nolan

As noted in the Preface, a distinguishing feature of the British Society of Gerontology (BSG) as a learned society is the diversity of its members. They are drawn from several academic disciplines and include both practitioners from the caring professions as well as professionals, advocates and activists from other occupations; for example, journalism, town planning and third world development. What all have in common, however, is the desire both to improve the understanding of ageing and to harness new approaches to raising the quality of life of older people.

The contents of this volume reflect this primary aim and also capture the catholicity of the BSG. Given this diversity, one would not expect the contributors to share a consensus about the priorities for the development of services for older people: indeed, the chapters reveal both common ground and disagreements. There are, for example, fewer remarks about the lack or underprovision of services to older people than one might expect, given that others have recently complained vigorously about the availability of community care packages, mental health services and primary care. Another surprise perhaps is that while age discrimination in the availability of acute hospital procedures has been castigated, it has only been mentioned in two chapters and the pervasive use of age to define eligibility to services has not been widely challenged. Nor has the feminisation of the ageing population proved a starting point for any of the analyses, despite the recognition of its key significance for public policy (Arber and Ginn 1991, 1996; Bernard and Meade 1993; Gannon 1998), although the importance of gender to issues of care-giving, the receipt of care and involvement in care services is raised in several chapters. The comparative silence on some issues contrasts markedly with virtually all analyses of the incomes of older people, which while recognising the considerable reductions in poverty in recent decades still decry its high prevalence among very old people, particularly widowed women living alone. With partial exceptions for residential, nursing, social and palliative care, the dominant criticisms in this book are much more about the poor quality of services and the lack of respect and humanity which accompany their delivery than either their non-existence or sparseness. Unless this emphasis is wholly idiosyncratic, one suspects that it marks the considerable progress in the availability of services over 30 years ago.

This final chapter concentrates on three themes which have emerged from the contributions and which reflect the distinctive 'gaze' of the BSG. The first reflects briefly upon the broad outline of our societies' (or governments') task in providing services for older people during the early decades of the new century. The second develops the points just introduced about the desired and desirable qualities of care delivery and thereby discusses a task mainly for practitioners. The third draws from the more specialised contributions to this book and applies theoretical and critical perspectives to the current array and arrangements of services: clear gaps and defects are identified which call for both policy makers' and practitioners' attention. The chapter and book conclude with a reflective commentary on the current British government's agenda for modernising and improving services for older people.

Meeting demands and expectations in the early twenty-first century

For several decades the implications of demographic ageing for our societies and particularly the welfare and care systems have been documented, debated and cynically recruited for ideological, political, institutional, professional and personal ends. Everyone now knows that 'we are living longer' and that the older population is growing. From the 1970s, many commentators predicted an increase of disability among older people, not only from rising numbers but also because improving medical technology would save people from dying without curing them, producing an exponentially increasing burden of health care services and costs (e.g. Teeling Smith 1989, p.3). Siegel's (1980) 'compression of morbidity' model attracted worldwide attention, but oddly most often prompted predictions of more extended disability. These were enabled in Britain by the absence of reliable time series data and by reference to self-report measures (as from the General Household Survey) and local surveys of presenting patients.

Governments have responded in a characteristic sequence, first with defensive cuts and retrenchment and then with constructive welfare proposals (well shown for the Netherlands by De Boer 1999). Gerontological issues and services have come much closer to the forefront of British policy and commercial concerns during the last decade (Harper 2000; Warnes 1999a). If the initial responses were as elsewhere most concerned with macro-economic management, the need to raise the quality of life of people with impairments and chronic conditions has also been recognised. It remains the case, however, that most politicians, economists and current affairs journalists are concerned more by the 'burden' of the growing number of older people on the rest of the population than the promotion of older people's interests – the inverse of the priorities of most members of the BSG (Jamieson, Harper and Victor 1997). Even the current mantra that statutory services should be reorganised to promote independence is inspired more by the government's wish to suppress utilisation than to meet the public's demands. How then do those with 'gerontological imagination' see the prospects of our 'ageing societies'?

Will the burden of disability grow?

Few are yet aware that the deterministic conclusion about a growing volume of disability is not now the most likely scenario. While this is not the place for a detailed account of demographic and health in later life trends (for which see Caselli and Lopez 1996; Charlton and Murphy 1997), the associations between the number of old people, the prevalence of disability and the demands for treatment, care and support repay scrutiny. During the late 1990s, a clutch of analyses of large US datasets have shown that the country's old age disability rates have recently been falling at an increasing rate (Crimmins, Reynolds and Saito 1999; Freedman and Martin 1998; Manton, Corder and Stallard 1997; Manton, Stallard and Corder 1998; National Institute of Aging 1999). One source has been four Long-Term Care Surveys between 1982 and 1994 which have categorised an individual as chronically disabled if he or she has a functional limitation lasting for at least 90 days. Age-specific disability rates declined between 1982 and 1989 at about 1.1 per cent per year, and between 1989 and 1994 at about 1.5 per cent p.a. At the current prevalence rate the number of older Americans with chronic disabilities will remain around 7 million even as the total older population grows. Manton's team have made projections of a 'disability adjusted support ratio'; that is, the number of adults aged 20 to 64 years for each chronically disabled person aged 65 or more. The current figure is 22 and if disability rates stay constant, by 2050 the ratio falls to 8, but if they continue to decline by 1.5 per cent p.a. the ratio will increase.

Similar trend data are not available for the UK, but since the 1960s there have been accelerating falls in age-specific old age mortality and it is highly likely that they have been accompanied by decreasing morbidity (Warnes 1999b). It would however be prudent to except disability from organic brain damage, for although age-specific stroke-induced deficits can be reduced by better management of at-risk patients, and despite some reports of an inverse association between educational attainment and the age-specific incidence of Alzheimer's dementia, age does appear to be the most influential factor. Just as the idea has recently spread that older people are not and need not be economically and socially unproductive, and the stereotype that all older people are frail and sick is now more often rejected than advanced, so will we see the realisation slowly spread that age-specific morbidity and disability rates are likely to fall.

Desirable qualities of treatment, care and support

The day when the dominant concern of policy makers turns from how on earth to 'cope' with the growing number of older people to finding the best ways of raising the quality and responsiveness of care cannot come too soon. The contributors to this book repeatedly call for improvements in the delivery of treatment, care and support to be improved but reveal contrasting emphases. One focus, for instance, is on the body, it being argued that medicine should shed its corporal fixation and adopt a more holistic paradigm. Others conversely suggest that the body should be a central concern in the provision of personal care. Such contrasts reflect in several ways the 'boundaries' between services which are a recurring theme and which, as Gillian Dalley notes, have repeatedly proved resistant to exhortations for 'seamlessness'. Central to Dalley's thesis is the need to move beyond 'theory-free' policy and practice and to recognise that services are constricted by their focus on 'technical' tasks, which ensures that personal and humane qualities are 'singularly absent'. Others contend that the barriers which inhibit older people from full citizenship will not be overcome until our notion of what it means to be a 'citizen' is based on 'relationality and interdependence' rather than autonomy. This means challenging the stereotype of what it means to be 'old and frail' and that it does not equate with being 'silent'.

The contributors advance disparate representations of old age and particularly of frailty. Coleman, for instance, in Chapter 13 gently chides 'experts' (including gerontologists) for their preoccupation with the negative aspects of ageing, and he calls for a move away from decline and disability towards well-being and independence. To him, our challenge is to enable people to reach old age in optimum health with the resources and attitudes that preserve independence and a good quality of life. In bold contrast, Dalley laments the emergence of rehabilitation and the new orthodoxy that independence and autonomy should be promoted, for she believes it creates the possibility that the very old and frail will be excluded from mainstream policy. She argues that by proselytising an ideal of 'successful ageing' based on these attributes, gerontologists are contributing to the further marginalisation of significant numbers of older people.[1]

Such tensions are of more than theoretical interest and lie at the heart of many contemporary debates about the future of care services. These are captured by a number of contributors who call for a change in the 'culture of care', with advocacy for person-centred care figuring prominently. Nowhere is this more apparent than in the National Service Framework (NSF) for Older People, the underpinning value of which, we are told, is person-centred care (see Chapter 5). The NSF aims to be 'ambitious but realistic' – the ambition extending to rooting out age discrimination and making horror stories about health and social care for older people a thing of the past. This is to be achieved by a focus on patients rather than the organisation of care and through generic quality standards and new indicators for the delivery of health and social care and the transitions between care environments. The size and difficulty of the task is clearly illustrated by the chapters on the transition to residential care. These eschew 'horror stories' but nonetheless highlight the relative powerlessness, passivity and exclusion still experienced by older people and their carers during one of the most difficult decisions of later life. Such studies seem to reinforce Dalley's assertion that the ideal of the seamless service is a chimerical 'pipe dream'.

It would be false to summarise the contributions as dominantly pessimistic for several have positive messages about the potential for new technology and design to aid decision making and involvement, to enhance empowerment and to reduce social exclusion. Arguably most important of all is the optimism that is expressed about the interaction between those providing and receiving support. Clarke and Hanson in Chapter 12 stress the positive personal qualities of care workers and their role in establishing close relationships. This opinion is shared in the previous chapter by Samuelsson, although he highlights the influence on 'trust' of both the continuity of the staff–client relationship and competence in the delivery of care. From the perspective of the recipients of domiciliary and nursing home care, the acceptability and

appreciation of care hinges on the extent to which they are delivered with 'personal and humane qualities'. It is therefore dismaying that, as the contributors point out, the 'therapeutic role' of the social worker has all but disappeared, and nursing moves away from personal towards technical care. These are not just the pieties of handwringing empathisers, they are shared by the studiously objective and hard-headed public finance auditors:

> [Personal qualities] are not added extras but are essential to a sense of personal security and quality-of-life for [older] people living with illness, disability and deteriorating health. National Health Service Trusts and Commissioners should recognise that, with pressure on services to increase efficiency and the rise in technical, as opposed to personal, nursing care, there is a danger that some of the things that patients say they value most highly will be lost. (Audit Commission 1999a, p.53)

Many studies of older and disabled people, carers and front-line practitioners similarly stress the importance of person-centred care by staff who combine technical competence with the skills of negotiation and mediation (Farrell, Robinson and Fletcher 1999). Yet they simultaneously point to the low status of work with older people and the continued denigration of the caring components. According to Easterbrook (1999), the main problem is a pervasive lack of vision about services for older people combined with tolerance of the current 'hotchpotch of innovation and good practice coupled with instances of poor standards, neglect and incompetence' (ibid., p.33).

In promoting the forthcoming NSF for Older People, the Minister John Hutton (1999, p.2) stated that the government will not tolerate poor standards of care for older people and argued that in adopting evidence-based care, it is essential to recognise that 'the views of older people and their carers, including personal experiences, are a key and essential part of this evidence'. As Barnes (1999) notes, there has been a general shift away from 'blind trust' in professionals and the emergence of a new discourse of partnership that provides a fundamental challenge to 'expert' authority, whether professional or academic. There are also the first signs of recognition that formal services (especially for older people) have made too many presumptions about what people need and prefer, and have been too slow to respond to the increased ethnic, cultural and behavioural diversity of the country, as well as to the significance of gender in patterns of care provision and use. It is to these issues that we now turn.

Implementing person-centredness: Diversity, participation and inclusion

Ethnic minority elders and care

For much of the life of the welfare state, care services have consistently failed to address the needs of certain sectors of the older population. Unresponsive and monolithic attitudes have persisted because they have been driven by rationalistic and bureaucratic approaches and producer interests in the absence of a conceptual framework for care (Bernard and Phillips 2000). The clearest demonstration is that the needs of people from ethnic minority groups have been low on the policy, practice and research agenda.[2] Consequently, responses by both health and social service agencies to variations in cultural background have been particularly ad hoc and patchy (Morton 1993). The rapid growth in the number of ethnic minority older people, especially those originating from the Indian subcontinent and the Caribbean, challenges the head-in-sand argument that there are too few to cause concern (Ahmad and Atkin 1996; Atkin, Lunt and Thompson 1999; Owen 1996). Explanatory concepts of 'jeopardy' have been advanced and critiqued to highlight the risks and barriers faced by ethnic minority elders (Blakemore and Boneham 1994; Butt and Mirza 1996; Norman 1985).

Critical gerontology offers ways of thinking about culture and ethnicity that go beyond minority group status. They are supported by empirical studies which have explored the experiences of older people as migrants and as immigrants, and the cultural and social context of their specific experiences of ageing. In Chapter 15, Chau and Yu's study of Chinese older people who have migrated to the UK for economic reasons reveals their social exclusion resulting from the difficulties they experience in balancing the life pattern of their place of origin with maintenance of an economic status, in this case typically gained through participation in the catering industries. The deterioration of their health and social ability is coupled with the deterioration of the caring capacity of their families. Language barriers and a severe underprovision of support for people from Chinese communities mean that many older Chinese people are unable to use care services to meet their needs effectively. As a result, they suffer 'double detachment' from both host and their own communities.

This sense of detachment is also highlighted in Chapter 16 by Phillipson *et al.* in their study of Bangladeshi families living in Bethnal Green. Older Bangladeshi people – described as 'first generation' – are aware of the simultaneous loss of one 'home' and, perhaps, a sense of rejection from the place where they have finally settled; problems which are magnified for those with poor physical and mental health. That they seek solutions to their situation in ways which echo those documented by Townsend in his influential study of post-war Bethnal Green, in turning wherever possible to extended family groups, reminds us, however, of the common patterns running through the lives of the majority of older people and of the crucial need to make policy more sensitive to the situation of family carers. At the same time, it is important to be suspicious of theories which see ethnic minority elders as defined simply by their disadvantages (Wilson 2000). Such approaches leave no place for the views of those elders themselves. As Barnes and Shaw argue in Chapter 8, they fail to highlight the ways in which organisations set up to support older people are often seen as primarily for white, middle-class people and do not address ethnic minority group concerns. More immediately, they do not allow for the ways in which migrants take charge of their own lives and resist or alter conditions in their country of destination.

Cultures of care

'Culture' does not belong exclusively to older people from ethnic minority groups. The ethnic identities of white majority older people are taken for granted or simply disregarded in much gerontological research (Atkin 1998; Blakemore and Boneham 1994). Yet, distinctive sets of norms and values are held about, as well as by, older people from the dominant white population with implications for patterns of care provision. Longino, in Chapter 2, shows how increasing support for complementary therapeutic health treatment is challenging medical practices and discourses of care, leading to a new paradigm which combines scientific knowledge with a humanistic approach. In parallel, Coleman calls for a shift in design culture that moves from an aids and adaptations approach based on expectations of deficit, decline, disability and dependency to an inclusive, age-aware approach based on active and user-centred independent living. In Chapter 12 by contrast, however, Clarke and Hanson illustrate how public attitudes continue to make death if not taboo then a hidden subject, which blocks older individuals' wish to talk about their care needs in the final stages of their lives. That death is seen as an inevitable part of older age means that palliative care approaches are typically not offered to older people who are terminally ill or whose health is in irreversible decline. Clarke and Hanson's subsequent call for a change in the culture of care echoes those who distinguish the 'gift' of care, which seeks to enable the cared for person and resists the discourse of the vigil (Fox 1995, p.107).

Participation, collective action and care

A key element in challenging discrimination, based both on ageist and racist assumptions and practices, is commitment to notions of empowerment and citizenship. These terms are, in fact, part of a 1990s policy language, which includes the additional concepts of advocacy, user involvement and participation. In Chapter 15, Chau and Yu refer, for example, to a 'start where Chinese older people start' approach. Yet, the ideas are not as new as they might appear. In the 1970s, commentators were arguing for users of services to have more 'voice' (Mayer and Timms 1970), while in the 1980s, Averil Osborn (see Chapter 17) spoke out for 'greater experimentation in participation and self-government' (Osborn 1985, p.11; see also Jacques et al. 1986).

Twigg (Chapter 7) reveals part of the problem to lie in the fact that policy remains predicated on an assumption that a clear distinction can be drawn between the health and social care needs of the individual. The energies and attention of agencies and professionals therefore continue to be focused on defending boundaries (with implications for the financing of care). In their disembodied approaches, aspects of being and of social exchange which care entails are commonly overlooked (Twigg 1997). Assessments thus remain characterised by a service-led rather than a needs-led approach and, as Davies, Sandberg and Lundh demonstrate in Chapter 9 with reference to the selection of a nursing home, older people exercise very little choice over formal sources of support (Bernard and Phillips 2000). If change has taken place within care services, then it has been 'more a shift in rhetoric than substance' (Harper 2000, p.113).

On the other hand, there have been a number of recent developments and measures taken at the local and national level to increase the participation of older people in 'having a say', as Chapters 8 and 17 both show. There is evidence that policy has 'initiated advocacy and elder support groups [as well as strengthened the foundations of existing organisations] that may in the future challenge some of the perceptions and realities of later life' (Harper 2000, p.113). Barnes and Shaw consider various forms of collective action among older people in Chapter 8, illustrating the potential and the dilemmas of such action through specific examples. As they argue, the idea of a 'good old age' offers a possible focus for solidarity which spans all cultural groupings, marginalised identities and ages, given that most of us hope to survive to old age and are likely to find ourselves caring for older relatives. However, support and resources are necessary to make participation possible and older people need to be convinced that the government has a genuine commitment to policies which respect their social rights as citizens.

It is perhaps not surprising, then, that while the spheres in which citizenship can be practised are varied, models of support, policy making and service delivery where older people are in control are most common at the local level. Warren and Maltby offer a review of such models which have been developed with support from the Averil Osborn Fund. In some projects, older people have not only been actively and creatively involved in having a voice, but have also themselves acted as researchers conducting policy-relevant investigations. Increasingly, academic researchers are joining Averil Osborn (Osborn and Willcocks 1990) in highlighting the crucial importance of working with older people and ensuring that research is both useful and usable. There is however still a considerable way to go before the research field ceases to be dominated by 'the other' – that is, younger people (Minichiello and Walker 1996). We are only just beginning to understand how to involve older people in research and how to enable policy makers to note and respond to user-led research.

In Chapter 14, Tetley, Hanson and Clarke demonstrate the important contribution to the participation and empowerment of older people which new technology may provide. Through the use of telematics, the ACTION project is exploring ways of facilitating communication between older carers and service providers and of delivering information in an accessible, user-friendly fashion. The initiative offers a means to reach individuals who are, to a greater or lesser extent, isolated within their own homes and/or who may have language and communication needs not typically met through traditional information channels. The fact that the video acts as a single source of information on a variety of needs also suggests that ACTION may go some way to breaking down some of the barriers between service agencies noted earlier.

Although the ACTION project is exploring the application of technology to care, Tetley, Hanson and Clarke in Chapter 14 warn us that as the new home-based communication technologies spread, older people without the hardware may become less able to be fully participating citizens. Indeed, other commentators have noted the widening gap between people who have easy access to information and those without the computers or the associated skills (Cahill 1994). In contrast, Bernard and Phillips (2000, p.45) are optimistic because of the pressures from older people to be regarded as 'active consumers', within professional groups to reorient their practices and question their professional autonomy, and from the government for older people to take rights-based action on their own behalf. These trends offer the possibility of developing a 'culture of empowerment' for policy making and service provision. Nevertheless, there are still questions about the extent to which empowering older people – whether as customers, consultees or researchers – will address the problems of very frail people who typically have been defined by their relationship with welfare services.

As Barnes and Shaw in Chapter 8 and Reed and Stanley in Chapter 10 point out, stereotypes of passivity and dependency still need to be challenged to protect the gains that have been made.

Gender and care

This desire to see users become agents rather than recipients has recently been promoted strongly with reference to older women. Barnes and Shaw express several commentators' advocacy of citizenship based on justice, an ethic of care and notions of relationality and interdependence within and between generations (see Chapter 8). Such an approach would help to recognise and respect the special position of older women in relation to care services. They are the main users of several services and often the main negotiators with care providers on behalf of their relatives. While for some women migration to this country may open up new possibilities for power and influence, for many others the transition is not empowering, as the interviews with the Bangladeshi women carers in Chapter 16 illustrate. There is a clear need for more research into perceptions and patterns of resistance and change among older women from ethnic minority groups, especially in relation to public service provision (Warren and Maltby 1998). Emphasis on an ethic of care approach in research as well as the forward agenda for care services has the potential to capture the values characterising the lives and motivations of older women. It would, moreover, benefit those working in the social work and social care sectors – typically women – where gendered distinctions between care and cure divide service provision and are played out in the ranking and subsequent resourcing of services (see Chapter 7).

Reform and modernisation

The book concludes with a brief examination of the many policy initiatives that the present British government has taken to reform and improve services for older people. Even in these early days, is it possible to see the likely successes and failures? To what extent will the measures address the issues raised in this book and its recommendations and, specifically, what chance do they have of raising the person-centredness of care and their responsiveness to diverse needs? The government's ten-year programme of modernisation specifies five objectives (including caring for vulnerable people) and eight diverse priorities, among which are 'older people's services'. Included are the proposals for governance, four 'quality' objectives and four relating to staff. The following undertakings are particularly relevant (some are edited):

- Implement the National Service Frameworks and promote the effective use of National Institute of Clinical Effectiveness guidance.

- Increase satisfaction by involving and responding to patients and the public.

- Implement joint charters for long-term care in line with *Better Care, Higher Standards* by June 2000.

- Implement a jointly agreed preventative strategy by March 2002.

- By March 2002, provide more diverse and flexible opportunities for carers to have a break, in line with *Caring About Carers.*

- Take action to improve quality in social services.

- For all registered services in health and social care, meet all requirements for frequency of inspection [and] working in partnership.

- Increase the number of doctors, nurses and another health and related professional staff. (DoH 2000, p.6)

Many of these emphases will be more welcome to older people's organisations than to the staff of the services involved: on paper, the ambitions are laudable and the priorities have been selected well. The problem as ever is implementation, for many times in the past similar aims have been announced but in the fullness of time no appreciable or beneficial change has come about.

The quality agenda

An important component of the modernisation plans for the NHS and personal social services is quality maintenance (DoH 1998a). Chapter 5 provides more details of the agencies and procedures that will pursue this agenda in the NHS, among which the National Institute of Clinical Excellence, the National Service Frameworks, new structures for clinical governance and lifelong learning (or retraining) are the most important. The equivalents in the social services are new measures to improve 'protection, standards in the work-force, partnerships, delivery and efficiency' (DoH 1998b); and in the social housing field there is the Best Value Performance Management Framework.[3]

A key ingredient is the promotion of evidence-based practice (EBP), now an orthodoxy in medicine (and more widely)[4] but too infrequently critically examined. One limitation is that while determining whether a drug has on balance a significant beneficial effect is relatively straight-forward, assessing the benefits of protracted, multi-agency treatment, care and support of multiply ill people is problematic. The task calls for intricate comparative studies of different organisational and personnel configurations and the use of hard to define non-somatic outcome measures such as morale, quality of life and satisfaction with a service. Alan Maynard and other contributors to this book raise these issues time and again but find little robust evidence, demonstrating that much more evaluation needs to be done to get away from reforms guided by hunches and good intentions.

Organisation and management of services

A perennial problem of older people's care services is their segmenta-tion between the health and social sectors and in many other ways, for example, between hospitals and community health, between profes-sional social work and (non-professional) social care, and between the treatment of affective mental health disorders (by non-specialists in primary care) and of psychotic and organic disorders (by specialist mental health services) (Norman and Redfern 1997). Not even the post-1993 community care arrangements have overcome the fragmen-tation for those with 'low intensity' needs. Since 1973 in Northern Ireland (with an interruption in the winter of 2000), personal social services have been run along with the NHS by four health and social service boards. It was anticipated that:

there are advantages in health and social care being combined under one agency…the needs of individual patients can be more comprehensively assessed and care provided on a co-ordinated basis. There is also less incentive for shifting costs from one agency's budget to another…[and] may also be economies of scale in management and administration. (Northern Ireland Economic Council 1994, p.95)

As late as 1995, however, community health services and personal social services were managed separately. There were no reports of significant service improvements and 'services had often not developed in an even and co-ordinated fashion and on occasions targeting has been poor' (*ibid.*, p.119).

Modern information handling and telecommunications should enable the smooth (if not entirely seamless) co-ordination of several professionals but have been counteracted by a shift to the care of more highly dependent people at home and the proliferation of specialised roles; for example, the diabetic nurse, the nutritionist and the incontinence adviser. As the Northern Ireland experience shows, more than organisational change is required and most would agree that the key to enduring change is to alter the funding streams and where financial responsibility lies. The Health Act 1999 specifies the new arrangements for Joint Investment Plans and in Sheffield at least rapid progress has been made. Plans are nearing agreement to create elderly 'intermediate care' resource centres in association with primary care trusts and with community health NHS trust and social services staff. These will provide:

- fully integrated assessment and treatment services including a range of rehabilitation and respite places, day places and home support

- formation of a core group of services within each primary care group (trust) accessible by both primary and secondary care including a dedicated multi-professional assessment team (nurses, therapists, social workers and community geriatrician) and community mental health team

- a breakdown of barriers between health and social services, by creating single sets of services with joint management, information systems, documentation and pooled budgets. (Sheffield Health Authority 2000)

Managing rising expectations

Harrison and Dixon (2000) have recently concluded that for all the many achievements and advances of the NHS (which they praise), successive governments have consistently failed to manage its 'crisis': the gap between the public's expectations and NHS performance. Both are rising strongly.

> The need to manage demand for health care [and, we can add, for social and residential care] and the methods to do it…have not been well appreciated in the UK. There has been no serious published analysis of rising utilisation and no visible attempt to forecast future demands. (Harrison and Dixon 2000, p.198)

If there are robust cross-sectional or time series models of the factors influencing the demand for any of health care, personal social services or residential and nursing care,[5] they are little known beyond welfare economics (probably data are unavailable). Tabloid journalism, the Internet, product promotions and telephone helplines are all spreading information and creating demands, while there is a decreasing tolerance of 'rationing', whether by government edict, spending limits or clinical prioritisation.

Whether meeting expectations is approached from a 'rights' or a 'needs' perspective, with the exceptions of general practice and acute conditions, services for older people are perceived to be capricious and generally deficient. Various mechanisms exist to collect, formulate, transmit and exert user-centredness in the human welfare services. In medicine, the role has traditionally been assigned to 'public health'. This works well for communicable diseases and infectious epidemics but has hardly touched service organisation and delivery. Democratic influence on local government services is virtually extinct and formal consultation councils and committees are tokenistic. The pressures to become more patient or user-orientated are exerted mainly now through (and by) the mass media, but could become an important byproduct of the evidence-based agenda. As the Audit Commission increasingly shows, 'evidence' refers as much to unmet need and dissatisfaction as to the efficacy of health technologies. The net effect will be further to challenge the clinician's traditional lead role in deciding the priorities for different types of services and how they should be organised. Over the next decade, finding non-market mechanisms which improve the management of expectations and demand will be crucial to the needs-led public health and social services, not least for domiciliary and residential and nursing home care.

Another dimension of change is however required. Particularly with respect to services for older people and their carers, a main source of much current public concern is the inconsistency and confusion about the categorisation of medical, nursing and personal care. As many analysts have concluded, there has recently been a narrowing construction of free-at-the-point-of-delivery NHS care. Both the Royal Commission on Long-Term Care and Julia Twigg in Chapter 7 propose that this should be reversed. At the same time, if, as in North America, an increasing share of frail and prospectively frail older people, whether encouraged by their concerned relatives or not, wish to enter residential institutions for the personal services, security and social activities they offer, all political parties will maintain that individuals must meet the 'hotel' element of the costs. A clear, widely understood and politically uncontroversial taxonomy of treatment, care and support and of who pays for each form of service would be a considerable advance. It would clarify the roles and long-term prospects for all sectors of the 'mixed economy' of care. To these changes, one other must be added, raising the status and prestige of the care of chronically frail older people, and particularly of those on very low incomes and with no family supporters.

Conclusions

Whatever the deficiencies in British care services for older people today, the variety and quantity of provision have never been greater and both exceed many times over the equivalents in all but a dozen other countries. Nor has there been a precedent for the spate of inquiries and committees during the last few years which have attempted to identify and disseminate good practice and to produce templates of model service organisation.[6] An outside observer would conclude that there is a determination to increase and improve the services that provide treatment, care and support for older people and their carers.

The principle which is most often cited or alluded to in this book is that services can and should become more 'fit for purpose' in several overlapping senses. They should be needs-led, more responsive to users' preferences, more guided by good practice and more efficient or effective. The abstract principle is hardly contentious. Its implementation is however enormously difficult, because it requires changes in policy priorities, in the ways the services are organised and in the balance of influence and control among politicians, executives, professional bodies, front-line staff, current users and the general public. As Tony Culyer (1991) wrote of the relatively lavish and heavily institutional system of support for older people in Sweden:

> The effectiveness of programmes for the elderly must be a high priority for more systematic investigation, using outcome measures that adequately represent those aspects of the lives of elderly people that are sensitive to the ways in which they are cared for. Given the vulnerability of this group, and the huge expense they represent, there is hardly any 'programme' in greater need of thorough investigation. (Culyer 1991, p.8)

There are encouraging signs that in Britain those investigations are under way and that older people's voices have begun to be influential.

Notes

1. This ideal is expounded more by American advocacy organisations than British or European analysts, although leading proponents have been the German psychogerontologists, Paul and (the late) Margret Baltes (1990). Policy presumptions and proposals in Britain sometimes reflect stronger support for American ideas than is found among British researchers and academics.

2. Although both the ESRC 1999–2002 Growing Older programme and the Joseph Rowntree Foundation highlight the ethnic sensitivity of services as key areas for research.

3. This scheme requires local authorities to achieve continuous improvements in services and greater local accountability in their initiatives to house and support vulnerable people. The key elements are setting objectives, adopting challenging performance targets, local perfor-

mance plans, independent audit and certification, and intervention by central government where necessary (Warnes and Crane 2000).

4. EBP has recently been imported into educational research by the British government. Following a highly critical report of recent educational research, the Department for Education and Employment in 1999 appointed Sir Michael Peckham, formerly (1991–95) Director of Research and Development at the Department of Health, as Chair of a new National Educational Research Forum to co-ordinate the structure, process and content of research in education. The forum will meet three times a year to identify research priorities, establish coherence and inform strategic developments.

5. For the difficulties and limitations of models of nursing home utilisation, even in the USA where there are strong insurance industry interests in developing robust models, see Garber and MaCurdy (1990) and the discussant's views.

6. Including Audit Commission (1997, 1999a, 1999b); HAS (1994, 1997, 2000); Help the Aged (1999).

References

Ahmad, W.I.U. and Atkin, K. (eds) (1996) Race and Community Care. Buckingham: Open University Press.

Arber, S. and Ginn, J. (1991) Gender and Later Life. London: Sage.

Arber, S. and Ginn, J. (1996) Connecting Gender and Ageing: A Sociological Approach. Buckingham: Open University Press.

Atkin, K. (1998) 'The Health of Britain's Ethnic Minorities.' Health and Social Care in the Community 6, 5, 389–391

Atkin, K., Lunt, N. and Thompson, C. (eds) (1999) Evaluating Community Nursing. Edinburgh: Baillière Tindall.

Audit Commission (1997) Coming of Age: Improving Care Services for Older People. London: Audit Commission.

Audit Commission (1999a) Forget Me Not: Mental Health Services for Older People. London: Audit Commission.

Audit Commission (1999b) First Assessment: A Review of District Nursing Services in England and Wales. London: Audit Commission.

Baltes, P.B. and Baltes, M.M. (1990) Successful Aging. Cambridge: Cambridge University Press.

Barnes, M. (1999) 'Users as Citizens: Collective Action and the Local Governance of Welfare.' Social Policy and Administration 33, 1, 73–90.

Bernard, M. and Meade, K. (eds) (1993) Women Come of Age. London: Edward Arnold.

Bernard, M. and Phillips, J. (eds) (1997) The Social Policy of Old Age. London: Centre for Policy on Ageing.

Bernard, M. and Phillips, J. (2000) 'The Challenge of Ageing in Tomorrow's Britain.' Ageing and Society 20, 1, 33–54.

Blakemore, K. and Boneham, M. (1994) Age, Race and Ethnicity. Buckingham: Open University Press.

Butt, J. and Mirza, K. (1996) Social Care and Black Communities: A Review of Recent Research Studies. London: HMSO.

Cahill, M. (1994) The New Social Policy. Oxford: Blackwell.

Caselli, G. and Lopez, A.D. (eds) (1996) Health and Mortality among Elderly Populations. Oxford: Clarendon Press.

Charlton, J. and Murphy, M. (eds) (1997) *The Health of Adult Britain 1841–1994*. Office for National Statistics, Decennial Supplement 12. London: HMSO.

Crimmins, E., Reynolds, S. and Saito, Y. (1999) 'Trends in Health and Ability to Work among Older Working-Age Population.' *Journal of Gerontology: Social Sciences 54*, 1, S31–S40.

Culyer, A. (1991) *Health Care and Health Care Finance in Sweden: The Crisis that Never Was; the Tensions that Ever Will Be*. Occasional Paper 33. Stockholm: SNS.

De Boer, A.H. (1999) *Housing and Care for Older People: A Macro–Micro Perspective*. Netherlands Geographical Studies 254. Utrecht: Faculteit Ruimtelijke Wetenschappen, University of Utrecht.

Department of Health (DoH) (1998a) *A First Class Service: Quality in the New NHS*. London: DoH.

Department of Health (DoH) (1998b) *Modernising Social Services: Promoting Independence, Improving Protection, Raising Standards*. Cm. 4169. London: The Stationery Office.

Department of Health (DoH) (2000) *Modernising Health and Social Services: National Priorities Guidance 2000/01–2002/03*. London: DoH.

Easterbrook, L. (1999) *When We Are Very Old: Reflections on Treatment, Care and Support for Older People*. London: King's Fund.

Farrell, C., Robinson, J. and Fletcher, P. (1999) *A New Era for Community Care: What People Want from Health, Housing and Social Care Services*. London: King's Fund.

Fox, N. (1995) 'Post-Modern Perspectives on Care: The Vigil and the Gift.' *Critical Social Policy 44/45*, 107–125.

Freedman, V.A. and Martin, L. G. (1998) 'Understanding Trends in Functional Limitations among Older Americans.' *American Journal of Public Health 88*, 10, 1457–1462.

Gannon, L.R. (1998) *Women and Ageing: Transcending the Myths*. London: Routledge.

Garber, A.M. and MaCurdy, T. (1990) 'Predicting Nursing Home UtilizationAmong the High-Risk Elderly.' In D.A. Wise (ed) *Issues in the Economics of Aging*. Chicago: University of Chicago Press.

Harper, S. (2000) 'Ageing 2000: Questions for the 21st Century.' *Ageing and Society 20*, 1, 111–122.

Harrison, A. and Dixon, J. (2000) *The NHS: Facing the Future*. London: King's Fund.

Health Advisory Service (HAS) (1994) *Comprehensive Health Services for Elderly People*. Sutton: HAS.

Health Advisory Service (HAS) (1997) *Services for People Who Are Elderly. Addressing the Balance: The Multi-Disciplinary Assessment of Elderly People and the Delivery of High Quality Continuing Care*. London: The Stationery Office.

Health Advisory Service (HAS) (2000) *Not Because They Are Old: An Independent Inquiry into the Care of Older People on Acute Wards in General Hospitals*. London: HAS.

Help the Aged (1999) *Dignity on the Ward: Promoting Excellence in Care: Good Practice in Acute Hospital Care for Older People*. London: Help the Aged.

Hutton, J. (1999) 'The National Service Framework.' Paper presented at 'Dignity on the Ward' – The Future of Hospital Care for Older People, Royal College of Physicians, 29 November.

Jacques, A., Forster, A., Mein, H. and Osborn, A. (eds) (1986) *Reaching Out to Dementia Sufferers and Their Carers*. Edinburgh: Age Concern Scotland.

Jamieson, A., Harper, S. and Victor, C. (eds) (1997) *Critical Approaches to Ageing and Later Life*. Buckingham: Open University Press.

Manton, K., Corder, L. and Stallard, E. (1997) 'Chronic Disability Trends in Elderly United States Populations.' *Proceedings of the National Academy of Sciences 94*, 6, 2593–2598.

Manton, K., Stallard, E. and Corder, L. (1998) 'Economic Effects of Reducing Disability.' *American Economic Review 88*, 2, 101–105.

Mayer, J. and Timms, N. (1970) *The Client Speaks.* London: Routledge and Kegan Paul.

Minichiello, V. and Walker, A. (1996) 'Introduction.' In V. Minichiello, N. Chappell, H. Kendig and A. Walker (eds) *Sociology of Ageing: International Perspectives.* Melbourne: International Sociological Association.

Morton, J. (ed) (1993) *Recent Research on Services for Black and Minority Ethnic Elderly People.* London: Age Concern, Institute of Gerontology, King's College London.

National Institute of Aging (1999) *The Declining Disability of Older Americans.* Research Highlights in the Demography and Economics of Aging 5. Bethesda, Maryland: National Institute of Aging.

Norman, A. (1985) *Triple Jeopardy: Growing Old in a Second Homeland.* London: Centre for Policy on Ageing.

Norman, I.J. and Redfern, S.J.R. (eds) (1997) *Mental Health Care for Elderly People.* Edinburgh: Churchill Livingstone.

Northern Ireland Economic Council (NIEC) (1994) *The Reform of Health and Social Care in Northern Ireland: An Introduction to the Economic Issues.* Belfast: NIEC.

Osborn, A. (1985) *Day Care for Older People in Day Centres: A Discussion Paper.* Ediburgh: Age Concern Scotland.

Osborn, A. and Willcocks, D. (1990) 'Making Research Useful and Usable.' In S. Peace (ed) *Researching Social Gerontology.* London: Sage.

Owen, D. (1996) 'Size, Structure and Growth of the Ethnic Minority Populations.' In D. Coleman and J. Salt (eds) *Ethnicity in the 1991 Census.* London: HMSO.

Sheffield Health Authority (SHA) and Sheffield Social Services (2000) *Modernising Health and Social Services for Older People: Sheffield Joint Investment Plan 2000–2001.* Sheffield: SHA.

Siegel, J. (1980) 'Recent and Prospective Trends for the Elderly Population and Implications for Health Care.' In S.G. Haynes and G. Feinleib (eds) *Second Conference on the Epidemiology of Aging.* Bethesda, MA: National Institute of Aging.

Teeling Smith, G. (1989) *Measuring Health: A Practical Approach.* Chichester: Wiley.

Twigg, J. (1997) 'Deconstructing the "Social Bath": Help with Bathing at Home for Older and Disabled People.' *Journal of Social Policy 26*, 2, 211–232.

Warnes, A.M. (1999a) 'A Decade of Gerontology's Development in Britain.' *Contemporary Gerontology 5*, 4, 120–124.

Warnes, A.M. (1999b) 'UK and Western European Late-Age Mortality Rates: Trends in Cause-Specific Death Rates, 1960–1990.' *Health and Place 5*, 1, 111–118.

Warnes, A.M. and Crane, M. (2000) *Meeting Homeless People's Needs: Service Development and Practice for the Older Excluded.* London: King's Fund.

Warren, L. and Maltby, T. (1998) *Older Women in the United Kingdom: Lives and Voices.* Paper delivered at the 14th World Congress of Sociology, Montreal, July–August.

Wilson, G. (2000) *Global Perspectives on Ageing: Issues and Policies.* London: Sage.

The Contributors

Emadad Alhaq, is a manager of several community care projects for the London Borough of Tower Hamlets Social Services. He has worked for the Carers' National Association as a development worker, and extensively on carers' issues, including Carers' Act implementation. He is a qualified counsellor and is currently undertaking an MBA at the University of East London.

Anne Ashe, BA (Hons), MA, MRTPI, is Research Associate at the Sheffield Institute for Studies on Ageing (SISA), University of Sheffield. She is currently involved in assembling the supportive evidence for the National Service Framework for Older People. Her earlier research at SISA was on health and social service needs of older people and on health and ethnicity in later life, and formerly was a research manager at the Department of Employment (now DfEE). She formerly worked and published extensively in policy-oriented social and environmental research at the Policy Studies Institute.

Marian Barnes, BA (Hons), MA, PhD, is Director of Social Research in the Department of Social Policy and Social Work at the University of Birmingham. Much of her work over the last 15 years has been concerned with user involvement and public participation in health and social care and she has written widely on this subject. Her current research includes a study of public participation and social exclusion in the ESRC Democracy and Participation programme. She also has lead responsibility for work on community involvement in the national evaluation of Health Action Zones.

Ruby C.M. Chau, MA, PhD, BSW, is Project Manager of the Lai Yin Association's New Direction Point. Her research interests include ethnic minorities and Chinese communities in Britain, Chinese women and social care, and social welfare and disability in China. She has published articles in *International Urban and Regional Research*, *International Social Work*, *Critical Social Policy*, and the *Hong Kong Journal of Social Work*.

Amanda Clarke, BA (Hons), MA, RGN, is a Lecturer and Research Associate, Department of Gerontological and Continuing Care Nursing, University of Sheffield. Her current research includes a doctoral study of older people's accounts of their experiences and attitudes towards ageing using a biographical approach. She is also working on the EU-funded project, *Assisting Carers using Telematic Interventions to meet Older Person's Needs* (ACTION), featured in Chapter 14.

Roger Coleman, MA (Hons), FRCA, is Senior Research Fellow and Director of the Helen Hamlyn Research Centre at the Royal College of Art (RCA). He delivered the 1992 Kelmscott lecture of the William Morris Society on 'By Accident or Design?', and he has established the DesignAge programme at the RCA and the European Design for Ageing Network. He is a director of R&D company London Innovation. Recent publications include 'Designing for Our Future Selves', in W. Preiser and E. Ostroff (eds), *Universal Design Handbook*, McGraw-Hill, New York, 2000, and articles in *Applied Ergonomics* and the *Journal of the Royal Society of Arts.*

Gillian Dalley, BA, MA (Econ), PhD, is Director of the Centre for Policy on Ageing, London. Her research interests include professional ideologies, community care and long-term care of older people. She led the CPA team which developed national standards for care homes, set out in *Fit for the Future?* which were published in 1999 by the Department of Health. Her recent publications include *Ideologies of Caring: Rethinking Community and Collectivism* (Macmillan, 1996) and *Patient Satisfaction: The Discharge of Older People from Hospital* (Centre for Policy on Ageing, 1997).

Sue Davies, Bsc (Hons), MSc, RGN, RHV, is a Lecturer in Nursing, Department of Gerontological and Continuing Care Nursing, University of Sheffield. She is currently working on a programme of research exploring experiences of nursing home entry and preparation for practice. She has recently completed a study of good practice in acute hospital wards for older people as part of the Help the Aged 'Dignity on the Ward' campaign. Her publications include *Research into Practice: Essential Skills for Reading and Applying Research,* co-edited with Patrick Crookes (Baillière Tindall, 1998).

Elizabeth Hanson, BA (Hons), PhD, RN, RGN, is a Senior Lecturer, Department of Community Nursing, Ageing, Rehabilitation, Education and Research of the School of Nursing and Midwifery, University of Sheffield. During 2000/1 she was seconded to the Department of Nursing, University of Götenborg, to assist in the development of a nursing programme. She is an adviser to the Swedish partners in the ACTION project. Her research interests include palliative care and family care-giving, and a study of a multi-media intervention to the latter was the subject of an article with Josie Tetley and Amanda Clarke that was published in 2000 in *The Gerontologist*

Charles F. Longino Jr, PhD, is Wake Forest Distinguished Professor of Sociology and Director of the Reynolda Gerontology Program at Wake Forest University, North Carolina. He is also Professor of Public Health Sciences and Associate Director of the J. Paul Sticht Center on Ageing at the Wake Forest University School of Medicine. He is interested in age-related population issues as they affect health care and economic development. Among his recent publications is *The Old Age Challenge to the Biomedical Model: Paradigm Strain and Health Policy,* co-authored with J.W. Murphy (Baywood, 1995).

Kate Lothian, Bsc (Hons), was the Research Assistant at the Sheffield Institute for Studies on Ageing who assembled the supportive evidence for the National Service Framework for Older People. She is contributing to an EU project concerned with carers of older people across Europe, and working as a behavioural therapist with a young boy with autism. She was winner of the British Psychological Society's annual student writer competition, with 'Detecting Depression in Older People' (*The Psychologist* 12 (7) (1999), 350–353).

Ulla Lundh, RN, PhD, is Senior Lecturer at the Division of Nursing Science, Linköping University, and at the University College of Health Sciences, Jönköping, Sweden. She is engaged in several international collaborations in Europe and South America. Her major research interests include family care, collaboration between family carers and educated carers and the integration of family carers in nursing homes.

Tony Maltby, BA (Hons), PhD, is Lecturer in Social Policy at the University of Birmingham. His main research interest is income variations and trends among older people in the EU and in Central European countries. He is joint author with Alan Walker of *Ageing Europe* (Open University Press, 1997) and a member of the Advisory Panel of the Centre for Research into Ageing and Gender at the University of Surrey. He is Honorary Treasurer of the British Society of Gerontology.

Alan Maynard, is Professor of Health Economics and Director of the York Health Policy Group in the Department of Health Studies at the University of York. He was Founding Director of the Centre for Health Economics at York (1983–1995), and Founding Editor of the journal *Health Economics*. He has worked as a consultant for The World Bank and The World Health Organisation and is Chair of the *York NHS Trust*.

Michael Nolan, BEd (Hons), MA, MSc, PhD, RMN, RGN, is Professor of Gerontological Nursing at the University of Sheffield. His principal interests are in family care-giving, long-term care and chronic illness, and he is involved in several comparative studies of the transition to long-term care with Swedish, America and Australian colleagues. Among his recent books are *Understanding Family Care: A Multidimensional Model of Caring and Coping,* with Gordon Grant and John Keady (Open University Press, 1996), and *Working with Older People*, with Gordon Grant and Sue Davies (Open University Press, 2001).

Jim Ogg is based at the Caisse Nationale d'Assurance Vieillesse, Paris. He is also Visiting Fellow to the Centre for Social Gerontology, University of Keele. Previously, he was Research Fellow to the ESRC-funded project 'Kinship and Family Change in the Urban Environment', based at the Department of Applied Social Studies, University of Keele. He has written several articles on research into elder abuse.

Chris Phillipson is Director of the Centre for Social Gerontology at the University of Keele, author of *Reconstructing Old Age* (Sage, 1999) and co-author of *The Family and Community Life of Older People* (Routledge, 2000). He is currently co-directing an ESRC-financed research project on 'Social Exclusion in Old Age', and a Nuffield Foundation-financed study of the lives of Bangladeshi women in East London.

Ian Philp is National Director for Older People's Services and Honorary Consultant Physician at the Northern General Hospital NHS Trust, Sheffield. During 1999–2000 he was Co-Chair (with the Chief Inspector of Social Services) of the External Reference Group for the National Service Framework for the Care of Older People, and until 2000 he was Director of the Sheffield Institute for Studies on Ageing. He chairs the British Geriatric Society's Special Interest Group for Health Services Research. Among his recent publications is *Outcomes Assessment in Health Care for Elderly People* (Farrand, 1997).

Jan Reed is Professor of Health Care for Older People, and Director of the Centre for Care of Older People at the University of Northumbria, Newcastle-upon-Tyne. She is particularly interested in care-home communities and privileging the voices of older people. She is evaluating a quality assurance system for care homes, developing a lifestyle plan for older people moving from hospital to care home; and undertaking a survey of older people and their service use; a study of nurses' preparedness to meet NSF guidelines, and an evaluation of Health Improvement Programmes for Older People.

Gillis Samuelsson, PhD, is Associate Professor in Social Gerontology and researcher at the Gerontology Center, University of Lund, Sweden. He is engaged in three multidisciplinary longitudinal studies of ageing. Other main interests are studies of the quality of care for older people, and of services for demented people and their carers (European collaboration project).

Jonas Sandberg, RN, is a Registered Nurse and a PhD student at the Division of Geriatrics, Linköping University, Sweden. His doctoral research is about the experience of placing a spouse in a nursing home setting. He is also the Secretary of the International Network for Studies Concerning Older Adults (INSCOA).

Sandra M.I. Shaw, BA (Hons), PhD, lectures in both sociology and social policy. She has several years' research experience, focusing on different groups of users (and carers) of health and social care services. Her current interests include mental health issues, carers, qualitative research methodology, interpretive theories and the construction of meaning.

David Stanley, BPhil, PhD, is Head of Division of Primary Care and Adult & Community Studies, and Co-Director, Centre for Care of Older People, at the Faculty of Health, Social Work and Education, University of Northumbria, Newcastle-upon-Tyne.

Josephine Tetley, Bsc (Hons), MA, PGCE, RGN, is a Lecturer in the Department of Gerontological and Continuing Care Nursing at the University of Sheffield. She has research interests in user consultation, gerontechnology and 'transitions in care'. Her current research includes a health needs survey of older people in a rural area, and doctoral research on decision-making and choice among older people. She has recently published co-authored articles in *Nurse Education Today, The Journal of Advanced Nursing* and *The Gerontologist.*

Julia Twigg, BA, Msc, PhD, is Redaer in Social Policy, Unversity of Kent and has had a long established interest in community care and the interface between health and social care services. Her earlier work was on informal carers, published as *Carers Perceived: Policy and Practice in Informal Care* (Open University Press, 1993, with Karl Atkin). Recently she has completed a study of the provision of help with bathing and personal care in the home, published as *Bathing: the Body and Community Care* (Routledge, 2000).

Saheed Ullah has been a social policy researcher since 1991. His research interests include ethnic minorities, health and social care, community renewal and regeneration. He has worked in Bangladesh where he undertook an evaluation of micro credit group lending schemes. He is currently the Policy and Research Officer for Social Services in the *London Borough of Tower Hamlets*.

Anthony M. Warnes, BSc (Hons), PhD, is Professor of Social Gerontology at SISA in the University of Sheffield. His interests centre on the sociodemography of ageing populations, and social and community health policies and delivery. During 1994–2000 he was Chair of the British Society of Gerontology. Recent books include *The Health and Care of Older People in London* (King's Fund, 1997), *Sunset Lives: British Retirement to the Mediterranean,* with Russell King and Allan Williams (Berg, 2000), and *Lessons from Lancefield: Tackling the Problems of Older Homeless People,* with Maureen Crane (National Homeless Alliance, 2000).

Lorna Warren, BSc (Hons), PhD, is Lecturer in Social Policy in the Department of Sociological Studies at the University of Sheffield. She has been working on studies of social care since the early 1980s. Her main interests are in research and development in the field of user involvement, with a focus on gender, ethnicity and older age. She is currently involved in the evaluation of the Sheffield Better Government for Older People programme and in a study of the lives and voices of older women from different communities living in Sheffield. She is a member of the Executive Committee of the Sheffield Institute for Studies on Ageing (SISA). Her recent books include *Changing Services for Older People* (Open University Press, 1996, with Alan Walker), and *Paths to Empowerment* (Policy Press, 1999, with Marian Barnes).

Sam W.K. Yu, BSW, PhD, is Senior Lecturer in the Division of Social Studies at City University, Hong Kong. His main research interests are social needs and the characteristics of Chinese communities in different societies. He has just completed a study of social care for Chinese older people in Britain (funded by the Joseph Rowntree Foundation). He has published articles in various refereed academic journals in the United Kingdom, Hong Kong and Taiwan. He is the author and co-author of three books on welfare institutions in Hong Kong and China.

Subject Index

All references to organisations and policies are British unless otherwise stated

abuse
    of carers 286–8
    of old people 31, 35–6, 59, 78, 299, 305
accidental injuries 92
activities, daily and 'meaningful' 56–7, 70, 126,
    219, 228, 238, 263, 300, 320, 321
Activities of Daily Living (scale) 57, 58, 79, 191,
    212
    Instrumental 226–7
acute care 18–9, 21, 30, 48, 51, 66, 70, 78, 79,
    91, 93, 96, 98, 100, 103, 108, 113, 115,
    123, 128, 132, 177, 244, 288, 325, 327
    emergency admissions 92, 244
advanced old age *see* 'old old'
Afro-Caribbean older people 145
Age Concern organisations 138
    AC Cookstown, Northern Ireland 299–300
    AC England 92, 94, 140
    AC Scotland 140, 292
    AC Sheffield 144
ageism, age discrimination 31, 55, 60–1, 93, 94,
    100, 115–6, 130, 142, 226, 311–2, 316, 320
age-related patterns of need and care 29, 32, 45–6,
    49, 81–2, 87, 153, 186, 206, 220, 222,
    224–5, 239, 263, 320
aids, aiding products 219–24, 234, 320
allocation of resources and services 24–5, 31, 36,
    75–88, 91, 200, 260, 328
    age-distribution 84, 199
almshouses 18
alternative medicine *see* medicine, alternative
altruism 142, 158, 266
Alzheimer's disease and AD Society 109, 246, 314
    see also dementia
arthritis 62, 115, 224, 226–7, 230, 266 *see also*
    osteoarthritis
Asian-origin older people 145
assessment of treatment or care needs 67, 79, 93,
    96, 108, 111, 115, 120, 153, 165, 176–7,
    186, 214, 252, 321, 326 *see also* community
    care, geriatric medicine, scales
    scales, assessment 58, 189–90
attitudes to old age, old people and patients 29,
    30, 60, 64–65, 82, 105, 148, 207–11, 303,
    316–7
Australia 226
auto-immune deficiency syndrome (AIDS) 41, 51
autonomy, prescriptions for 57, 58, 94, 100, 115,
    137, 245, 316 *see also* dignity, independence
avoidable morbidity and mortality 91

babies, low birth weight, ascribed relative value 83
Bangladesh, Sylhet region 276–7
Bangladeshi-origin older people 273–89, 300,
    319, 323

bathing *see* washing
beds 235–6
    getting in and out of 109, 110, 239, 281, 283
    blocking 80, 125, 177, 180
behavioural medicine 43
bereavement 26, 50, 160, 208, 211–2, 268
Better Government for Older People 138, 149,
    296–7
biographical perspective 63, 66, 208, 215, 301
    Bangladeshi 276–7
    informing practice 66, 69, 145, 162, 301
biological ageing 31, 44, 224–5
biomedicine, biomedical model of medicine
    39–40–1, 43, 46, 50, 122, 125, 129, 244
biotechnology companies 32, 244
Birmingham 301
blindness *see* visual impairment
body 31, 40–1, 44–5, 49, 52, 119, 122, 126–7,
    131, 132–3, 321
    representations of 40, 41, 131, 315
Booth, Charles 18
breast screening 100
British Geriatrics Society 94, 111, 112
British Society of Gerontology 9, 19, 291, 307,
    311
    Averil Osborn Fund 291–307, 321
building codes and regulations 226

Callahan, Daniel 84
cancer and treatment 27, 75, 115, 205–6
care 119–33, 243–56, 288
    assistants 26, 109, 126, 130, 132–3, 161, 167,
    169
    ethics 137, 323
    intermediate 326
    management *see* community care
    models of 152, 187, 288, 319–23
    personal (distinguished from nursing) 114,
    119–33, 168, 197, 328
    personal care plans 101, 169, 244
    quality of 31, 54, 75, 78, 90, 100, 108, 110,
    145, 146, 160, 168, 185, 188, 196, 214,
    243, 312, 316, 324 *see also* clinical
    governance
carers 32, 35, 58, 61, 64, 68, 90, 93, 94, 96, 97,
    100, 110, 135, 152–69, 174, 179, 201, 208,
    243, 245, 247, 255, 273–88, 300, 317, 319,
    324
    Carers' (Recognition and Services) Act 1995 19,
    179
    groups 139, 161, 169, 245–6, 270, 300
    daughters (in-law) as 110, 161–4, 213–4, 276,
    280, 284–5
    role in nursing homes 160–4
    spouses as 35, 155, 158–60, 165, 212, 251,
    281–4
    views of 13, 106, 179, 245, 253, 270, 300–2
case studies
    Alzheimer's disease patient at home 109–10,
    250–2
    carers' involvement in admission to nursing
    homes 158–60, 162–3
    depressed, bereaved man found unconscious 50

frail people in multi generational Bangladeshi households 275–87
nursing home patient (Ms Coughlan) 114
nursing home residents 114–5
spouse carers anticipating bereavement 212–3
stroke patient with visual impairment 110
cemeteries 207
Centre for Policy on Ageing 18, 109, 168, 307
cerebrovascular disorders 19, 60, 62, 79, 80, 92, 93, 94, 99, 101, 110, 115, 142, 279, 281, 285, 286, 314
subdural haematoma 96
China 269
Chinese-origin older people 258–71, 301, 318–9, 320
chronic disorders and care 29, 42, 45–46, 48, 49, 58, 62, 123, 128, 130–1, 206, 208, 314, 328
citizenship, basis for eligibility to service 121–4, 135–49, 258–71, 273–89, 291, 315, 320, 321, 327
clinical decisions 24, 81–2, 90, 327, 328
clinical effectiveness 81–82, 90
clinical governance 78, 86, 90, 91, 122, 324–5 see also staff, accreditation
clinical sciences, see medicine–as science
clothing, protective 241
clubs, social and recreational 138, 266
Cochrane reviews 84–85 see also research
cohort (birth) differences 39–40, 41–2, 49, 148, 187, 198, 304
first generation migrants 276–7
Commission for Health Improvement 86, 90
community care 56–57, 69, 105–10, 130, 142, 166, 253, 295, 302, 325
assessment, management and packages 19, 21, 79, 80, 93, 104, 109, 110, 124, 155, 178–80, 253
community health services 20, 28, 46, 56, 92, 93, 100, 101, 103, 105, 108, 128, 130–1, 132, 140, 288, 325, 326
and nursing homes 114
compensation for inappropriate intervention 78
complementary medicine, see medicine–alternative
consultation on policy see involvement, participation
consultations, medical 32, 42
consumer groups, consumerism 43, 138, 221, 226, 238
Consumers' Association 234
continuing care see long term care
coronary angioplasty see surgery–heart
cost effectiveness 69, 75, 81–82, 90, 93
crime 144
victims 143–4
cultural identity see ethnicity
Cumberledge Report 1986 19

day centres 17, 21, 108, 247, 266, 282, 284, 292, 303
day clinics and hospitals 326
death and dying 204–16
euthanasia 212–3
finitude 24, 29, 81–2, 207, 209–12

'good death' 206
deference and fatalism of older people and carers 31, 60, 143, 148, 161–2, 174, 177–8, 187, 224, 260, 304, 316–7, 323
dementia 45, 92, 94, 96, 109, 166, 241, 251, 314, 325
demography and ageing 45–6, 48, 92, 135, 139, 153, 186, 219–20, 238, 262–3, 274, 313
Denmark 123–4
dental hygiene 229–30
Department of Health 34, 89–101
Department of Social Security 27, 107, 156
Department of Trade and Industry 241n
dependency 46, 47–8, 58, 62, 69, 143, 147, 208, 225, 238, 320, 323
depression, clinical 31, 50, 67, 94, 215, 285
deprivation, disadvantage 20, 31, 144, 147, 187, 199, 255, 260, 322
design 219–41, 256, 316, 320
designers 220, 247
packaging 229, 239
Descartes, René 40
diabetes 89, 110, 269, 280–1, 285, 326
dignity, individual 119
prescriptions for 35, 58, 85, 94, 100, 137–8 see also autonomy
disability, disabled people 29, 46, 49, 56, 58, 62–4, 68, 91, 119, 138, 155, 220, 226–8, 245, 313–4, 317, 320 see also Activities of Daily Living
Disability Adjusted Support Ratio 314
disability movement 129–30, 135, 145, 296
discharge from hospital 55, 61–2, 78, 115, 142, 171–82, 205, 247, 254
doctors, influence of see medicine
doctor-patient relationship 26, 41, 43, 66, 81, 215
domestic work and servants see house work
dressing (clothes) 59, 70, 110, 131, 176, 194, 282, 287
drugs, therapeutic see medication

efficiency see cost-effectiveness, evidence-based, health economics
electoral influence of older people 139
employment among older people 263
empowerment 34, 55, 58, 140, 142, 148, 178, 204, 252–4, 295, 320, 322 see also involvement, participation
end-of-life care 92, 204–16, 320
endocrine system 44
English National Board for Nursing, Midwifery and Health Visiting 94
environment, environmental 221–3, 228, 261
influences 44, 63, 64
medicine 43–4, 46, 49, 115
modifications 42, 221
epidemiology of disease and disorder, old age 49, 126 see also age-related
equity in care 25, 36, 76, 81–4, 94, 119–20, 135, 137, 267 see also allocation
ergonomics 221, 223, 237, 239, 241n

ethnicity, ethnic minorities 138, 144, 149, 246, 267, 271, 273–89, 299–302, 318–9, 323 *see also* Bangladeshi, Chinese-origin
  adaptation of services to 63, 68, 93, 96, 98, 260, 288–9, 295, 300–2
  Standing Conference of Ethnic Minority Senior Citizens 149
Europe 228–9, 231, 243, 244, 258
  health care 81
  home care 125, 248
  social assistance and insurance 121, 123
evidence-based medicine and care 30, 58, 67–68, 79–80, 84, 86, 93, 94, 95–99, 125, 291, 317, 325, 328, 330n *see also* research
  Health Evidence Bulletins 97, 101n
exclusion, social *see* ageism; citizenship, deprivation; health and social services–marginalisation
extended family 278–80, 319
excretion, human 131–2
exercise 224

'fair innings' (duration of life and allocation of health care) *see* allocation
falls, personal 92, 93, 94, 97, 101, 115, 241
family medicine or practice *see* general medical practice
family relationships *see* inter-generational relations
feeding (eating) 70, 115, 131, 281–3, 287
feminism, feminist 137, 139, 312
follow-up care (after acute episode) 79, 108
'frail' older people 22, 31, 70, 92, 94, 99, 109–11, 116, 119, 140–3, 145, 158, 175, 184, 200, 243, 245, 247, 268, 280, 322, 328
France 123
functioning, individual 48, 57, 58, 60, 62, 200 *see also* Activities of Daily Living
funerals 211
furniture 235–8

gender 63, 84, 127, 131, 137–8, 145, 186, 280, 285, 288, 323
  adaption of services to 58, 84, 312
  and care staff 127, 132, 323
genes, genetic medicine 41
general medical practice 13, 22, 28, 32, 34, 45, 52, 77–9, 92–4, 100, 104–7, 115, 125, 128, 141, 180, 252–3, 325–7
  and nursing homes 114, 251
  medical centres 247
  NHS Primary Care Groups and Trusts 104, 105
geographical boundaries of organisations, inconsistent 107
geographical variations in care provision 75, 87, 105
geriatric
  descriptive adjective 22, 60
  medicine and assessment 18–20, 45, 49, 51–52, 57, 92, 96, 111, 128, 247, 326
  in nursing homes 113–4
Germany 80, 123, 124, 235
gerontology 9–10, 52, 59, 116–7, 208, 222, 240–1, 271, 291, 292, 293, 303, 313, 315–6, 329n

critical 69, 318
gerontechnology 226, 240, 244
global economic restructuring 135
governments 28
  Conservative (1979–97) 33–4, 77, 83, 92–3, 104
  Labour (1997-) 16, 34–5, 54, 77, 83, 89, 100–1, 114, 115, 120, 148, 167–8, 245, 296–7, 317, 323–8
  Inter-Ministerial Group for Older People 297
grandchildren 275
Griffiths Report 1988 19, 107

handicap *see* disability
health
  as a want and policy goal 24, 43, 77, 79, 92, 137, 140, 149, 327
  checks 101
  definitions and concept 76, 129, 146, 200, 244
  education and promotion 42, 44, 92, 94, 96, 97, 100, 115, 141
Health Action Zones 115, 138, 148
Health Advisory Service 55, 92, 94
health and social services for older people 68, 75–88, 90–93, 98, 100–1, 103–17, 140, 156, 171, 240, 243–56, 260, 292, 301, 312, 315–28
  charges for 111, 119–20, 122–3, 131, 133, 164–5, 186, 253, 328
  co-ordination and service agreements (inter-agency working) 16, 91–2, 94, 99, 100, 104, 107–8, 125, 182, 214, 296, 324, 326–7
  costs, expenditure and funding 16, 28, 42, 52, 77, 91, 92, 101n, 107, 110, 112, 120, 122, 131, 155, 164, 166, 198, 238, 255, 260, 294, 326
  democratic control 122, 136, 148, 260, 293, 304, 321, 327
  dichotomy of sectors 21–2, 92, 103, 108, 111–2, 119–33, 320–1
  employment in 28 *see also* staff, workforce
  fragmentation 11, 15–16, 20, 21, 30, 63, 103, 107, 108, 110, 135, 171, 320, 325
  ideologies of 105, 106, 121, 125, 132, 317
  influences upon 16, 121, 125, 132, 136, 140, 193, 201, 253, 260, 292, 301, 317, 328
  interpreters, need for 270, 288, 300, 302
  key worker or co-ordinator for individual 110, 216
  marginalisation and exclusion 17, 22, 28, 30, 31, 35, 51–52, 108, 113, 115–7, 135, 141, 246, 255, 260, 273, 288–9, 317
  pathways of care 91, 95, 100
  plethora of providers to an individual 108, 171, 195–8, 214
  policy 19, 54, 77, 83, 90–93, 106, 112, 119–25, 130, 135, 148, 201, 294, 313, 323–8
  pooled or joint budgets and working 16, 30, 104, 108, 125, 172–3, 182, 326, 327

reorganisations and reform 16, 21, 33–34, 79, 83, 91, 99, 104, 120, 148, 156, 182, 184, 253, 317, 323–8
'seamless services' 31, 63, 108–10, 181, 315
tendency for increasing specialisation 106, 198, 326
Health Authorities 107, 163, 164
health (care) economics 24, 34, 42, 52, 75–88, 187, 327
Health Improvement Programmes 91
hearing impairment 238, 275
heart disease 27, 62, 89, 115, 269, 280–1, 283, 285
Helen Hamlyn Research Centre 241
Help the Aged 19, 92, 93
hip replacement 19, 75, 78, 79, 80, 141
Hippocratic tradition 81, 86
holistic medicine and care 24, 30, 40, 43–4, 64, 68, 126, 127, 171, 205, 250, 315, 317, 320
home and housing 48, 51, 229, 252, 263, 268, 277–8, 300, 302–3, 325
    adaptations and improvement 42, 101, 223–4, 233, 286
    home-delivery of personal services 229
    homeliness in nursing homes 162
    lifts, absence of 283
    local authority 19, 28, 107, 325, 329n
    sheltered 19, 144, 155, 237, 241
    multi-generational households 268–9, 275, 277–81
    overcrowding 276, 288
    remaining in own, preference and prescription 48, 56–57, 156, 220
    security 233–4, 328
home care, home helps 20, 31, 56, 108–10, 120, 124, 130–2, 142, 156, 158, 184–201, 213, 266, 268, 286, 326
    charges for 124
    expectations of and satisfaction with 142, 187, 199, 214, 253, 268
    private sector agencies 110, 255
homeless people, older 19
homeopathy 47
Hong Kong 269–70
hospices 112, 205
hospital care see acute care
housebound 141, 269
house work 131, 192, 197, 268
housing for older people
human resources see workforce planning
hygiene 238

iatrogenic harm and disease 26, 47, 77–8, 206
identity, individual 62, 142, 147, 149, 262 see also ethnicity, gender
impairment see disability
images of old age 29, 147
immune system 44, 50–1
inappropriate treatment or care 47, 48, 59–60, 106, 164, 206, 245, 273
incomes of older people 29, 263, 312, 328
incontinence 55, 67, 234, 282, 326

independence, promotion of 55, 56, 58, 62, 69, 115, 147, 184, 186, 187, 200, 219, 234, 239, 313, 316 see also dependency
inequality 84, 85, 87, 120, 135, 255, 322
influence, of various stakeholders see power
information and communications technologies 25, 47, 91, 98–99, 108, 229, 235, 240, 243–56, 322, 326, 327
    informed care choices 153, 164, 175–6, 250, 254
    Internet 25, 47, 101, 229, 235, 243, 255, 270, 327
    mobile phones 238
    telephone advice lines 25, 101, 245, 327
    television as 248, 254
    video-phone 245, 247, 249, 322
informal care 20, 35, 264 see also neighbours' care and support, voluntary care associations
innovations in treatment and care 91, 100, 249, 289
institutional care see long-term care, nursing homes, residential care
insurance and companies 32, 80, 122–3, 228–9, 330n
inter-generational
    contract 149, 288, 323
    distance and tensions 30, 144, 159, 267, 268, 276, 281, 285
    relations and support 56, 64, 110, 135, 137, 146, 147, 152–69, 175, 245, 265, 267–9, 273, 277–81, 319
inter-personal skills of staff 42, 65, 67–8, 126, 176, 179, 187, 192, 197, 209, 216, 289, 316
    see also doctor-patient relationship
intimacy of care 119, 132, 198, 213
involvement of older people in policy and practice decisions 32, 63, 93, 135, 140–5, 159, 168, 175, 271, 292, 301, 305, 320, 327
Ireland 140
    Northern 244–5, 300, 325–6
isolated old people 31, 50, 67, 265, 277, 292, 301, 322

Japan 226

kidney dialysis 18
kin relationships see inter-generational relations
kitchen, design 223–4, 227, 233, 239
knowledge-base see evidence-base; research
Kuhn, Maggie 135, 137, 146

laboratory tests 244
language barriers 260, 264, 266, 267, 277, 288, 300–1, 305, 319, 322
law and litigiousness 27, 32, 42, 78, 114, 264
learning difficulties, personal 115, 128, 130, 283, 305
life course 148
life-long learning
    among professionals 90, 325
lifting a person 286
London 16, 20
    Bethnal Green and Woodford 273–89, 319

Tower Hamlets Bengali Carers Development Project 285
long-term care 47–48, 51, 54, 59, 64, 100, 111–5, 119, 123, 124, 130, 147, 152, 164, 324, 328 *see also* nursing homes, residential care
longevity and its increase 29, 77, 84, 210, 221, 313
longitudinal studies 60
lunch clubs 266, 300

malnutrition *see* nutrition
managed care organisations (USA) 52, 80
management 24, 34, 77, 83, 86, 98, 105–6, 112, 121–2, 125, 148, 165, 181, 239, 244, 304, 326, 327
  costs 77, 200
  data *see* operational data
Manchester 302
market forces and mechanisms 24, 34, 42, 131, 167, 226–8 *see also* NHS–internal market
mass media 25, 34, 77, 91, 116, 144, 147, 167, 187, 233–4, 313, 327, 328
meals-on-wheels 20, 108, 109, 120
means testing 100, 111, 120, 122–4, 131, 168
mediation 28, 299, 305, 317
medical model, spread of 106, 206
medical-social boundary 119–33
medication 28, 123, 284
medicine 40, 122, 127, 177 *see also* general practice, geriatric medicine
  alternative, complementary and traditional 23, 25, 47, 261, 320
  as a commodified service 24, 42–3, 46–7, 77, 79, 131
  community based 128
  Royal Colleges 26, 34, 77, 86, 87, 93
  education and training 41, 50, 86, 98, 100, 126, 205, 325
  mechanical analogy 40
  occupational 115, 263
  paradigms and principles 39–52, 62, 63, 69–70, 77, 83, 85, 94, 106, 111, 113, 126, 129, 177, 328
  therapies and technologies 23, 47, 67, 82, 84, 90, 99, 115, 119, 122, 125, 128, 316, 320, 328 *see also* specific treatments, e.g. hip replacements
  as a profession 12, 22, 33–34, 42, 45, 55, 57, 64, 77, 85, 93, 104, 121–2, 125, 127, 129
  as science 23, 31, 40, 43, 45, 47, 64, 86, 98, 122, 125, 126, 128, 320
mental health and ill-health 27, 40, 48, 56, 57, 78, 79, 93, 130, 135, 165, 206, 247, 275–6, 280, 284, 319, 325
mental health services 27, 31, 89, 94, 99, 101, 125, 180, 325, 326 *see also* psychiatry
migration 165, 168, 266, 269–70, 273, 274, 276–7, 283, 318, 319, 323
Ministry of Health 18, 20
'mixed economy' of care 21, 27, 109, 328 *see also* residential care
Modernising Social Services (1998) 35

morale *see* depression, mental health
mortality of older people 45–6, 78, 91, 147, 204–16, 314, 320
motor skills, personal 250, 269
multiple sclerosis 223
myocardial infarction *see* heart disease

National Assistance Act 1948 18, 124
National Care Commission 168
National Carers' Association (formerly National Council for Carers and their Elderly Dependants) 19, 93
National Committee for Older People's Welfare 18 *see also* Age Concern
National Corporation for the Care of Old People 18 *see also* Centre for Policy on Ageing
National Health Service 16, 20, 33, 35, 75, 77, 83, 89–101, 104, 107, 121, 245, 325, 327–8 *see also* the following indexed 'National' organisations and bodies
  Care Direct 101
  internal market 33, 34, 131
  Health Act 1999 326
  management 34, 35, 327
  NHS and Community Care Act 1990 19, 104, 124, 156, 294
  NHS Direct 245
  nursing homes 114
  scope of 'free' care 111–5, 119–20, 328
National Institute for Clinical Excellence (NICE) 55, 86, 90, 324–5
National Patient Survey 32, 90
National Pensioners' Convention 139, 148
National Service Frameworks (for treatment and care) 55, 89, 324–5
  for Older People's Services 70, 89–101, 297, 316, 317
  Carers', External and Older People's Reference Groups 93, 95, 297
need for treatment, care and support 76, 81–83, 111, 115, 120, 122, 126, 141, 153, 175, 177, 182, 195, 216, 246, 250, 253, 261, 319, 320, 327, 328, 329
neighbours' care, support and surveillance 50, 141
nerve system, central 44
Netherlands 83, 313
New Deal for Communities 148
night sitting 109, 110, 246
nomenclature for old and sick 116
Nuffield Foundation, The 18
nurse training 10, 70, 87
nurses, role of, and nursing 27, 34, 42, 46, 54, 65, 67, 77, 86, 87, 105, 113, 125, 127, 132–3, 153–4, 161, 172–4, 176, 317, 326
  Central Council for Nursing 94
  community 108, 128–9, 131, 326
  district 109, 110, 121, 129
  training 10, 132, 167
nursing homes and their residents 18, 27, 29, 48, 57, 80, 86, 92, 100, 101, 112–4, 152–69, 174–8, 186, 215–6, 237, 251, 330n
  expectations 167
  'lounge-standard' resident 59

National Health Service 114
placements in 25, 109, 152–69, 171–82, 207, 250, 254, 316, 321
ideal types 158
trial residence 165
regulation and standards 27, 164, 168, 177
receptivity to ethnic minorities 267–8
nutrition 44, 47, 50, 55–6, 67, 101, 268, 326

occupational therapy 27, 108, 125, 180, 326
Office of Science and Technology 241n
Older People's Welfare Committees 20
'old old' 22, 39, 45–6, 62, 64, 92, 114–6, 146, 186, 198, 274
operational data 77, 78, 244, 327
Organisation for Economic Co-operation and Development 28
Osborn, Averil 292–5, 320
osteoarthritis 50
outcomes and indicators 25, 54, 56, 60, 61, 69, 75, 77–8, 82, 87, 95, 99, 142, 154, 215, 305, 316, 329
Disability Adjusted Support Ratio 314
Quality Adjusted Life Years 81–82
outpatient clinics and appointments 77

pain and control of 57, 75, 78, 79, 92, 126, 205, 206, 214
palliative care 10, 25, 31, 84, 92, 101, 112–3, 130, 204–16, 248, 320
participation in treatment or care policy and decisions 55, 93, 140–5, 149, 159, 165, 179, 181, 186, 215, 253, 259, 270, 292, 296, 300–2, 304, 320 see also involvement
patient-centred treatment and care see person-centred
patient held records 108
patient knowledge of treatments and outcomes 25, 47
expectations 100, 207
patient support groups 47
pensioners' action and support groups 138, 299–302, 321
drama groups 302
performance of services or staff 76, 78, 85, 90
Performance Assessment Framework (NHS) 90
personal social services see social services, home care
person-centred treatment and care 24, 35, 43, 54–70, 93, 94, 96, 99, 100, 201, 205, 213, 316
pharmaceutical companies 32
phlebitis 266
physiotherapy 125, 246
placebo effect 40
pneumonia 50
policy see health and social services, policy
political parties and groups 138, 139, 145
Poor Law and institutions 20, 121, 187, 199
population-based perspectives 86 see also public health medicine
Portugal 245
positive ageing see successful ageing

postcode rationing see geographical variations
power of various stakeholders 32–4, 47, 64, 84, 328, 329
practice, types of knowledge informing 65–66 see also evidence-based
preferences, older people's 132, 137, 189, 317–8, 329 see also home, patient knowledge
prejudice, ethnic and racial 264, 273, 320
pressure sores 110
prevention of disease and disorder 42, 46, 54, 58, 61, 92, 96, 97, 186, 200, 244, 324
primary health care see general medical practice
private (for-profit) sector 27, 42, 59, 86, 109, 110, 112, 124, 132, 155–6, 164, 174, 176, 185, 219, 239, 246, 254
products, retail 229–32, 235, 239, 247
Comfacto bed 235
Good Grips™ 230–2
professions and their associations 26, 34, 105–7, 182 see also medicine – Royal Colleges
ancillary or supplementary to medicine 125
prosthetics 227 see also aids, hip replacement, wheelchair
psychiatry 128, 163, 180, 325
old age 19, 92
psychological state and well-being see depression, mental health
psychology, clinical 64, 180, 205
psychosomatic effects 40, 44
public expenditure 16, 27, 28, 34
public health medicine 12, 44, 46, 48, 82, 115, 327
Our Healthier Nation and Saving Lives (Green Papers) 115
public opinion 34, 86, 91

quality-of-life 56, 57, 58, 69, 78, 79, 83, 105, 168, 205, 220, 241, 250, 252, 265, 291, 294, 313, 325

racism see prejudice
radiography 125
rationing of care 75–88, 327
reciprocity, as cultural norm 187
rehabilitation 29, 46, 48, 51, 54, 60, 78, 79, 96, 97, 101, 112, 116, 128, 225, 241, 326
normative models 60–64, 94, 315–6
religion 138, 209–11
reminiscence therapy 248 see also biographical
research and researchers 43, 58, 90, 99, 108, 125, 126, 129, 172–82, 244–52, 261, 271, 274, 293, 297, 299–304, 319, 321–2 see also longitudinal studies, scales
abstracts journals 97–99, 101n
design 234, 240
dissemination 293, 296, 298–9, 302, 306
ESRC Growing Older programme 297, 306, 329n
'grey' literature 98
informal care 244–52, 285
health services 32, 98, 327
literature reviews 61, 83, 84–85, 95–99, 185
nursing homes 152–69, 174–8, 327, 330n

palliative care 206, 208–9
participation of older people 291–307
randomised control trials 79, 85, 96
social services 104, 106, 107, 109, 125, 140–1, 187–200, 327
social work 79, 85, 98, 172
residential care 27, 29, 80, 92, 112–4, 144, 146, 168, 174–82, 237
placements in 25, 109, 152–69, 171–82, 250, 316
receptivity to ethnic minorities 267
translation into policy and practice 291, 293
resource allocation *see* allocation
Registered Homes Act 1984 19, 29
respiratory diseases 50
respite and care 113, 245, 251, 282, 324, 326
retirement, early 263, 266–9
rheumatism 224
rights, civil and social 135–49, 262, 267, 327 *see also* citizenship
Robert Wood Johnson Foundation (USA) 49
Royal College of Art 232–3, 241
Royal College of General Practitioners 94
Royal College of Physicians 83, 94
Royal Commission on Long Term Care (1999) 13, 60, 114, 119, 130, 131, 167–8, 249, 328
Royal Commission on the Aged Poor (1895) 18

Saga Holidays 231
scarcity (of resources) 80
Scotland 140
Edinburgh and the Lothians 300
Fife User Panels 140, 141, 145–8
Seebohm Report 1968 21
self-care, self-help 57, 138, 141
sensory decline 224 *see also* visual
sexuality 41, 138
Sheffield 96, 140, 144, 157–69, 245–50, 261, 301, 326
AgeWell 140, 144
Chinese community 264–9
Institute for Studies on Ageing 10
Lai Yin Association 265
Pensioners' Action Group 140, 145–7
University of 10, 152
Shipman, Harold 78
social security benefits 123, 147, 251, 283
social integration 56, 261–71, 301 *see also* inter-generational relations
social isolation 262
social services and care 35, 55, 56, 67, 79, 82, 85, 90–93, 100, 104, 119–25, 127, 140, 178, 185, 223, 255, 260, 266, 286, 293, 323, 324, 326
charges for 111, 119, 122
local authority 17, 19, 20, 28, 105, 107, 109, 110, 111, 112, 121–2, 124, 156, 181, 186, 260, 286, 296
perceived to be for 'whites' 267
reorganisations and reform 21, 90–93, 100, 106, 130, 294, 324
training 10, 126, 130, 132, 325

trend for concentration on intensive services 186, 199, 255
social work 17, 79, 86, 104, 106, 174–7, 246, 317, 326
profession 12, 46, 105, 125, 127, 323
socio-economic class 144, 186, 187, 191, 197, 259, 319
variations in health 49
sociology 60, 64, 105, 207–8
Spain 248
spirituality 40, 44, 94, 98, 205, 209–10, 282
staff and professions, medical and social care 32, 109, 125, 127, 171–3, 179, 185, 227, 243, 249, 289, 303, 320, 323 *see also* attitudes, medicine, nursing
accreditation and regulation 26, 27, 30, 87, 90, 93, 94, 125, 324
morale 12, 87, 109, 215–6, 253
multidisciplinary working 171–82, 326
nursing home 154
performance 76, 85, 94, 109, 176, 190, 196, 317
training and development 26, 27, 35, 40, 66, 85, 87, 90, 91, 96, 98, 100, 105, 107, 126, 172–3, 180, 199, 200, 205, 325
stereotypes of older people or patients 22, 30, 60, 147, 148, 149, 207
strokes *see* cerebrovascular disorders
'successful ageing' and critiques 58, 116–7, 220, 226, 316, 329n
suicide and suicidal tendency 31
surgery 51, 78
heart 19, 51, 75
survival 24, 62, 78, 83, 91, 126
swallowing 67
Sweden 83, 123, 152–69, 184–201, 245
Malmö 193–4

taxes, taxation 120, 267, 268
technology 25, 47, 51, 82, 122, 126, 207, 221, 316, 322 *see also* information, medicine-therapies
telematics and telecare *see* information
terminal care *see* palliative
theory 64, 70
absence of 63, 104, 107, 315, 318
grounded 157
thrombolysis 19
tissue viability 101
toilets and toileting 70, 131, 233, 282, 284, 286 *see also* incontinence
touching of patients or clients 119, 132, 213
training, retraining *see* staff, training
transport of patients or clients 113, 143, 149, 175, 252, 300, 303
travel 220
Trollope, Anthony 83

ulcers of skin 51, 110
United States of America 28, 39–52, 57, 80, 226, 235, 241n, 243, 328
disability trends 314
Gray Panthers 135

health care system 48, 52, 77, 123
  Medicaid 123, 124
  Medicare 80, 123, 124
  Oregon health care 83
  Townsend movement 139
utilitarian concepts 24, 82

varicose veins 266
viagra 80
video recorder 221 *see also* information
visual impairment 75, 110, 165, 224, 250, 268,
    275, 284
voluntary (care) organisations 17, 20, 23, 113,
    121, 138, 146, 157, 185, 221–2, 246, 254,
    265, 289, 299–302
  Retired and Senior Volunteer Programme 139

Warren, Marjorie 57
washing self or patient 70, 109, 110, 131, 133,
    194, 214, 282, 283
welfare policy and state 91, 119–21, 131, 135,
    149, 186, 260, 274, 318
welfare rights officers 251–2
well-being, wellness 44, 56–57, 78, 94, 100, 115,
    137, 139, 140, 149, 184, 219, 225–6, 241,
    259, 301, 315
  age and perception of 146
wheelchairs and bound 223, 283, 286
widows, widowers and widowhood 50
Wiltshire 303
Wolverhampton 273–89
women 127–8, 145, 185, 186, 265, 280, 285–8,
    301, 323
workforce issues and planning 12, 27, 28, 45, 52,
    91, 93, 198, 324
workhouses, poor-law 29

Author Index

Italicised page references are bibliographic

Abbey, J. 212, 215, 216, *216*
Abel-Smith, B. 17, *36*
Abrahamson, P. 259, *271*
Acker, J. 127, *133*
Addington-Hall, J. 206, 207, 214, *216, 217*
Ahmad, W.I.U. 273, *290*, 318, *330*
Age Concern Cookstown 300, *308*
Albright, B. 153, *170*
Allen, A. 243, *257, 258*
Allen, L. 141, *151*
Altmann, D. 214, *216, 217*
Amenta, E. 139, *150*
Andrew, T. 128, *133*
Angus, J. 153, 154, *170*
Anon 263, *271*
Applebaum, R. 184, 197, *201, 202*
Arber, S. 312, *330*
Ashby, M. 247, *257*
Askham, J. 273, 288, *290*
Atchley, S. 184, 197, *202*
Atkin, K. 318, 319, *330*
Audit Commission 27, *36*, 55, 67, 70, 107, *117*, 317, *330n, 330*

Baker, M. 60, *70*
Bain, C. 97, *101*
Baines, D. 141, *151*
Baldwin, N. 57, *70*
Baldwin, S. 54, 61, *73*
Ballabio, E. 246, *256*
Balloch, S. 128, *133*
Baltes, M.M. 64, *70*, 329n, *330*
Baltes, P.B. 329n, *330*
Bamford, C. 206, *217*
Banerjee, S. 19, *38*
Barer, B.M. 64, *72*
Barker, J. 97, *101*
Barker, P.J. 64, *71*
Barnard, D. 64, *71*
Barnes, C. 296, *308*
Barnes, M. 136, 140, 141, 142, 143, 145, 148, *150, 151*, 249, 253, *256*, 304, 307, *308*, 317, *330*
Barolin, G.S. 61, *71*
Barron, A. 249, *256*
Beauvoir, S. de 29, *37*
Becker, G. 60, *71*
Benjamin, A.E. 124, *133*
Bennett, G. 140, 143, 145, *150*, 304, *308*
Beresford, P. 292, 296, 297, 305, *308*
Berg, S. 185, *203*
Bernard, M. 138, *150,* 273, 274, 289, 290, *290*, 304, *308*, 312, 318, 321, 322, *330*
Berthold, H. 245, 247, 248, *257, 258*
Berthoud, R. 263, *271*
Better Government for Older People 296, *308*

Bhatnagar, A. 300, 301, *308*
Biggs, S. 58, 62, *73*
Binney, E.A. 125, *134*
Black, D. 114, *117*
Black, N. 97, *101*
Blakemore, K. 273, *290*, 318, 319, *330*
Bleissner, R. 48, *53*
Bloor, K. 83, *88*
Blythe, R. 29, *36*
Boaz, A. 297, 304, *308*
Boer, A.H. de 313, *331*
Bond, J. 61, *71*
Bond, S. 59, *73*
Boneham, M. 273, *290*, 318, 319, *330*
Booth, A. 57, 62, 63, 70, *73*
Booth, C. 18, *18*
Bornat, J. 215, *217*
Bosanquet, N. 215, *217*
Bowling, A. 69, *71*
Bowman, C. 114, *117*
Boyer, C. 251, *257*
Bradshaw, A. 247, *257*
Brändstädter, J. 64, *71*
Brito, L. 245, 248, *257, 258*
Britton, A. 97, *101*
Brocklehurst, J.C. 18, 19, *36*
Brooker, C. 70, *71*
Brouwer-Janse, M.D. 220, 238, *242*
Brown, A. 116, *118*
Brown, H. 130, *133*
Brown, J. 70, *71*, 92, *102*
Brown, S. 178, 181, *183*
Brun, C. 197, *202*
Buckwalter, K. 154, *169*
Buckman, R. 211, 216, *217*
Burns, F. 245, 246, 255, *256*
Bury, M. 210, *217*
Butler, A. 19, *36*
Butt, J. 300, *308*, 318, *330*

Cabinet Office 297, *308*
Cahill, M. 322, *330*
Callahan, D. 84, *88*
Carstensen, L.L. 64, *70*
Carter, T. 292, 296, 297, 305, *308*
Cartwright, A. 206, 207, *208*
Caselli, G. 314, *330*
Cassel, E.J. 50, *52*, 64, *71*
Centre for Policy on Ageing 19, *36*, 109, 114, *117*, 168, *169*
Challis, D. 56, *71*, 156, *169*
Chalmers, I. 84, *88*
Chambers, M. 245, 248, *257, 258*
Chan, C. 263, *271*
Chan, Y.M. 263, *271*
Charlton, J. 314, *331*
Charmaz, K. 64, *71*
Charnley, J. 19, *36*
Chau, C.M. 261, 265, *271*
Chinese Action Group 260, 265, *271*
Chiu, S. 264, *271*
Choudhury, Y. 276, 277, *290*
Clare, J. 116, *118*

Clark, D. 205, 207, 208, *217*
Clark, P.G. 58, 64, 69, *71*
Clarke, A. 244, 247, 248, 249, 251, *256, 257*
Clarke, C.L. 58, 59, 69, *71, 73*
Cole, T.R. 29, *37*
Coleman, P.G. 19, *37*, 70, *71*
Coleman, R. 220, 226, 228, 230, 233, 235, 238, *242*
Connidis, I.A. 201, *202*
Connis, R.T. 62, *72*
Cook, G. 167, *170*
Cooper, M. 307, *308*
Corder, L. 49, *53*, 314, *332*
Cormie, J. 140, 141, 145, *150, 151*
Corrigan, J.M. 77, *88*
Cotterill, P. 215, *217*
Cowan, D. 246, 249, 249, 250, 256, *257*
Craig, Y. 299, 305, *308*
Crane, M 19, *37*, 330n, *332*
Crichton, M. 141, 145, *150*
Crimmins, E. 314, *331*
Cullen, K. 256, *257*
Culyer, T. 329, *331*
Curran, M. 64, *73,* 153, 158, 159, *170*
Cusack, D. 154, *169*
Czaja, S.J. 246, *257*

Daatland, S.O. 185, *202*
Dalley, G. 105, 109, 115, *117*
Daly, T. 245, *257*
Davies, C. 127, *134*
Davies, S. 70, *71*, 92, *102*, 156, *169*
Day, H. 58, 69, *71*
Dean, H. 136, *150*
Dellasega, C. 153, 169, *169, 170*
Department of Health 27, *37*, 54, 55, 56, 60, 61, 69, *71*, 89, 90, *102*, 104, 105, 113, 114, 116, *117*, 156, *169*, 244, 253, 255, *257*, 324, 325, *331*
Department of Health and Social Security 104, 105, 107, *117*
Department of Social Security 296, *308*
Dickens, C. 29, *37*
Dickinson, E. 54, 55, 60, 61, *74*
Dingwall, R. 18, *37*, 97, *102*
Dixon, J. 327, *331*
Dodd, H. 307, *308*
Donaldson, M.S. 77, *88*
Doolittle, G. 243, *258*
Ds Fi 185, 198, *202*
Dubos, R. 43, *52*
Duggan, M. 180, *182*
Dunamel, L.M. 57, *72*
Duncan, M.T. 154, *169*
Dunkle, R.E. 48, *53*
Dunlop, B.D. 48, *52*
Dunning, A. 297, *308*

Eade, J. 276, 290, *290*
Easterbrook, L. 54, 60, *72*, 317, *331*
Ebrahim, S. 61, *71*
Edelbalk, P.G. 184, 185, 188, 189, 190, 196, 197, 198, 199, *202, 203*

Edwards, W. 189, 190, *202*
Ekman, S. 64, *73*
Eliasson, L.R. 184, 186, 197, *202*
Elliot, H. 249, 253, *257*
Ellis, L. 70, *71*
Elmér, Å. 187, *202*
Emery, D. 245, *257*
Entwistle, V. 244, 253, *257*
Eraut, M. 64, *72*
Essex, S. 181, 182
Estes, C.L. 125, *134*
European Community 259, *271*
Evandrou, M. 255, *257*
Evans, J.G. 19, *37*
Evans, R.L. 62, *72*
Evers, H.K. 59, *72*

Fagerstedt, B. 197, *202*
Fakhoury, W. 206, 214, *217*
Fardel, J. 60, *70*
Farquhar, M. 58, *72*
Farrell, C. 317, *331*
Fast, J.E. 201, *202*
Feldman, P.H. 124, *134*
Field, D. 204, 206, 207, 208, *217*
Fillit, H.M. 19, *36*
Fisk, J. 224, *242*
Fisk, M. 307, *308*
Fleetwood, H. 241, *242*
Fletcher, P. 317, *331*
Flowers, J. 244, 254, 255, *257*
Forster, A. 116, *118,* 293, *309,* 320, *331*
Foss, L. 44, *52*
Fossbinder, D. 65, 67, *72*
Foucault, M. 129, *134*
Fox, D. 42, *52*
Fox, N. 320, *331*
Fozard, J. 220, 238, *242*
Freedman, V.A. 314, *331*
Freemantle, N. 86, *88*
Freudenthal, A. 241, *242*
Freund, P.E.S. 39, *52*
Fridberg, T. 124, *134*
Friedland, R.B. 46, 49, *52, 53*
Friedman, J.P. 235, *242*
Fulton-Suri, J.L. 220, 238, *242*
Fruin, D. 68, *72*

Gannon, L.R. 312, *331*
Garber, A.M. 330n, *331*
Gardner, K. 290, *290*
Giddens, A. 207, *217*
Gilchrist, C. 92, *102*
Ginn, J. 128, *133*, 149, *150*, 312, *330*
Glendinning, C. 123, *134*
Glennerster, H. 19, 20, 21, 26, *37*, 180, *183*
Goodman, D. 307, *309*
Gotzsche, P.C. 86, *88*
Gough, R. 185, *202*
Government Statistical Service 28, *37*
Grant, G. 64, 65, *73, 74,* 152, *170,* 213, *217,* 255, *257*
Greatbatch, D. 97, *102*

Greve, J. 19, *36*
Greve, W. 64, *71*
Griffin, F.N.U. 68, *72*
Griffith, V. 153, 154, *170*
Gustke, S. 243, *257*

Haas, B.K. 58, *72*
Haldorsdottir, S. 66, *72*
Hambleton, R. 181, 182
Hanford, L. 54, 60, *72*
Hanson, E. 208, *218*, 244, 247, 248, 249, 251, 256, *257*
Hardy, B. 108, *118*, 182, *182*
Harel, Z. 48, *53*
Harper, S. 313, 321, *331*
Harris, J. 57, *70*
Harrison, A. 327, *331*
Harrison, S. 243, *258*, 304, *309*
Haselkorn, J.K. 62, *72*
Hassell, K. 252, *257*
Hasselkus, B. 154, *169*
Hayden, A. 304, *308*
Hazan, H. 207, *217*
Health Advisory Service 27, *37*, 55, 67, *72*, 92, *102*, 330n, *331*
Health and Welfare Canada 184, *202*
Hecht, R. 303, *309*
Hegeman, C.R. 153, *170*
Help the Aged 330n, *331*
Henderson, C. 153, *170*
Henderson, J.N. 64, *72*
Hendricks, R.T. 62, *72*
Henshaw, L. 273, 288, *290*
Henwood, M. 56, 69, *72*, 108, *118*, 182, *182*
Hiscock, J. 108, *117*
Hollingbery, R. 303, *309*
Holme, A. 210, *217*
Home Office (Seebohm) Committee 21, *37*
House of Commons Health Committee 111, *118*
House of Commons Home Affairs Committee 260, 264, *271*
Howarth, G. 206, 208, 210, 211, *217*
Hoyland, J. 206, *217*
Hudson, B. 108, 112, *118*, 182, *182*
Hughes, B. 58, 69, *72*, *74*, 147, *150*
Hugman, R. 182, *182*
Hull, K.V. 154, *170*
Humpherys, D.R. 116, *118*
Hunt, M.E. 189, *202*
Hunter, M. 131, *134*
Huntingdon, J. 125, *134*
Hutton, J. 317, *331*

Illich, I. 129, *134*
Impallomeni, M. 156, 157, *169*
Ingvad, B. 184, 185, 188, 189, 190, 196, 197, 198, 199, *202*, *203*
International Association of Gerontology 56, *72*
Ivory, M. 149, *150*

Jacques, A. 293, *309*, 320, *331*
James. J. 107, *118*
Jamieson, A. 313, *331*
Jankey, S.G. 58, 69, *71*

Jennett, B. 22, *37*
Jensen, E.M. 241, *242*
Johansson, J. 185, *202*
Johnson, C.L. 64, *72*
Johnson, M.A. 153, *169*
Joseph Rowntree Foundation 54, *72*
Jones, A. 263, 264, *271*
Jones, B. 60, *70*
Jones, D. 260, *272*
Jones, K. 18, *37*
Juul-Andersen, K. 241, *242*

Kahn, R.L. 116, *118*
Kane, N.M. 124, *134*
Kane, R.A. 56, 62, *72*, 184, *202*
Kane, R.L. 184, *202*
Katona, G. 187, *202*
Katz, J.T. 207, 216, *217*, *218*
Katz, S. 48, *53*
Keady, J. 152, *170*, 213, *217*, 255, *257*
Keating, N.C. 201, *202*
Keefe, J. 201, *202*
Kelly, D. 57, *70*
Kent, B.C. 64, *73*
Kirkwood, T. 221, 225, *242*
Kitwood, T. 45, *53*, 64, *72*
Kivnick, H.Q. 58, 65, 69, *72*
Kohn, L.T. 77, *88*
Komaromy, C. 207, 216, *217*, *218*
Knapp, M. 82, *88*
Kose, S. 226, *242*
Kruckeberg, T. 154, *169*

Lacey, P. 180, *182*
Laker, S. 70, *71*, 156, *169*
Lancaster, J. 97, *101*
Langlinais, T.C. 235, *242*
Lannerheim, L. 189, *202*
Laslett, P. 222, 232, *242*
Lau, B. 261, *272*
Law, C.M. 19, *38*
Lawler, J. 127, 132, *134*
Lawton, M.P. 57, *72*
Lay, M. 214, *216*, *217*
Lee-Treweek, G. 59, *72*
Le Fanu, J. 17, 19, *37*, 244, *257*
Letherby, G. 215, *217*
Levine, D. 153, *170*
Lewis, J. 19, 26, *37*, 180, *183*
Lewisham Older Women's Health Project 307, *308*
Liaschenko, J. 65, 66, 68, *73*
Lindeiberg, S. 64, *74*
Lister, R. 137, 142, *150*, 261, *272*
Littlewood, J. 132, *134*
Livingston, G. 59, *73*
Loane, M. 243, *258*
Longino, C.F., Jr 42, 43, 49, *53*
Lopez, A.D. 314, *330*
Lund, U. 196, *202*
Lundberg, L. 198, *202*
Lundh, U. 167, *170*
Lunt, N. 318, *330*

Mabileau, A. 306, *309*

Macaualy, V. 247, 248, *256*
McAuley, W.J. 48, *53*
McCarthy, M. 206, 214, *216, 217*
McCormack, B. 215, *217*
MaCurdy, T. 330n, *331*
McDonald, G. 79, 82–83, *88*
McFee, G. 270, *272*
McGuire, M.B. 39, *52*
McKee, M. 97, *101*
McLaughlin, E. 123, *134*
McLean, J. 128, *133*
McLernan, A. 243, *258*
McNamara, B. 206, *217*
McPherson, K. 97, *101*
Magnusson, L. 245, *257*
Maire, F. 243, *258*
Major, L.E. 306, *309*
Maltby, T. 301, *310*, 323, *332*
Mandelstam, M. 227, *242*
Manela, M. 59, *73*
Manton, K.G. 49, *53*, 314, *332*
Marck, P. 65, *73*
Marshall, M.N. 114, *118*
Marshall, V.W. 211, *217*
Martin, L.G. 314, *331*
Martin-Matthews, A. 199, *202*
Martlew, B. 58, *73*
Mastrian, K. 153, *169*
Mathias, P. 180, *183*
Matthiesson, V. 153, *170*
Mayer, J. 320, *332*
Mayers, C.A. 61, *73*
Maynard, A. 75, 83, 84, 85, 86, *88*
Meade, K. 138, *150*, 312, *330*
Means, R. 18, 19, 20, *37*, 121, 124, *134*
Mein, H. 293, *309*, 320, *331*
Mellor, P. 207, *217*
Mercer, G. 296, *308*
Miller, W.I. 132, *134*
Mills, L. 181, *182*
Minkler, M. 58, 64, 69, *73*
Minichiello, V. 271, *272*, 322, *332*
Mirza, L. 300, *308*, 318, *330*
Mittelmark, M.B. 45–46, *53*
Mooney, R. 307, *308*
Moore, A. 97, *102*
Moore, A.A. 49, *53*
Moran, R. 246, 256, *256, 257*
Morgan, D.L. 154, *169*, 173, *183*
Morris, J. 296, *309*
Mort, M. 304, *309*
Morton, J. 318, *332*
Moss, M. 57, *72*
Mosse, E. 307, *309*
Moutray, M. 243, *258*
Munro, A. 300, 301, *308*
Murphy, E. 97, *102*
Murphy, J.W. 42, *53*
Murphy, M. 314, *331*
Murray, J. 147, *150*
Murray, S.U. 58, 65, 69, *72*
Myerson, J. 233, *242*

Nalleppa, M.J. 153, *170*
National Insitute of Aging (USA) 314, *332*
Nay, R. 153, 154, *170*
Nazroo, J. 290, *290*
Neuberger, J. 204, *217*
Newman, J.R. 189, 190, *202*
Nicolass, G. 252, *257*
Nilsson, M. 64, *73*
Nocon, A. 54, 61, *73*, 296, *309*
Nolan, J. 58, 62, 63, 64, 70, *73*, 153, 158, 159, *170*
Nolan, M.R. 58, 62, 63, 64, 65, 70, *71, 73*, 92, *102, 152*, 153, 158, 159, 167, 169, *170*, 213, *217*, 255, *257*
Norman, A. 261, *272*, 318, *332*
Norman, I.J. 325, *332*
Norris, B. 241, *242*
Northern Ireland Economic Council 326, *332*
Nusberg, C. 142, *151*, 248, *258*

Oakley, A. 304, 305, *310*
O'Boyle, C.A. 58, 59, 69, *73*
Ogg, J. 273, 274, 289, 290, *290*
Oldby, B. 197, *202*
Oldman, C. 19, *36*
Oliver, M. 130, *134*
Onyejiako, S. 261, *272*
O'Reilly, A. 248, *258*
Ordsall Local History and Drama Group 302, *309*
Organisation for Economic Cooperation and Development 28, *37, 38*
Ornel, J. 64, *74*
Ory, M.G. 61, *73*
Osborn, A. 292, 293, 294, 295, 298, 306, 307, *309, 310*, 320, 321, *331, 332*
Ostroff, E. 226, *242*
Outram, S. 307, *309*
Øvretveit, J. 180, *183*
Owen, D. 262, 263, *272*, 318, *332*

Pahl, J. 128, *133*
Pain, R.H. 144, *150*
Paley, J. 64, *73*
Palmer, A. 173, *183*
Parker, D. 264, *272*
Parker, J. 20, *38*
Parker, M. 156, *170*
Parker, R.A. 18, 19, 20, *38*
Parker, S. 97, *102*
Parry Jones, W.L. 18, *38*
Paterson, B. 65, *74*
Payton, V.R. 174, *183*
Peach, C. 276, 290, *290*
Peace, S.M. 57, *73*, 305, 306, *309*
Pearson, A. 153, 154, *170*
Pearson, M. 108, *117*
Peebles, L. 241, *242*
Pencheon, D. 244, 253, 254, 255, *257*
Penhale, B. 305, *309*
Penning, M. 201, *202*
Personal Social Services Research Unit 124, *134*
Pescosolido, B. 251, *257*
Pharoah, C. 273, *290*

Phillips, J. 273, 274, 289, 290, *290*, 318, 321, 322, *330*
Phillips, P. 184, 197, *201*, *202*
Phillipson, C.R. 58, 62, *73*, 273, 274, 289, 290, *290*
Philp, I. 70, *71*, 156, *169*
Philpot, M. 19, *38*
Philpot, T. 130, *134*
Pillemer, K. 153, *170*
Poland, F. 64, *73*, 153, 158, 159, *170*
Popay, J. 304, 305, *310*
Porter, E. 58, *73*
Porter, R. 274, *290*
Poulson, D. 247, *257*
Prather, J. 142, *151*, 248, *258*
Preiser, W. 226, *242*
Price, D. 115, *118*
Prior, D. 137, *150*
Prior, P. 148, *150*
Prophet, H. 54, *73*
Putnam, R. 139, *150*

Qualitative Solutions and Research 157, *170*
Qureshi, H. 296, *309*

Ranson, S. 136, *151*
Rappert, B. 298, *310*
Raynes, N.V. 167, *170*
Razzaque, K. 181, *182*
Redfern, S.J.R. 325, *332*
Reed, J. 58, 59, *73*, 167, *170*, 173, 174, 178, 181, *183*
Reents, H. 226, *242*
Relatives' Association 153, 154, *170*
Reuben, D.B. 49, *53*
Reynolds, S. 314, *331*
Reynolds, W. 64, *71*
Richardson, S. 247, *257*
Rivett, G. 17, 19, *38*
Robertson, A. 294, *310*
Robinson, I. 64, *73*
Robinson, J. 317, *331*
Roche, M. 137, *151*
Rogers, A. 244, 249, 252, 253, 254, 255, *257*
Rolland, J.S. 62, *73*
Rosenmayr, L. 187, *202*
Room, G. 259, *272*
Ross, L.E. 189, *202*
Rostgard, T. 124, *134*
Rothenberg, K. 44, *52*
Rowe, J.W. 116, *118*
Rowley, N. 270, *272*
Royal College of Nursing 114, *118*
Royal Commission on Long Term Care 60, *74*, 114, *118*, 119–20, 123, 125, 130, *134*
Ruler, A. 153, 154, *170*

Saito, Y. 314, *331*
Samuelsson, G. 184, 185, 187, 188, 188, 189, 190, 196, 197, 198, 199, *202*, *203*
Sandberg, J. 167, *170*
Sanderson, C. 97, *101*
Sandvick, H. 25, *38*
Sapienza, A.M. 124, *134*

Sarvimäki, A. 64, *73*
Scheidt, R.D. 116, *118*
Schön, D. 64, *74*
Schunk, M. 123, *134*
Scottish Office 109, *118*
Seale, C. 204, 206, 208, *217*, *218*
Sevenhuijsen, S. 137, *151*
Seymour, J. 205, 207, 208, *217*, *218*
Shardlow, P. 136, *150*
Sharit, J. 246, *257*
Shaw, S.M.I. 140, 147, *151*
Sheffield Health Authority 327, *332*
Sheldon, S.H. 276, *290*
Shewan, J. 247, 248, *256*
Shoemaker, A. 154, *169*
Shortliffe, E.H. 243, 244, *257*
Siddell, M. 146, *151*, 208, 211, 216, *217*, *218*, 307, *308*
Siegel, J. 313, *332*
Siim, B. 139, *151*
Sinclair, A. 54, 55, 60, 61, *74*
Siu, A.L. 49, *53*
Sivananthan, S. 243, *258*
Sjöbeck, B. 187, 189, 196, *203*
Slack, K. 19, 20, *38*
Slack, R. 156, *169*
Smith, H. 130, *133*
Smith, J. 204, 209, *218*
Smith, M.H. 49, *53*
Smith, R. 18, 19, 20, *37*, 121, 124, *134*
Socialdepartmentet (Sweden) 167, *170*
Social Services Inspectorate 55, 67, *74*, 109, *118*
Socialstyrelsen (Sweden) 155, 156, *170*
Song, M. 265, *272*
Stallard, E. 49, *53*, 314, *332*
Stanley, D. 167, *170*, 178, 181, *183*
Starr, J. 156, 157, *169*
Starr, P. 42, *53*
Statens Offentliga Utredningar (Sweden) 185, 198, *203*
Statistical Abstract of Sweden 186, *203*
Sternberg, J. 197, *202*
Stevenson, C. 64, *71*
Stevenson, J. 54, 60, *72*
Stevenson, O. 17, *38*
Steverink, N. 64, *74*
Stewart, J. 136, 137, *150*, *151*
Strode, S. 243, *257*
Ström, P. 196, 197, *203*
Summer, L. 49, *53*
Sundin, O. 248, *258*
Sundström, G. 185, *203*
Swann, A. de 121, *134*
Szebehely, M. 184, 186, *202*

Tallis, R. 19, *36*, 207, *218*
Tarpey, M. 273, 288, *290*
Taylor, B. 153, 154, *170*
Teeling-Smith, G. 313, *332*
Tester, S. 123, *134*
Tetley, J. 244, 247, 248, *256*, *257*, *258*
Thomas, A. 198, *203*
Thomas, C. 296, *310*

Thompson, C. 318, *330*
Thompson, T. 180, *183*
Thomson, D. 18, *38*
Thorne, S. 65, *74*
Thornton, P. 307, *309, 310*
Thorslund, M. 156, *170*
Thulin, A.B. 197, *203*
Thursz, D. 142, *151*, 248, *258*
Tickle, E.H. 154, *170*
Tilse, C. 153, 154, *170*
Timms, N. 320, *332*
Tinker, A. 18, 19, *38*, 253, *258*
Titmuss, R.M. 20, *38*
Toffaleti, C. 302, 306, *310*
Tornstam, L. 187, *203*
Tout, K. 270, *272*
Townsend, P. 18, 19, 29, *38*, 273, *290*
Tozer, R. 307, *310*
Trieschmann, R.B. 58, *74*
Trombly, C.A. 61, *74*
Tucker, C. 153, 154, *170*
Turner-Smith, A. 246, 249, 250, 256, *257*
Twigg, J. 133, *134*, 321, *332*

Unruh, D. 209, 211, *218*

Vamplew, T. 276, 290, *290*
Vesperi, M.D. 64, *72*
Victor, C.R. 56, *74*, 313, *331*
Vries, G. de 220, 238, *242*

Walker, A. 56, *74*, 135, 142, *150, 151*, 270, *272*, 297, *310*, 322, *332*
Walker, D. 307, *310*
Walker, G. 64, *73,* 153, 158, 159, 170
Wall, A. 123, *134*
Walsh, K. 137, *150*
Walsh, N. 141, *151*
Walter, T. 207, 208, *218*
Ward, L. 130, *134*
Wärneryd, K-E. 187, 199, *203*
Warnes, A.M. 19, *38,* 70, *71*, 208, *218*, 262, *272*, 274, 290, *290*, 298, 307, *310*, 313, 314, 330n, *332*
Warren, L. 142, *151*, 255, *258*, 297, 301, 306, 307, *310*, 323, *332*
Watkin, V. 60, *73*
Watson, P. 97, *102*
Wattis, J.P. 18, *38*
Webb, B. 17, *38*
Webb, S. 17, *38*
Webster, C. 17, 20, *38*
Weightman, A.L. 97, *101*
Weissert, W.G. 48, *53*
Wenger, G.C. 64, *74*
Wilkin, D. 58, *74*
Willcocks, D. 292, 293, 295, 306, *309*, 321, *332*
Williams, A. 24, *38*, 75, 83, 85, *88*
Williams, B. 64, 65, *74*
Williams, C. 307, *308*
Williams, F. 61, *73*, 304, 305, *310*
Williams, J. 128, *133*
Williams, R. 209, *218*
Williams, S. 64, *73,* 153, 158, 159, *170*

Willmott, P. 276, *290*
Wilson, F. 70, *71*, 92, *102*
Wilson, G. 145, *151*, 319, *332*
Winkler, M.G. 29, *37*
Wistow, G. 69, *74*, 108, *118*, 182, *182*
Wong, D. 264, *272*
Woodroffe, D. 18, 19, *38*
Wootton, R. 243, *258*
World Health Organisation 205, *218*

Yawitz, M. 220, 238, *242*
Yorgason, J.B. 116, *118*
Young, J. 61, *74*, 116, *118*
Young, M. 276, *290*
Yu, W.K. 261, 265, *271*

Zanner, R. 42, *53*
Zylan, Y. 139, *150*

What are the implications of current economic, social and political trends in Britain for older people? Social and demographic changes have led to traditional areas of welfare being transformed. The contributors to this book take a critical look at the current situation and assess the implications for future practice. They debate the assumptions and values underlying established welfare programmes and consider the case for change as growing demands put health and social services under increasing pressure. The second part of the book discusses specific areas in detail, ranging from the organisation of effective domiciliary social care to the impact of new technologies on older people's lives. This book provides a comprehensive and practical overview of the provision of services for older people and will be a valuable and thought-provoking resource for anyone involved in caring for and supporting them.

The editors are all at the University of Sheffield. **Anthony M. Warnes** is a professor of Social Gerontology and during 1995–2000 was Chair of the British Society of Gerontology. **Lorna Warren** is a lecturer in the Department of Sociological Studies and has been carrying out research on and with older people for seventeen years. **Michael Nolan** is a professor of Gerontological Nursing and is involved in several international comparative studies of formal and informal care-giving.

Jessica Kingsley *Publishers*
116 Pentonville Road
London N1 9JB

ISBN 1-85302-852-5